Poverty, Growth, and Institutions in Developing Asia

This page intentionally left blank

Poverty, Growth, and Institutions in Developing Asia

Edited by

Ernesto M. Pernia

and

Anil B. Deolalikar

Published for the
Asian Development Bank by
palgrave macmillan

First published 2003 by
PALGRAVE MACMILLAN
Houndmills, Basingstoke, Hampshire RG21 6XS and
175 Fifth Avenue, New York, N. Y. 10010
Companies and representatives throughout the world

PALGRAVE MACMILLAN is the global academic imprint of the Palgrave Macmillan division of St. Martin's Press, LLC and of Palgrave Macmillan Ltd. Macmillan® is a registered trademark in the United States, United Kingdom and other countries. Palgrave is a registered trademark in the European Union and other countries.

ISBN 978-1-4039-1806-2

This book is printed on paper suitable for recycling and made from fully managed and sustained forest sources.

A catalogue record for this book is available from the British Library.

Library of Congress Cataloging-in-Publication Data

Poverty, growth, and institutions in developing Asia / edited by Ernesto M. Pernia and Anil B. Deolalikar.
p. cm.
"This book is an outcome of ADB's regional technical assistance research project, Pro-Poor Economic Growth and Institutional Constraints to Poverty Reduction in Developing Asia"--P..
Papers and discussion from a conference held in October 2001 in Manila, climaxing the project.
Includes bibliographical references and indexes.
ISBN 978-1-4039-1806-2 (cloth)
1. Poverty--Asia--Congresses. 2.Income distribution--Asia--Congresses. 3.Political planning--Asia--Congresses. 4. Asia--Economic policy--Congresses. 5. Asia--Social policy--Congresses. 6. Asia--Economic conditions--Congresses. I. Pernia, Ernesto M., 1943- II. Deolalikar, Anil B.

HC415.P6P683 2003
330.95'009172'4--dc22

2003058076

10 9 8 7 6 5 4 3 2 1
12 11 10 09 08 07 06 05 04 03

Contents

Tables

Figures

Appendices

Foreword

In the Asian Development Bank's (ADB) first *Medium Term Strategic Framework* (1992-1995), "reducing poverty" was identified as one of the five strategic development objectives along with promoting economic growth, supporting human development, improving the status of women, and managing natural resources and the environment. In 1999, poverty reduction was accorded even higher prominence and was declared as the overarching goal of the institution.

Since the early 1990s, ADB has actively encouraged and supported research on poverty and related issues. Output of such effort included, among others, several volumes devoted to issues of rural poverty and urban poverty in Asia. Poverty research in ADB contributed to the formulation in late 1999 of the institution's poverty reduction strategy. However, poverty reduction strategy, like development strategy in general, is not static but is a dynamic process that improves with better data and the continuing search for new knowledge.

The present volume contains a set of general issues papers and quantitative country case studies. While confirming that economic growth is key to poverty reduction, the papers attempt to elaborate on the theme that institutions and other factors matter as well, and paying attention to them can contribute to sustaining both growth and poverty reduction in the long run. The book will be of interest to readers both inside and outside ADB.

Ifzal Ali
Chief Economist
Asian Development Bank

Preface

This book is an outcome of ADB's regional technical assistance research project, Pro-Poor Economic Growth and Institutional Constraints to Poverty Reduction in Developing Asia. The project focused on seven Asian developing countries: Bangladesh, Indonesia, Lao People's Democratic Republic, Pakistan, Philippines, Thailand, and Viet Nam; and, for purposes of further comparison, two relatively developed Asian economies: Republic of Korea (or Korea) and Taipei,China. The project began with an organizational and planning meeting in March 2001. The research undertook extensive reviews of the literature; field interviews with key persons in government, academia, private sector, and nongovernmental organizations (NGOs); and selected country case studies.

A mid-term conference to present and discuss preliminary papers was held in October 2001 in Manila. It was the climax of the project and was a high-profile event, with the inaugural address given by Philippine President Gloria Macapagal-Arroyo, and the keynote speech by Professor Assar Lindbeck of Stockholm University. Apart from the paper authors and ADB staff, several experts from government, academia, international organizations, and NGOs participated in the conference as designated discussants. These included Werner Konrad Blenk, Ramesh Khadka, Mario B. Lamberte, Suparat Manmin, Peter McCawley, Solita C. Monsod, Tae Kyu Park, Atiur Rahman, and Ching-lung Tsay. Pan-long Tsai and Suk Bum Yoon prepared background papers on Taipei,China and Korea, respectively. From ADB's operational and other departments, session chairs, panelists and discussants included Jose Edgardo L. Campos, Edward M. Haugh, Jr., Frank Harrigan, Gunter Hecker, Anita Kelles-Viitanen, Shoji Nishimoto, Arvind Panagariya, Cedric D. Saldanha, Christine Wallich, Clay Wescott, and G.H.P.B. Van der Linden. M. G. Quibria was also a designated discussant representing the ADB Institute.

The research project was carried out by the Economics and Development Resource Center (EDRC, the precursor of the Economics and Research Department [ERD]) with the collaboration of the operational and other departments represented by an interdepartmental working group (IWG). The IWG included Paul L. Chang, Siew Tuan Chew, Merrel Chin-Yee, Neeraj K. Jain, Sudipto Mundle, Stephen J. Pollard, Adrian H. Ruthenberg, William Staub, Susan D. Tamondong, Caroline Vandenabeelle, and Etienne R. Van de Walle.

Jungsoo Lee, Charles Adams, and Arvind Panagariya, who headed EDRC during different periods, and subsequently Ifzal Ali, ERD, provided general direction and encouragement to the project. Several others deserve special mention for the valuable help and support they extended. Aludia Z. Pardo assisted in the preparation of the research proposal. Pilipinas F. Quising, the principal technical assistant of the project, provided substantial research support, apart from taking charge of administration and coordination matters. She was very ably complemented by Gemma B. Estrada for research assistance, and Ma. Lourdes L. Antonio and Anna Karmina V. Ong for administrative assistance. Emmanuel de Dios served as economics editor, Regina Capuno as copy editor, and Glenn Concepcion as graphic designer. Cherry Lynn T. Zafaralla gave valuable editorial and production advice, and Lynette R. Mallery liaised with the publisher.

Ernesto M. Pernia, Manila
Anil B. Deolalikar, New Delhi
March 2003

Contributors

Abuzar Asra is Senior Statistician, Economics and Research Department, Asian Development Bank, Manila. He was Research Professor at the Central Agency of Statistics, Indonesia. His main research interest is poverty and income distribution.

Arsenio M. Balisacan is Professor of Economics, University of the Philippines, and was Undersecretary of Agriculture. His research interests are poverty, inequality, agricultural and rural development, and political economy of policy reforms.

Alex B. Brillantes, Jr. is Director, Center for Local and Regional Governance, University of the Philippines. Earlier, he was Executive Director, Local Government Academy of the Department of Interior and Local Government.

Marita Concepcion Castro Guevara is Research Associate, Institute of Philippine Culture, and faculty member of Sociology and Interdisciplinary Studies, Ateneo de Manila University. Her main research area is urban poverty.

Anil B. Deolalikar is Professor of Economics, University of California, Riverside. He was Lead Human Development Economist, World Bank's Resident Mission in New Delhi, and previously was Professor of Economics at the University of Washington, Seattle.

Gemma Esther B. Estrada is a consultant, Economics and Research Department, Asian Development Bank. Earlier, she was Technical Assistant to the Undersecretary for Policy and Planning, Department of Agriculture.

Raghav Gaiha is Professor of Public Policy, Faculty of Management Studies, University of Delhi. He has held visiting faculty positions at Cambridge, Harvard, Yale, Stanford, and MIT. His research interests include poverty, decentralization, rural institutions, and macro policy reforms.

Ernesto M. Pernia is Lead Economist, Economics and Research Department, Asian Development Bank. Earlier, he was Professor of Economics, University of the Philippines, and Research Fellow, East-West Center, Honolulu. His main areas are regional and urban economics, human resource economics, and poverty.

Mary Racelis is Research Scientist, Institute of Philippine Culture, Ateneo de Manila University, and its former Director. She has published extensively on poverty and well-being, urbanization, community organization and people's empowerment, civil society, gender, children, and socio-cultural change.

Acronyms and Abbreviations

ADAB	Association of Development Agencies in Bangladesh
ADB	Asian Development Bank
ADC	Asian developing country
ANGOC	Asian NGO Coalition for Agrarian Reform and Rural Development
APO	Asian Productivity Organization
BARD	Bangladesh Rural Development Academy
BKK	Badan Kredit Kecamatan
BOT	Build-operate-transfer
BRAC	Bangladesh Rural Advancement Committee
BPS	Biro Pusat Statistik (Central Bureau of Statistics)
CARL	Comprehensive Agrarian Reform Law
CARP	Comprehensive Agrarian Reform Program
CBO	Community-based organization
CD	Cumulative distribution
CDF	Cooperative Development Foundation
CIDA	Canadian International Development Agency
CIDSS	Comprehensive and Integrated Delivery of Social Services
COTI	Central Officials Training Institute
CPAR	Congress for People's Agrarian Reform
CPI	Consumer price index
DFID	Department for International Development
DMC	Developing member country
DPC	District Planning Committee
DRDA	District Rural Development Agency
EPI	Expanded program of immunization
ESCAP	Economic and Social Commission of Asia and the Pacific
FDI	Foreign direct investment
FIES	Family Income and Expenditures Survey
FSFE	Fixed-stage fixed-effects
GDP	Gross domestic product

GMO	Genetically modified organisms
GNP	Gross national product
GSK	Gono Shasto Kendro
GSO	General Statistics Office
HCE	Household consumption expenditure
HDI	Human development index
HEPR	Hunger Eradication and Poverty Reduction
HUDCC	Housing and Urban Development Coordinating Council
IA	Irrigation Association
IFAD	International Fund for Agricultural Development
IG	Irrigation group
IGF	Intergovernmental fiscal
ILO	International Labour Office
IMF	International Monetary Fund
IPD	Institute for Popular Democracy
I-PRSP	Interim Poverty Reduction Strategy Paper
IRDP	Integrated Rural Development Program
IT	Irrigation team
IV	Instrumental variable
JRY	Jawahar Rozgar Yojan
KALAHI	Kapit Bisig Laban sa Kahirapan (Linking Arms Against Poverty)
Lao PDR	Lao People's Democratic Republic
LATI	Local Autonomy Training Institute
LGC	Local Government Code
MKSS	Mazdoor Kisan Shakti Sangathan
MMR	Maternal mortality rates
MNDC	Metro Naga Development Council
MOLISA	Ministry of Labour, War Invalids and Social Affairs
Naga SPEED	Naga Socialized Program for Empowerment and Economic Development
NAPC	National Anti-Poverty Commission
NCPC	Naga City People's Council
NEDA	National Economic and Development Authority
NESDB	National Economic and Social Development Board
NGO	Nongovernmental organization
NIA	National income accounts

NILG	National Institute of Local Government
NOVIB	Netherlands Organisation for International Development Co-operation
NRB	National Reconstruction Bureau
NSCB	National Statistical Coordination Board
NSO	National Statistics Office
OECD	Organisation for Economic Co-operation and Development
OLS	Ordinary least squares
OPP	Orangi Pilot Project
PARCode	People's Agrarian Reform Code
PATC	Public Administration Training Center
PCE	Personal consumption expenditure
PO	People's organization
PPA	Participatory poverty assessment
PRC	People's Republic of China
PRSP	Poverty Reduction Strategy Paper
PSR	Public sector reform
RDA	Rural Development Academy
SCOL	Spatial cost-of-living
SES	Socioeconomic survey
SEWA	Self-Employed Women's Association
SMC	School Management Committee
SSA	Social Security Act
SUSENAS	Survei Sosial Ekonomi Nasional
SWS	Social Weather Stations
TDRI	Thailand Development Research Institute
UMP	Urban Management Programme
UNCHS	United Nations Centre for Human Settlements
UNDP	United Nations Development Programme
UNICEF	United Nations Children's Fund
UP	Uttar Pradesh
VLSS	Viet Nam Living Standards Survey
WCED	The World Commission on Environment and Development
WDR	World Development Report
WEP	World Employment Program
WTDP	Well-to-Do Program

1 Introduction

ANIL B. DEOLALIKAR AND ERNESTO M. PERNIA

A main feature of Asia's success story has been the remarkable social transformation and poverty reduction that accompanied rapid economic growth in the region. Some three decades ago, more than half the region was poor, only two of five adults were literate, and the average person could hope to live only 48 years. At present, the proportion of poor people is down to one third, 70 percent of adults are literate, and life expectancy has risen to 68 years. And while the region's population has increased from 1.8 billion to 3.0 billion, the number of poor people has dropped from more than 1 billion to less than 900 million.

Because Asia is so vast and heterogeneous, however, its success story is not equally true for all economies. Large disparities in economic and social progress persist between and within countries in the region. There is a sharp contrast between economies in South

Asia and those in East and Southeast Asia. Even the more dynamic East and Southeast Asia have suffered some setbacks, with transient poverty increasing in countries hardest hit by the recent Asian financial crisis.

Whether they intended to or not, some countries have adopted economic growth strategies that were more pro-poor than others and met with remarkable success. What are the key policy ingredients of such growth strategies? What factors apart from differences in economic growth account for the differential progress in social development and poverty reduction across Asian developing countries (ADCs)? These and similar other questions continue to challenge policymakers and scholars alike.

The purpose of this book is to identify and discuss the main institutions that have an impact on poverty reduction, either directly or indirectly via their impact on economic growth. In addition, it explores the various pathways through which institutions may inhibit or promote poverty-reduction efforts of a country and examines the impact of institutional policies and reforms on poverty reduction. Some of the questions it tries to address are the following: To what extent have institutional constraints inhibited some ADCs from being able to reduce poverty rates as rapidly as other ADCs? How might one explain vast intercountry differences in social, cultural, and political institutions? Are these differences exogenous, or can they be changed by policy interventions? What types of institutional reforms can improve the poverty reduction efforts of countries?

POVERTY REDUCTION IN ASIA

Both the extent and depth of poverty vary markedly across ADCs. Using national definitions, poverty incidence ranges from a low 6 percent in the People's Republic of China (PRC) to 53 percent in Bangladesh (Table 1.1). Under the dollar-a-day international definition, poverty varies from less than 2 percent in Kazakhstan and Thailand to as high as 50.3 percent in Nepal (David et al. 1999). Likewise, the extent to which poverty has fallen over time varies substantially across Asia. In South Asia poverty incidence barely changed between 1987 and 1996, falling only slightly from 44.9 to 42.3 percent. In contrast, the incidence of poverty in East Asia fell from 26.6 to 14.9 percent over the same period (World Bank 2000b). In addition, there are

Table 1.1: Changes in Poverty Incidence and GDP Per Capita, Asian Developing Countries, 1990s

ECONOMY	POVERTY INCIDENCE				ANNUAL PERCENT CHANGE	
	YEAR	PERCENT	YEAR	PERCENT	POVERTY INCIDENCE	REAL GDP PER CAPITA
Bangladesh	1992	58.84	1996	53.08	- 2.54	3.10
Cambodia	1994	39.00	1997	36.10	- 2.54	3.18
PRC	1994	8.40	1996	6.00	-15.48	10.52
India	1992	40.90	1994	35.00	- 7.49	3.33
Indonesia	1990	15.10	1996	15.70	0.65	6.21
Korea	1994	16.40	1995	12.30	-25.00	7.29
Lao PDR	1993	45.00	1998	38.60	- 3.02	4.23
Malaysia	1995	9.60	1997	6.80	-15.84	6.37
Nepal	1992	49.00	1996	42.00	-3.78	2.36
Pakistan	1993	22.40	1997	31.00	8.46	1.47
Philippines	1994	40.60	1997	36.80	-3.22	2.60
Sri Lanka	1991	20.00	1996	25.00	4.56	4.05
Taipei,China	1996	0.54	1997	0.54	0.00	5.26
Thailand	1994	16.30	1996	11.40	-16.37	7.70
Viet Nam	1996	19.23	1997	17.70	- 7.96	7.42

Sources:

Poverty Incidence:

Bangladesh: ADB (2000a).

Cambodia: World Bank (2001e).

PRC: World Bank Global Poverty Monitoring database (*http://www.worldbank.org/research/povmonitor*).

India: World Bank (2001e).

Indonesia: World Bank (2001) Global Poverty Monitoring database (*http://www.worldbank.org/research/povmonitor*).

Korea: Yoon (2001).

Lao PDR: Government of Lao PDR (2000a).

Malaysia: Jomo and Aun (2000).

Nepal: World Bank (2001e) Mahbub ul Haq Human Development Centre (1999).

Pakistan: Kemal (2001).

Philippines: NSCB (1997).

Sri Lanka: World Bank (2001e).

Taipei,China: Tsai (2001)

Thailand: NESDB (1999).

Viet Nam: MOLISA (2000).

Real GDP per Capita:

World Bank,Global Development Network Growth database (*http://www.worldbank.org/research/growth/GDNdata*).

large intercountry differences in the extent to which social services, especially health and education, reach the poor. Countries such as Sri Lanka have been more successful than others, such as Pakistan, in targeting social services and subsidies to the poor (Streeten 1995).

There is no single explanation for these disparities. Some conjecture that the diversity of experience stems from cross-country variations in geographical characteristics, natural resource endowments, demographic trends, and urbanization rates (UN-ESCAP 1998, ADB 1999c, World Bank 1997b). An enumeration of such factors, however, merely demonstrates that poverty is the outcome not only of economic processes but also of social and political phenomena and their interactions. Mediating such interactions are various institutions that are important in understanding poverty and in devising needed policies. Thus, while economic growth is widely recognized as the principal engine to promote poverty reduction and improve living standards, it cannot fully explain intercountry differences in poverty reduction. Of course, the adoption of policies that promote rapid economic growth is influenced in turn by social, political, and institutional processes.

Significant progress in poverty reduction requires a strategy that not only promotes rapid economic growth but also addresses other determinants of poverty, such as institutional factors. The new poverty reduction strategy of the Asian Development Bank (ADB) adopts just such a comprehensive approach: "Since poverty causes and characteristics differ from country to country, the starting point must be a comprehensive examination of the constraints and opportunities for poverty reduction in each country. This will require understanding the nature, intensity, and spread of poverty; the distributional effects of macroeconomic policies; the focus and efficiency of public expenditures; and the effectiveness of government programs and institutions" (ADB 1999a, 15).

WHAT ARE INSTITUTIONS?

We adopt in this book a broad definition of institutions as "...the rules of the game in a society or, more formally, [are] the humanly devised constraints that shape human interaction. In consequence they structure incentives in human exhange, whether political, social, or economic" (North 1990, 3). Institutions range from informal ones such as social networks, norms of behavior, and gender roles, to formal ones such as the legal system, corporate organizations, the politico-administrative system or the state in general—all of which interact with each other. State institutions cover many aspects, including the public provision of basic education and health services, public order and safety, and infrastructure. The nature of governance determines the availability and quality of these public services and, hence, the poor's access to them.

Nonstate institutions include organized social institutions as well as informal values and norms. Social capital may be considered as a social institution. It typically consists of informal norms and relationships that enable people to pursue objectives and act in concert for common benefit. Social capital is particularly important for the poor. Ethnicity and gender roles, which remain pronounced in Asia and lead to discrimination against minorities and females, are other institutions that underpin poverty and inequality.

Thus, apart from economic growth, various institutions and sociocultural factors can explain why some countries have reduced poverty and inequality faster than others, or why in particular circumstances poverty and inequality prove difficult to tackle. Institutions and policies influence all three pillars of ADB's poverty reduction strategy: pro-poor, sustainable economic growth; social development; and governance. Analyzing the nature of these institutions and policies will contribute to a deeper understanding of poverty and propoor growth and the formulation of more effective country poverty reduction strategies.

INSTITUTIONS AND POVERTY REDUCTION

What is the nature of the linkage between economic growth, institutions, policies, and poverty reduction? Figure 1.1 illustrates in a simplified fashion how these factors are related to each other, with respect to poverty reduction outcomes. Institutions affect poverty both directly and indirectly via a number of mediating factors. The choice of policies and their implementation is critical. While this book is concerned with all the linkages between institutions and poverty reduction shown in the simple schema, it lays relatively greater emphasis on the direct effects of institutions and policies on poverty, about which less has been written. By contrast, there is already a large, three decades-old literature on how political, social, cultural,

Figure 1.1: Relationships between Institutions, Economic Growth, and Poverty Reduction

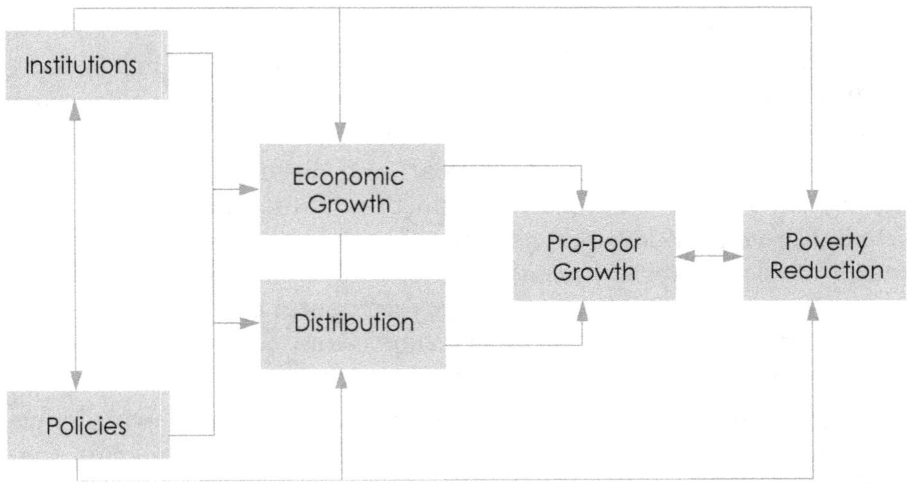

and administrative institutions affect economic growth and income distribution in a country via its choice of macroeconomic and trade policies, such as outward orientation, financial liberalization, exchange rate flexibility, macroeconomic stability, and labor market flexibility (see, e.g., Little, Scitovsky, and Scott 1970).

ORGANIZATION OF THE BOOK

This book has two parts. Part I—comprising Chapters 2 to 5—brings together a number of essays on the role of various types of institutions in poverty reduction. Part II—covering Chapters 6 to 9—is a collection of quantitative country case studies that examine the relationships between poverty, economic growth, and other factors.

The second chapter in this volume—Poverty Reduction: Approaches and the Role of Political Institutions by Deolalikar and Pernia—discusses the various approaches to poverty reduction that have evolved over the years, as well as the political economy of poverty reduction. It examines the literature on the relative roles of economic growth, direct poverty alleviation policies, social service provision, institutions and governance in overall poverty reduction.

The authors also address the importance of political will and political commitment to poverty reduction,[1] and discuss how such political will is often shaped by the competing interests of dominant coalitions and interest groups.

The third chapter—Sociocultural Institutions Affecting Poverty and Poverty Reduction by Racelis and Castro Guevara—begins with a multidimensional perspective on poverty, defines the concept of exclusion (social, economic, and political) and discusses how exclusion and poverty reinforce each other, and then enumerates the types of excluded groups in developing Asia. The chapter also addresses the concept of social capital and its relationship to poverty reduction, as well as the role of civil society (nongovernmental organizations, community-based organizations, labor unions, and cooperatives, among others) as poverty reduction intermediaries.

In the fourth chapter—Public Sector Reform and Poverty Reduction—Brillantes discusses the types of administrative reforms that have been implemented in various ADCs, and how these reforms have directly or indirectly served to reduce poverty. He argues that the success of the bureaucracies in Republic of Korea (Korea) and Taipei,China can be attributed to the insulation of the technocratic elite in charge of policy making and implementation from the ravages of short-run pork-barrel politics. Most other developing countries in Asia have, however, found it difficult to achieve such insulation.

One type of administrative reform is decentralization of rights and responsibilities from central government agencies to local institutions and communities. Chapter 5—Decentralization and Poverty Reduction by Gaiha—focuses on the types of decentralization that have been undertaken in Asia, and how these have influenced poverty reduction. Gaiha argues that the extent, form, and outcomes of decentralization have varied considerably across countries in Asia. In some countries, decentralization has been top-down and politically motivated, guided largely by the narrow self-interest of political leaders seeking legitimacy and mass support, while in other countries it has been guided by a genuine desire to empower local governments and communities. Gaiha stresses the need for incentive-compatible organizational structures to ensure the smooth and effective functioning of local governments. His contention is that a glaring weakness of many decentralization efforts in developing Asia is the absence of incentives for the bureaucracy to serve the interests of elected local government officials.

Extending the general theme of the essays in Part I that institutions and other factors, besides economic growth, matter to poverty reduction, the country papers in Part II analyze subnational data pertaining to Indonesia, Philippines, Thailand, and Viet Nam. In effect, these papers go beyond the common practice of employing cross-national regressions to document the growth-poverty nexus.

In Chapter 6—Revisiting Growth and Poverty Reduction in Indonesia—Balisacan, Pernia, and Asra show that while the growth–poverty nexus appears tight, indeed, at the aggregate level, panel data on the country's 285 districts reveal huge differences in poverty changes, subnational economic growth, and local attributes. Results of econometric analysis show that besides growth, other factors influence the welfare of the poor by altering income distribution, apart from their impact on growth itself. Among the critical ones are infrastructure, human capital, agricultural price incentives, and access to technology. Thus, while fostering economic growth is evidently crucial, a more complete poverty reduction strategy should take into account these relevant factors. In the context of decentralization, subnational analysis can be an instructive approach to examining local governance in relation to growth and poverty reduction.

A parallel analysis is done for the Philippines in Chapter 7—Poverty, Inequality, and Growth in the Philippines. Examining provincial data, Balisacan and Pernia show that economic growth explains a lot but not all about poverty. The balance that seems fairly large can be accounted for by other factors (e.g., infrastructure, human capital, and location-specific characteristics) and institutions (e.g., political economy and agrarian reform). Thus, while growth is indeed good for the poor, it is not good enough. For policy purposes, an intracountry examination of the determinants of poverty reduction seems superior to cross-country analysis.

In Chapter 8—Poverty, Growth, and Inequality in Thailand—Deolalikar explores the impact of economic growth as well as changes in income inequality on poverty reduction using provincial data over the period 1992-1999. The results suggest that, while income growth has a strong positive effect on poverty reduction, income inequality has a sharply negative effect. Income inequality reduces the rate of poverty reduction in two ways: first, increased inequality is associated with increased poverty after controlling for economic growth, and second, high levels of initial inequality reduce future growth rates, thereby impeding the poverty reduction that would have taken place in the presence of rapid growth. This suggests that income inequality can critically affect the rate of poverty reduction, especially in a low-growth environment. Given that the near-term prospects for growth in Thailand are guarded, it may be particularly important for poverty reduction strategy to focus on improving income inequality, or at least preventing its further worsening.

Finally, in Chapter 9—Economic Growth and Poverty Reduction in Viet Nam—Balisacan, Pernia, and Estrada analyze provincial data from two household surveys in the 1990s to see how local attributes and institutions contributed to the remarkable poverty reduction during that decade. The results suggest that economic growth was the single most dominant determinant of the improved living standards of the poor. Economic reform that began in the 1980s laid the foundation for dynamic growth that resulted in sharp poverty reduction. The implication is that the higher the growth rate, the lesser becomes the role of distributive factors that directly influence the poor's well-being. Nevertheless, these factors could contribute to reinforcing both growth and poverty reduction in the long run.

Note

1. Throughout this volume, the terms "poverty reduction," "poverty alleviation," and "anti-poverty" are used interchangeably.

PART I
General Essays

2 Poverty Reduction: Approaches and the Role of Political Institutions

Anil B. Deolalikar and Ernesto M. Pernia

EVOLUTION OF POVERTY REDUCTION STRATEGIES

The policy concern about poverty and income distribution among multilateral organizations goes as far back as 1970 when the United Nations Committee for Development Planning, in preparing for the United Nations' Second Development Decade, referred to the necessary 'war on poverty' (United Nations 1970). The Committee declared poverty reduction through accelerated development, improved income distribution, and other social changes (including employment, education, health, and housing) as the paramount objective of an appropriate international development strategy.

The World Bank in 1974 published a seminal volume on redistribution with growth (Chenery et al. 1974), which emphasized that policies of wealth redistribution were not only consistent with promoting growth, but actually conducive to it. The suggestion that no trade-off existed between economic growth and the fight against inequality and poverty was fairly novel. Nonetheless, the idea won acceptance in policy circles fairly quickly.

In the 1980s, the International Labor Office (ILO) launched the World Employment Program (WEP), under which a number of studies on income distribution and poverty were undertaken. Many of Sen's early writings on the entitlement-capability approach (Sen 1981), for instance, were published under the ILO WEP program.

The World Bank took this concern for poverty further by making it the theme of its *World Development Report* (WDR) in 1990. According to the *WDR 1990*, a successful attack on poverty needed to be mounted simultaneously on three fronts: (i) broad-based (labor-intensive) economic growth that generated employment and incomes for the poor; (ii) development of human capital (education, health, and nutrition) of the poor that would allow them to better exploit the opportunities created by economic growth; and (iii) social safety nets for those among the poor who were unable to benefit from growth and human development opportunities owing to physical and mental disabilities, natural disasters, civil conflict, and physical isolation.

The Asian Development Bank's (ADB) poverty reduction strategy, although broadly similar, differs from the *WDR 1990* in explicitly considering the importance of governance. According to ADB (1999a), the three pillars of a poverty reduction strategy are: (i) pro-poor, sustainable economic growth; (ii) social development, comprising human capital development, social capital, improving the status of women, and social protection; and (iii) sound macroeconomic management and good governance, required for the successful achievement of the first two pillars.

In addition, the ADB approach emphasizes the importance of understanding the nexus between poverty and the environment. Two of the major environmental issues are (i) air and water pollution in mega-cities that affects the poor disproportionately (Pernia 1994); and (ii) deforestation, natural resource depletion, and land degradation that can deepen poverty (Quibria 1993).

In its *WDR 2000*, the World Bank put forward a new analytical framework—built on three pillars, namely empowerment, security, and opportunity—to attack poverty. Empowerment is the process of enhancing the capacity of poor people to influence the state's institutions that affect their lives, by strengthening their participation in political processes and local decision making. Security is the protection of the poor against adverse shocks, through better management of macroeconomic shocks as well as more comprehensive safety nets. And opportunity is the process of improving the access of the poor to physical and human capital and increasing the rates of return to these assets.

Despite superficial differences, it should be noted that the various approaches to poverty reduction are actually quite similar. All of them emphasize the importance of broad-based, labor-intensive, and inclusive growth; good governance and accountability; human and social development; and social protection and special poverty alleviation policies.

Another important issue relating to poverty reduction that has arisen in recent years, thanks to the success of East Asian countries in reducing poverty, is globalization. The East Asian countries' success is often attributed to their pursuit of economic openness. Opponents of globalization insist that by requiring developing countries to reduce barriers to the movement of goods, services, and capital, and enforce global property claims, globalization destroys domestic industries and traditional crafts, and threatens the food security of poor families. Proponents of globalization, on the other hand, point out how globalization offers enormous opportunities to developing countries through easier access to the world's knowledge, better technologies for delivering products and services, and expanded markets.

A recent review by the UK's Department for International Development (DFID 2001) does point to some serious concerns, including the fact that, although globalization has an important role in promoting economic prosperity, it has not influenced the lives of the poor living in remote or inaccessible areas so far. In addition, globalization is also said to have exposed developing countries to systemic risks, as illustrated by the Asian crisis of 1997/1998. On the other side of the argument, it might be pointed out that the lack of impact on marginalized areas and sectors is less an argument against globalization per se than an argument for inclusion. Similarly, the fact that financial and other crises do occur is less about globalization and more about the need for a sound macroeconomic position, adequate domestic regulation, and transparency in relationships between companies and banks. At any rate, a more critical and nuanced view would recognize that the potential benefits of market reforms and globalization cannot be realized in the absence of appropriate institutions including regulatory frameworks. At least during the transition, therefore, the poor could be and often are subject to acute hardships, while social inequalities could widen.

Specific concerns over globalization have also been expressed in the context of rural poverty alleviation. The International Fund for Agricultural Development (IFAD 2001), for example, points out how trade liberalization influences the rural poor in diverse ways. Removing or reducing biases against farm prices may help food sellers among the rural poor but harm net food buyers. However, what is important is access to competitive market channels. If, for instance, monopsonistic marketing boards are merely replaced by private monopsonists, trade liberalization may bring only little gains to smallholders. Moreover, supply responses are conditional upon infrastructural support (e.g., roads and communication networks). Finally, trade liberalization is associated not just with higher food crop prices but also higher variances of these prices, especially rice. So, even if smallholders benefit under certain conditions from higher prices, they are also exposed to greater variability of farm incomes (for illustrations, see Lustig and Stern 2000 and Gaiha 2001a). Worries over food security add to the already high levels of tension among the poor.

Growth and Poverty Reduction

In the last few years, there has been increasing interest in the question of whether the poor share the benefits of growth. One strand of literature analyzes the cross-country relationship between economic growth and income per capita in the first quintile of the distribution (i.e., the poorest of a country's population). Using essentially the same data and similar econometric techniques, Roemer and Gugerty (1997), Gallup et al. (1999), and Dollar and Kraay (2001) estimate the growth elasticity of per capita incomes of the poorest quintile to be practically one, implying that growth in average income leads to a one-for-one increase in the incomes of the poor. However, Timmer (1997) obtains an elasticity of around 0.8, indicating less than proportionate gains for the poor from economic growth.

A second strand of literature examines the effect of economic growth on absolute poverty. Ravallion (2000), Ravallion and Chen (1997), and Bruno et al. (1998) find that the elasticity of the poverty headcount ratio is typically greater than two—viz., when average income increases by 10 percent, the proportion who are poor declines by more than 20 percent. Other studies such as those of Morley (2000), De Janvry and Sadoulet (2000), and Smolensky et al. (1994) report smaller elasticities of around 1 percent, but these are obtained from a smaller sample of countries. Ravallion and Chen (1997) also use poverty lines that combine an absolute and a relative component, but their elasticities are highly sensitive to where the poverty line is located. They estimate elasticities of poverty ranging from -2.6 to -0.7, depending on whether the threshold is established at 50 percent or 100 percent of the average income observed at the initial period of observation.

A third strand probes the growth-poverty nexus using data on regions, states, provinces, or districts within a country. Subnational econometric analysis of the effect of growth on incomes of the first quintile in Indonesia and the Philippines reveals a still large but lesser role of growth in poverty changes (elasticity much less than one). In Indonesia, human capital, infrastructure, agricultural price regime, and access to technology directly influence the welfare of the poor by altering income distribution (Chapter 6). In the Philippines, local governance and agrarian reform, in addition, have significant favorable effects on the poor's well-being (Chapter 7). In India, literacy, higher rural-to-urban income levels, and other state-specific attributes contribute importantly to poverty reduction (Datt and Ravallion 1998). In Thailand, income inequality and dependency burden raise poverty incidence, while education and economic growth reduce it (Chapter 8). Subnational analysis seems superior to cross-country regressions: first, because the concepts and measurements of poverty, inequality, and income vary widely across countries; and, second, because the relationship between growth and poverty is highly country-specific, and so must be poverty reduction strategies and policies.

Whether across or within countries, however, the existence of differences in the effect of growth on poverty reduction inevitably raises the question whether and under what conditions a greater response can be effected. It is in this context that the term "pro-poor growth" is often used. Pro-poor growth, as distinguished from "trickle-down growth", is economic growth that is explicitly biased in favor of the poor so that they benefit more than proportionately relative to the nonpoor. Obviously, pro-poor growth is possible only under an enabling environment in which poor households can rapidly increase their production, income, and earnings. Since the most important asset—often the only asset—that the poor possess is their own labor, labor-intensive development projects will tend to be pro-poor.

Kakwani and Pernia (2000) define a pro-poor growth index that compares the actual reduction in poverty due to growth with the reduction in poverty that might have occurred with no change in inequality. Using this definition, they find that during the 1990s growth in Korea was significantly more pro-poor than growth in Thailand and Lao PDR. Thailand's growth became progressively more pro-poor over time, however. Moreover, growth in rural areas was found to be more pro-poor than that in urban areas.[1]

Direct Poverty Alleviation Policies

Obviously, no one would argue that growth is all that is needed to improve the lives of the poor. Many developing and developed countries have supplemented macroeconomic growth with direct antipoverty interventions. Such interventions include land reforms, microcredit, and public employment schemes.

Land reforms are critical in less industrialized countries, since access to land is an important source of livelihood in the rural areas. To the extent that many empirical studies have shown smallholders to be more efficient users of land than large landholders, and sharecropping to be inefficient vis-à-vis owner-operated cultivation (Shaban 1987, Binswanger et al. 1995, Otsuka 2000, Ravallion and Sen 1994), the implementation of land reforms may pose no trade-offs between equity and efficiency.[2] In addition, land reform is said to give a 'voice' to landless workers and sharecropping tenants, who are typically the poorest in most countries, through greater participation in local institutions.[3]

Special employment schemes have also figured prominently in poverty alleviation programs of many Asian developing countries (ADCs). The two most common types are self-employment creation schemes and wage-employment schemes. Most self-employment creation schemes seek to place income-generating assets, such as dairy cattle, power looms, small retail stores, or street-hawking equipment in the hands of the poor. This is typically done by giving the poor access to credit and various forms of marketing assistance. A good example is India's Integrated Rural Development Program (IRDP), which offers subsidized credit for the purchase of income-generating assets. Dubbed as one of the largest self-employment schemes in the world, the IRDP benefits nearly one third of all rural poor households in India (Bandopadhyaya 1985). Indonesia has also had two similar schemes with very wide coverage—Kupedes and Badan Kredit Kecamatan (BKK). The BKK serves more than 35 percent of Java's 8,500 villages (World Bank 1990). Another well-known self-employment creation (microcredit) scheme is the Grameen Bank of Bangladesh (Khandker 1998).

Wage employment schemes provide labor opportunities to the poor, typically in public works projects. These schemes have long been used in many developing countries in emergency situations, such as during periods of famine and drought and, more recently, during periods of macroeconomic stabilization and adjustment, when there is large-scale, transitory unemployment and underemployment in the rural sector. In recent times, however, many developing countries have incorporated such schemes as regular elements of an antipoverty strategy. Particularly in South Asia, wage employment schemes in the form of rural works constitute the core of government antipoverty strategies. For instance, the government of India operates the National Rural Employment Program, a national wage employment scheme based on public works projects. Another well-known scheme is the Employment Guarantee Scheme in the Indian state of Maharashtra. In the Philippines, in the mid-1960s, a pump-priming program that centered on the construction of roads and other infrastructure was implemented to generate employment in the countryside. Again, in 1986, the Philippine government launched the Community Employment Development Program, which also focused on building farm-to-market roads and other similar infrastructure as part of rural job creation.

Which of the three types of policies—land reform, microcredit, or public employment programs—is likely to be most effective in reducing poverty? A combination of all three will typically be more effective than any single policy, since each addresses different aspects of poverty (e.g., chronic versus transitory poverty). It is important to

Figure 2.1: Public Works versus Means-tested Credit Subsidy Maharashtra, India, 1987-1988

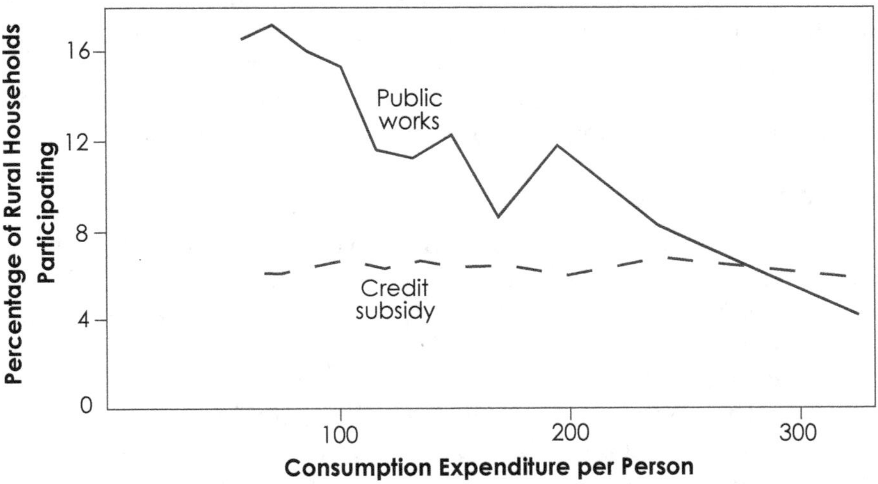

Source: Ravallion and Datt (1995).

note, however, that direct poverty alleviation policies alone are unlikely to result in sustained poverty decline. What is needed is a combination of pro-poor economic growth and direct poverty interventions.

A study comparing the beneficiaries under a credit scheme (viz., the Integrated Rural Development Program) versus those under a workfare scheme (the Employment Guarantee Scheme) in the Indian state of Maharashtra found the workfare scheme to be well targeted at the poor. That is, participation in the scheme declined with economic status (Ravallion and Datt 1995). By contrast, participation in the credit scheme bore virtually no relationship with the economic status of beneficiaries (Figure 2.1). This may have been because a large number of individuals misrepresented their incomes to qualify for subsidized loans or due to widespread corruption in the administration of the program.

A few studies have drawn attention to the disincentive effects of direct antipoverty interventions. In has been argued, for instance, that rural public works may discourage job search and investment in income-augmenting skills (Besley and Coate 1992). Food subsidies in Sri Lanka have been associated with a reduction in labor supply and work effort (Sahn and Alderman 1988). Another study for South Africa found that public pension support to parents of migrant workers significantly decreased the remittances from migrant children (Jensen 1998). If these effects are confirmed through detailed empirical analyses, their implications for the cost-effectiveness of antipoverty interventions can be serious. An important issue then is whether incentive-compatible designs of such interventions are feasible.

Basic Social Services

Another instrument for combating poverty is improved access to social services, especially health and education (Sen 2000a, World Bank 2000b). Not only are basic levels of health and education a right, they are also important in accelerating poverty reduction, as they allow the poor to take advantage of the opportunities created by economic growth.[4] But in many countries, the poor have less physical (geographical) and economic access to education and health services than the nonpoor, resulting in lower rates of utilization and, hence, worse health and literacy outcomes. A vicious circle of poverty is thus formed, leading to ill health, malnutrition, and illiteracy, which in turn perpetuate poverty.

The physical remoteness of the poor from public facilities such as hospitals, health centers, and schools is often exacerbated by community financing of public schools and health centers. Since richer communities are better able to raise matching funds for public investments, they are likely to receive more and better public facilities. Studies in Cambodia and Viet Nam have shown that average distances to secondary schools and higher levels of health care (viz., polyclinics and hospitals) are significantly greater for the poor than for the nonpoor (Pradhan and Prescott 1998, World Bank 1999).

Even if geographical access to social services were the same for both the poor and the nonpoor, as in urban areas, the high cost of these services would serve as a significant barrier to their use by the poor. Although many publicly provided services, such as health care and schooling, are supposedly available free of charge to the poor, in practice these services are rarely obtained without some form of payment. Fees are typically charged for medicines, textbooks, and supplies. In addition, public officials may extract informal payments to provide otherwise "free" public services.

Institutional Factors and Governance

Social, cultural, and institutional factors exert a pervasive influence on poverty reduction—both directly as well as indirectly—via their effects on growth, poverty alleviation policies, and provision of social services. Political exclusion, for example, can result in some groups being denied access to publicly provided social services and poverty reduction programs. Agricultural growth may benefit the poor less to the extent there are institutional obstacles to legislating and implementing effective land reform. In addition, sociocultural taboos and beliefs can result in some groups deliberately excluding themselves from public antipoverty programs. These issues are discussed in detail in the succeeding chapters.

There has likewise been growing recognition that good governance is an important factor that contributes to poverty reduction. Good governance implies transparency and accountability in public decision making, greater participation by citizens and civil society in decision making, and devolution of administrative and fiscal powers to local governments and communities. A major intervention to bring about good governance is the continuing attempt to introduce wide-ranging reforms in the public sector.

POLITICAL INSTITUTIONS AND THE POLITICAL ECONOMY OF POVERTY REDUCTION

Political will and commitment are primary prerequisites for poverty reduction. All the factors that cause poverty to decline, including pro-poor growth, social development, and good governance, depend on a prior commitment to reduce poverty and a determination to implement the measures required to succeed. The question remains, of course, how the political will for poverty alleviation can be engendered.

Democracy, Political Will, and Poverty Reduction

An emerging literature holds that democracy is important for poverty alleviation. The argument is that basic civil liberties, such as freedom of expression and dissent, hold governments accountable for their actions, thus improving performance. The most well-known proponents of this hypothesis are Sen (1981) and Drèze and Sen (1989), who have pointed out, among other things, that no country with a free press has ever experienced a major famine. They hypothesize that the fear of the media focusing on the government's failure forces governments into prompt famine-avoidance action. As Sen (1981) himself has noted, however, a free press does not necessarily eliminate persistent hunger since relatively moderate starvation does not attract much attention in newspapers. The case of India is pertinent in this regard; while India has been able to avoid large-scale starvation and famine because of its free press, it has been much less successful than other countries, such as the People's Republic of China (PRC) and Sri Lanka, in eliminating malnutrition.

Likewise, a cross-country study of 1,488 World Bank-financed government projects in developing countries over the period 1974-1987 finds that the performance of these projects was better in countries where civil liberties are greater (Isham, Kaufmann, and Pritchett 1997).[5] The effect of civil liberties on project performance was strong and positive even after controlling for other political and economic variables.[6]

It is simplistic to think, however, that democracy or civil liberties alone can guarantee poverty reduction. After all, only until recently it was widely believed that a strong and autocratic leadership was an essential factor common to all the ADCs that had experienced rapid economic growth and poverty reduction, such as the Republic of Korea (hereafter Korea) and Taipei,China in the 1960s and 1970s; Thailand in the 1970s and 1980s; and Indonesia in the 1980s and early 1990s. Some scholars credit the success of Korea and Taipei,China in implementing far-reaching land reform to their 'enlightened dictatorships' (e.g., Haggard 1990). At the same time, poverty reduction in one of Asia's most democratic countries, India, had been among the slowest rates in the region, at least until the 1990s.[7]

In a review of antipoverty programs in India, Kohli (1987) has argued that there are differences in regime types even within a democratic setting, and that these differences matter to poverty reduction. Three important elements of a pro-poor political regime in a democratic setting are: (i) coherent and stable leadership; (ii) market-oriented economic policy coupled with good governance; and (iii) clear pro-lower-class ideology. Even this, however, merely brings us to the next natural question, which is: Why do regimes possess these three attributes in different degrees? In other words, what determines the "pro-poor" bias of the political regime at the national and subnational levels?

Interest Groups and Dominant Coalitions

Modern theories of the state recognize that governments are rarely monolithic and impervious to social and political pressure from interest groups.[8] Politicians, bureaucrats, businesses, and consumers frequently use the authority of government to influence economic and other transactions for their own benefit. Citizens use political influence to obtain access to benefits allocated by the state; politicians use public resources to retain power; businesses seek special favors (such as protection from competition) from the government; and bureaucrats offer access to government benefits for personal reward. The frequent result is an inefficient and inequitable allocation of resources.

Lobbying by special-interest groups is thus critical to understanding government actions. Within this framework, the political feasibility of antipoverty interventions depends greatly on the distribution of benefits from the antipoverty intervention, which in turn depends on the prevailing configuration of pressure groups in the country (e.g., labor unions, landlords, peasant movements, consumer groups, women's groups) (de Janvry et al. 1992). Thus, poverty reduction outcomes (and more generally, development itself) are conditioned by the dominant coalitions prevailing in the country (Bardhan 1984).

The prospects for poverty alleviation in a country will be better, the stronger are the coalitions of the poor. In turn the relative strength of such coalitions depends on several factors, such as their awareness of potential gains from collective action, their willingness and ability to cooperate with other groups, and their degree of politicization. Many mechanisms exist through which coalitions of the poor can influence the state. These include periodic consultations, lobbying through mass media, street protests, and other forms of activism and confrontation.

To these traditional interest groups must be added another set that has lately become important, namely global institutions. Developing countries act within the context of rules under the global economic system, which is largely dominated by global organizations such as the International Monetary Fund, World Bank, Asian Development Bank, World Trade Organization, foreign governments, and businesses. Such organizations often have an important say in influencing a developing country's choice of poverty-related policies. For example, labor market flexibility may be required of a country like Korea as a precondition for joining the Organisation for Economic Cooperation (OECD). A country like Cambodia or Viet Nam may be required by a multilateral organization to put in place a clear and donor-approved poverty reduction strategy if it is to continue receiving loans at preferential rates (such as the Asian Development Fund or International Development Association credits). Thus, external actors can be regarded as another pressure or interest group influencing government action.

Land Reform

Nowhere is the importance of dominant coalitions and interest groups in bringing about poverty reduction more evident than in the case of land reform. Effective land reform has been recognized as a *sine qua non* for agricultural and economic development.[9] Even more importantly, land reform is critical to poverty reduction, since landlessness is a root cause of poverty in rural Asia (ILO 1977, Khan and Lee 1984, Breman and Mundle 1991). Countries that have effectively implemented land reform have not only experienced more robust agricultural growth and productivity,[10] they have also enjoyed a better distribution of income and lower rates of poverty. In addition, an often underemphasized by-product of land reform is, as Bardhan (1997) notes, that changing the local political structure gives more voice to the poor and enables them to participate in local self-governing institutions and in managing local public goods.

Overwhelming evidence exists to show that land reform was critical in bringing about agricultural development, poverty reduction, and even industrial growth in Korea and Taipei,China. The sweeping land reforms enacted by the former in 1948-1950 and the latter in 1949-1953 redistributed between one quarter and one half of all available land (Haggard 1990, Ho 1978). Korea, which had one of the most unequal distributions of land in the world in 1945 (with 3 percent of the rural population owning 60 percent of the land and a vast 80 percent of the rural population being landless tenants or semitenants), transformed itself into a country having one of the world's most favorable land distributions. In 1970, Korea's Gini coefficient of land inequality was merely 0.37—a great deal lower than that in countries such as Brazil (0.83) or Mexico (0.77) (Shin 1998). This reversal was entirely the result of sweeping land reforms, first by the American military government in 1948, followed by the Korean government in 1950.

It is often believed that the occupying American occupation forces were responsible for implementing the land reform in Korea. However, the real impetus for land reform came from social conflict in the form of agrarian struggles that began under Japanese colonial rule in the 1920s (Shin 1998). Widespread tenancy disputes in the 1920s resulted in the colonial (Japanese) government abandoning its earlier landlord-based policy and its reluctance to intervene in land disputes. The Tenant Arbitration Ordinance was enacted in 1932, which enabled landlords or tenants to submit claims to nonbinding arbitration by local representatives of county tenancy offices. This was followed in 1934 with more land laws that further constrained landlord rights.[11] The power of landlords was also circumscribed when Japanese rule ended, since many of them were tainted with having been collaborators of the colonial forces. Against this backdrop, many grassroots organizations that dominated local politics in 1945, such as peasant unions and people's committees, proposed sweeping land reform to redress inequity and unfairness in rural society. Far from supporting land reform, the United States (US) occupation forces suppressed many of these organizations as communist and restored the Japanese colonial framework. This had the consequence of breeding frustration and discontent among peasants that led to a major agrarian rebellion in the country in 1946. While the US military government made some concessions and distributed some Japanese-owned lands to peasants in 1948, real land reform did not take place until 1950, when the National Assembly passed a sweeping land reform bill (Shin 1998).[12]

Land reform in Taipei,China took place under a different set of circumstances. It was carried out in three stages between 1949 and 1953: the compulsory reduction of land rent; the sale of public land to actual tillers; and the "Land-to-the-Tiller Program", which imposed a limit on the amount of land that could be held by landlords.[13] Land reform was initiated just before the Chinese Communist victory on the mainland, which posed a threat to the island's internal security. Against this background, the Nationalist Party began implementing land reform both as a means to gain political legitimacy and to prevent Communist penetration into the rural areas (Tai 1974).[14] In addition, it helped that the Nationalist Party leaders, coming from the mainland PRC, did not include any representatives of the local landed gentry. It was thus conveniently sheltered from the protests of indigenous landlords against land redistribution. Likewise, the bureaucracy that had accompanied Chiang Kai-shek from the mainland had no indigenous connections and was thus more effective in implementing land reform legislation. Thus, a coalition between a nonindigenous ruling party interested in seeking political legitimacy and a bureaucracy lacking connections to indigenous landlords, united by a common interest in averting a Communist rebellion, were instrumental in bringing about comprehensive land reforms in Taipei,China.[15]

Unfortunately, Korea and Taipei,China are atypical among ADCs in terms of the sweeping nature of their land redistribution and the success of their land reform programs. Many ADCs have encountered difficulties in enacting and implementing meaningful land reform. Indeed, in some ADCs, such as Pakistan, rates of landlessness have actually increased over time (Irfan and Amjad 1984), and this has been a significant factor in the rising rates of rural poverty. An important reason for the lack of progress on land reform in Pakistan has been the continued dominance of landlords in ruling party coalitions.[16] After Independence, activists in the Muslim League developed political influence on the basis of their wealth, mainly in land. Landlord families extended and perpetuated their power by entering politics and getting themselves elected to influential positions in village, provincial, and national governments. But even when they do not hold elective office, landlords can still exert considerable influence in government decision making (Irfan and Amjad 1984, Stern 2001). Having thus secured political influence, the landlord lobby has been able to thwart efforts to pass and implement meaningful land reform. The resulting feudalism in Pakistan has been blamed for the lack of progress on several fronts, including agricultural development, industrialization, and eradication of illiteracy.

The Philippines also has an uneven history of success in implementing land reform. Initial attempts at land reform were motivated by a rebellion by Communist guerrillas (known as the Huks) during the 1940s. Under the leadership of President Ramon Magsaysay, a number of reform laws were enacted during the 1950s to avert forceful change of the existing political order. Since these reforms were not implemented effectively, there was a need for another set of reforms—as embodied in the Agricultural Land Reform Code—in 1963 (Tai 1974). Indeed, the Philippines has a long history of land reform legislation that has only been implemented half-heartedly. President

Marcos launched the Operation Land Transfer program in 1972,[17] which was followed in 1988 by yet another land reform—the Comprehensive Agrarian Reform Law—under the leadership of President Aquino. Owing to weak implementation, as much as 72 percent of rural families were still landless at the end of her term (Putzel 1992). Not surprisingly, agricultural growth has been poor in the Philippines relative to other countries in Asia. Rice yields in 1991 were less than half those obtained in PRC, Japan, or Korea.

With a former NGO leader designated in 1992 as Secretary of the Department of Agrarian Reform, substantial progress was achieved during the Ramos administration through the transfer of public land to cultivators and private land voluntarily sold by their owners to the tenants. Newly created agrarian reform communities, composed of the new owner-beneficiaries, received targeted support services for increased production. Nonetheless, the political will needed to sustain this momentum declined from 1998 onward, owing to insufficient funds allocated to the land acquisition process, coupled with mounting resistance from the large private landed elites and plantation owners. The targeted number of hectares for land transfer has been reduced, while prospects for an accelerated program appear unlikely to come from a landlord-dominated legislature.

Countries that have delayed implementation of land reform find themselves in a quandary, since land reform becomes increasingly difficult to implement the longer it has been delayed. Extensive delays not only lead to uncertainty among farmers, but also undermine land markets by allowing landowners to convert their lands to other uses to circumvent the law.

Mobilizing Action for Poverty Reduction

Given the nature of the modern state, how can action for poverty eradication be mobilized within the often chaotic, free-for-all power grab by various special-interest groups? Surprisingly little attention up to now has been devoted in the development economics literature (although it abounds in NGO literature) to issues of how to build constituencies for poverty eradication; how to form coalitions and alliances that can bring about meaningful land reform; and how to rally and organize support for rational social policies that benefit everyone in the long run.

Coalitions of the Poor

Poverty reduction is obviously not a task that governments, NGOs or development institutions can do on their own. It ultimately requires the efforts and participation of the poor themselves. To be effective, however, the poor need to build coalitions with other groups, such as governments and NGOs. As the IFAD report on rural poverty puts it (IFAD 2001, 214):

> ...it is misguided bureaucratic centralism to plan for the poor; partnerships for poverty reduction, wherever possible, start with the agency of the poor themselves, with their preferences and potentials. But it is naïve to suppose that the poor can make bricks without straw; technologies, information, schools and skills have to be built in conjunction with outsiders... This requires putting the poor at the center of the [development] process, as full partners in determining the priorities and the directions of change, emancipating them from the constraints that trap them in poverty, empowering them.

In Korea, it took coalitions of tenants and grassroots organizations such as peasant unions and people's committees to pressure the government to enact and implement land reform. More recently, coalitions of the rural poor and civil society organizations in Thailand succeeded in moving poverty to the top of the government's agenda. During the 1980s to the mid-1990s, a period of rapid growth of the Thai economy, poverty incidence in Thailand fell dramatically, and the government saw little need to devote much attention to poverty reduction programs. A number of poverty alleviation programs existed on paper, though these amounted to little in practice.[18] With the onset of the economic crisis in 1997, however, the decade-long decline in poverty quickly came to an end, and poverty rates increased sharply.[19] As the situation of the poor continued to deteriorate, rural unrest began to rise. In 2000, thousands of villagers took to the streets of Bangkok to clamor for action against rural poverty. The rural poor also staged widespread protests in Bangkok against the impact on their livelihoods of the Pak Moon dam, a state hydroelectric facility in northeastern Ubon Ratchathani province. The street protests and other demonstrations received organizational and other support from

NGOs, such as the Forum of the Poor, a grassroots movement for change in Thailand.[20]

The coalition of the poor, with civil society support, has brought concrete gains. The National Assembly in 1997 passed a new constitution that, for the first time in Thai history, guarantees community rights to self-determination. There is also growing consensus in the country on the need for an alternative development model and the importance of developing sustainable communities in which people, especially the poor, have the power to manage their own resources in an equitable manner. The Thai Rak Thai party, which ran on a strong rural poverty alleviation platform, won the national elections in early 2001. The new government has already begun implementing major antipoverty projects, such as a village-based fund for poor villages and debt relief for farmers. Poverty alleviation has turned almost overnight into the new government's overriding objective.

There are numerous examples of successful coalitions of the poor and civil society organizations throughout Asia. One of them is the Self-Employed Women's Association (SEWA) in the Indian state of Gujarat, which had a long history of organizing textile workers in the city of Ahmedabad, but which adapted those lessons to organizing self-employed women in the informal sector. Starting from an urban base in Gujarat, it expanded to rural areas. SEWA is both a trade union and a grassroots movement for the empowerment of the poorest women in Indian society. Case studies in Carr et al. (1996) indicate that, despite initial skepticism among the members, the organization has not only led to significant income gains for the members on a regular basis, but the experience of managing producer groups has also imparted greater security and independence to the women members both within and outside the household. The sense of solidarity is strengthened and caste divisions are weakened. Women now advise their husbands on cropping decisions. Their advice is also sought on community matters (e.g., sanitation). Greater political awareness has led to more active participation in local elections (Carr et al. 1996).

In the Philippines, the Congress for People's Agrarian Reform (CPAR)—a coalition of 22 NGOs working with 14 large peasant alliances that represent 1.5 million small farmers, peasant women, landless cultivators, agricultural workers, and fisherfolk—lobbied in the late 1980s for the incorporation of the People's Declaration of Principles on Agrarian Reform into a new agrarian reform law. With thousands of farmers and civil society members throughout the country marching, protesting, lobbying inside the legislature, and camped daily at a tent city outside it, Congress and the Senate ultimately passed the Comprehensive Agrarian Reform Law (CARL) in 1991. Although weaker than its proponents had envisioned, CARL was more progressive than any previous agrarian reform law passed. Without the massive peasant lobbying effort, a law with weaker provisions would have been passed.

CPAR had a profound impact on society. It gave national and local peasant leaders the experience of attempting to unify the organized peasantry, and some idea of the issues that divided them. They learned how to build consensus and democratic management, and got to know better the leaders of other ideological persuasions. These personal friendships undoubtedly sustained the largest coalition in Philippine history for a longer period than anyone would have predicted. Fisherfolk issues surfaced separately from those of farmers; peasant participation in congressional debates was institutionalized; and government's interest in managing dissent rather than responding to peasant demands emerged clearly. Peasants and their NGO supporters learned how organizationally strong they needed to be in countering the power of entrenched elites (Goño 1996).

Other ADCs may not currently have similarly strong NGOs and peasant organizations but it may only be a matter of time before these emerge. At the same time, it should be realized that forming coalitions of the poor may not always be easy, since they are far from being homogeneous and may have different ideologies. Various coalitions of the poor with differing ideologies and agenda could actually work at cross purposes, undermining each other's positive efforts.

Obtaining Support from the Non-Poor

Antipoverty programs may find little support or even face outright rejection because the dominant coalition of the nonpoor perceives that it would lose from such programs. In such cases, however, the political support of some nonpoor groups can be enlisted if they also stand to gain from pro-poor policies. Higher incomes for the poor, for example, create a greater demand for goods and services produced by the nonpoor. This multiplier effect provides an objective basis for the nonpoor to provide political support to policies that increase the productivity and incomes of the poor (Streeten 1995). However, such beneficial effects from antipoverty programs need to be publicized among the nonpoor, especially the middle class. This suggests in turn that the success of poverty alleviation programs may well depend upon how the programs are "packaged" and "marketed" to the non-target population.

Likewise, to overcome political opposition to pro-poor policies, especially in times of financial crises, (nonpecuniary) compensation may have to be paid to the nonpoor, even though this may seem inequitable (Streeten 1995, IFAD 2001).[21] Streeten (1995) cites the case of urban wage earners who are often the losers in periods of structural adjustment. Although these groups are generally better-off than farmers, some redeployment payments or retraining schemes to these vocal and powerful groups may be necessary, if only to "buy" their support for pro-poor, progressive reform. As Streeten (1995, 13) puts it, "...the objective of benefiting all the poor and only the poor is [politically] impossible to achieve; excess coverage is preferable to deficient coverage, both for political and administrative reasons." This idea—of not strictly limiting the benefits of antipoverty programs to the poor—has been gaining ground in recent years (Gelbach and Pritchett 1995, Lanjouw and Ravallion 1998, van de Walle 1995).

A difficulty with this argument, however, is that leakages of antipoverty program benefits to the nonpoor are not self-limiting. There is a real risk that the nonpoor may capture the dominant share of public resources and crowd out the poor completely (Bardhan 1984). This is especially likely when resources for antipoverty programs are limited. But while the problems have been identified, there is still no clarity over where a government should draw the line.

Timing of Program Capture

Where the nonpoor manage to capture the benefits of pro-poor programs, it frequently happens in the initial stages of program implementation. This may be due to imperfect targeting, lack of information, or incentive incompatibility. As the antipoverty program expands over time, however, the incremental benefits derived by the poor from the program typically increase. This implies that the average participation rates of the poor in antipoverty programs may understate their marginal participation rate. Using household survey data from the Indian National Sample Survey, Lanjouw and Ravallion (1998) test this hypothesis, and find that the marginal benefits to the poorest quintile of households from the three main antipoverty programs in India—viz., public works, the Integrated Rural Development Program, and the Public Distribution System (a food subsidy program)—are significantly greater than either the average or marginal benefits derived by the richest quintile. In addition, they find that although average primary school enrollment rates are lower for children in the poorest quintile than in the richest quintile, the marginal odds of primary school enrollment are significantly greater for the poorest quintile. These empirical findings support the early-capture theory—i.e., they suggest that the nonpoor benefit from public programs early in the program cycle, while the benefits to the poor accrue later.

Another example of the early-capture model is the social security program in Thailand. In late 1998, as a response to the 1997/1998 financial crisis, the Thai government implemented a far-reaching change to the social security system that had been in place in the early 1990s. The change included the establishment of pension and child allowance schemes for private-sector employees. The idea behind the change in coverage benefits was to offer social protection to the poor affected by the economic crisis.

However, as of 1999, only 15 percent of Thai workers were reported to be covered by the Social Security Act (SSA), with wide variations across different types of workers (World Bank 2000c). Since enrollment in the SSA is mandatory for employees of large private-sector firms and for public employees, social security coverage is strongly biased toward the better-off (high-wage) workers. Figure 2.2 shows that 82 percent of private-sector wage employees earning more than B15,000 per month were covered by SSA as of August 1999, but only 14 percent of those earning B3,001-4,000 per month were covered. Indeed, according to the SSA rules, only workers who were paid more than the minimum wage were eligible for social security coverage, which meant that the lowest-paid workers were automatically excluded from program participation.

This bias toward high-wage employees is not a failure of the Thai social security program per se, which is relatively new in that country. The history of social security programs in more developed countries suggests that initial coverage rates are typically low and biased toward formal-sector employees, who tend to be better-off than infor-

Figure 2.2: Percent of All Employees and Private-Sector Employees with Coverage under the Social Security Act, by Employee's Monthly Wage Rate, Third Quarter of 1999 (Thailand)

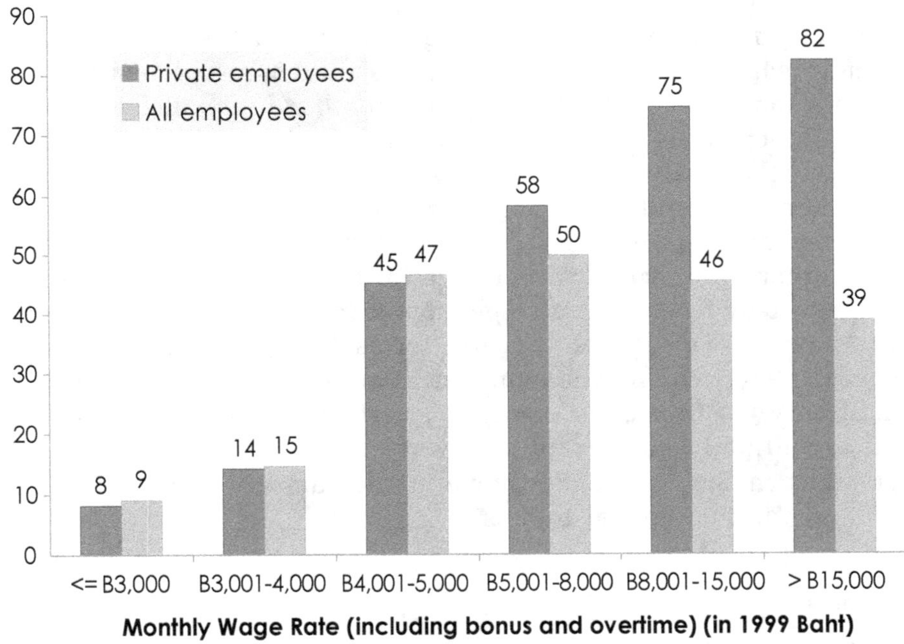

Source: World Bank (2000c).

mal-sector and own-account employees. The relatively higher incomes and salaries of formal-sector employees, in fact, make the social security program financially viable and sustainable. Over time, however, population coverage of the program expands and reaches the low-income and informal-sector groups, with the better-off salaried employees often cross-subsidizing the lower-paid informal-sector and own-account employees.

The Thai government has definite plans to expand the social security program rapidly over the next few years to cover employees of companies with ten or fewer employees. Workers set to benefit from the program's expansion include those working in garages, restaurants, beauty parlors, and other independent ventures. By some accounts, domestic helpers will also be covered by the social security program. Thus, the poor, who did not benefit from the program in its early stages, are expected to eventually obtain social protection from this program.

CONCLUSION

Poverty reduction strategies have evolved over the years, becoming more sophisticated in line with the increasing recognition of poverty's multidimensionality. Approaches have included economic growth, direct poverty alleviation programs, basic social services, and, more recently, institutional factors and governance. The experience of the more successful Asian countries suggests that a strategy with a strong emphasis on economic growth supplemented synergistically by the other approaches is more likely to lead to better outcomes than a strategy focused on a single approach. Institutions and governance have grown in importance in terms of their influence on the delivery of services and the administration of antipoverty programs, apart from their impact on economic growth itself. Above all else are political will and commitment to poverty reduction. They need to be kept intact in the face of the competing demands of dominant coalitions and various interest groups.

Notes

The authors thank Pilipinas F. Quising for very able research assistance.

1. Timmer (1997) also touches upon this issue. He finds that in countries in which the income gap between the poor and the rich is relatively small, growth of labor productivity in agriculture has larger positive effects on the incomes of each quintile than the growth of nonagricultural productivity. But in countries with large income gaps, growth in agricultural productivity is no more effective than nonagricultural productivity in alleviating poverty. Not surprisingly, the rich in these countries benefit substantially from agricultural growth, presumably because of the highly skewed distribution of land.
2. In a somewhat qualified endorsement of land redistribution, Banerjee (2000) does not dispute the efficiency and equity gains. However, given that all forms of redistribution cost money as well as bureaucratic and political capital, it is unclear whether redistributing land is the best way to redress inequality.
3. From the perspective of broadening the constituency for antipoverty interventions, Herring (2000, 31) observes: "Whether policy promotes more or less state intervention, agrarian reform remains a means of restructuring the field of power to which state functionaries respond, and therefore enables more possibilities for

building an effective and responsive state, without which all other anti-poverty options—including growth—are reduced in efficacy."

4. There is a large literature on pecuniary and non-pecuniary returns to schooling in developing countries (Psacharopoulos and Woodhall 1985, Schultz 1988). Several econometric studies have also estimated large productivity gains from improved health and nutrition (Strauss 1986, Deolalikar 1988, Sahn and Alderman 1988).
5. A very large number of indicators of civil liberties were used, including (but not limited to) media free of censorship, open public discussion, freedom of assembly and demonstration, freedom of political organization, and nondiscriminatory rule of law in politically relevant cases.
6. Rather surprisingly, the authors also found a positive association between civil unrest in a country (e.g., protest demonstrations and strikes) and project performance. This, according to the authors, "... suggests that some degree of civil tension reflects a citizen's ability to agitate and influence government's behavior without negative repercussions—a mechanism that plausibly leads to greater accountability and hence better choice and implementation of projects... (Thus) basic civil liberties—such as the freedom of individual expression, a pluralistic and free media, the ability of groups to organize, and freedom of dissent and criticism—facilitate citizen voice and hence more effective government action" (pp. 223, 235)
7. There is some evidence to suggest that, during the 1990s, absolute poverty declined significantly in India, coinciding with the period of economic liberalization and reform.
8. Indeed, what distinguishes "strong states" from "weak states" is the extent to which social control is vested in a large number of local-level social organizations that continually try to extract contracts, jobs, goods, services and authority through the bureaucratic networks of the state. Such states that end up being "weak states" are those unable to govern effectively because their leaders are too busy brokering conflicting demands from various constituencies, often for their own survival, to pursue broad social and political agendas (Migdal 1988).
9. The manner in which land is owned and organized affects (i) the incentive framework within which the farmer makes his production and investment decisions, (ii) the sharing of cropping risk between the tenant and the landlord, and (iii) the need for supervision in farming. There is a great deal of evidence from around the world that owner-cultivators have greater incentives than tenants to increase their work effort, to make longer-term productivity-enhancing investments in their land, and to adopt new and more appropriate agricultural technologies, because they know that the resulting economic gains are largely theirs. Also, when farm workers own their land, there is less need for supervision of labor. Thus, the shift of a large number of tenants to owner-cultivators can have a

significant positive impact on agricultural productivity, and rising productivity is necessary before resources, such as capital and labor, can be transferred successfully out of agriculture to the rest of the economy.

10. However, it has been argued that while there may exist a marked inequality in terms of land ownership in many agrarian economies in Asia, there is much less inequality in terms of operational holdings (Otsuka 1993). The inequality in the distribution of land is further reduced when adjustments are made for soil quality differences across farm sizes, since, in most ADCs, small farms typically are located on superior quality soil than large farms. These facts tend to weaken the equity argument in favor of land reform. Moreover, in many poor countries (such as Bangladesh), the large size of the population and the small amount of land make further redistribution economically infeasible. In these countries, the main plank of antipoverty policies in rural areas would have to be based on enhancing land productivity through new seed-fertilizer and irrigation innovations, and not through further redistribution (Pernia and Quibria 1999).
11. The 1934 Agricultural Lands Ordinance guaranteed contract lengths of at least three years, allowed tenants to propose reduction or remission of rent upon crop failure, made contracts renewable unless violated by tenants, and forbade agreements in which the tenant waived certain rights (Cho 1989).
12. Interestingly, under the Korean land reform, landlords whose plots were expropriated were compensated for their land loss with land bonds— (financial assets that could be reinvested elsewhere). The government encouraged the use of these land bonds for industrial capital formation through the purchase of vested nonagricultural enterprises. The land bonds constituted an important vehicle of the capital formation that was needed for Korean industrialization, and many landlords, especially the largest ones, profitably used land bonds to become industrial capitalists (Shin 1998).
13. The rent reduction program, initiated in 1949, limited farm rents to a maximum of 37.5 percent of the annual yield of the main crops. Rent reduction was followed by the sale of public land (mostly land previously owned by Japanese colonists and confiscated after the war) to tenants, with the price set at 2.5 times the annual yield, which was well below the market price. Under the land-to-the-tiller program, initiated in 1953 and the final step in the land reform process, land owned by landlords in excess of approximately three hectares of medium-quality paddy field, or its equivalent, was compulsorily purchased by the government and resold to the tenants at 2.5 times the land's annual yield. The government paid for the land in commodity bonds (70 percent) and in shares of stock in four government enterprises (30 percent). In turn, the tenants paid for the land—in rice for paddy land and in sweet potatoes (converted to cash) for dry land—in 20 installments over a period of ten years (Ho 1978).
14. In India land reform was also used as a means to gain legitimacy for a new regime. The Congress Party abolished the *zamindari* (sharecropping tenancy)

system in 1935 as a way of widening its base beyond a small group of intellectuals and becoming a mass independence movement (Tai 1974).

15. On the other hand, land reform in Thailand only marginally affected the farmers, yet agriculture has performed well (Rashid and Quibria 1995).
16. Naseem (1977) notes that a total of only 5 percent of farming families were favorably affected by the two major land reforms implemented in Pakistan in 1959 and 1972. Neither of the two land reforms measures improved the lot of the landless laborers directly.
17. As Putzel (1992, 374) puts it, "...since the colonial period, landowning interests have shackled the (Filipino) bureaucracy and blocked every attempt at comprehensive land registration.... The Marcos years proved that an authoritarian form of government has no special proclivity toward reform implementation."
18. For instance, a World Bank poverty assessment noted: "... The principal conclusion of this evaluation of targeted anti-poverty programs in Thailand is that, despite impressions to the contrary, the level of government spending on these programs is small, and what money is being spent appears to be having little impact on the lives of the poor. Therefore, effectiveness of these programs in reducing the incidence and severity of poverty is limited. The widespread perception within Thailand that a lot of public spending is devoted to poverty alleviation efforts is not borne out by the reality. Rather, this impression probably reflects the number and variety of publicly-funded programs that are aimed directly or, in most cases, tangentially at helping the poor" (World Bank 1996a, 49-50).
19. The headcount ratio of poverty in Thailand increased from 11.4 percent in 1996 to 13 percent in 1998 and 15.9 percent in 1999. This meant that an additional one million persons became poor in 1998, with 1999 seeing another 2 million persons added to this number (World Bank 2000d).
20. Forum of the Poor is also referred to sometimes as Assembly of the Poor. In addition to compensation for loss of land and means of livelihood due to dam construction, another issue put on the front burner by the coalition of NGOs and the poor is the eviction of farmers from forest areas.
21. For example, the IFAD report on poverty argues, "... in some cases, the poor may benefit by uniting with some of the rich in a coalition... Many non-poor, for whatever reason, often support forms of insurance or universal coverage amounting to pro-poor redistribution: for example, to provide basic health care or social safety nets" (IFAD 2001, 192).

3 Sociocultural Factors Affecting Poverty and Poverty Reduction

MARY RACELIS AND
MARITA CONCEPCION CASTRO GUEVARA

INTRODUCTION

Until fairly recently, discussions of poverty have largely dwelt on assessments of income and expenditure, with "social analysis" rarely proceeding beyond issues of health and education. Such discussions unfortunately neglect decades of rich sociological, anthropological and psycho-social research that sheds light on poverty, its differential causes, expressions and consequences in societies the world over. Central to this discussion are key concepts from sociology (e.g., social class, family, cooperation, conflict). Anthropology contributes such concepts as culture, values, norms, ethnicity, and alliances, while social psychology adds such notions as vulnerability, self-esteem, insecurity, and discrimination.

This chapter focuses on poor people and their social environments, drawing on the works of sociologists, anthropologists, and social psychologists. The next section introduces a multidimensional perspective on poverty, exploring how men, women, children, and youth view their own poverty and ways of overcoming it. The third section considers the social structures and processes that divide people into groups affected by discrimination, prejudice, marginalization, ostracism, and lack of access to the benefits of society—or what has recently been termed social exclusion. The fourth section is devoted to socially reinforced institutional arrangements that help poor people survive and prosper. The fifth section focuses on nongovernment organizations (NGOs) and their contributions to poverty reduction. The last section reviews government pro-poor interventions through expanded social welfare and other safety net programs, and summarizes key points and important sociocultural guidelines for poverty reduction.

A MULTIDIMENSIONAL PERSPECTIVE ON POVERTY

The most broadly used standard for measuring poverty is the adequate consumption of food and other essentials. This yardstick—the *poverty line*—is expressed in terms of the minimum level of income or expenditure necessary to purchase a basic caloric intake. Its popularity stems from the need for a simple and basic measure of poverty (ADB 1999c).

Nonetheless, a consensus is growing among governments and international organizations that poverty dimensions go beyond this traditional view to embody a multitude of nuanced definitions as well as causes and effects. Key to understanding poverty, especially in sociocultural terms, is the notion of *deprivation*. Poverty represents a deprivation of essential assets (physical, social, and psychological) to which every human being is entitled (ADB 1999a, c). It means a lack of adequate food, shelter, education, and health. It implies vulnerability to ill health, economic dislocation, and natural disasters. It highlights ill treatment on the part of institutions of the state and society. Poverty is equated with powerlessness to influence key decisions affecting one's life (World Bank 2000b). It is "living without fundamental freedoms of actions and choice that the better-off take for granted" (Sen in World Bank 2000b, 1).

Well-being is the converse of poverty, and also has multiple definitions and dimensions. It is closely identified with good health and disposition, the ability to exercise one's rights and live a life of personal dignity, the freedom to make economic and political choices, and the opportunity to participate in decisions that affect one's life (CIDA 2000). The absence of these opportunities or the inability of some people to enjoy these conditions is generally equated with poverty, or ill-being.

Notions of poverty and well-being are culture-specific and thus call for assessments within a specific context and which consider the views of the poor themselves. Vulnerable groups are in the best position to define poverty and well-being, and to formulate appropriate poverty reduction efforts (Racelis-Hollnsteiner 1979, Racelis 1999). Since the poor themselves live and breathe poverty daily, they constitute the most reliable source of information about their experiences and needs. They are in effect "poverty experts" (Narayan et al. 2000). Social scientists, therefore, need to incorporate into their traditional analytical frameworks data contributed by poor people themselves.

Poor People's Perspectives on Poverty and Well-being

How do poor people in Asia define poverty and well-being? Participatory poverty assessments and related studies sponsored by the Asian Development Bank, World Bank, and some bilateral agencies illustrate the value of listening to the voices and formulations of the poor.

People from fishing and farming villages in Pakistan viewed poverty as not having life's essentials, as suffering from deteriorating family relationships, and as forced out-migration. Isolation is a common theme. The poor feel they are increasingly disadvantaged and marginalized, with the rich having more productive land and access to modern equipment. Increasing their sense of isolation from mainstream development is the inaccessibility of markets and facilities, plus the unreliability and high costs of needed communications and transportation infrastructure. Lack of employment and education opportunities, coupled with unresponsive government policies, also emerged as key factors that increase their poverty. As a consequence, fisherfolk and farmers must supplement their incomes by taking on second jobs. Even older persons are no longer exempt from work (CIDA 2000).

Well-being was defined conversely as being able to meet basic needs—having enough to feed, clothe, and house the family; and having access to education and health care. A small family was sometimes seen as a sign of prosperity. Farmers regarded having access to productive land as crucial. The state of the environment also related closely and directly to local perceptions of well-being. As for the government, many among the citizenry perceived it as unable or unwilling to enforce existing policies, invest in education (seen as the most important factor in attaining a better quality of life), or deliver modern infrastructure or services (CIDA 2000).

In Lao PDR, villagers from various ethnolinguistic groups[1] cited self-sufficiency in rice as the key to determining poverty or well-being. Livestock was another primary indicator of wealth. Secondary criteria for poverty included the lack of arable land, livestock disease, poor health and the inability to afford medical treatment, women working harder than men, having to hire out one's labor, lack of technical knowledge and skills, lack of accessibility (especially roads), insufficient clothing, and poor housing.

Many of these responses reflect people's current resource base. These are seen in the main solutions to poverty offered by Lao PDR villagers, who underscore the importance of rice sufficiency and livestock. They speak of resolving issues related to rice cultivation (particularly, expanding production areas), increasing livestock holdings and obtaining the needed funding assistance to do so, solving problems of livestock disease, developing functioning paddies, having land to cultivate, enhancing reliable cash cropping, building better roads and gaining access to markets, obtaining better schoolbuildings and teachers, expanding medical assistance, and generating clean water and electricity.

In Bangladesh, a participatory poverty assessment conducted in 10 locations (un Nabi et al. 1999) identified five common features of well-being or a good quality of life. First, a household with a high level of well-being has year-round employment opportunities. Second, it owns cultivable land with cattle and draught power. From these two household endowments flow savings and capital, which represent the third feature of well-being. Fourth, to maintain a satisfactory quality of life, a household or an individual should also own a good house (built with brick or in some areas tin), and enjoy a healthy life with family members, free from anxiety. The fifth feature of a household's well-being centers on good clothing, satisfactory food consumption, and the ability to send children to school. Noteworthy in this enumeration are, first, the multidimensionality of the values that constitute well-being, e.g., between present and future, between capital and income, between physical and social values, and, second, the apparent hierarchy among them.

The poor distinguish between five levels of well-being: the rich, the "middle" stratum, the "socially poor", the "helpless poor", and the "bottom poor." In rural areas, the rich are large landowners able to employ wage labor, while in urban slums, they are house-owners earning from house rentals. "Socially poor" households farm land of moderate size (one to two acres) and own cattle draught animals and agricultural implements. In the slack season they have only two regular meals a day, owing to serious food deficits.

In the main the "helpless poor" own neither land nor homestead and depend on wage labor and sharecropping for their livelihood. They are poorly clothed, settle for inadequate health care and education, and cannot provide dowries or entertain guests. The "bottom-poor" households own neither land nor homestead and are headed by women or elderly men who have no income-earning members to help them. They lack access to loans and interact minimally with other social groups.

The Bangladeshi men and women interviewed estimate that about three fourths of rural and urban households fall into the three lowest categories: social poor, helpless poor, or bottom poor. Poverty means confronting certain forms of deprivation daily: job scarcity; natural calamities which unleash further problems such as crop failure, infertility or salinity of land, landlessness, and homelessness; absence of health care facilities; insufficient numbers of schools; poor communications; burden of dowry; insecure housing tenure for those living on government land; inadequate electricity; declining land productivity coupled with increasing production costs; and insufficient food.

A similar hierarchy of levels of well-being is recognized by the poor in Thailand. Men and women from both urban and rural areas (Bangkok and its vicinity, Central region, North, Northeast, and South) classify well-being into five levels: (i) *mee un ja kin* (very rich); (ii) *mee kin* (rich/well-to-do); (iii) *por yu dai* (average); (iv) *jon* (poor but coping); and (v) *jon mak* (very poor) (Paitoonpong 1999). The very rich live comfortably, have power and enough money to extend loans, possess property and inheritance, have significant savings, and own more than 50 *rai* of land. The rich/well-to-do have the same characteristics as the very rich but possess less of an inheritance. Those with an "average" level of well-being are debt-free and live well, have a job and savings, and own a small piece of land. Those who are poor but coping earn their living on a daily basis, buy things on credit and from hawkers, actively seek loans, and have land of a size enough to accommodate only their dwelling. The fifth category, the very poor, have no land, lack a place to live or must live with others, buy goods on credit and from hawkers, possess no assets, and regularly resort to borrowing. Plagued by chronic hardship, their life is a daily struggle.

Thai villagers and urban residents equate well-being with having a permanent place to live, a response that reflects the insecurity faced by many who, having occupied government property, are chased off the land as "squatters." Well-being also signifies having sufficient means to live a comfortable life and raise a loving family. Stability is linked to well-being and means having money and a job. With material security come other endowments, such as good health and the ability to pay for medical expenses and send the children to school. In summary, a house, money, and à job were the three recurring responses of Thai villagers and urbanites when discussing their indicators of well-being and a good quality of life.

Poverty, on the other hand, is deprivation. In Bangkok and its environs and in the Central area, deprivation includes the lack of permanent tenure or ownership of land on which to live; unemployment; high-interest loans; high cost of electricity; and lack of income, farmland, and markets for farm products. In the South, unemployment together with lack of income, financial resources, and farmland also emerge as key problems. In the slum areas, congested living conditions rank high as a major problem, while in rural areas, unemployment, the high cost of living, debt, and low prices for farm products are the most important. In the Northeast, the most serious problems are unemployment, debt, low prices of farm products, and high cost of farm inputs and consumer goods.

In Viet Nam participatory poverty assessments were conducted in 1999 among over 1,000 households in four very different parts of the country. Despite the diversity of the study areas, common themes emerged.

Well-being means having an income that was enough to cover food consumption and sufficiently stable to withstand periods of misfortune or hardships. In terms of basic assets in rural areas, this translates into adequate landholdings of reasonable quality, employment that brings about a favorable ratio of workers and dependents in the household, cash to buy inputs, ownership of livestock, off-farm employment, a diversified farm base, and ability to access formal sector financial services on favorable terms. In urban areas, well-being again signifies sufficient employment and a satisfactory dependency ratio in the household. In addition, well-being also means a permanent and sturdy dwelling with basic furniture and equipment and proximity to one's place of work. For the urban poor, proximity of one's dwelling to the main road and alleys is of utmost importance, since this ensures greater access to public facilities.

Viet Nam households also regard nonmaterial aspects of well-being as important, though less so than material assets. Well-being means freedom from debt along with the anxiety and humiliation debt engenders. Respect from the community, or conversely, not being regarded as inferior because of poverty, are crucial to a sense of well-being. Participating in community and social activities and having a network of contacts that can facilitate access to services and informal safety nets in times of emergency and need also emerge as important to adults in all sites (Viet Nam-Sweden Mountain Rural Development Programme, Actionaid, Save the Children Fund/UK and Oxfam/GB 1999). For Viet Nam children, nonmaterial aspects of well-being include having good friends; not being despised, scolded, or beaten by rich children; no quarrels between their parents or in the neighborhood; and resisting being lured into drug use by addicts (Save the Children as cited in Racelis et al. 1999).

Poverty means facing frequent human or material crises. Human crises include family members becoming ill or addicted to drugs, alcohol, or gambling, while material crises refer to property damage from natural calamities and crop or investment failures. Poverty also entails limited literacy, numeracy, language, and technical skills; and the consequent diminution of one's chances of obtaining a job in an extremely competitive market for unskilled labor.

Finally, poverty entails cultural and physical marginalization. This is the testimony of migrants living on the fringes of Ho Chi Minh City. Unlike registered, bonafide urban residents, migrants perform unskilled tasks in the informal sector[2] where there is little security. They are unable to obtain formal-sector credit, free health care, or subsidized education. They lack social connections and networks of informal support. Ethnic groups in remote areas feel marginalized, have low literacy levels, and often find themselves victimized by the rest of society, partly owing to their inability to speak the national language (Viet Nam et al. 1999).

In the Philippines, Social Weather Stations (SWS), a private survey-research institute, has pioneered the use of a self-rated, bottom-up approach to track poverty. Survey respondents give their own interpretation of the word "poverty." Based on a showcard with the word *mahirap* (poor) at one end, *hindi mahirap* (not poor) at the other end, and a line between these, respondents simply point to where they think their own family falls (Mangahas 1999).

SWS survey responses in March 2001 indicate that 59 percent of all households in the Philippines considered themselves poor or *mahirap;* 16.1 percent of them had experienced hunger (or having had nothing to eat) at least once in the last three months. The self-rated poverty incidence of 59 percent was almost twice the official poverty incidence of 32 percent, last estimated by the government in 1997 (Mangahas 2001). Comparing the time-series of self-rated poverty incidence (SWS surveys) with the time series of official poverty incidence (government) reveals that the former always registers roughly twice as many poor. This suggests that officially defined poverty really refers to those in much deeper distress, utilizing a criterion like not having enough income to cover food consumption. Twice as many Filipino households saying they consider themselves poor and explaining why, implies that their definition of poverty contains nuances beyond food security which the official definition fails to capture. As Sen (2000b) points out in his commentary on conventional indicators for estimating absolute poverty levels, poverty is a general state of deprivation that has more to do with entitlement and capacity than mere income or nutritional levels.

A participatory poverty assessment by the Canadian International Development Agency in 1998 similarly reveals that Filipinos go beyond the traditional definition, specifying the characteristics of well-being as food security, good quality housing, personal savings, and access to education and health care. The ability to ride out "shocks" is seen as an indicator of well-being, while the inability to provide life's necessities constitutes ill-being. The latter means eating less than three meals a day, having insecure or no employment or income, and being deprived of access to land or capital. Ill-being, or poverty, also represents a failure to exercise control over one's life, not being able to plan for the future, and vulnerability to manipulation by corrupt businessmen/women and government officials (CIDA 2000).

The Annual Poverty Indicators Survey conducted by the National Statistics Office of the Philippines from April to September 1999 gives a sense of how Filipinos define both an improving as well as worsening quality of life. The top five reasons cited by 13 percent of households for why they became better off over the past 12 months are: more earnings, abundant harvest, better health, new job with higher salary, and more remittances from abroad. On the other hand, the top five reasons given by 34 percent of households for becoming worse off are: higher food prices, reduced income, loss of a job, natural disasters and droughts, and poor health. The responses indicate that material well-being is of utmost importance to a good family situation, as seen in more earnings (even leading some to seek overseas employment) and an abundant harvest. However, physical well-being (better health) and security (protection from natural disasters and drought) are also critical.

Well-being involves access to economic assets, first and foremost. It is significant, however, that the aspiration for economic assets is not always stated in the form of a money metric-like income or a sum of wealth, but is frequently stated as a demand for concrete goods or physical resources, which often reflect the poor's current resource base or economic activity. Even more significant is how well-being is almost everywhere seen to include nonmaterial values, such as the care and the welfare of children, self-respect and dignity, informal support networks, and peace and good relations within the family, community, and country. Security implies a physically safe and secure environment (referring especially to protection from natural disasters) as well as personal physical security. Freedom of choice and of action entails a whole range of activities, including helping others, gaining education and skills, traveling freely, and making political and other decisions that affect one's life (Narayan et al. 2000).

SOCIAL EXCLUSION

Concept of Social Exclusion

If poverty or ill-being is not limited to income and material deprivation, then the poor need access not only to resources needed for productive and survival needs but also to opportunities for enhancing their creative human potential. To be deprived of the capacity to do valuable things or achieve valuable states of being is what Sen refers to as "capability poverty" or "capability deprivation" (ADB 2000f). As a concept, social exclusion reflects capability deprivation, comprising all "deprivations that diminish a person's life and freedom" (Sen in ADB 2000f, 2). Social exclusion refers to the norms and societal and institutional processes that exclude certain groups from full participation in the social, economic, cultural, and political life of societies (Narayan 1999).

> Individuals or even entire groups can be excluded by being deprived of: a livelihood; secure, permanent employment; earnings; property, credit, or land; housing; minimal or prevailing consumption levels; education, skills, and cultural capital; the welfare state; citizenship and legal equality; democratic participation; public goods; the nation or the dominant race; family and sociability; humanity, respect, fulfillment and understanding (Silver 1995, 60).

The complex reality that perpetuates poverty cannot, however, simply be visualized in a binary mode of exclusion-inclusion. Disadvantaged groups find themselves included differentially from varying aspects of development, or included so minimally that dependency prevails and they are rendered powerless to exert any significant influence in society. Moreover, exclusion does not necessarily mean the total absence of integration into wider systems, since most poor people do belong to both horizontal and vertical networks of social relations. The key element lies, rather, in the social practice of power and the ways in which it spawns unequal patterns of integration that promote unjust or destructive outcomes (Kelles-Viitanen 2001).

Social exclusion is not a radically new concept. It is rooted after all in the Aristotelian notion of the richness of human life (Sen 2000c). Nonetheless, it contributes significantly to the discourse on poverty by emphasizing the multidimensionality of deprivation and the relational roots and processes that generate capability deprivation (Sen in ADB 2000f). Social exclusion occurs at different levels. In the *household*, it is manifested in the distribution of resources, responsibilities, power and authority among household members. In the *community*, exclusion appears in the differential treatment of people in terms of social status, allocation of power and resources, access to basic services, and levels of participation in political and social events. At level of the *nation*, state policies, cultural practices, and the mass media often reinforce these exclusionary tendencies. At the *global* level, policies often overlook the well-being of the poor.

Excluded Groups

Who are the excluded groups in Asia and how are they excluded? Among the most disadvantaged and vulnerable groups are the rural poor, urban poor, women, children, indigenous peoples, refugees, migrants, youth, disabled, and older persons. Distinctive as they are, each category is actually a mix of most of the others. Thus, one could focus on rural-urban linkages rather than either the rural or the urban sector. Women can be disabled and indigenous. Limits of space permit discussion of only three examples.

Excluded Rural Poor

Poverty in Asia remains a largely rural phenomenon (Rosegrant and Hazell 2000). Of the world's 1.2 billion poor people, three quarters totaling 900 million live in rural areas (IFAD 2001), the vast majority of them in Asia. The rural poor in Asia depend on agriculture as small cultivators, tenants, or workers on and off farms. By and large, they own no assets, are trapped in debt, and lack access to technology and credit. Compared to their urban counterparts, rural households are usually larger, with illiterate or barely literate heads. They have limited access to social services (like education, health care, family planning, adequate shelter, safe drinking water, standard toilets and sanitary facilities, and electricity), which is exacerbated by their lack of information about available services. Their low social status further disenfranchises them politically and makes them a highly vulnerable group (ADB 2001b).

Access to Assets. Asia's rural poor are economically excluded, as seen in their *lack of income and economic assets*. The incidence and severity of rural poverty almost always exceeds that of urban poverty (IFAD 2001). Except for the Republic of Korea (Korea); Taipei,China; and Thailand, the countries covered in this study have rural poverty incidences ranging from one third to one half of the rural population:

37 percent for Pakistan in 1991; 40 percent for Bangladesh in 1995-1996; 51 percent for the Philippines in 1997; 53 percent for Lao PDR in 1993; and 57 percent for Viet Nam in 1993 (World Bank 2000b). On the other hand, the proportion of urban households living below the poverty line in these countries ranges from less than 2 percent (Korea) to 28 percent (Pakistan) (World Bank 2000b).

Since land is the most important economic resource for poor farmers, many rely on its produce to meet their subsistence needs while struggling also to generate additional income. Most rural poor have two or fewer hectares of landholdings. Given existing technology and access to complementary inputs, this size of landholding often represents too limited an asset to produce enough to meet even the basic subsistence needs. Many households with no land at all fall into the poorest category of agricultural or off-farm rural workers.

Land distribution data for the countries in this study show that the arable land per head of agricultural population declined for the period 1979-1981 to 1995-1997. This implies that the rural poor have lost a significant share of their access to land over the last two decades. The pattern of land distribution is, moreover, highly unequal. Four of the countries in this study had land Gini coefficients greater than 0.5: Bangladesh, Pakistan, Philippines, and Viet Nam. Those with lower land Gini coefficients in the 0.3 range were Korea; Taipei,China; and Thailand (IFAD 2001).

In countries with large numbers of landless and land-deficient households, many of the rural poor are tenants and sharecroppers. Pakistan shows a relatively high incidence of sharecropping at 18 percent. On the other hand, at least 30 percent of all farm families are tenants in Bangladesh, Philippines, and Thailand. The relationship between landlords and tenants is often highly unequal. In areas where landless laborers compete fiercely for land, tenants are highly dependent on the landlords, who can charge tenants high rents. This leads to a rapid tenant turnover and increases the vulnerability of cultivators excluded by tenure insecurity (Okidebe 2001).

The lack of access to land exacerbates low incomes and sustains rural poverty. To reduce the vulnerability of the poor, a number of countries have embarked on land reform schemes, with Korea and Taipei,China being among the most successful. The fairly low land Gini coefficients for these two countries attests to the effectiveness of their programs, and their experience suggests that an effective agrarian reform program can significantly alleviate poverty and reduce inequality. The Philippine experience, on the other hand, indicates that unless land transfer is accompanied by effective programs of credit, agricultural extension and training services, technical inputs, marketing assistance, and price information, beneficiaries of agrarian reform may not be able to generate significant increases in productivity. Even worse, they may eventually yield to the pressure to sell their newly acquired land illegally to eager middle-class buyers or builders of residential subdivisions and commercial enterprises.

Aside from land, *livestock* is another important economic asset for Asia's rural poor. In Lao PDR, for example, livestock was identified as the primary indicator of wealth, and the lack of it a determinant of poverty. Accordingly, livestock disease was cited as one of the top two causes of income shortages.

The rural poor in Asia suffer not only from insufficient income and economic assets, but also from *inadequate infrastructure* (roads and electricity) *and communication* (telephones, radio, and newspapers). The poor infrastructure characteristic of rural Asia has an important bearing on the growth of rural economies—affecting prices, diffusion of technology, and use of inputs. All are necessary for spurring agricultural production and increased incomes in developing countries (IFAD 2001). Further, compared to their urban counterparts, rural households have far less access to electricity, telephones, radio, and newspapers. More than the size of the farm holdings, the isolation of farms from major economic and social centers is the factor most likely to contribute to rural poverty (Okidebe 2001).

In the face of both increasing competition for markets and new technological opportunities, poor rural dwellers need connectivity to address their needs and support their endeavors. Unless the state of technology improves in the countryside, small farmers and fisherfolk are likely to be left out of the most important communication innovations occurring around the world.

Access to Basic Social Services. It is evident that educational and enhanced functional skills, coupled with good health, constitute human capital or human assets crucial to people's achieving healthy and productive lives. Yet, poor Asian rural dwellers lack these opportunities.

Rural households generally possess low educational attainment owing to their limited access to schools or their children's tendency to drop out in the early grades. In Pakistan from 1990-2000, only 46 percent of rural children were enrolled, compared with 75 percent of urban children. Rural health status remains low owing to poor nutrition and poor quality care. These deficiencies in education and health further reduce the productivity and earning capacity of the rural poor. Moreover, in almost all the countries studied, the public provision of education, health services, water, sanitation and shelter is strongly biased toward urban areas. The urban poor, nonetheless, receive a disproportionately low share of the city's benefits, compared to better-off residents.

The rural-urban disparity in *access to health services* was greatest for Pakistan in the period 1985 to 1995. Only 33 percent of rural Pakistani households enjoyed access to health care, as against a reported 99 percent for urban households. In the Philippines, the proportion of rural households with access to health services, at 74 percent, is only slightly lower than the proportion of urban households, at 77 percent. Among the countries involved in this study, Korea provides the highest levels of health care, with virtually everyone in the country, rural and urban poor alike, enjoying these services. Thailand's public provision of health services is similarly impressive, with 90 percent of both rural and urban households having access in 1985 to 1995. Viet Nam also performed well, with 80 percent of rural households and nearly all urban households receiving health benefits (UNICEF 1996).

As for *access to safe water*, the proportion of rural households enjoying this basic service in 2000 was invariably lower than that of urban households. Viet Nam, Korea, and Thailand had the lowest proportions of rural households with access to safe water, at 50, 71, and 77 percent, respectively. The corresponding proportions for their urban populations were much higher at 81, 97, and 89 percent, respectively. In the Philippines, 80 percent of rural, and 92 percent of urban households enjoyed safe water. The rural-urban disparity in Pakistan was 84 versus 96 percent. In Bangladesh the disparity was less, with nearly all rural and urban households drinking safe water, at 97 and 99 percent, respectively. The only country where rural households had better access to safe water than urban households was Lao

PDR, where virtually all rural households enjoyed safe water, compared with only 59 percent of urban households (UNCHS 2001).

Rural households also fared worse than urban ones with respect to *sanitation*. The problem appeared to be most severe in Lao PDR, Pakistan, and Bangladesh, where the proportions of rural households with improved sanitation were only 34, 42, and 44 percent, respectively. In contrast, the proportions for urban populations were significantly higher at 84, 94, and 82 percent. In Viet Nam and the Philippines, 70 and 71 percent, respectively, of rural households had improved sanitation; the corresponding proportions for their urban populations were higher at 86 and 92 percent. Thailand showed the highest scores, with 96 percent of rural households and 97 percent of urban households enjoying access to improved sanitation.

What all these figures demonstrate is that the rural poor have been left behind in terms of income, physical assets, and human assets, even as economies achieve remarkable progress and transformation. Indeed, growth alone is not enough to reduce rural poverty in Asia. What is needed is growth that raises agricultural productivity and incomes of small-scale farmers and landless laborers. Moreover, the rural poor are benefited most when land is distributed relatively equitably. Additionally, investments in rural physical infrastructure and in the rural poor's human capital (health, nutrition, and education) are particularly crucial in reducing rural poverty.

Excluded Urban Poor

Rapid urbanization has been an unmistakable hallmark of the 20th century, and this is particularly true for the Asian and Pacific region. In 1960, roughly one in five people lived in urban areas; by 1980, the ratio was one in four. Today, with 37 percent of Asia's 3.7 billion people staying in urban areas, the ratio is one in three. By 2025, half of Asia's population will be living in urban areas (UN-ESCAP 1998, UNCHS 2001). In the Philippines, the transition came as early as 1992.

Of the eight countries included here, three can already be considered predominantly urban societies. In Republic of Korea, Taipei,China, and Philippines, 82, 77, and 59 percent, respectively, of their total populations live in urban areas. In contrast, Viet Nam, Thailand, Lao PDR, Bangladesh, and Pakistan remain largely rural, the proportions of their urban population being 20, 22, 23, 25, and 37 percent, respectively (UNCHS 2001, Population Reference Bureau 2000).

Among Asia's 1.35 billion urban population are its urban poor—typically defined as people living in informal and "squatter" settlements in urban and urbanizing areas and whose income falls below the poverty threshold set by the government (Ngolaban 1999). They depend on the informal economy for their livelihood, live in miserable housing conditions, are constantly threatened with eviction for illegal occupancy, and have little or no access to basic social services like running water, sanitation facilities, schools, or health clinics (ADB 1994).

Urban poverty incidence in the eight countries is below 30 percent. Based on national poverty lines, the proportion of urban poor households for Pakistan is estimated at 28 percent (1991); Viet Nam at 26 percent (1993); Lao PDR at 24 percent (1993); Philippines at 23 percent (1997); Bangladesh at 14 percent (1995-1996); and Thailand at 10 percent (1992). Korea shows less than 2 percent of its urban population as poor or living on less than one dollar a day (1993). Urban-rural comparisons indicate that the incidence of poverty in urban areas is less than that in rural areas. Moreover, the proportion of urban poor households has been declining over the years. In Bangladesh, for example, urban poverty incidence declined to 14 percent in 1995-1996 from 23 percent in 1991-1992. In the Philippines, it dropped to 23 percent in 1997 from 28 percent in 1994 (World Bank 2000b), although 2001 data show 726,000 informal settler households in Metro Manila alone (over 4 million individuals, or some 42 percent of the total metropolitan population) (HUDCC 2001).

Falling urban poverty incidence, however, tends to hide the reality that Asia's urban poor continue to live under conditions of extreme deprivation and suffer social exclusion in many ways—at times even more brutally than their rural counterparts.

Lack of income is a major constraint facing urban poor households. In the poor countries of Asia, the dwindling capacity of the formal sector to generate employment means that only low-paying informal sector jobs are available to the great majority of urban poor residents (Karaos 1997). Accordingly, the informal sector keeps growing to accommodate the large number of men and women seeking a living in urban areas (Balisacan 1994b). Indeed, informal sector workers help make life possible for the entire urban population. Men work in the construction, transport, and small-scale manufacturing sectors. Women peddle goods on streets and sidewalks, or do laundry and other domestic tasks for wealthier households. All across Asia, the informal economy accounts for at least an unrecorded half of gross domestic product (Racelis 1999).[3]

Informal sector workers suffer from low and unstable incomes, their average earnings being much lower than those in the formal sector (Ratanakomut et al. 1994). Informal sector workers also lack the employment benefits that their counterparts in the formal sector usually enjoy. When they have difficulty making ends meet, many resort to borrowing from moneylenders at exorbitant rates. They also pay more for public goods and services, like water and electricity, than do better-off groups. Catastrophic illness wipes out savings and depletes the good will of lenders. For these reasons, urban poor settlers are hard-pressed to accumulate assets or savings.

The irony lies in the realization that many of the urban poor are rural folk who migrated to the city, fleeing rural poverty and seeking better income opportunities (Balisacan 1994b, Khundker et al. 1994). Gainful urban employment, however, is typically hard to find. As a consequence, many migrants endure conditions far worse than those they left behind. Yet a return to the countryside presents daunting problems—landlessness, limited economic opportunity, inadequate social services, relative isolation, and even civil strife. At the same time, the ability to survive in cities and, for a significant proportion, even move up the socioeconomic ladder through hard work, plus the vitality of urban living, raise expectations that keep millions in cities despite their degraded surroundings. In many of the older informal settlements, urban-born children and grandchildren of the original migrants now comprise the majority.

Unaffordable housing heightens the exclusion of the urban poor. Land policies fail to yield enough developed residential sites for them. Moreover, because of the way formal markets are structured and regulated, poor people in cities cannot afford the choices available in these markets. In the Philippines, for example, the prices of raw land in the peripheral areas of major cities like Metro Manila, Metro Cebu, and Metro Davao have been rising by 25 percent annually in real terms over the past two decades (Institute on Church and Social Issues 2000).

In Korea, the shortage of urban land sites has likewise resulted in high prices for urban land. As housing costs escalate, decent housing becomes almost inaccessible to the urban poor (Kim 1994). This serious imbalance between housing supply and demand forces the urban poor to resort to self-built housing in informal settlements, a decision that automatically confers illegal status upon them.

Tenure insecurity confronts urban poor households that have built or rented houses on public or private property without construction or occupancy permits. These "informal settlers" live in constant fear of forced evictions, demolitions, and distant relocation. In many cases, this fear turns into reality as houses are demolished by city authorities or destroyed by mysterious fires in the night to give way to roads, commercial establishments, or housing for middle- and upper-income classes.

Throughout the year 2000 in Karachi—home to an estimated 4.5 million people living in *katchi abadis* (urban informal settlements)—government agencies bulldozed over 800 houses in four different settlements. Investigations by the Urban Resource Centre (2001) revealed that these operations were carried out to free up land for the construction of high-rise buildings. The developers reportedly used government agencies to evict the residents forcibly without prior notice. In the Philippines, 8,067 families lost their homes in demolitions in 1997, and another 3,754 in 1998 (Urban Poor Associates, as cited in Ngolaban 1999).

Forced eviction and relocation to distant and poorly served areas are twin horrors stalking the lives of informal settlers. Evictions cause serious trauma for those who must watch their homes being bulldozed or gutted by fire; they also erode the social capital that has been built over years of mutual assistance and friendship. Ill-prepared and distant relocation sites cause severe problems for the urban poor. In the worst cases, basic services like clean water and electricity are lacking, and neither schools nor teachers are in place. No housing structures or only partially constructed shelter exists, forcing the relocatees to make do with makeshift, salvaged materials.

By far the most serious problem in distant relocation sites is the lack of livelihood opportunities. Proposed income-generation programs typically promise eventual earnings but fail to provide for immediate subsistence. All too often government programs focus on skills training that have little relevance for earning in a poor community. With transport costs back to the city now prohibitively high, entire families give up and move back to the city to squat anew. Or, they split up so that one or two members move back to in-city residence to earn for the rest.

Poor people in urban areas suffer *poor living conditions*. Unable to afford safe, well-serviced sites, many inhabit congested communities on marginal land—disaster-prone areas under bridges, along fetid canals, on riverbanks or steep slopes, near garbage dumps, and along railway lines. Given the insecurity of tenure in illegal settlements and the ever-present threat of eviction, many urban poor hesitate to improve either their housing or their settlements. Evidence shows that this situation is gradually reversed with assured security of tenure.

Harsh living conditions prevail not only because people live on marginal land and in congested communities, but also because municipal services, such as a safe and adequate water supply, sewerage connections, and regular waste collection are denied them owing to their illegal status. In Lao PDR and Viet Nam in 2000, only 59 percent and 81 percent, respectively, of the urban poor had access to improved water services (UNCHS 2001).

Sanitation remains a problem in urban areas in Korea, Bangladesh, Lao PDR, and Viet Nam, where in the year 2000, only 76, 82, 84, and 86 percent, respectively, of urban households had access to improved sanitation (UNCHS 2001). Municipal services can be worse in the major cities of these countries than in small urban centers. In Lahore, Pakistan, only 74 percent of households have a sewerage connection, with only half benefiting from regular waste collection. In Hanoi, less than half of the households are linked to a sewerage and waste collection system, at 40 and 45 percent, respectively (World Bank 2000b). In Manila, only 44 percent of the urban poor use sanitary toilets, the majority using rivers and canals, open pits or "wrap-and-throw" for their toilet needs (Jimenez in Soco 2000).

Poor sanitation, lack of potable water, overcrowded and poorly ventilated living and working environments, together with air and industrial pollution—all take a toll on the health and safety of the urban poor. Higher rates of disease and accidents, along with garbage avalanches and fires in the densely packed settlements, are but some of the consequences of their miserable living conditions. Add to this the anxiety of daily trying to make ends meet, and grappling with eviction notices, and one can understand why the urban poor can face some of the most difficult situations in any country.

Lack of access to education and health services means that poor urbanites must endure low educational levels and chronic nutritional deficiencies. Although overall statistics show that urban areas are better served than rural areas, these figures hide the reality of urban poverty and exclusion. For the period 1990-2000, the proportion of urban households in the Philippines, Bangladesh, and Pakistan with access to basic education stood at 67, 72, and 75 percent, respectively (Okidebe 2001). This indicates that at least a quarter of the populace, inevitably the urban poor in these countries, are beyond the pale of formal systems of basic education.

With regard to health, only 77 percent of the urban population in the Philippines had access to health services for the period 1985 to 1995 (UNICEF 1996). The immunization rate in slum areas of Bangladesh comes to only 38 percent, compared to about 80 percent reported for rural areas (Sen n.d.). The illegal status of urban poor settlers further deprives them of regular health services.

The urban poor create wealth in society and make city life possible through their wide-ranging skills and services, but they themselves face difficulties accumulating assets. All too often, they are perceived as parasites, felons, and eyesores by society, which, at best, ignores their needs, and at worst, shunts them off to distant, ill-served relocation sites. Government programs frequently fail to recognize the range of poverty among the urban poor, and develop interventions based on averages rather than on differentiated levels of poverty. As a result, the poorest are often left out of these programs or are deemed recalcitrant because of their unwillingness or inability to participate in these intended solutions.

Until their need for, and right to, adequate income, employment, tenure security, decent housing, social services, greater participation in social and political processes, and treatment with dignity is recognized, a huge proportion of striving people living in the midst of plenty will continue to be deprived of the benefits due them. This in turn will undermine their capacity to contribute fully to their respective societies.

Excluded Women

In Asia as in many parts of the world, women experience pervasive and profound exclusion. Unequal gender relations often result from socialization processes that ascribe differential roles, rights, and values to women and men. While the culture of each society shapes the forms of their exclusion, Asian women experience comparable forms of exclusion—in the household, the economy, and the polity.

High maternal mortality rates (MMR) for some countries reflect women's exclusion from adequate *health care*. The MMR for South Asia and for Southeast Asia and the Pacific are 551 and 449 per 100,000 live births, respectively, higher than the world average of 437 deaths although much lower than the 979 for Sub-Saharan Africa. Bangladesh, in 1990, had the highest MMR at 850, followed by Lao PDR at 650, then Pakistan at 340. On the other hand, the Republic of Korea and Viet Nam had the lowest MMRs at 130 and 160, respectively (UNDP 1999).

High MMRs in Bangladesh, Lao PDR, and Pakistan are correlated with poor performance in other health indicators. The proportion of the population with access to health services for the period 1990-1995 was only 45 percent for Bangladesh, 67 percent for Lao PDR, and 55 percent for Pakistan, as compared to 90 percent for both Thailand and Viet Nam, and 100 percent for Korea (UNDP 1998). Additionally, in 1995, only a small proportion of the population in Bangladesh, Lao PDR, and Pakistan (at 35, 32, and 39 percent, respectively) had access to adequate sanitation. Compare this with the higher rates for Thailand and Korea (96 and 100 percent, respectively) (UNDP 1998a).

Women make up the majority of illiterates in the region. As of 1997, in the low-income countries of Pakistan, Bangladesh, and Lao PDR, literacy rates among female adults were low at 25, 27, and 27 percent, respectively. In contrast, female adult literacy rates in Southeast Asia approach 100 percent (including Viet Nam at 89 percent). Adult Korean women enjoy the highest literacy rate at 96 percent (UNDP 1999). Similar trends can be observed in female primary net enrolment rates. In 1997, Bangladesh and Lao PDR had the lowest rates at 69 and 70 percent, respectively, whereas Korea, Philippines, and Viet Nam had almost universal net enrolment (UNDP 1999). The latter figures portend a better level of education among the next generation of women.

Employment patterns highlight the exclusion that women suffer through gender discrimination. Women comprise about 40 percent of the Asia-Pacific labor force. The disparity in labor force participation already partly reflects the differential social assignment of tasks between men and women, with men more likely to seek economic employment and women relegated to domestic tasks. Even among the employed, however, the proportion of women earning incomes is lower than among men, since most women, especially in the agricultural sector, carry out unpaid family labor on land. Thus, in addition to lower income earnings, women suffer from the undervaluation of their unpaid work.

In developing countries, women's contributions to the national product are not adequately captured in national statistical systems, first because such systems intrinsically exclude domestic or household work, and secondly because of the difficulties in representing the large informal sector where many women work and unpaid family labor predominates. The result is a lack of attention to the gender-specific effects of economic policies. In recent years, protests from women's groups have at the very least led to attempts to quantify the economic contribution of women's unpaid labor, either by measuring the number of hours women spend at work (and the intensity of work), the economic value of this time, the volume of their production, or the value of what they produce (UN-ESCAP 1998).

It is worth noting that the social status of women in Korea has not advanced at a rate corresponding to that country's outstanding economic progress. While women's health and basic education have improved remarkably, their social, economic, and political participation has lagged.

Moreover, schools continue to teach children that girls should be subservient and take responsibility for the house, while boys must be independent and oriented to the larger world of economy and society. This assignment is in keeping with the Confucian cultural tradition that upholds the patriarchal family system and extends such family values toward other areas of social life. As a result, many Korean women end up with relatively low-paying jobs or as full-time homemakers after graduation from school or college, unable to apply their learning professionally (UNDP n.d.).

Korea ranked 27th in terms of the Human Development Index, but was only 61st in the Gender Empowerment Measure in the *Hu-*

man Development Report of 2001. The point is that economic progress does not automatically translate into improvements in the social status of women, that is unless such progress is coupled with efforts to challenge patriarchal stereotypes. As Drèze and Sen (cited in Mahbub ul Haq Human Development Centre 2000, 30) have stated, "On their own, the forces of development and modernization do not necessarily lead to a rapid reduction in gender inequalities."

Asia-Pacific women not only occupy inferior positions in the workplace but are also relegated to the periphery of *politics*, despite having won the right to vote at least five decades ago. On average, women occupy a meager 10% of legislative seats, which is hardly representative of the women that comprise half of the population (UNDP 1999). The weak political participation of women makes it unlikely for poor women's interests to be taken seriously and in proportion to their numbers and specific situations of deprivation.

More than in the workplace and in the polity, however, it is at home where women experience the most damaging consequences of their exclusion. *Violence against women and girls* is a major problem that continues to inflict both physical and psychological damage. A government survey in the Philippines indicates that one of every 10 women had been battered (Illo 1997). In Bangladesh, of 1,961 reported cases of women subjected to violence in 1998, 72 percent were severely beaten by their husbands. Equally distressing are reports that 50 percent of all murders in Bangladesh are attributable to marital violence, almost all the victims being women. In Pakistan, domestic violence occurs in every third household (Mahbub ul Haq Human Development Centre 2000).

Women in South Asia clearly lag behind their sisters in Southeast and East Asia, as shown by such indicators as literacy, health, and employment patterns. Southeast Asian women benefit from bilateral kinship systems that trace descent through both parental lineages and enable women to inherit equally with men, subject to variations in the application of Islamic law. Accordingly, when Southeast Asian women engage in petty trade and other micro-enterprises, they are culturally allowed to retain control of their earnings, a source of significant power in the household.

In contrast, the status of South Asian women is developed through the patriarchal social system, such as that in Bangladesh and Pakistan, which fosters a strong dependence of women on men. The institution of *purdah* (literally, curtain) encompasses a set of culturally and religiously justified ideals and practices embodying gender segregation. In traditional circles, the onset of puberty requires the complete seclusion of women and the confinement of women's socioeconomic roles to the domestic sphere. Purdah has generally restricted the mobility of many Muslim women and given men authority over them. Men are reluctant to permit women to do outside work, even among poor households (de Haan 1994, Mahbub ul Haq Human Development Centre 2000), although poor women in rural areas do work in the fields.

The patriarchal perception of women as male property has resulted not only in the exclusion of many women from economic activities, but also in numerous cases of violence against them. In Pakistan these include incidents of *karo-kari* or honor killing. If women are even suspected of being involved in an illicit relationship, they may be killed for "tainting the family honor." There are also cases of murder or attempted murder of women by deliberate stove-burning in Pakistan (as many as 272 reported in 1999), and incidents of jealous male friends, spurned suitors, and irate husbands throwing acid onto a woman's face or body (Mahbub ul Haq Human Development Centre 2000). Further, South Asian gender exclusion is compounded by caste or caste-like distinctions that prevent low-caste women and their families from competing equitably for societal resources and standing.

Regional comparisons have their own pitfalls, however. Pointing to the advantages of Southeast Asian over South Asian women may divert attention from the more important task of assessing how women in a particular country are faring vis-à-vis the men in their own society. Similarly, linking violence against women with poverty should not make one lose sight of the violence occurring even in well-to-do countries and among high-income families.

In various ways disadvantaged men, women, and children in Asia experience exclusion from mainstream social processes. Among the factors contributing to this marginalization are the stigma of poverty, age, and gender; and the alienation attached to belonging to a minority ethnic, linguistic, racial, or cultural group. Exclusion also operates against those who suffer physical or mental disabilities, or who manifest behavior that flaunts community norms. In time, poor people may internalize these societal criteria and exclude themselves from mainstream society.

Whatever the form of exclusion, however, the effect is always a lower quality of life and diminished well-being for the people who experience it. Despite this, or maybe in response to it, vulnerable groups have learned with varying degrees of success to manage their lives in remarkable displays of resilience.

RESILIENCE OF THE POOR: COPING STRATEGIES AND SOCIAL CAPITAL

Despite deprivation and neglect, poor people find creative ways not only of surviving but also of forging a better future for their families and themselves. Whether on farms or in slums, male or female, elderly or young, they eke out a living somehow and seem to pull through by resorting to multiple coping strategies. On the other hand, these exact a heavy toll on already vulnerable groups, since they include cutting back on expenditures, selling assets, increasing labor, migrating to the city or remote rural areas, seeking overseas employment, borrowing, and calling on support networks.

Coping Strategies

The primary strategy adopted by poor households is *expenditure reduction*. Major adjustments are made in food consumption by replacing expensive, higher-quality sources of calories with cheaper food. For the bottom-poor, the change in food consumption means a reduction in food intake—say from three meals a day to only two or even one (Knowles et al. 1999). Education, health and recreation are further expense items that can be cut, together with water and electric consumption, and purchases of clothing. House and equipment repairs may also be deferred.

Women bear the brunt of adjusting to chronic emergencies. Attending to their family's needs before their own, they sometimes skip one meal during the day so that their children can have three. Studies have shown that rising food prices lead to larger reductions in nutrient intake for women than for men (Atinc 1998, World Bank 2000b). In addition, women are also burdened with the responsibility of stretching meager household budgets, sourcing credit, and locating money with which to pay past loans. This can put a tremendous strain on marital and familial relations. Desperate husbands confronted with wives appealing for more resources for their children often respond with beatings and abuse (Reyes et al. 1999). Women and children suffer most in the grueling struggle for survival.

Vulnerable groups also cope with crisis by *selling off, pawning, or renting out assets.* The rural poor may sell their livestock and, if necessary, their land. The urban poor, on the other hand, may sell or pawn their personal belongings such as watches, jewelry, and appliances, or may offer a room in their house for rent. Those with access to electricity and water may also sell these at a gain. Since the poor have few physical assets to begin with, some of them begin to consider their own bodies as assets that can be sold. Urban poor residents in the Philippines and Viet Nam sell their blood to small blood banks. Male unemployed residents of Baseco, a large slum community in Tondo, Manila, go as far as to sell their kidneys (Racelis et al. 1999). Even more desperate, however, are those who sell their babies for adoption (at US $70-$650 in Viet Nam), or give their children over to prostitution. In Ho Chi Minh City, daughters are also sold off to be married at $1,000-$7000 (Viet Nam et al. 1999).

Poor people augment their income by *increasing their labor supply* (World Bank 2000b); this is done by looking for secondary sources of income or working longer hours. If these efforts are not enough to satisfy basic consumption needs, other members of the household are mobilized to expand the labor supply. Older family members engage in piecework at home. Children stop schooling in order to scavenge, guard other people's cars, and sell newspapers, lottery tickets, candy, chewing gum, and flower garlands. Where local labor markets cannot generate sufficient demand for unskilled labor, households move to the uplands or begin their *migration to the city or overseas.* Reverse migration also occurs as unemployed urban dwellers return to their home communities in hopes of finding some support there.

Borrowing money and food constitutes another coping strategy. Poor households first seek assistance from their extended families, then their friends, then neighbors and other community members, or occasionally a former employer, in that order. They seldom qualify for formal credit from banks or government institutions, whose application processes are arduous and slow, in any event. If potential lenders in the family or neighborhood do not come through, desperate seekers turn to loan sharks who charge exorbitant interest rates and ruthlessly enforce repayment.

Some coping mechanisms victimize others, as when the better-off poor charge their worse-off counterparts inflated prices for miserable living spaces and basic utilities like water and electricity, or engage in loan shark operations. Some forms of child labor, such as prostitution and pornography, or the use of children in theft operations or as drug couriers, expose them to physical and moral hazards, not to mention psycho-emotional trauma. Forcing women into prostitution or into early marriage are still other ways of exploiting already vulnerable people. Finally, activities like dynamite and cyanide fishing, uncontrolled cutting of trees, and gold panning with mercury, destroy the natural environment and ecosystems. Environmental degradation not only puts present-day communities at risk, but also imperils the patrimony of future generations.

Poor people respond to their poverty with a wide range of behavioral responses and strategies that provide largely short-term solutions. However, such responses and strategies can have unforeseen consequences and can expose the already desperate to even worse conditions of vulnerability, as well as threaten their long-run survival (Racelis et al. 1999). Selling assets, particularly land, during times of crisis for example has obvious profound repercussions on the household's future productive potential. Delays in seeking health care can lead to serious illness, if not death. A reduction in the quantity or quality of nutritional intake may cause debilitating physical and psychological effects, particularly among children and pregnant women. Disrupted schooling may mean irreversible losses in human capital and income earning potential for the dropout. Selling blood too frequently, not to mention the sale of internal organs for transplant, can seriously damage body functioning and lead to death or disability. Resorting to substance abuse threatens one's own well-being and may bring harm to others. The other acute examples include instances of incest or rape of children among families with mothers working overseas. Similarly, many young women sold into prostitution end up in a worse situation when they contract AIDS. It remains a challenge for government policies and programs to ensure that families do not invite destructive long-term results as they struggle to cope with immediate problems (Atinc 2000).

Social Capital

The ability of the poor to survive depends greatly on their own ingenuity and perseverance. Their creativity in preparing nourishing meals at reduced costs, or their ability to take on multiple jobs and extended work hours represent noteworthy contributions to their own survival. Laudable though their sheer grit and determination may be, they also need help in coping with shocks, and thus tap into the social capital built up in the community. This operates at the micro level, as in illness, disability, or death in the family; the meso level, such as floods and landslides; or the macro level, when national financial crises hit them so hard that they can no longer feed their children, pay school fees, afford hospital treatment, or bury their dead.

Social capital refers to the norms and social relations embedded in social structures that enable people to coordinate action and achieve desired goals (Narayan 1999). Unlike physical and natural capital, which focus on access to means of production and consumption, or human capital, which is based on access to education and training, social capital is *relational*. It concerns people's relationships with others that can be harnessed to their advantage (Portes cited in Narayan 1999).

Social capital is created when people form social connections and networks based on principles of mutual trust, reciprocity, and norms for action (Racelis 1999). These relationships and connections can be either horizontal or vertical, and embody implicit contracts sustained by cultural norms and values. The concept of social capital is broad enough in principle to encompass a wide range of relationships, from face-to-face personal interactions whose character and efficacy depend on the individual characteristics of the transacting parties, to the more formal and impersonal relations entailed in dealings that invoke the law or involve organs of the state. An important part of the problem of understanding poverty has been the failure to realize, first, the significance of social capital and, second, the nature of the social capital that is available to the poor. It is evident that the poor have less access to those types of social capital that are abstract and more formally organized under legal contract and state protection, such as wide-reaching business and financial organizations including entitlements and redress promised by civil and political rights.[4] Clearly, the condition of poverty is partly based on an exclusion from types of social capital that are potentially wider in scope and application.

It would be a mistake, however, to think that the poor are totally bereft of social capital themselves. Rather, the social capital they build up frequently assumes forms that tend to be more implicit and self-enforcing. *Bonding social capital* refers to the horizontal (egalitarian) associations among people, consisting of social networks and associated norms that have an impact on community productivity and well-being. In Asia, where family and kinship ties remain strong, the family structure serves as the most reliable source of bonding social capital. On the other hand, *bridging social capital* pertains to vertical or hierarchical associations that enable people to link with groups having access to influence and resources. Such ties are tapped in times of need under cultural principles of reciprocity (Racelis-Hollnsteiner 1963).

Studies of rural communities in Malaysia and the Philippines reveal a working social redistribution system that underlies class and status relations in the peasant economies of these countries (Scott 1985, Kerkvliet 1990). In what Scott (1985) calls the "moral economy", peasants willingly serve the better-off members of society (e.g., landlords and capitalists) and place themselves under the latter's patronage in exchange for the assurance of economic well-being and protection against forces that could undermine the survival of their families.

The ability of the poor to survive adverse conditions and create resilience measures depends, for the most part, on their access to both bonding social capital and bridging social capital. Bonding social capital, derived primarily from family and neighbors, gives communities a sense of identity and common purpose and can serve as an important day-to-day safety net. Bridging social capital, obtained from wealthier and more influential individuals and groups, provides poor people with access to resources critically needed to lift them out of poverty.

The main sources of social capital for the poor include the family, the community, and civil society. Each generates social capital, which the poor can apply to enhancing their economic and social welfare. It is normally within and through the family that children develop *trust, reciprocal actions,* and *concern for others.* These traits, especially trust, are essential for the formation of relationships with people outside the family (friends, neighbors, community members, co-workers, and other groups in society). The family's ability to meet children's needs for physical and emotional nurturance has a strong bearing on children's perceptions of the trustworthiness of nonfamily members. In healthily functioning families, the care and protection given by parents to their children instills an implicit desire to return such support, thereby establishing the basis for reciprocity and exchange.

The family also represents an important *informal safety net*. In Asia, where family and kinship ties remain strong, the family structure assumes a role in social security, cushioning members from adverse effects of poverty. Transfers in cash and in kind from parents to children, between siblings, or among relatives, are common. Other forms of assistance include taking in and supporting relatives who have nowhere to live or who cannot manage on their own. When parents advance in years, children take care of them as well. In Asia, older persons often live with their children in extended families. Out of sheer tradition or because they find themselves in financial or other difficulties, adult children may bring their own children to live in their parents/grandparents' households, which may then come to comprise three generations.

The spread of globalization and urbanization, as well as the trend toward smaller families, are making significant inroads into the extended-family system and long-standing cultural practices across Asia. Traditional caregivers for older persons are declining in number, especially in the better-off countries. Consequently, the social safety nets and support normally provided by family structures are becoming increasingly unavailable to many older persons.

The *community* augments the family as a source of social capital. In Asia, social networks abound in urban and rural communities, with many examples of neighbors, friends, and members of local associations coming to one another's assistance for overcoming survival, safety, and social problems. Many villages designate one day in the week for every household to participate in cleaning up the community grounds and repairing community infrastructure. At the same time, such ties can yield negative consequences if they lead to the formation of gangs victimizing passers-by, or antisocial groups that engage in theft in the poor community itself.

In Viet Nam, villages and neighborhoods have mechanisms of immediate support for households facing hardship. People lend cash or food to friends and relatives, and contribute to wedding and funeral expenses. Money or food donations are organized for the very sick or elderly, and battered women are assisted. People find work for jobless friends and relatives, or even share work or contracts with them. Some communities exhibit a strong sense of obligation to help poorer households by providing childcare while the parents are at work. Revolving credit and savings associations, and informal savings clubs are common, as are instances of communities working together to upgrade their alleys and pathways (Viet Nam et al. 1999).

In Bangladesh, men in the village of Dhamrai raise funds for suddenly widowed women, as well as offer food to starving neighbors. In the village of Gowainghat, a youth club raises funds from which interest-free loans are extended to the Hindu poor. In one incident, when flash floods occurred, everyone cooperated to protect the community—Muslims and Christians, poor and nonpoor alike. In yet another demonstration of social cohesion, Muslim women in Madaripur village mobilized villagers to raise the money needed for the dowry of a Hindu woman, whose parents could not marry her off for lack of money (un Nabi et al. 1999).

In Korea, a movement of various social, religious, labor, and management groups contributed immensely to relief operations for the poor and unemployed most affected by the Asian financial crisis. Voluntary donations for the poor rose in terms of both the total amount (by 8 percent) and the number of contributors (by 28 percent). Volunteers serving at food shelters or social welfare institutions likewise increased. Women's associations and religious organizations were encouraged to organize a campaign to distribute free sack-meals for students without lunch. Christian communities, such as the Dail Community and the Christian Doctor's Association, assisted the homeless and the poor near Seoul Station by establishing food shelters, providing temporary accommodations, and arranging free medical consultations. A voluntary association of artists held free performances of plays, dances, and "sing-alongs" for the unemployed and homeless (Moon, Lee, and Yoo 1999).

In the Philippines, the spirit of volunteerism and mutual support is perhaps best embodied in the traditional practice of *bayanihan*, which originally involved community members helping a neighbor transfer residence by lifting the hut on bamboo poles, and carrying it all the way to its new location. Another manifestation of community solidarity is found in the custom of *paglalamay*, or attending the wake of a friend or neighbor whose parent, spouse, or child had just died; and giving *abuloy,* or a monetary contribution to help with funeral expenses. In a country that frequently experiences a wide range of natural calamities, Filipinos have become expert at mounting local relief operations virtually overnight, always with impressive results, as shown in the participation of different sectors and social classes. Even on a daily basis and outside of crisis or calamity situations, neighbors provide mutual assistance in myriad ways: they borrow money or food from one another, mind one another's children, and inform one another of upcoming community events, job prospects, or government assistance programs.

In Pakistan, a system of community-level food security and welfare revolves around the *zakat*, a tax levied on the wealthy to benefit the poor and needy. Redistribution occurs through the mosque. Those eligible to receive zakat, called the *mustahiqueen*, include the poor (especially widows and orphans), as well as people with disabilities. There are currently 1.5 million mustahiqeen in Pakistan who are served by the zakat system (Social Policy and Development Centre 2001).

The support networks provided by the community are vital for poor households, but have their limitations. The kind and level of help provided by friends and neighbors who themselves possess limited resources or might even be in a similar plight are usually not adequate to lift the poor out of poverty. Repeated shocks or long-term stresses can overwhelm informal support systems, which are more effective at meeting short-term security needs than at fostering changes in the underlying causes of exclusion. Moreover, as already noted, larger social and demographic trends, including globalization, migration, and urbanization, have begun to erode much of the social and economic foundations for these types of social capital. For households in chronic poverty or that face serious shocks, therefore, it is necessary to look for systems that are more encompassing and that mobilize larger amounts of resources and which, while supporting people-generated efforts, have the capacity to go beyond them. State-level and state-initiated systems obviously offer the widest opportunities. Civil society offers others.

CIVIL SOCIETY

Civil society consists of both formal and informal organizations operating outside the state and market to promote various interests in society. These include nongovernmental organizations (NGOs), community associations, labor unions, cooperatives, religious groups, professional associations, student organizations, media and academic institutions, among others.

These organizations fall into three major categories: community-based organizations[5] (CBOs), civic or professional organizations, and NGOs. CBOs feature a mostly poor grassroots membership operating on a voluntary basis through associations, unions, or cooperatives. Civic/professional organizations are also mostly voluntary and revolve around the interests of the members, who fall into the better-off socioeconomic category. NGOs are intermediary organizations with salaried professional organizers and development workers. They focus on promoting the equitable distribution of resources, expanding economic opportunity and productivity especially for poor and powerless sectors, and enhancing people's empowerment and self-reliance.

Recent research has shown the direct relationship between a vital associational life and economic development. A study of poverty in Tanzania demonstrates that social capital, measured by the extent of membership in a village's civil society group, correlates with household income in the community. Villagers with higher levels of social capital have higher incomes (Narayan et al. 2000). This may be partially explained by the attraction that dynamic communities hold for prospective donors.

Together, NGOs and CBOs all over Asia are at the forefront of organizing and advocacy efforts to bring justice, peace, and equity to poor people (Racelis 2000b). They have proven instrumental in helping communities draw upon and expand their social capital. At the same time, while NGOs have reached significant numbers of poor people in ways that governments have not, they face limitations that are well-acknowledged. On the one hand, they often fail to reach the very poorest, notwithstanding numerous projects, programs and advocacy thrusts. On the other, they realize that short of dismantling unjust and discriminatory elite structures of power, preferably through democratic means, reform can bring only limited relief to poor communities.

Asia boasts of many examples of how trust, mutual assistance, and supportive institutional mechanisms embedded in the activities of civil society organizations facilitate the realization of shared goals and promote the economic and social well-being of the poor. Prominent examples of how NGOs can successfully work with poor people to reduce poverty and sustain that outcome include the Grameen

Bank in Bangladesh, Orangi Pilot Project in Pakistan, and Urban Land Reform Task Force in the Philippines. The Grameen Bank is an innovative banking system that draws upon and augments the elements of social capital—mutual trust, accountability, participation, and creativity (Khandker 1994). The Orangi Pilot Project (OPP) demonstrates how urban informal settlers can bring dramatic improvements to their communities when they unite to contribute their own funds and labor to a local project (Racelis 2000a). The Urban Land Reform Task Force is a coalition of urban poor organizations, NGOs, and concerned individuals that succeeded in pushing for the passage of the Urban Development and Housing Act (Karaos et al. 1995).

NGOs as Poverty Reduction Intermediaries

In Asia, civil society movements are generally equated with non-governmental organizations, most of which are composed of middle class social activists. This stems in part from NGOs having consistently dominated the front lines of democratization in developing societies for more than 30 years. In terms of their dominant orientations they may be classified as being either mainly (i) service-provider NGOs, (ii) development NGOs, or (iii) empowerment NGOs.

At one end, service-provider NGOs strive to reduce the adverse effects of poverty on people's lives through poverty alleviation programs. They initiate projects dealing with livelihood, health, child feeding, and credit, as well as training and education activities. At the other end, empowerment NGOs undertake poverty eradication programs to transform the socioeconomic system into one that distributes the fruits of a productive economy more equitably by addressing the structural causes of poverty and exclusion. Enabling people to obtain power through community organizing is the key approach. Development NGOs endeavor to do both, that is, meet immediate and medium-term poverty reduction goals through specific project interventions, bolstered by community organizing.

NGOs have assumed a variety of roles in promoting poverty-oriented economic approaches (San Juan 1996): (i) socioeconomic empowerment of poor communities through holistic sectoral and community organizing and different levels of socioeconomic education and training (e.g., skills training in enterprise development and in business management); (ii) delivery of services needed for enterprise and cooperative development (e.g., technology, credit); (iii) development of models and technologies in enterprise development for poor communities; (iv) advocacy against environmentally destructive and wasteful business/industry practices; (v) advocacy for pro-people economic strategies and approaches (e.g., agrarian reform); and (vi) checking unsustainable and inequitable economic development strategies.

In Asia, the NGO sector has grown steadily. Bangladesh and the Philippines are each listed as having more than 40,000 NGOs. In contrast, Lao PDR and Viet Nam have very few local NGOs, although their number is increasing. At the same time, under political party leadership, mass organizations of farmers, women and youth in these two countries have taken on a number of the service, organizational, and advocacy functions of NGOs.

The burgeoning of NGOs in many Asian countries reflects certain global trends. First, decreasing resources available for development assistance from funding agencies has necessitated increased NGO involvement to ensure benefits for the poor. Second, trends toward globalization and privatization have reduced the role of governments in providing essential public services, with local communities expected to take more responsibility for meeting their own needs. Third, demands for democratization and popular participation have brought an end to several authoritarian regimes, allowing the installation of more democratic governments. This has created an enabling environment for people to be active, speak out, organize, and become genuine partners in development (ADB 1999d).

The heterogeneity of experiences in the eight countries as regards NGOs emerges clearly. Lao PDR and Viet Nam, which share common histories of centrally planned economies shifting to free market systems, have relatively few local NGOs. The few existing ones operate under the watchful eye of government; on the other hand, international NGOs abound. Bangladesh and Pakistan have common early histories vis-à-vis NGOs, but the Bangladesh government gives NGOs far more leeway in their operations than does Pakistan. In the Philippines, as in Thailand, NGOs have taken on strong advocacy and community support roles toward pro-people and pro-poor strategies and approaches. They openly criticize government and private sector entities that undermine or resist these approaches and have no hesitation to take to the streets or highways in protest, together with their grassroots partners.

Despite the energy expended by NGOs in supporting people's development, a working relationship is needed with the State if the results are to make a difference for poor people. It is noteworthy, for example, that in Bangladesh—which holds the Asian record for the largest number of NGOs relative to the population—even all NGOs taken together are unlikely to serve more than 20 percent of the rural poor. Accordingly, NGO collaboration with the government, and increasingly also with the private sector, is necessary if poverty is to be addressed on a comprehensive, national scale. The issue then is less whether NGOs and government should work together (they have no choice); it is a question of *how*.

Much of government-NGO collaboration depends on the constraints placed upon NGO activities in a political climate created by government regimes (Farrington and Lewis 1993). A useful classification, therefore, might be one that recognizes the amount of political space and "room for maneuver" afforded NGOs in Asia.

In environments of political repression, NGOs work in "safe" localized sectors, trying not to compromise their overall political and community-based ideals. They focus on "safe" projects as venues for building people's organizations in the hope that when political change does come, these groups will be able to participate more directly in program development, monitoring and policy formulation. Such conditions prevailed in Bangladesh before independence, the Philippines under Marcos, and Korea under Park.

NGOs may also work with relatively nonantagonistic but bureaucratic government agencies under *stable but nondemocratic conditions*. In such cases, NGOs carry on grassroots and poverty-focused work that includes consciousness-raising and development projects that people can pursue with some success under the watchful, often skeptical or outright suspicious, eyes of the authorities (Lao PDR, Pakistan, Viet Nam).

Under conditions of *relative democracy*, NGOs strive to build new levels of accountability into government activities and improve government's responsiveness to the demands of poor people. This is accomplished by encouraging poor and disadvantaged groups to articulate their demands. Increased networking, communication and coordination are facilitated among NGOs and through carefully nurtured partnerships, between them and government. Bangladesh; Korea; Philippines; Taipei,China; and Thailand provide examples of such conditions (Farrington and Lewis 1993).

A key element that defines the NGO landscape in any country is therefore the amount of democratic space allowed by its government for citizens to organize poor people and to criticize or seek to reformulate government programs and policies. The wider the democratic space, the larger the number of local NGOs and the higher the ratio of local to international NGOs. Where a country's political leadership severely restricts the democratic space, local NGOs find difficulty operating effectively and remain few relative to international NGOs. The latter then dominate in the work with poor communities, sometimes finding their foreign status to be advantageous and other times disadvantageous vis-a-vis government.

Assessing NGOs in Asia

NGOs in Asia are at the forefront of change. Their focus remains that of enabling the poor to take steps to overcome their poverty through collective efforts. These efforts have an impact not only in villages and neighborhoods but even at municipal, state, or higher levels of program and policy formulation. Yet, government officials frequently accuse NGOs of "creating trouble" and misconstrue their efforts to encourage community-based organizations that question or resist government actions (or inaction). Rather than work with NGOs to tap all sources of local development initiatives, government officials and local elites often hinder their efforts, to the extent of threatening POs that collaborate with NGOs.

Elites become uneasy, even resentful, when POs articulate their exclusion from asset distribution and identify the structural basis for it. Many feel threatened when they see the erosion of dependency relationships that have kept poor people beholden to them. This weakening of traditional ties happens as the poor organize around their own interests, and become bolder about their needs, more demanding of their rights, and less dependent on landlords and traditional patrons for support. Indeed, a key role of NGOs is to enable POs to connect with new networks and make outside contacts that enable them to sidestep traditional links. Some noteworthy examples of Asian networks are Focus on the Global South, Asian NGO Coalition for Agrarian Reform and Rural Development (ANGOC), Third World Network, and groups that focus on specific issues, like globalization, intellectual property rights, genetically modified organisms (GMOs), and landmine eradication.

In some cases, however, government officials do have reason to be critical of NGOs and their operations. NGOs are alleged to be too quick to criticize government decisions, yet remain ignorant of the technical, legal and administrative frameworks that mandate these decisions. NGOs may, for example, agitate for the inclusion of an expenditure item in a municipal budget that was finalized a whole year earlier in line with regulations. The bureaucracy is pilloried for slow implementation, although project personnel are at the mercy of unavoidable and time-consuming auditing procedures. Some officials cite the arrogance that some NGOs exhibit as self-appointed watchdogs over government actions, even as the NGOs themselves lack accountability for their own activities and the money entrusted to them.

NGOs have generally taken these criticisms to heart and begun collaborating more closely with government officials who seem to be genuinely interested in implementing pro-poor programs. They, for example, are learning about government budgeting and auditing procedures, the economics of low-income housing, and laws or regulations governing indigenous peoples' rights. Many are seeking or already successfully developing self-funding mechanisms to reduce their dependency on foreign donors. Included here are strategies aimed at leveraging public funds to prioritize poverty-reduction programs. Nonetheless, most NGOs realize the need for vigilance, lest they be co-opted into becoming action arms of the government and lose their privileged position of trust and partnership with organized poor groups.

In the Philippines, where the NGO network and experience is widest, the National Economic and Development Authority (NEDA) admits that no evaluation of the experience of government-NGO cooperation has yet been undertaken, but the agency is convinced nonetheless that the benefits outweigh the shortcomings (ADB 1999d, 24). Other government officials and business groups recognize the value of NGO work with local community groups, viewing it as a way to simplify and facilitate government's efforts to reach the poor. Particularly admired are the NGOs' quick-response approaches and adaptability to local requirements, their ability to interact closely with particular groups of poor people, to have a committed staff ready to set aside personal discomforts to be of service to people, and their capacity to introduce resources and ideas to the community (Farrington and Lewis 1993, 333).

People's Movements

Nongovernmental organizations are not the only influential groups in civil society. People's movements are gaining ground in terms of drawing government's attention to poverty through their potential threat of violence. Consisting of masses of organized poor with the capacity to assert their interests through nonviolent or more militant means, people's movements figure prominently on the Asian scene. Class-based resistance movements, such as the peasant mobilizations of Lao PDR and Viet Nam, which led to the ousting of France as the colonial power and later to the Socialist struggle for supremacy, were all rooted in people's movements.

Similarly, the Communist Party of the Philippines and its military wing, the New People's Army, and earlier the Huk movement in Central Luzon near Manila, spread rapidly, based on agrarian unrest, open conflict against landlords, and guerrilla warfare. The rebellion also caused a major government-initiated transmigration scheme that allocated public land in Mindanao to large numbers of landless peasant families. Ironically, however, this incursion into largely Muslim or indigenous people territory would later fan the flames of a secessionist Muslim movement against the encroachment of Christian Filipino settlers in their home territory, as well as pose serious threats to the cultural integrity of indigenous peoples.

Owing to peasant pressure in various forms, agrarian reform legislation in the Philippines moved slowly from one presidential administration to another, with the landlord-dominated legislature making just enough concessions to mitigate rural social unrest. It is instructive to examine the case of Philippine peasant movements, which in 1998-1999 linked up with NGOs and other civil society supporters in nonviolent ways to demand comprehensive agrarian reform.

One such movement turned out to be the most ideologically varied coalition in Philippine history (Goño 1998). The Congress for a People's Agrarian Reform, or CPAR, came into being in 1987, soon after the People Power uprising that ousted President Ferdinand Marcos and catapulted Corazon Aquino into the presidency. Given the low priority she appeared to give to agrarian reform, 22 NGOs and several peasant organizations soon ran a series of nationwide consultations with peasant groups and other disadvantaged rural people. They aimed to reach the broadest possible peasant consensus on the kinds of legislation needed. Twelve of these rural organizations, claiming to have a combined membership of 1.5 million small farmers, peasant women, landless cultivators, agricultural workers and fisherfolk, formed a coalition, the Congress for a People's Agrarian Reform (CPAR).

In the ensuing months, CPAR successfully lobbied the Office of the President to issue an executive order on agrarian reform and Congress to pass the appropriate bill. However, when the bill was passed as the Comprehensive Agrarian Reform Law, many CPAR member-federations rejected the watered-down text that the progressive legislators could not prevent from approving. CPAR then campaigned in favor of a draft bill, the People's Agrarian Reform Code (PARCode).

Members mobilized around a signature campaign calling for 2.9 million signatures on a petition for a citizen's initiative to set aside CARL and pass PARCode into law. In addition, CPAR broadened its advocacy scope to include additional issues like the price of rice and corn, the appointment of the agrarian reform secretary, a Magna Carta for Small Farmers, and the rights of fisherfolk. It joined campaigns for reforms in foreign debt management, reduced militarization in the countryside, and the removal of American military bases. Further, it decided to participate in the 1992 presidential and local elections, determined as it was to promote peasant issues, like agrarian and aquatic reform, land use conversion, and participatory governance; and to demonstrate the existence of a strong peasant vote.

Assessments of CPAR agree that it had a profound impact on the society (Goño 1998). It gave national and local peasant leaders the experience of attempting to unify the organized peasantry, and some idea of the issues that divided their ranks. Leaders gained considerable experience in consensus building and democratic management, and became acquainted with their counterparts of differing ideological persuasions. Such personal friendships undoubtedly kept the largest coalition in Philippine history going much longer than anyone would have predicted. The power of political influence came to the fore and demonstrated how organizationally strong poor peasants had to be to change entrenched power alignments.

Social movements in Asia demonstrate that class is not the only mobilizing variable. Gender disparities have led to active women's movements in many countries. Ethnic or religion-based conflict has also inspired independence movements, such as those in East Timor and Mindanao. Owing to the international media attention they generate, as well as their disruptive impact on the political and economic scene, these movements virtually compel governments who want to avoid military action to allocate more resources and services to those excluded sectors.

On the other hand, there are also people's organizations composed of organized poor sectors, who are no less resolute in their demands, such as the slum-dwellers of Bombay and informal settlers in Quezon City and along Metro Manila's Pasig River. Their successful organization and mobilization, notwithstanding the insecurity they face, have resulted in their stopping evictions, resisting resettlement in distant and ill-prepared sites, demanding security of land tenure, and negotiating the terms of social service benefits. Recognizing that the urban poor are a force to be reckoned with, city officials throughout the region have been more willing to listen and respond more positively to urban poor concerns. As Carroll (1997, 11-12) has pointed out, "long-term change for the better in the lives of poor people is rarely achieved without the pressures generated by strong and united poor people's movements."

Successful or not, the experience and skills NGOs acquire in previous struggles can serve them well in future movements. The NGOs involved in CPAR, for example, acquired valuable experience in dealing with people's organizations and in coalition building. This facility came into play once more in the sequence of events in which civil society mobilized effectively for People Power II in January 2001. The result was the removal of President Estrada from office and the assumption of then Vice President Gloria Macapagal-Arroyo to the presidency. The Filipino NGOs have learned how to initiate and manage civil disobedience campaigns using nonviolent means. They also expertly utilize advocacy mechanisms to bring an issue to a head so that wide-ranging action can get underway. In this sense, NGO networking and coalitions to hold governmental accountable for its policies and actions in favor of the poor may be considered its own kind of movement—a citizens' movement.

Unfortunately, despite ample evidence across Asia and elsewhere that pressures from below are the most effective catalysts for meaningful social reform, governments, particularly military governments, still view the emergence of people's movements as threats to the state. Rather than view protests as responses to untenable human situations, some governments regard them as efforts at destabilization to which the only proper response can be violent suppression.

Since the poor are meant to be the ultimate beneficiaries of poverty reduction strategies, however, it is crucial for governments and the private sector alike to address the interests and concerns articulated by people's movements. The tension between recognizing the validity of demands of excluded groups, on the one hand, and assessing the extent to which the latter may undermine the legitimacy of government authority, on the other, is one that every political administration must face squarely.

GOVERNMENT ANTIPOVERTY STRATEGIES THROUGH SOCIAL WELFARE AND SAFETY NETS

Most governments in Asia would regard it as their mandate not only to protect their citizens, dispense justice, and enforce contracts, but also to ensure that even the poorest and most vulnerable citizens have sources of income and access to basic social services that permit them to enjoy a dignified life. Toward this end, governments set up a variety of agencies and arrangements to provide these services, such as public health centers, education ministries, and water authorities, among others. They also enact redistributive measures such as land and aquatic resources reform, and the affirmation of indigenous people's ancestral land rights. More recently, they have worked with NGOs and other civil society groups to improve ways of reaching and mobilizing the poor for self-development and capacity building.

Because these regular antipoverty programs typically have a long gestation period, their impact on poverty reduction is felt only over the medium or long term. In the meantime, the poor may experience temporary adverse conditions that can push them further into destitution. These include illness and physical injury, violence and lack of peace and order, temporary and permanent loss of employment, old age crises, abrupt changes in food prices, shocks arising from natural disasters, and unpredictable swings in the macroeconomy. Government interventions that yield immediately felt effects are therefore essential to prevent the poor from sliding even farther down from already precarious levels of well-being.

Social assistance or welfare programs aimed specifically at the poor are regular government programs that seek to maintain at least a minimum living standard. These involve relief in cash or in kind to the poorest groups, and special services to marginalized groups, such as battered women or children in situations of armed conflict. Social security and insurance programs may mitigate risks arising from retirement, unemployment, illness and disability. Because they tend to require prior contributions from the poor, with only a few of the program benefits receiving partial subsidies, poor people find themselves left out of the contributory and subsidized programs.

Finally, *safety net programs* are bridging mechanisms that mitigate the adverse impact of economic dislocations and shocks, disasters and calamities, and structural adjustments on specific disadvantaged and vulnerable groups. These are short-term and time-bound interventions that include emergency assistance, food subsidies, emergency employment, retraining, and emergency loans.

Commentaries on government approaches to poverty reduction in five of the countries studied—Bangladesh; Philippines; Korea; Taipei,China; and Viet Nam—will highlight some of the key features of social policy development in Asia.

Both Taipei,China and Korea attained high levels of economic growth and social welfare protection through a long process that began several decades ago (UNDP n.d.). The two countries can look back on similar initial conditions as having fueled their rapid economic growth (Booth 1999). First, both countries built upon a favorable legacy of education developed under Japanese colonial rule; the two free governments then reinforced this advantage through massive spending on education.

Second, at the start of their periods of accelerated growth, both countries enjoyed highly equitable distributions of income and wealth, which for the most part were maintained in the ensuing decades. This reform stemmed in no small measure from forcefully introduced land reform programs during military rule, facilitated in Korea by the pressures of peasant movements and weakened local elites, and in Taipei, China by rulers from the mainland who disempowered indigenous elites and broke their resistance.

Targeted poverty alleviation programs in the two countries created support programs also aimed at building up the productive capacities of the poor. In Taipei,China, poor families, including aboriginals, received food subsidies, job placement, vocational training, housing and houses for older persons, family planning, community welfare benefits and disaster assistance, among others, as part of the Well-to-Do Program (WTDP). Similarly, Koreans obtained government assistance for food, housing, medical expenses and child delivery, educational costs, funeral expenses, and livelihood.

Policies encouraging growth and redistribution yielded programs for savings promotion among poor households, protection of rural and fishery communities, and public works employment. Basic education through high school was guaranteed, with strong vocational skills built in, and substantial university scholarship possibilities especially in science and technology for poor but promising students. Support to small and medium enterprises complemented the government drive for large-scale industrialization. Moreover, values common to the two countries emerged in government affirmations that poverty was not a personal but a social issue, and that citizens had a right to expect assistance and social protection from their government. This orientation formed the underpinnings for the development and improvement of the social welfare system from the 1980s onward. It found reinforcement in the cultural value given in both societies to family solidarity, diligence, and hard work.

Both countries adopted a fourfold social strategy of asset distribution, income support and livelihood protection, universal basic education, and human resource development. This was sorely tested during the Asian economic crisis in 1998-1999. Korea's remarkable economic growth came to a halt. The number of unemployed increased threefold, from 0.56 million in 1997 to 1.46 million in 1998 (Park and Kim 1998). The proportion of the poor in cities rose from 7.5 percent just before the crisis, to a peak of 23 percent in the third quarter of 1998, tapering off to 16 percent in the last quarter of 1998 (Atinc 2000).

Faced with the economic slowdown, the government increased spending for safety nets, unemployment benefits and public works, and condoned interest payments for loans. It reduced spending on education, civil service salaries, rural development, and defense. Because unemployment emerged as the most serious consequence of the crisis, a comprehensive policy package included the expansion of unemployment insurance, the Wage Claim Guarantee Fund, a large wage subsidy program, public works programs and temporary livelihood protection, and loan programs for the unemployed. Of these measures, the expansion of unemployment insurance and public works programs appear to have had the strongest potential for real impact (Moon et al. 1999).

Other strategies for temporary livelihood protection and income support included transfers in cash or in kind. The means-tested Livelihood Protection Program, which provided cash and in-kind aid to those unable to work, was expanded in May 1998, both in terms of coverage and budget allocation (Moon et al. 1999). Finally, to target the in-between group ineligible for either unemployment benefits or livelihood assistance, the government offered loans through the Life Stabilization Fund, the Resettlement Allowance Fund, and National Pension Fund (Moon et al. 1999).

Compared to other countries in the region, Korea went the furthest in expanding safety nets during the financial crisis (Atinc 2000). Its decision to do so reflects the greater demand for public action on the part of the citizenry, as well as a greater government capacity to respond in terms of both will and resources. Especially significant is the government's extensive net of pro-poor programs that was already in place *before* the crisis, which the government could then expand rapidly and effectively. A bureaucracy familiar with managing social welfare coverage programs in normal times made it possible to add new programs quickly that responded well to the differential needs of a wide range of affected groups.

This shows that even when economic growth and full employment are present, social welfare coverage for the population at large and social safety nets may be needed to tide over its most vulnerable groups in more trying times.

In the Philippines, poverty has challenged every administration since independence in 1946. Despite a steady decline in Philippine poverty incidence from 49 percent in 1985 to 32 percent in 1997, the Asian economic crisis, coupled with the El Niño drought, both of which occurred in 1997-1998, arrested that positive trend. By 2000, poverty incidence had risen again to 34.2 percent, or approximately 4.5 million families of the total 14 million. In rural areas, the proportion of families with incomes below the food threshold stood at 16.8 percent, making up 2.6 million subsistence incidence families (NSCB 2001 as quoted by Dancel 2001, NAPC 2001b).

Over three quarters of the poor in the Philippines live in rural areas (NAPC 2001a). However, poverty in the country is fast acquiring an "urban face", suggesting that it is no longer simply a rural phenomenon (Balisacan 1999). One of every two rural families now lives in poverty, while the comparable ratio for urban families is one of every five. Four regions in the country have high poverty incidence rates (with over half of their population considered poor), including the Autonomous Region of Muslim Mindanao (70 percent), Bicol (56 percent), and Northern and Central Mindanao (51 percent) (NSCB 2001 as quoted by Dancel 2001).

Despite the decline in poverty levels up to 1997, however, inequality increased in the last half of the 1990s. This is reflected in the rise in the national Gini index from 0.47 in 1994 to 0.51 in 2000 (Reyes 2002). Reasons given include the benefits that upper income groups enjoyed from liberalization policies in the early to mid-1990s. Recent episodes of economic growth appear not to have not benefited the poor (Balisacan 1999).

The slow progress in poverty reduction can be attributed to a number of factors: (i) the slow pace of economic growth resulting from past policies that have favored capital-intensive, inward-oriented development, and which have given low priority to agriculture and exports; (ii) the highly inequitable distribution of incomes and assets dating back to the Spanish colonial era; (iii) the limited access to social services, particularly primary health care, quality basic education, and credit; and (iv) the limited coverage and impact of official safety net programs and targeted poverty reduction programs.

Despite his election on a pro-poor platform, President Joseph Estrada never achieved his goal of reducing poverty incidence from 32 to 25-28 percent by 2004. Massive citizen protests against gross economic mismanagement and widespread corruption forced him out of office less than halfway through his term. At the time of his departure, a clearly enunciated antipoverty strategy had not yet been put in place (NAPC 2001b). Instead there was a nationwide targeted antipoverty program, the *Lingap para sa Mahihirap* (Caring for the Poor), which envisioned livelihood, medical insurance, waterworks, food subsidies, socialized housing, and social welfare programs at the legislative district level.

However, that program failed for several reasons (Balisacan et al. 2000). First, it had a weak targeting design. The program's aim of reaching the poorest 100 families in each of the 78 provinces and 83 cities in the country diffused resources and resulted in high program costs. Poverty could have been reduced more effectively if resources had been focused on the poorest provinces or municipalities. Moreover, the program was plagued with leaks. Second, it lacked the participation of local governments and beneficiaries in the identification of program beneficiaries, as well as in monitoring and assessment. Third, it utilized a politicized process of beneficiary selection by national legislators. These findings are corroborated by two studies (World Bank 2001b, IPD 1991), which revealed that nonpoor communities and households benefited more from the program than did the poor. Lingap was only the latest among many other programs in the country since the mid-1980s that were plagued by similar deficiencies: substantial undercoverage; lack of convergence among agencies; low levels of awareness and information; lack of consultation with beneficiaries and local government units; highly politicized process of program implementation; and poor monitoring and evaluation of program impact (NAPC 2001a).

Under the current Macapagal-Arroyo Administration, the antipoverty strategy, as drafted by the National Anti-Poverty Commission (NAPC 2001c), is anchored on *redistributive reform.* This focuses on asset reform, human development services, participation in governance and institution-building, security from violence, employment and income generation, and social protection for the poorest and most vulnerable groups through targeted interventions, social welfare assistance, safety nets, and social insurance. Immediate and medium-term responses in the most depressed communities are being organized through the *Kapit-Bisig Laban sa Kahirapan* (Linking Arms Against Poverty), or KALAHI, which is characterized by extensive consultations with communities and their local governments.

Bangladesh has made considerable progress in income-poverty reduction since the crisis-ridden 1970s. That decade was marked by a massive cyclone and floods, a war of independence, and a major famine, simultaneously imposed on an already poor populace. Not surprisingly, poverty rose sharply to 80 percent. It subsided in the first half of the 1980s but rose again in the second half. By the 1990s, a more significant and sustained decline in poverty was evident along with the per capita GDP growth of 1.5 percent in 1973-1990 and 2.4 percent in 1991-1996 (Sen 2000). Significantly, while the incidence of the *poor* declined from 59 to 53 percent in the period 1991-1992 to 1995-1996, the *very poor* also dropped from 43 to 36 percent of the population[6] (World Bank 1998).

The impact of higher growth rates on poverty has been tempered by rising inequality, especially in urban areas (World Bank 1998). The Gini coefficient was in the 0.36-0.39 range between 1973-1974 but it had risen to 0.43 by 1995-1996. Depending on the poverty measure used, some 20 to 30 percent of the potential poverty reduction from growth may have been lost to rising inequality. In 1994, the bottom 40 percent of all households owned only 16 percent of total rural income, while the top 10 percent owned 32 percent (Cook et al. 2001).

Poverty in Bangladesh is conditioned by locational, climatic, economic, and social factors (Cook et al. 2001). It reflects a strong rural dimension, with 89 percent of the poor and 93 percent of the very poor living in rural areas. Natural calamities annually challenge Bangladesh's growth prospects and exacerbate the condition of the poor. The nonownership of productive assets is likewise a determinant of poverty in a largely agrarian economy. Land is scarce and highly valued, and poor people tend to be landless. Around 70-80 percent of those with less than half an acre of land are poor; 60 percent are very poor. Finally, gender and caste sharpen the experience of poverty.

Bangladesh has a long tradition of safety nets that are funded largely by external food aid. The three largest government programs are: (i) Food for Work, which provides wheat and rice in exchange for work on rural infrastructure projects; (ii) Food for Education, which provides wheat and rice to poor children in return for regular primary school attendance; and (iii) the Vulnerable Group Development, which provides food grain and training to disadvantaged women. Test Relief is a smaller program that supports activities like cleaning ponds and bushes, and making minor repairs on rural roads, schools, mosques, and *madrasah* (Islamic schools) during the rainy season (World Bank 1998).

Heavy dependence on a multiplicity of aid donors for poverty reduction programs can lead to dire consequences (Sobhan 1998). The first is the high cost of aid delivery to the poor. A study of externally funded aid to poverty projects implemented by various agencies of the government revealed that almost 50 percent of expenditures did not go to the target beneficiaries but rather into overhead costs, hardware, and foreign and local consultancies. While not mentioned, corruption almost surely exacerbates the problem.

Also a subject of concern is the government's persistently strong tendency to delegate policy reform initiatives to external donors. These often come in the form of conditionalities in a variety of aid programs. Donor-driven policy initiatives have pressed for financial sector reform, privatization of public enterprises, import liberalization, discontinuation of agricultural subsidies, sale of irrigation equipment, jute sector reform, railway reform, and capital market reform. Yet, the success of any move to eliminate poverty will depend on whether the government can establish its own vision for poverty reduction and recapture its autonomy in the policy and operational spheres (Sobhan 1998).

Since the reunification of *Viet Nam* in 1976, poverty reduction has been a central goal of the government, and the driving force since 1986 behind *doi moi* (the reform process aimed at transforming the Viet Nam economy from a centrally planned to a market-based system). The country has achieved substantial progress, slowed down only by the recent Asian economic crisis. Poverty had been reduced from a high of 70 percent of the total population in the mid-1980s, to around 50 percent in 1992 (UNDP Viet Nam 1996). Using World Bank poverty lines the poverty rate further declined from 58 percent in 1993 to 37 percent in 1998 (World Bank 1999). This dramatic drop is clearly related to faster economic growth and the creation of employment opportunities (Jansen 2000). However, indicators of inequality show an increase between 1993 and 1998 with the Gini coefficient rising from 0.33 in 1993 to 0.35 in 1998 (ADB 2000d). Poverty thus remains widespread. According to the Ministry of Labour, Invalids and Social Affairs (MOLISA), of Viet Nam's population of 77 million, as many as 12.5 million people (16 percent) live in poverty, and 1.5 million people face hunger regularly. Based on a broader definition of poverty adopted by the World Bank, no less than 28 million people (37 percent) lack the minimum income to maintain a decent level of living (United Nations in Viet Nam 1999).

Geographic location, ethnicity, household size, and age figure closely in the poverty equation (United Nations in Viet Nam 1999).

Rural households are most affected and make up about 90 percent of the poor. In urban centers, the poverty rate is lower and features concentrations of new migrants. The Northern Uplands, Northern Central Region, and Central Highlands have the highest poverty rates (MOLISA 2000). Moreover, a majority of the poor are ethnic minorities, primarily Hmong and Tay, who live virtually isolated from basic services. Poverty is also pervasive among larger households with several children under the age of 15. The brunt of poverty's impact is felt most by children. Some 52 percent of them are malnourished, 14 percent of whom suffer from severe malnutrition.

The government's National Target Program for Hunger Eradication and Poverty Reduction (HEPR), established in 1998, provides a framework to address some of the most pressing concerns of poor people in Viet Nam. As the government's *targeted poverty reduction strategy*, the HEPR incorporates many pro-poor services and programs of the government. It has nine components, namely: (i) sedentarization, resettlement and New Economic Zones; (ii) infrastructure development in poor communes and resettlement; (iii) promotion of agriculture and off-farm production; (iv) extension services for agriculture, forestry and fisheries, and income generation; (v) training for HEPR staff; (vi) assistance to ethnic minorities facing extreme difficulties; (vii) credit and saving facilities for the poor; (viii) education for the poor; and (ix) health for the poor (World Bank 1999).

The HPER strategy suffers from a number of important weaknesses, however (World Bank 2001c). Institutional arrangements and division of responsibilities between ministries are unclear; this fragmentation of the program's administration thus undermines efficiency. Projects are inappropriately targeted and insufficiently monitored and evaluated. Little opportunity is provided for people and communities to participate, and the roles of potential actors are not clearly defined. Planning and decision-making are assigned only to central authorities, whereas people's initiatives at the grassroots level, such as savings groups, receive scant attention (World Bank 2001c).

Aside from its targeted poverty reduction framework, the government has developed *formal social safety nets* to protect vulnerable groups. It spends around 14 percent of its budget on social transfers, and has been formulating a number of social insurance schemes and relief funds (United Nations in Viet Nam 1999). Allocations to basic social services have increased from 6.1 percent of total government spending in 1990, to 8.5 percent in 1997 (Jansen 2000). However, the majority of the beneficiaries are not the poor but special priority groups, such as former government employees and war veterans (World Bank 2001c). The only formal protection available to the poor consists of the Social Guarantee Fund for Regular Relief and the Contingency Fund for Pre-Harvest Starvation and Disaster. The benefits of the Fund for Regular Relief reach only a minority of those qualified to receive assistance: 24 percent of orphans, 15 percent of the disabled, and 46 percent of the solitary elderly.

In many programs intended for the poor, there is overwhelming evidence that anticipated benefits often fail to reach them, especially the poorest among them. This happens for a number of reasons. First, inadequate planning, management, and monitoring divert relief and safety net programs to better-off recipients, with the collusion of corrupt officials. Second, poor people lack the information needed about relief or safety net programs to ascertain whether they are entitled to them or to understand how to gain access to benefits; moreover, if they do not organize themselves effectively, they lack the power to hold officials accountable for inequitable or corrupt allocation decisions. Third, poor and informal sector workers generally fall outside government social assistance schemes because they have not made the mandatory contributions over their working lives that entitle them to claim benefits later on.

SUMMARY AND CONCLUSION

Understanding poverty—its reduction and eventual elimination—calls for going beyond narrow income or consumption measures or strictly economic analyses to incorporating the wealth of sociocultural knowledge at hand. This entails multidimensional insights and drawing on wide-ranging data analyses from the noneconomic social sciences, experiences of NGOs and other civil society groups active in working with disadvantaged communities, and from poor people themselves.

While poverty is a state deeply felt by the poor, equally deserving of attention are the concepts of well-being and happiness that give meaning to their lives. Disadvantaged community residents can identify who of their neighbors are poor (but with some resources), poorer (with only few resources), and poorest (virtually no resources). Moreover, they can describe the characteristics defining each marginalized cluster; suggest some key reasons for its poverty or vulnerability; and propose ways of gaining access to assets, resources, services, participation, information, and dignity.

Poor Asians view well-being as having enough food, decent shelter, clothing, and stable livelihoods. It embodies good health, strength, and a fine appearance. Harmonious family and community relations contribute to it. Being accorded respect, no matter how poor one is, emerges as a strong theme, along with the desire to exert greater control over one's life individually or collectively. All this makes it incumbent upon government and private sector leaders to help identify and dismantle exclusionary structures and processes that create, sustain, and exacerbate poverty. This in turn will enable marginalized groups to take advantage of new opportunities that give promise of a better, more inclusive life.

Intrinsic to poverty is social exclusion. This refers to the norms, societal processes, and institutional arrangements that inhibit certain groups from full participation in the social, economic, cultural, and political life of societies. Exclusionary norms operate at household, community, national, and global levels. They encompass everything from differential allocation of food and education among household members; to discrimination within communities on the basis of social status and through differential access to basic services; to the national level where cultural practices and state policies reinforce the power of some to the disadvantage of the many; and to the global level where trade or structural adjustment policies could push the poorest groups deeper into poverty.

Social groups experience social exclusion in different ways. For rural people, it centers around land, environmental degradation, and isolation from services. For the urban poor, exclusion means deplorable slum environments, insecure residential tenure, and constant threat of eviction to distant relocation sites with a corresponding separation from existing sources of employment and income. Poor women worry about their inability to feed, clothe or educate their children, their limited or virtually non-existent opportunities for earning income or participating in decision-making, and violent behavior from abusive husbands. Similar commentaries can be applied to children, indigenous peoples, disabled, elderly, and other disadvantaged groups.

Despite their poverty or perhaps because of it, poor people remain remarkably creative and resilient. This is seen in their coping behavior. Strategies include further reducing expenditures; selling or renting out their meager assets; increasing their work activities; borrowing money, food, and other necessities; and migrating within or outside the country. The costs of pursuing these approaches take their toll on the most vulnerable groups. Thus, young children become more malnourished, risking permanent disability or even death. Children, women, and older persons become sick more often but cannot afford health care; young girls and boys drop out of school for full-time work; and adolescents are sold into prostitution or pornography rings, while desperate young adults try to make ends meet through theft or the drug trade. Also affected is the natural environment as destitute people move into the uplands to harvest trees for firewood and overuse other natural resources, or engage in illicit fishing in coastal areas causing the destruction of coral reefs and mangrove forests.

Civil society organizations, particularly NGOs, work extensively with poor people to help improve their economic, political, and social well-being. Especially when the state is weak or virtually absent and chronic poverty afflicts large numbers of people, or when severe shocks deplete traditional safety nets, NGOs strengthen poor people's ability to meet their daily needs and enhance their capacities through education, training, organizing, and advocacy. These forms of empowerment expand poor people's demand and decision-making opportunities. They may also lead to a reorganization of institutional and power relationships that enable disadvantaged groups to gain greater access to society's resources.

NGO networks, made up largely of an active middle-class citizenry, have mobilized fellow civil society organizations to advocate and develop new paradigms of society that are more favorable to the poor. These attempts to reorient government and its institutions have had varying degrees of success in Asia, depending on how well or badly the state has related to NGOs and civil society. More recently, NGOs have also been expanding mutually supportive relationships with the business sector in line with the latter's growing interest in corporate philanthropy and local development.

NGOs may be classified in terms of their dominant orientation to addressing poverty. At one end of the continuum lies the promotion of welfare services for poverty alleviation, and at the other, community empowerment for poverty eradication through structural change.

In between is a combination of welfare-enhancing projects and empowerment thrusts toward poverty reduction. Although long engaged in working with disadvantaged men, women, and children in society, NGOs and other social development groups acknowledge the difficulty of reaching the poorest among them in a sustained way. As in the case of government, how to develop better-targeted approaches remains a continuing challenge.

Asian countries harbor a mix of local NGOs organized and run by their own citizens, along with international (or foreign) NGOs, coming largely from the North. The democratic space allowed by its government for citizens clearly exerts a large influence on the number of NGOs and their effectiveness as poverty-reduction intermediaries.

Asian governments regard NGOs with mixed reactions. On the one hand, they recognize the capacity of their dedicated and modestly paid professional staff to reach the poor quickly and flexibly with innovations leading to effective poverty reduction. On the other hand, many officials regard NGOs as troublesome carping critics, who are largely ignorant of government constraints and procedures. Moreover, they complain that even as NGOs exact transparency and accountability from government, NGOs themselves tend to avoid transparency and evade accountability. Suspicious officials even accuse some of mobilizing poor groups to destabilize the government and threaten those in authority. Thus, varying modes of collaboration and conflict play out among NGOs and governments in Asia over time, with reasonably effective collaboration among some, and animosity and repression among others. By and large, Asian societies acknowledge the roles NGOs and civil society have played in drawing attention to the poor and powerless, and to the exclusionary systems that must be overcome for people's development and empowerment toward the elimination of poverty. Many NGOs are now developing strategies that encourage governments to realign their budgets in favor of pro-poor programs. In the process, their earlier dependence on foreign funding for this purpose is diminishing.

Still, it is not only NGOs that catalyze significant social change. People's movements in Asia have often forced governments—through violent or nonviolent means—to engage in widespread land and other asset reforms. In the transition economies, mass organizations carry out the mobilizing functions undertaken by NGOs elsewhere. However, since mass organizations operate under government auspices, they are not classified as NGOs or civil society groups.

Governments have also ventured into social reform through a variety of welfare or social assistance programs. Focusing on the poorer and disadvantaged citizens, their approaches take several forms. *Relief*—in cash or in-kind transfers—is targeted at chronically poor and vulnerable groups or those affected by natural or man-made disasters. *Safety nets* are short-term, time-bound bridging mechanisms that mitigate the adverse impact of economic dislocations and shocks, calamities, and structural adjustment measures. *Social security and social insurance* programs, whose coverage varies widely in Asia, draw on legislation to decrease risks arising from retirement, unemployment, illness, and disability.

A summary of the sociocultural determinants and sustaining factors that have prevented or enhanced poverty-reduction in Asia highlights the following points:

(i) Social structure and cultural outlooks, together with the discriminatory processes they engender in a country, bring about inequitable and often highly skewed resource allocations, thereby promoting continuing dependency and powerlessness in large sectors of the populace.

(ii) The failure of governments and ruling elites to understand poor people's perspectives on poverty and variations in vulnerability at differing points in their lives has seriously undermined efforts to help and enable the poor to overcome their poverty.

(iii) The barriers erected by social exclusion processes remain resistant to change and discourage opportunities for the poor to overcome them through greater empowerment and productivity; nonetheless, breakthroughs toward poverty reduction do occur.

(iv) The resilience and social capital generated by the poor surface not only in their capacity to survive (albeit often at great cost to certain marginalized groups) but also in the reciprocal services and community-wide benefits that accrue to members through extensive interaction with family, kin, neighbors, friends, employers, public officials, and other allies.

(v) The democratic space that governments leave open for poor people to express their grievances and seek redress affects civil society efforts to bring about effective reform. The larger the space, the more effective are civil society efforts toward poverty reduction. The more open the government to collaborating on development and empowerment of NGOs, the greater the chances for sustainable transformation of small but successful community-based efforts into scaled-up local and national government programs.

(vi) High poverty levels in South Asia versus lower levels in Southeast and East Asia can be partially explained by differences in gender relations and opportunities for women and girls in the two regions. Traditional social structures and cultural norms in South Asia, much more than in Southeast or East Asia, still keep large numbers of South Asian women isolated from public life and virtually powerless in economic, political, and social terms. Targeted programs for women and girls in both regions, cognizant of levels of need and formulated in consultation with them, will go far toward enhancing their developmental capacities. Accelerated programs in South Asia must be regarded as urgent.

To put the above learning points into practice, governments in Asia will clearly need to reduce the negative elements cited and build on and enhance the positive elements. They can most effectively do this through poverty reduction policies and programs that pursue multiple approaches:

(i) creating abundant employment opportunities for all groups with particular attention to the poor in differing types of vulnerability;

(ii) promoting small and medium enterprises with the capacity to grow and contribute to strong local economies, also giving particular attention to strengthening women's earning and other capacities;

(iii) developing human resources through providing access to basic services—health, education, shelter, water and sanitation;

(iv) accelerating rural development, asset reform, and agricultural and fisheries modernization for small farmers, fisherfolk and rural workers; promoting urban development through secure land tenure, employment, and basic services for the urban poor;

(v) protecting and augmenting budgetary allocations for social sector programs;

(vi) identifying the poorest and most vulnerable groups and developing with them programs targeted to address their particular needs in sustainable ways, including psycho-social and community organizing approaches aimed at raising their self-esteem and self-confidence on taking action to change their lives;

(vii) systematizing government peer consultations with representative groups of poor and vulnerable people, support-NGOs, and civil society allies through effective training and institutional reform in the implementation of pro-poor government and private sector programs;

(viii) gaining a better understanding of poverty in its multifaceted dimensions, drawing on economics and the behavioral social sciences, and developing partnerships among government, the private sector, NGOs and most of all, poor people who live the problem; and

(ix) recognizing that the roots of poverty lie in social relations that reinforce the power of privileged elites, and keep large numbers of men, women, and children poor and powerless.

Notes

The authors are grateful to Liza L. Lim and Naina Shakya for valuable research assistance.

1. These consisted of 50 ethnolinguistic groups in 43 districts and 90 villages, including the four major ones, Tai-Kadai, Mon-Hkmer, Hmong-Mien, and Tibeto-Burma.
2. The informal sector in general refers to the large number of subsistence enterprises and individuals that have the following characteristics: ease of entry, very small scale of operations, unregulated and competitive markets, and skills learned outside of formal education (International Labor Organization as cited in Yu 1994). The roots of the informal economy are found in the weakness of modern industry to provide sufficient employment and productive resources, forcing the poor and unemployed to rely on their resourcefulness (Yu 1994).
3. Some of the informal sector output is already inputted in the gross domestic product statistics, although the exact extent may vary from one country to the next.
4. This corresponds to what North (1990) would term "formal constraints" entailing third-party enforcement.
5. These are also known in the Philippines as people's organizations (POs).
6. Based on the cost of basic needs (CBN) method of measuring poverty incidence, the poverty line represents the sum of the cost of a representative fixed food bundle and either a lower (less generous) or upper (more generous) allowance for nonfood consumption for each area. The percentage of the population falling below the lower poverty line refers to the very poor, while those falling between the lower and upper poverty lines are the poor. Please see World Bank (1998) for the Bangladesh Bureau of Statistics estimation of the poverty line for various geographic areas in Bangladesh.

4 Public Sector Reform and Poverty Reduction

ALEX B. BRILLANTES, JR.

INTRODUCTION

A major challenge confronting developing countries is implementation as evidenced by the gap between policy pronouncements and results. This is addressed in the works of Grindle (1980, 1997) who focused on the imperfect correspondence between the statement of policy goals and their achievement in society and Iglesias (1976) who had earlier pointed out this fundamental politico-administrative problem. Iglesias cites studies evaluating the UN First Development Decade of the 1960s, which invariably concluded that the failure of most development plans in developing countries could be attributed to deficiencies in the planning process or to obstacles encountered during plan implementation.

Failure of implementation has been attributed to a number of factors. One is the lack of capacities of implementing agencies and institutions due to either: (i) the lack of skilled personnel, funds and resources to implement identified development interventions; or (ii) the unclear and undefined relationships, including lack of coordination between and among the various government institutions, and between government and civil society. Another is the leadership's lack of political will arising from patronage and personalistic politics prevalent in most developing countries. A related issue is the lack of legitimacy due to either the leadership's manner of ascendancy to power (e.g., through a coup), or its inability to deliver basic services after assumption to power, or corruption, even after being installed through democratic means. Finally, failure of implementation may also be attributed to noncooperative elements of the bureaucracy that, due to entrenched self-interest, purposely resist and even subvert the implementation of development interventions.

One of the most visible evidences of the failure of implementation is the prevalence of poverty in many developing countries today. Indeed, the reduction of poverty has become one of the most pressing challenges confronting Asian developing countries (ADCs).

The question may therefore be asked at this point: How may poverty reduction interventions be more meaningfully and effectively implemented? In the context of the foregoing observation on the factors responsible for the failure of implementation, capacity building seems a valid solution. De Dios and Hutchcroft (2002) underscore the importance of the enhancement of the administrative capacity of key institutions in the politico-administrative system, in any project on institution building.

The need for capacity building to ensure success in implementation therefore establishes the significance of institutional reform. Based on North's (1990, 3) definition that institutions are "the rules of the game in a society", institutional reform then means altering the rules of the game. Grindle (1997) suggests areas where capacity building through institutional reform may be directed at, namely, the development of legal systems, policy regimes, mechanisms of accountability, regulatory frameworks, and monitoring systems that transmit information about and structure the performance of markets, governments, and public officials. He adds that at the broadest level, institutional reform involves the structures that affect economic and political interaction and the way states relate to markets and civil society.

This chapter addresses the general question: What role do public sector reforms play in a country's efforts to reduce poverty? The literature exploring the linkage between public sector reforms and poverty reduction is still in its infancy. This chapter attempts to link public sector reforms to poverty reduction through good governance. It has been widely recognized that good governance is a *sine qua non* for sustained economic growth and poverty reduction (UNDP 1997, 1998c, 1998b; World Bank 1996, 2000b; ADB 2001a; Eid 2000; Pernia 2001).

Analytical Framework

Reviews and assessments of previous poverty reduction efforts conducted by international institutions such as the World Bank, United Nations Development Programme, and Asian Development Bank, among others, have shown that issues relating to governance have been critical to the success of poverty reduction efforts.

The UNDP (2000) points out that governance has been the missing link between antipoverty efforts and poverty reduction. It adds that faulty governance can nullify the impact of pro-poor national policies and targeted interventions. Indeed, good governance is the single most important factor in the war against poverty and in the struggle to promote development (Anand 2000, 12).

The OECD (2000) recognizes the complexity of the issue noting that good governance may be difficult to ensure because of its various dimensions and political implications.

The standard and widely accepted definition of "governance" is offered by the UNDP (1997, 9) as "the exercise of political, economic and administrative authority to manage a nation's affairs. It is the complex mechanisms, processes, relationships and institutions through which citizens and groups articulate their interests, exercise their rights and obligations, and mediate their differences." Four types of governance are identified: economic governance, political governance, administrative governance and systemic governance. The concern of public sector reform as discussed in this chapter is on political governance, which "refers to decision-making and policy implementation of a legitimate and authoritative state," and mostly on administrative governance which is "a system of policy implementation carried out through an efficient, independent and accountable public sector" (UNDP 1997, 10).

Good governance lays the ground for legitimacy of the state. When there is public order, when there is observance rule of law, when basic services are delivered, in other words, when there is implementation, the authority of the state is accepted and hence becomes legitimate. This is part of the social contract. It overcomes the so-called "legitimation crisis" (Habermas 1975) being experienced by most soft states that are simply unable to enforce fundamental laws and deliver basic services owing to the weakness of their politico-administrative structures and institutions.

The next logical question therefore is the type of government that is able to deliver and is accepted as legitimate. This issue is at the core of the continuing debate between authoritarianism and participative (sometimes referred to as "democratic") forms of government. The examples of Korea and Taipei,China come to mind which, at some point in the 1960s, adopted authoritarian forms of government to consolidate the power of the state resulting in the provision of basic services to the people. The same is true with Malaysia and Singapore. Traditional participation, marked by direct election of leaders, was certainly low in the authoritarian setup but enforcement of laws and efficient delivery of services was high. On the contrary, there are democratic governments that have been high in participation but low in implementation. Bangladesh and Philippines are examples, although these states have also had their bouts with authoritarianism. Interestingly, post-authoritarian Republic of Korea (Korea) and Taipei,China now have participative and democratic forms of governments and continue to be high in implementation.

Indeed, the jury is still out as far as the question of authoritarianism and participative democratic forms of government is concerned. Is the adoption of some form of authoritarianism part of the political development process of developing countries? Why do some move on to democratic forms of government, while others don't? Can there be good governance under democratic and authoritarian setups that have been legitimated through the provision of order, delivery of basic services, and implementation of laws? Indications are that there can indeed be good governance in various types of governments as long as laws are enforced and as long as basic services are delivered, and of course, as long as accountabilities are clear to obviate corruption. These continue to be some questions that have to be addressed in the continuing discourse on good governance. Perhaps there are really no clear answers or "models" as far as the correlation between the type of government and good governance is concerned. A critical point that may be pursued, as suggested earlier, is operationalizing good governance in terms of the delivery of basic services and rule of law, which provide the context for legitimation of the form of government.

Equally significant is the role corruption plays as an obstacle to good governance and thereby poverty reduction. The chances of economic growth—a vital prerequisite to poverty reduction—are very low where corruption predominates and where neither citizens nor private investors can be certain that the law will be obeyed (Eid 2000, World Bank 2000a, ADB 2000a, UNDP 2000). Many of the public sector reform interventions, including the massive reorganization of bureaucracies, decentralization of powers to local governments and institutions, and empowerment of citizens to participate in the processes of governance, when properly implemented and sustained, can help prevent, or at least minimize graft and corruption in the politico-administrative system. Indeed the reasoning is quite simple: resources freed from graft and corruption would mean more resources for development, which means the delivery of more basic services to the people. These means better roads, more doctors, more medicines, more heath centers, more schools, more teachers, more shelter, more agricultural extension, better irrigation systems, more opportunities, and therefore more rural and even urban development. Reducing corruption in the public sector makes a country more attractive to investors (World Bank 2000a). Again this means more investments and more jobs created, and eventually more development. More development means less poverty. In other words, when we eradicate or at least minimize corruption, we reduce poverty.

Another key feature of good governance is people participation. This means that when the people themselves identify the specific development programs, projects and activities at their level, then the probability of interventions being *responsive* is much higher. For instance, decisions on where footpaths, roads and bridges are to be built are made in consideration of the most benefit to the majority, rather than catering to narrow political and business interests. Such interventions that are owned by the people have a higher probability of being sustained.

Reforms in the public sector may be implemented on three levels: at the national level, specifically in the bureaucracy; at the local level, specifically among local institutions and local governments; and at the level of civil society, specifically in terms of encouraging people participation in the processes of governance. Among the ADCs studied, reforms in the public sector have been among the priorities of most governments. Reorganizing the bureaucracy and decentralizing powers to local authorities have been among the reform priorities articulated by various governments as they assumed power. As the experience of the selected ADCs illustrates, such reforms take time; they cannot be fast-tracked and may take decades before they actually bear fruit and contribute to the general effort of bringing about good or better governance. Public sector reforms should be seen and appreciated as a long-term effort. Frequent political changes in governments and regimes—whether brought about by normal changes in administration (Philippines, Thailand); or political and military upheavals (Bangladesh, Pakistan); or transition governments from centrally planned economies to market economies (Lao PDR, Viet Nam)—have caused the implementation of such reforms to be disrupted or discontinued, in the process, hampering general poverty reduction initiatives. Others early on (such as Korea and Taipei,China) carried out public sector reform and have been relatively successful in their efforts to reduce poverty.

Stability, continuity, and sustainability in the implementation of public sector reform are key factors to their success. More specifically, stability insulates development interventions from disruptions caused by political changes and even upheavals; continuity ensures implementation of programs and projects in spite of changes in administration; and sustainability provides the context for ownership of development interventions and, in some cases, continuous implementation even after the donors have pulled out. This is one dimension in the implementation of public sector reforms that has tremendous implications upon poverty reduction efforts.

Building upon Grindle (1997), this chapter argues that public sector reform may be targeted at specific institutions: legal systems, policy regimes, mechanisms of accountability, regulatory frameworks, and monitoring systems. Three strategies that can bring this about are (i) reorganization; (ii) decentralization, and (iii) citizen participation. How such institutional reforms lead to good governance and better implementation, and hence contribute, albeit indirectly, to poverty reduction is seen in the following:

(i) *The implementation of reorganization.* Reorganization streamlines processes and addresses fundamental problems associated with bureaucratic red tape and graft and corruption. This would therefore lead to increased accountability and transparency in the bureaucracy, an institution once described as "the weak link in national development efforts" (in De Dios and Hutchcroft 2003).

(ii) *The decentralization of powers to the lowest levels possible in accordance with the principle of subsidiarity.* As a management tool, this would enhance the responsiveness of policies and decisions to the actual needs of the people, considering that decisions are made "as close to the ground" as possible. As a tool for empowerment, decentralization provides the avenue for participation. It also means strengthening the capacities of the lower-level institutions (see next chapter).

(iii) *Citizen participation.* This is sometimes referred to as civil society participation. Citizen participation in the processes of governance, i.e., in the delivery of basic services to the people, carries with it an implicit recognition of the limitations of the formal structures and processes of government, considering the lack of resources and also inherent graft and corruption. It has also led to a fundamental redefinition of the notion of governance.

Figure 4.1 is a schematic presentation of the analytical framework adopted by this chapter that suggests the relationships among *public sector reforms, implementation, good governance,* and *poverty reduction.*[1]

Figure 4.1: Public Sector Reforms, Implementation, Good Governance, and Poverty Reduction

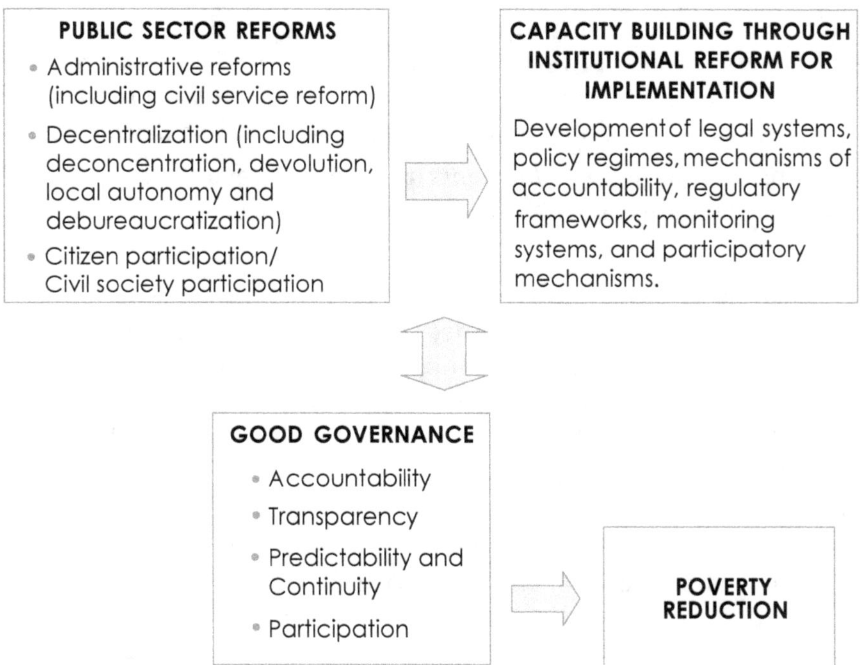

Note: This analytical framework builds upon the works of Grindle (1980, 1997); Iglesias (1976); North (1990); and De Dios and Hutchcroft (2003).

Mechanisms for Public Sector Reforms

Public sector reforms (PSRs) have been the preoccupation of many administrations upon assuming power. They embark on massive reforms of the politico-administrative system ostensibly to make government more efficient, effective, responsive, and less corrupt. However, the perspective situating PSR within the context of the broader poverty reduction strategy is of recent vintage. For instance, the poverty reduction strategy of Pakistan under the Musharaff government includes "civil service reforms, devolution of powers and people participation" as a major component. Viet Nam embeds public sector reform within the framework of good governance to achieve "poverty elimination." The Philippines highlights decentralization as a strategy in its National Action Plan Against Poverty. Thailand recognizes the crucial role of the decentralization of powers to its Tambon Administrative Organization in its poverty reduction strategy. People participation has been one of the key factors behind the relative success of NGO-initiated poverty reduction efforts in Bangladesh. Viewing PSR as a strategy for poverty reduction imbues it with more meaning and relevance, and elevates it to a higher level of discourse.

Among the major *mechanisms* that promote public sector efficiency and good governance are the following (World Bank 2000a):

(i) internal rules and restraints, e.g., internal accounting and auditing systems, independence of the judiciary and the central bank, civil service and budgeting rules, and rules governing ombudsmen and other internal watchdog bodies (that often report to parliaments);

(ii) "voice" and partnership, e.g., decentralization to empower communities, service delivery surveys to solicit client feedback, and "notice and comment" regulatory rule making; and

(iii) competition, e.g., competitive social service delivery, private participation in infrastructure, alternative dispute resolution mechanism, and privatization of certain market-driven activities, which may involve a fundamental rethinking of the role of the state, often a key component of reform.

With the above as basic guideposts, three major areas of public sector reform that are essential to achieve the goal of poverty reduction may be identified:

(i) *Administrative reforms.* Designed to improve the "internal rules and restraints," these reforms, which aim to promote efficiency in the public sector include streamlining and reorganizing the bureaucracy, and implementing civil service reform through downsizing, rightsizing, reinventing, upgrading/updating salaries and wages, addressing graft and corruption, and introducing accountability in the bureaucracy.

(ii) *Decentralization.* This aims to empower local communities through their local governments (or subnational governments) and provide them opportunities to be heard and to participate in public decision-making institutions and processes. This provides voice and partnership that would lead to public sector efficiency. More specifically, this covers transferring functions, powers and authorities to local governments, especially in the area of financial decentralization; and developing and strengthening local capacities in the areas of organization and management, personnel, and most especially fiscal administration.

(iii) *Citizen participation.* This mechanism allows communities access to policy making and service delivery, and enables their participation in oversight and accountability mechanisms. Thus public sector efficiency is promoted by providing citizens voice and partnership in such areas as the design, formulation, implementation, and monitoring of the delivery of basic services; the process of governance; and the monitoring of government programs and projects, thereby promoting accountabilities.

Public sector reforms are usually associated with comprehensive changes in the institutions, organization, and processes in the bureaucratic machinery of the state. These changes may be brought about through comprehensive reorganization plans such as "reinventing"[2] and reengineering government.

In recent years, there have been general shifts in the focus of administrative reforms moving away from the traditional concerns of public administration, i.e., general management concerns like organization and management, personnel management, and fiscal administration, to emphasis on empowering processes such as decentralized forms of governance, extensive participation of the citizens (now viewed as clients and partners), accountability, and transparency in

Table 4.1: Trends and Shifts in Governance and Public Sector Reform

FROM	TO
Centralized, uniform, "top-down" service delivery	Decentralized, diverse, localized service delivery
Citizen as client and beneficiary	Citizen as customer and partner
Self-sufficiency	Interlinked sectors
Hierarchical control	Empowerment
"Upward" accountability	"Outward" accountability
Standardized procedures	Performance orientation
Apolitical civil service	Advocacy-oriented civil service
Individual skill building	Organizational competence
Law and order, institutions and institution-building, and general functional areas of government	Modified orientations of development, general systems modeling, middle-range theory formulation

Sources: Adapted from Ellison (1998) and Farazmand (1998).

public administration concerns (Ellison 1998, Farazmand 1998, APO 1998; see Table 4.1). The shifts have been necessitated by the imperatives to cope with the increased demands and expectations upon government, the general failure of implementation, and the recognition of the role of the private sector and civil society in enhancing governance. Over and above these are the demands and challenges brought about by a rapidly changing environment responding to the imperatives of globalization and the information technology revolution (Asian Productivity Organization 1998). These challenges have provided the context for a bureaucracy that would be more socially oriented and hospitable to the implementation of poverty reduction programs.

ADMINISTRATIVE REFORMS FOR POVERTY REDUCTION

One of the major approaches to institutional development and reform, especially in terms of "changing the rules of the game" is in the area of administrative reform. This encompasses wide-ranging concerns such as changes in structures and systems, inculcating values of excellence, changing the mindsets of civil servants, and increasing the use of information technology to increase transparency, accountability and effectiveness of government (APO 1998). Indeed, administrative reforms—central among which are reforms in the civil service—will foster economic growth and sustained poverty reduction by reducing obstacles posed to private sector development by a poorly performing public sector. Such reforms will increase the resources for priority spending by containing personnel expenditures. Finally, these will contribute to good governance through increased accountability by addressing the serious problems of governance and corruption.

Caiden (1991) observed the trend to implement massive administrative reforms in many bureaucracies in the Third World. In trying to be more responsive to the demands to bring about development and reduce poverty, and the pressures of increased globalization, governments have pinpointed the "dead hand of the bureaucracy", plagued by problems such as poor performance of public bureaucracies, cumbersome procedures and red tape, and corruption. Government itself had become too big and therefore had to be downsized through administrative reform.

Administrative Reform and Poverty Reduction: Exploring the Linkage

The implementation of administrative reform has been a concern of many countries. It is interesting that the countries that have been relatively successful in their poverty reduction efforts—Korea and Taipei,China—have been among those that have early on launched massive administrative reform programs. In 1934, Korea recognized the need to improve its administrative capacity by setting up the Committee for Studying Administrative Efficiency. In 1947, Taipei,China enacted the National Civil Service Act to improve its bureaucracy and make it more responsive to the needs of the public. This was followed by several reorganization interventions in 1937, 1940, 1956, and 2001.

Other countries that continue to struggle with their poverty reduction strategies have likewise embarked on massive administrative reforms. For instance the Philippines adopted a comprehensive reorganization plan in the mid-1950s. Thailand enacted its Civil Service Acts in 1928, 1975, and 1992. Bangladesh launched a series of comprehensive reorganization interventions beginning with the Administrative Services Reform Committee and the National Pay Commission in 1972. This was followed by several reorganization strategies in 1975, 1981, 1982, 1989, 1993, 1996, and 1997. Lao PDR set up a Committee for Organization and Personnel in the early 1990s. Pakistan studied the reorganization of its public sector through the Hafeez Pasha report in 1997 and the Committee for Government Organization Improvement in 2000. Viet Nam conducted a comprehensive Public Administration Review in 2000. Indeed, the above suggest a possible correlation between the relative success in poverty reduction efforts and the implementation of reforms in public administration. (Appendix Table 4.1 provides a summary of administrative reform interventions in selected ADCs).

Administrative reforms provide the vehicle for the implementation of poverty reduction programs. However, they are not sufficient to launch administrative reforms. These have to be sustained, periodically evaluated, and improved upon. This is where the dimension of leadership—many times also referred to as political will—comes in. Reform efforts supported by the leadership have greater chances of being successfully implemented and sustained. This brings us to a discussion of the extent to which the type of government (whether authoritarian, or democratic and hence participative) plays a role in the success or failure of poverty reduction efforts. As pointed out by de Dios (1997), the current discussion over the exact relationship between the form of governance and economic growth or development is one of the most interesting and fertile interfaces between political science and economics.

Many ADCs have at one point or another in their political histories adopted some form of authoritarian government. Foremost among those that have achieved dramatic success in poverty reduction are Korea and Taipei,China. The other countries that have experienced authoritarian rule in contemporary history, including Bangladesh, Lao PDR, Pakistan, Philippines, Thailand, and Viet Nam continue to struggle in their poverty reduction efforts. The Philippines had a long period of authoritarian rule under Marcos in the 1970s into the mid-1980s. Thailand had its share of authoritarian rule imposed by the many generals who assumed power mostly through coup d'etat in the

1970s into the 1980s. Bangladesh had its military dictators in the 1980s and early 1990s, although it now enjoys some form of participative democracy. Pakistan over the past three decades has shuttled back and forth between the authoritarian rule of generals who forcibly took power, and participative democracy. Viet Nam and Lao PDR are still ruled by their authoritarian communist parties. The interesting problematique that may be raised is the possible relationship between the form of government and poverty reduction. At this point, it is not possible to draw any conclusive correlation between these variables.

Related to the issues of sustainability and design and implementation of reforms in the public sector is the presence of institutions and think tanks—academic, government, and nongovernment. These would provide research and training support to carrying out and sustaining public sector reform. Most ADCs are not wanting in terms of the presence of such institutes. Table 4.2 provides a listing of such institutions that can provide support to the government for the conceptualization, design, implementation, monitoring, and evaluation of public sector reforms.

Administrative Reform in Bangladesh: Formalisms and Fuzzy Governance?

Administrative reform has been a concern in Bangladesh ever since independence in 1971 (Ahmed and Khan 1990, Siddiqi 1995, Shelley 2000). For instance, from 1971 to 1985, the various governments of Bangladesh undertook six major reforms. Centralism was—and continues to be—a major feature of the Bangladesh bureaucracy. Considering that the administrative system was dominated by the military and civilian bureaucrats, the approach of government was akin to that of a "stern headmaster" and was more paternalistic, autocratic, and "tutorial rather than participatory" (Shelley 2000). Among the major recommendations repeatedly made by various administrative reform bodies were improvement in the pay scale of the civil servants and the decentralization of administration within the context of restructuring and rationalizing public administration and civil service. The reforms recommended were wide-ranging but, in most cases, were either rejected or implemented in radically modified forms and in an unintegrated fashion (Shelley 2000, Barenstein 1994). Reform interventions that entailed increases in the salaries of the civil

Table 4.2: Capacity Building and Training Institutions in Selected ADCs for Local or National Officials

Bangladesh	Bangladesh Public Administration Training Center (PATC) Bangladesh Rural Development Academy (BARD) Rural Development Academy (RDA) National Institute of Local Government (NILG) Ministry of Local Government, Rural Development and Cooperatives
Korea	Graduate School of Public Administration, Seoul National University Central Officials Training Institute (COTI) Local Autonomy Training Institute (LATI) Korean Institute of Public Administration
Lao PDR	Committee for Human Resource Development National School for Administration and Management (1991)
Pakistan	Civil Service Academy Pakistan Administrative Staff College National Institute of Public Administration Pakistan Academy for Rural Development Central Superior Services Academy
Philippines	Development Academy of the Philippines Civil Service Commission Local Government Academy National College of Public Administration and Governance
Thailand	King Prajathiphok Institute National Institute of Development Administration
Viet Nam	National Institute of Public Administration

Sources: Various sources, including Islam (1990), Tiep (1998), Aminuzzaman (1992), Brillantes (1998), Siddiqi (1994), Pakistan Government (2001), and Wescott (2001).

servants did not go beyond policy pronouncements. The same was true with the incessant call for more decentralization. The implementation of these policy pronouncements was hampered by constant changes in government, disruptions, and frequent strikes (*hartal*) called by the political opposition. Resistance to reform and the lack of commitment among entrenched bureaucrats subverted the implementation of reforms. This resistance to reform may be rooted in the fact that civil service reforms encroach into the little kingdoms of bureaucrats and erode their sources of power.[3] Consequently, well-meaning administrative reforms were hardly implemented, much less sustained, leaving little impact upon poverty reduction interventions.

The experience of administrative reform in Bangladesh has been mostly at the level of formalisms, lacking the commitment that goes beyond rhetoric, and with a record wanting in implementation (Sobhan 1998, Shelley 2000). Such policy dissonance has led Barenstein (1994) to label Bangladesh's type of governance as "fuzzy governance." As pointed out by Ahmed and Khan (1990), the system of public administration in Bangladesh retains several characteristic features including centralization, passion for rank, caste differentiation of officials, and lack of subsystem autonomy. Its historical experience of military-bureaucratic dominance, coupled with pervasive graft and corruption, has nullified the gains of most administrative reform efforts and thus hardly contributed to overall poverty reduction in the country.

Implementing Massive Reforms in Pakistan: The National Reconstruction Bureau

In October 1999, a military-led coup headed by General Pervez Musharaff ousted the civilian regime of Nawaz Sharif. Ostensibly, Musharaff mounted the coup to replace the regime of Sharif that was widely perceived to be corrupt. Musharaff declared that he would eliminate graft and corruption and introduce massive reform in the government. Among the major moves of the Musharaff government was to create the National Reconstruction Bureau (NRB) under the Office of the Prime Minister. The NRB would play a key role in designing and implementing massive reforms for Pakistan. General Musharaff (who proclaimed himself President in June 2001) early on enhanced the powers of the National Accountability Bureau and the Federal Public Service Commission to restore accountability in the government and ensure merit-based recruitment in the civil service. Finally, the regime announced plans to implement a massive decentralization and devolution plan to local bodies.

The Musharaff government took power at a time when Pakistan was trying to recover from what has been referred to as the "lost decade" (Stern 2001, Finance Minister of Pakistan 2001). Indeed, the political administrative history of Pakistan has seen many attempts by both civilian and military governments to address many fundamental issues that have always recurred upon the assumption of each new regime (ADB 2001a), including the type of political system the country should have; the role of the military in the system; the role of religion (Islam) in the polity; and the balance between provincial autonomy and the federal system.

The continuing expansion of the bureaucracy, political patronage, excessive centralization, and unclear delineation of responsibilities between the central and subnational institutions including local governments have led to a "total lack of effective governance" (Siddiqui 2001, 202). The continuing lack of accountabilities, lack of participation, weak political institutions, pervasive corruption, and poverty have always been among the challenges confronting the various governments of Pakistan (Siddiqui 2001, ADB 2001a).

It was within the context of the above that the government of Musharaff has embarked on a massive effort to reform and reshape the civil service. It has enhanced the powers of the Federal Public Service Commission. Among the major thrusts of the reforms for the civil service are the following (ADB 2001a):

(i) a frontal attack on corruption resulting in the dismissal of more than 1,000 civil servants;
(ii) a comprehensive scheme of interprovincial transfer of civil servants especially among the district management group and the police;
(iii) a downsizing of the bureaucracy through the consolidation and merging of ministries, divisions, and departments; and a review of the salary structure of the civil service;
(iv) training and career planning of civil servants through civil service exams and performance-based promotions; and
(v) efforts to encourage transparent and merit-based decision making.

The government has declared that it will adopt a holistic approach in revamping the civil service at the federal, provincial, and local levels. This meant that, in contradistinction to previous reform efforts, Musharaff's reforms were to cut across all levels, and involve as many sectors as possible. Hopefully, this will lead to more responsive governance and consequently contribute to the reduction of poverty in the country. The creation of the powerful National Reconstruction Bureau with its mandate to push for massive reforms throughout the bureaucracy, backed by the military, may indeed provide the push for serious implementation. However, other factors such as resistance among entrenched bureaucratic interests have to be considered. The capacities to implement such massive reforms—including availability of much needed financial and human resources—should likewise be addressed. Finally, political will continues to be an imperative. The military nature of the Musharaff government might indeed be able to provide such a will, and in the process, gain legimacy if it were to succeed in its reform and poverty reduction efforts. It must be recalled that the government of Musharaff continues to be wanting in political legitimacy and acceptance owing to the nature of its ascendancy. Its effectiveness in implementing reforms, including its poverty reduction strategy, might just contribute to the legitimation of his government.

As part of its overall comprehensive administrative reform program, the new government of Pakistan crafted a comprehensive poverty reduction strategy, the Three–Year Poverty Reduction Programme, 2001 to 2004. Leadership in the implementation of the Programme is to be provided by the Planning Commission.

From the framework for poverty reduction, one can see that civil service reforms, devolution of powers to subnational institutions, and people participation in governance have been identified among the major factors that can contribute to the reduction of poverty in the country. Chaudri (2000) has noted how devolution can hasten the process of bringing the government closer to the people under the principle of subsidiarity. The process includes the following:

(i) changing the role of the civil service from central to public service. Essentially, this means reorienting the centralist mindsets of the bureaucrats and recognizing the equal importance of lower levels of government considering that they are all in the service of the people ("public");

(ii) enhancing professionalism, transparency, and service orientation in the departments involved in the delivery of social and development services;

(iii) setting in place a merit-based system of incentives to enable the civil service to make the shift from a control-minded bureaucracy to service-oriented public servants;

(iv) strengthening of local government institutions through a deliberate process of devolution, capacity building for local governments, and formulation of a wide-ranging local government code; and

(v) setting in place a policy framework that would encourage civil society organizations and nongovernmental organizations to participate in governance especially in the areas of development of human capital such as education, mass literary, education and nutrition, and social action programs.

Good Governance: A Pillar of Viet Nam's *Doi Moi*

The case of Viet Nam illustrates how the introduction of massive reforms through *doi moi* has contributed to good governance and poverty reduction.

Since 1986, the centerpiece of the socioeconomic development strategy of Viet Nam has been doi moi. According to the UNDP/UNICEF study (1996), poverty has been reduced after the *doi moi* was initiated in December 1986. Years later, estimates further show that from 1993 to 1998, poverty has been significantly reduced from 58 to 37 percent.[4] Wescott points out that indeed the case of Viet Nam is "a very successful case of poverty reduction."[5]

Doi moi is the overall reform process that aims at transforming the Viet Namese economy from a centrally planned system to one that is dynamic and market-based (UNDP/UNICEF 1996). The government declared in its country report to the World Summit for Social Development held in Copenhagen in 1995 that high and sustainable economic growth is critical if it is to be successful in its poverty reduction efforts. Its doi moi strategy is anchored on three major aspects: (i) high and sustainable economic growth; (ii) stability, and (iii) equity. It should be noted that the strategy points out that good governance and its features, including transparency and accountability, are imperative in the attainment of stability and equity.

Embedded in the poverty elimination[6] framework of Viet Nam are aspects pertaining to improving governance in general, and bringing about public sector reforms in particular. More specifically, these aim to develop and strengthen the capacities of the various institutions involved in the task of poverty elimination. Among the major strategies for capacity development are restructuring public administration and legal reform. These include professionalizing the civil service, rationalizing salary structures of the civil servants, and reviewing regulatory measures and codification of laws.

Administrative Reform and Poverty Reduction Strategies

Most ADCs have some broad framework for development and poverty reduction at various levels (see Table 4.3). An example would be the Poverty Reduction Strategy Paper (PRSP) adopted by the government with the support of international agencies, such as ADB and the World Bank. PRSPs are seen as comprehensive development strategies aimed at poverty reduction (Whaites 2000). They likewise provide a more systematic approach to poverty reduction and address uncoordinated and sometimes contradictory poverty interventions implemented by previous governments and donors. A fundamental feature of the PRSP is that it is prepared and *owned* by the government. Equally important is the fact that the preparation of the PRSP is highly participatory.[7] Building upon these PRSPs, the United Nations Development Programme (UNDP) sponsors innovative pilot projects and connects countries to global best practices and resources that may serve as a basis for replication and adaptation by similarly situated countries.

Thailand: Sustaining the Gains in Poverty Reduction

The past 40 years in Thailand have seen the formulation of eight development plans that essentially provided the framework for the country's development strategy for the period. The plans underwent many phases, from the construction of infrastructure to reduction of income inequality, to project and program approaches, to the imperative for trade liberalization, and finally to the imperative to be economically self-reliant (TDRI 2000, Suphachalasai and Patmasiriwat 1991).

Table 4.3: Poverty Reduction Strategy Frameworks in Selected ADCs

Korea	Livelihood Protection Law 1961 Implementation Act of Livelihood Protection Law (Presidential Act 4218) 1969 National Basic Life Assurance Law 1999
Lao PDR	Interim Poverty Reduction Strategy Paper 2000 Focal Site Strategy 2000
Pakistan	Three-Year Poverty Reduction Programme 2001-2004
Philippines	Social Reform Agenda and Poverty Alleviation Act of 1997 Comprehensive and Integrated Delivery of Social Services 1994 National Anti-Poverty Action Agenda 2000
Taipei,China	Means Test Act Governing the Poverty Relief in the Taiwan Providence 1963; 1977 Current Stage Social Policy of the Principle of People's Livelihood 1965 Four-Year Program to Enhance Social Welfare in the Taiwan Providence 1971 Outlines for Eliminating Poverty in the Taiwan Providence (Well-To-Do-Program (WTDP) Social Assistance Law 1980
Thailand	Fifth National Economic and Social Development Plan 1982-1986 Sixth to Eighth Economic and Social Development Plans 1987-2001
Viet Nam	Interim Poverty Reduction Strategy Paper (I-PRSP) 2000

Sources: Constructed from data in Yoon (2001); Dennis (2000); Lao PDR (2000a, 2001); Pakistan Government (2001a); Philippine National Anti-Poverty Commission (1999); Thailand Development Research Institute (2000); Suphachalasai and Patmasiriwat (1991); Tsai (2001); and Viet Nam Socialist Republic (2000).

However, it was only with the Fifth Plan that a comprehensive rural development plan for poverty alleviation was crafted. This was mostly in response to the problems of insurgency then besetting the country. Accompanying the Plan was a development plan for the rural areas, which aimed at poverty eradication in the "backward areas" (TDR1 2001).

The National Committee of the Rural Poverty Program enjoined the cooperation of four ministries—Interior, Health, Agriculture, and

Education—to implement the program, with the National Economic and Social Development Board (NESDB) as the chair of the Committee. To a certain extent, the Committee was responsible for orchestrating the various poverty reduction efforts and initiatives emanating from the other ministries. Such a high-level committee was needed to give prominence to the poverty reduction thrust of the government. The creation of the Committee was seen as part of the overall package of reforms to streamline the government. It is interesting to note that the committee was set up to bypass the usual bureaucratic impediments to program implementation (Suphachalasai and Patmasiriwat 1991). Actually, "bypassing" regular established bureaucratic structures through the creation of ad hoc bodies has been a time-honored tradition in public administration where the objective is to fast track the process of reform yet avoid disrupting the bureaucracy.[8]

Subsequently, three other National Development Plans were crafted building upon the earlier ones. These were the Sixth Plan (1987-1981) that addressed education and manpower issues; the Seventh Plan (1992-1991) that embraced the concept of sustainable development; and the Eighth Plan (1997-2001), formulated before the Asian crisis, that focused on people's participation and addressed specific problems such as urban poverty. Thailand's Ninth Plan (2002-2006) once more underscores the goal of poverty reduction.

Over the past few years, especially after recovering from the effects of the Asian crisis in the late 1990s, the approach to poverty reduction in Thailand emphasized new dimensions. These focused on "people centered development," the participatory approach (a key element in the Fifth Plan), and an active stakeholder participation through the NGOs (as highlighted in the Eighth Plan). The challenge for poverty reduction in Thailand is how to sustain the gains of the past few decades that saw Thailand, before the Asian crisis, exhibit remarkable economic growth and poverty reduction to a point of being identified as the emerging newly industrializing economy in the region. While extensive stakeholder participation may certainly be helpful, TDRI points out that this has to be complemented by sound rules, regulations and monitoring systems. In other words, traditional public administration and management concerns should continue to provide the foundation for citizen participation in poverty reduction.

Lao PDR: Focal Site Strategy for Poverty Reduction

The Laotian strategy for poverty reduction, referred to as the Focal Site Strategy, was crafted after the conduct of a Participatory Poverty Assessment (PPA), which aimed to record the experiences and concerns of the poor (Lao PDR 2000b). The State Planning Committee conducted consultations in the formulation of the PPA in October 2000. As a general policy for poverty reduction, the PPA argued for the continued emphasis on economic growth and development but targeting socially defined groups in specific environments where the poor are located, hence "focal site strategy." Focal sites are essentially area-based approaches to integrated area development (Dennis 2000, Lao PDR 2000a). Focal site approaches to poverty reduction will enable the implementation of targeted and area-specific poverty reduction programs. The PPA concludes this will have the effect of lessening inequality and improving the living conditions of the poor.

Through its Focal Site Strategy, the government declared its strong commitment to reduce poverty in the uplands. As in the case of other ADCs however, there is still a need to develop capacities, considering that the capacity to implement this program remains limited (Dennis 2000, UNDP/UNICEF 1996). Since these poverty reduction programs and projects will have to be implemented through the regular institutions of the bureaucracy of Lao PDR, the current government has underscored the importance of professionalizing the bureaucracy to enable implementation.

Civil service reform has been considered a high priority in the national development agenda in general, and in poverty reduction efforts in particular. However, the problem is the continued politicization of the civil service, which may serve as an obstacle to meaningful reform. Klauss (1997) points out the difficulties for civil servants to be "professional" and non-politicized within the context of a politico–administrative system dominated by the political party of the government. What we have here is dissonance between a "professional" bureaucracy and its "proper" role as an instrument of the political party of Lao PDR. The professional operations of the civil service are hampered by the politicization of the civil servants themselves considering the blurred division between politics and administration, between being a member of the communist party and being a member of the civil service. In other words, differing views on policy, politics, and government program priorities are to be worked out in a participatory process at the grassroots level through party deliberations. Regardless of one's technical and professional perspectives, the civil servant is expected to buy into and support the policies and programs that grow out of the process (Klauss 1997).

Then there is the problem of corruption. According to a World Bank report (1999), surveys of entrepreneurs, businesses, and prospective foreign investors reveal pervasive controls and red tape, creating opportunities for graft and corruption, thus increasing the cost of doing business.

Such fundamental issues and concerns have to be addressed first before even going further into discussions of implementing administrative reforms for poverty reduction. This is where the need for capacity building comes in. This means not only streamlining structures and processes, pinpointing accountabilities, strengthening the capacities of upland institutions, but also, equally important, shifting perspectives and developing mindsets.[9]

Korea: Bloated Bureaucracy as the Price of Growth?

Korea's achievements in terms of rapid economic development and the consequent advances in poverty reduction have been widely recognized as a model for many countries (Yoon 2001). Indeed, Korea's success has been attributed to the Korean Civil Service System that orchestrated the industrialization through a series of five-year economic development plans starting from 1961. This contributed to the transformation from an agrarian society to a post-industrial one within a period of three decades (Young-Pyoung Kim 1997).

However, an unintended consequence of the rapid economic development was the increase in the number of employees during the 1960s and the 1970s. The growth in the size of the bureaucracy was brought about by the "revolution of rising expectations" that led to the creation of new agencies and institutions to respond to these expectations. Toward the end of the 1970s, government was evolving into some kind of an "inefficient monolith," unresponsive and unable to provide quality services to the people (Pan Suk Kim 1999, 2).

The Korean bureaucracy was seen to suffer from the common problems confronting most bureaucracies: excessive governmental regulation and intervention in the market economy which has stifled Korea's competitiveness at home and abroad, too much centralization, lack of transparency and flexibility, and low competitiveness vis-a-vis other bureaucracies in the region that were relatively less bureaucratic (Kim 1999, Kim 1997).[10] Excessive bureaucratization was likewise seen as a contributory factor to the crisis in the 1990s. The ultimate objective of Korea's public sector reform was to make the public sector conform with the shift toward a social and economic system governed by market principles, individual initiative, and democratic values.

To address the above, Kim Dae Jung's government included the implementation of administrative reforms in the reform agenda in the late 1990s, not only to cope with the effects of the crisis but also to open the economy and encourage the private sector. The government continued to pursue the implementation of these administrative reforms at the turn of the century. It has made headway in some areas, specifically in streamlining government functions, but needed to put more effort in the area of achieving a "highly competitive government." One area where Korea has made some significant advances is in addressing graft and corruption.

Taipei,China: Political Will in Administrative Reforms Supports Poverty Reduction

Like Korea, Taipei,China has demonstrated how rapid economic growth can lead to the reduction of poverty (Tsai 2001). Placed within the context of administrative reform, Taipei,China has, since the mid-1930s, launched a series of comprehensive administrative reform programs, beginning with the Committee for Studying Administrative Efficiency in 1934. This evolved into the Committee for the Improvement of Administrative Efficiency three years later.

Subsequently, other administrative reform measures were implemented. These included the one initiated by Chiang Kai-Shek in the early 1940s called "Three Connected States of Administration" that viewed the administrative process as consisting of the planning, implementation, and evaluation stages. Other reforms were aimed at improving the salary structure of civil service personnel.

The key to the success of administrative reform initiatives was implementation, also referred to as political will (Sun and Gargan 1996, Tsai 2001). For instance, toward the late 1950s, a study showed that 75 of 88 (85 percent) of the recommendations for administrative reform were implemented. The serious implementation of reforms in the bureaucracy of Taipei,China provided the positive context and reinforcement for the implementation of the various poverty reduction strategies, including the highly successful Well-To-Do-Program. Another demonstration of strong political will that led to the successful implementation of a poverty reduction program was in the area of land reform.

Sun and Gargan (1996) conclude that many problems result from conflicts among traditional culture, democratization, and industrialization. Formal administrative structures and processes in the civil service system have to adapt to the specific culture of the society. There are indeed certain ways of doing things that may be the norm in the western culture but which may clash with what is acceptable in local culture. Proposed administrative reforms must therefore be sensitive to the local politico–administrative culture and environment. This also demands more flexibility on the part of the agents of reforms.

Dealing with Corruption through Administrative Reform

The World Bank and other multilateral institutions have offered a standard and universally accepted definition of corruption: the abuse of public office for private gain (Ofosu-Amaah, Soopramanien, and Uprety 1999). It "involves behavior on the part of officials in the public and private sectors, in which they improperly and unlawfully enrich themselves and/or those close to them, or induce others to do so, by misusing the position in which they are placed" (ADB 2000b, 5). Among the ways of addressing the problem is institutional reform, reducing the size of the state and mobilization of the population (Kpundeh and Hors 1997). These will bring about good governance and a sound public administrative system that facilitate the delivery of goods and services and contribute to the reduction of poverty (Kpundeh 1997).

Among the major causes of corruption are cumbersome, nontransparent, over-regulated, and nonparticipatory state policies, as well as low salaries paid to civil servants (UNDP 1998b). These provide the context for corruption. The bureaucrat essentially has the power and discretion to enforce such regulations, and may decide not to enforce the rigid rules in consideration of a fee or some other favor from the public.

Table 4.4: Accountability and Anticorruption Policy Frameworks and Measures in Selected ADCs

Korea	Suhjonghoeshin Movement (General Administrative Reform Movement) 1975
Pakistan	Poverty Reduction Program 2001 National Accountability Bureau 2001
Philippines	Anti-Graft and Corrupt Practices Act 1967 Code of Ethics for Public Officials (RA 6713) 1989
Taipei,China	Pushing Forth Administrative Reform and Establishing Clean and Efficient Government 2001
Thailand	Discipline in Civil Service, Chapter 4, Civil Service Act of 1975

Sources: Various sources, including Raksasataya (1989) and Rahman (1986).

Administrative reform, including reorganization, streamlining, simplifying systems and procedures, and encouraging citizen participation can address one of the fundamental causes of corruption, help advance the development of the society, and contribute to overall poverty reduction efforts (Kpundeh 1997, Ofosu-Amaah et al. 1999, Mahbub ul Haq Human Development Center 1999).

Most ADCs have their share of graft and corruption. Table 4.4 shows the specific policies, laws, and institutions established by selected ADCs to address corruption in the society and thus help reduce poverty.

Taipei,China: Eliminating "Black Gold" for Poverty Reduction

Reforms in the administrative system of Taipei,China have played an important role in the country's development and, consequently, in the significant reduction of poverty in the country (Hwa 1991). However, the system continues to be criticized for the persistence of corruption and inefficiencies. It is therefore within this context that reforms continue to be pursued.

Taipei,China has adopted a comprehensive approach in its latest development strategy (Taipei,China GIO 2001) which identifies 20 areas ranging from social welfare programs to technological development. One of these areas is administrative reform and establishing clean and efficient government. By 2000, anticorruption efforts have resulted in 102.18 percent more indictments and an increase in conviction rate to 63.59 percent. Likewise, three organizations, 36 units, and 30 special task forces were ordered dissolved and 22,578 government employees were dismissed, leading to a 24 percent decrease in the number of government employees.

These significant accomplishments sent a powerful message to the bureaucracy about the government's no-nonsense approach to anticorruption. Taipei,China has demonstrated a strong track record in implementation, which helps explain its advances in poverty reduction. In fact, Premier Chang, referring to the oft-repeated "Asian values" as an explanation for developments in the region, said that the anticorruption campaign is the "new Asian value" in the new millennium. He added that "eliminating black gold" (referring to wealth acquired through corrupt means) was the highest expectation that people had of the new government. By the end of June 2000, the Executive Yuan (branch) of government set up the Operational Center for Investigation and Seizure of Black Gold Criminals. More than 2,200 cases concerning "black gold" have been investigated and some 600 people have been prosecuted (Chang Chun-hsiung 2000).

Korea: Targeting Corruption, 1970s to the 1990s

As early as 1975, a campaign to bring about economy, efficiency, and honesty in public life was launched in Korea through the *Suhjongshoeshin* Movement, also referred to as the General Administrative Reform Movement. This marked the beginning of an era of drastic administrative environmental reform in Korea. Officially, the Suhjongshoeshin hopes to achieve "National Restoration" through the enhancement of administrative and political efficiency, elimination of corruption in officialdom, elimination of social waste and injustice, and values and mental revolution (Rahman 1986). The Movement had three major sets of measures, namely: (i) the improvement of personnel administration through training, recognition, awards, compensation, and benefits; (ii) institutional reforms including revision of regulations, improvement of general administrative procedures and reporting practices, upgrading administrative knowledge and skills, and effective budgetary procedures; and (iii) environmental cleansing, which included requiring officials to conduct their official and private lives according to strict standards.

The Suhjongshoeshin Movement was evaluated to be quite effective. In 1975 alone, the year the program started, close to 22,000 civil servants were punished. Several implementation concerns were raised that included politicization of the cases filed as well as the need for a central coordination agency to orchestrate the massive anticorruption drive. However, though corruption was not totally eliminated, the drive did have an impact in bringing about integrity and honesty in Korean public service. This may also have contributed to the relative success of its poverty reduction programs. The fact that Korea was under authoritarian rule at that time may also explain the quick implementation of reforms and the lack of visible resistance among those affected.

Toward the end of the 1990s, after the 1998 elections, the new democratic government targeted the elimination of corruption in the public sector. As in the 1970s, strong leadership and political will were demonstrated by the widely popular leadership of the charismatic Kim Dae Jung who was once imprisoned for his resistance to the dictatorship. In both cases, the authoritarian rule of the 1970s and the democratically elected leadership of the late 1990s gained legitimacy and acceptance among the people because of the no-nonsense implementation of reforms and anticorruption programs. In other words, at the end of the day, the Korean case suggests that it is really the leadership that matters, one that is able to demonstrate resoluteness and political will in the implementation of reforms.

Among the elements of the anticorruption package of Korea are the following (World Bank 2000a):

(i) Implement administrative reforms in *corruption-prone sectors*, e.g., the construction industry, tax administration, police force, environmental policy and administration, food and sanitation businesses, education, military conscription, government procurement, and customs.

(ii) Establish an anticorruption infrastructure, e.g., an anticorruption law and an independent anticorruption committee with representatives from the academia, business, and civic organizations.

(iii) Expand citizen participation in anticorruption activities, e.g., provide support for NGOs to conduct awareness campaigns and voluntary monitoring.

(iv) Build a social environment for anticorruption, including an educational and public awareness program, review of administrative procedures to improve transparency, and disclosure of more information to the public.

(v) Implement specific measures such as increasing salaries for public servants to match those in the private sector within five years, compensating those who report corruption with cash rewards, launching inspections of large local governments upon the request of 1000 or more citizens, and making it obligatory to disclose the contents and use of public funds.

Korea's goal is to become a *transparent state* by the year 2003, and rise from 43rd to 20th place in the ranking of Transparency International.

Addressing Corruption: The Experience of Other ADCs

Pakistan's Poverty Reduction Program recognizes that the elimination of corruption is necessary for integrity in the formulation and conduct of economic policy and in the discharge of government functions and provision of basic services. Hence, to reduce corruption and increase accountability among government officials, the National Accountability Bureau was set up with investigatory and prosecutorial powers. As of May 2000, some 1,000 corrupt officials have been charged by the new regime (Government of Pakistan Interim PRSP 2001b).

The emerging and continuing problem of corruption has been recognized as challenges to good governance in the Lao People's Democratic Republic. These have been significant hindrances in managing the economy and fostering long-term sustainable growth and development. Thus steps have been taken to address some corruption-related issues. Among other things, the Auditor General's Office has been set up, procurement legislation has been issued, the accounting and auditing profession has been liberalized and licenses issued, state-owned enterprises are being audited, and the Lao People's Revolutionary Party's (LPRP) inspection board has stepped up its oversight (Lao PDR 1998).

In Thailand, Phongpaichit (1998) identified four major patterns of corruption that need to be addressed: syndicated corruption; procurement kickbacks; rent seeking, maintenance (or concessional privileges); and bid fixing. The low salaries of those in the public sector compared to those in the private sector have also been identified as a concern that must be addressed by administrative reform (Thamrongthanyavong 1998). Indeed, increasing the salaries of public officials may address continuing corruption in the bureaucracy. Wescott (2001) cites the example of Cambodia where the government has begun to raise the salaries of civil servants by 10 percent as a first step toward addressing the root cause of corruption.

Within the context of bureaucratic reform, a major issue that must be addressed in Thailand is how to stamp out the widespread sale of positions. Additionally, in the area of corporate governance, two areas were targeted for reform, namely: eliminating the conflict of interest in the selling of shares and extension of loans among the shareholders, directors, and managers themselves (Phongpaichit 1998); and the passage of an antitrust law. As early as 1975, the Civil Service Act devoted a whole chapter (Chapter 4) to discipline in the civil service to address the problem of corruption (Raksasataya 1989).

The problem of corruption is therefore one that the ADCs continue to address. Strategies range from broad administrative reform efforts (such as those launched by Korea; Philippines; and Taipei,China) to massive reorganization interventions after a political upheaval (such as those in Bangladesh and Pakistan). Increasing the salaries of the people in the bureaucracy has always been a component of the reform efforts. In the end, however, what really counts is the success in reforming and changing the mindsets of the people in the bureaucracy and, more importantly, "political will" in implementing reforms, as demonstrated by the Korean model.

CITIZEN PARTICIPATION FOR POVERTY REDUCTION

Participatory governance is a key factor that can spell the success or failure of poverty reduction programs and projects. Participation has been defined as "a process through which stakeholders influence and share control over development initiatives and the decisions and resources, which affect them" (World Bank 1996b, 3). Alternatively referred to as "voice and freedom", the participation of citizens in the different phases of poverty reduction programs and projects including conceptualization, design, implementation, and evaluation may lead to the choice of appropriate interventions (Sen 2000b, World Bank 1996). Greater voice would lead to more transparency and accountability and help in the continuing struggle against corruption.

Participation can be operationalized as partnerships through various mechanisms. This could include consultations (direct or indirect) with the citizens in various phases of the project cycle.[11]

There is this school of thought that argues that, based on the experience of some ADCs, including Bangladesh and the Philippines, the increased involvement of civil society groups and NGOs in the governance processes may be attributed to the general inability of the state to govern, mostly in terms of the delivery of services. NGOs have come in as complementary or alternative service delivery mechanisms.

Citizen Participation for Good Governance: The Bangalore Score Card

A classic example of citizen participation for good governance and poverty reduction is in the area of monitoring and evaluation as illustrated by the concept of governance scorecards pioneered by the Public Affairs Center in Bangalore, India[12] (Paul 1996, World Bank 2001a). The score cards were prepared by the City of Bangalore in partnership with committed community-based organizations. The general objective was to assess the efficiency and adequacy of governance *from the recipients' point of view* (World Bank 2001a). Its specific objectives were:

- (i) Obtain citizen feedback on the quality and adequacy of public services
- (ii) Catalyze citizens to adopt a pro-active stance by demanding accountability, accessibility, and responsiveness from service providers
- (iii) Compare service providers across various indices

(iv) Identify areas in which citizens experience high levels of stress in accessing the service
(v) Estimate the hidden costs incurred by the citizens
(vi) Measure the efficiency and effectiveness of the grievance redress mechanism

Score cards have been used to evaluate and obtain feedback on the quality of delivery of basic services including general urban services, health, and public distribution system. The score card approach for poverty reduction in Bangalore was successful in obtaining feedback from the citizens and has been used as the basis to identify areas that needed improvement or strengthening. It has actually become part of the process of governance and has been institutionalized, with citizens actually looking forward to rating various aspects of governance on a periodic basis. Due to its success, the Bangalore score card system has been replicated and adopted in other cities, including Ahmedabad, Calcutta, Chennai, Delhi, Mumbai, and Pune. The World Bank has further proposed the adoption of governance score cards for the cities of Chittagong, Dhaka, Khulna, and Rajshahi.

NGOs in Bangladesh: A Paradigm of Citizen Participation

Civil society and nongovernment organizations have played a key role in the poverty reduction efforts of Bangladesh. Bangladesh has been recognized worldwide as among the countries with the most dynamic NGO sector.[13] It is through this sector that citizen participation in poverty reduction efforts is operationalized.

The emergence of NGOs in Bangladesh is due largely to the failure of government, whose operations have been characterized by waste, mis-targeting, corruption, and inefficient delivery of programs (Sobhan 1998, Mahbub ul Haq Human Development Center 1999). NGOs have emerged as alternative development institutions "designed to deliver aid more purposefully and efficiently to the poor" (Sobhan 1998, 11). Many of the poverty reduction programs that have been considered successful in poverty reduction at the micro level have been those implemented by NGOs (such as the Grameen Bank and the BRAC) at least in terms of raising household income levels. *Participation* and *ownership* by the poor have been identified as key factors in the relative success of NGO-initiated poverty reduction programs and projects in Bangladesh (Sobhan 1998, Smillie 1997).

NGOs have been considered to be "moderately effective in their efforts to empower the poor in Bangladesh" (Sobhan 1998, 24). As part of their overall attempt to coordinate their work and exercise political leverage as an advocacy body, the NGOS in Bangladesh have forged the Association of Development Agencies in Bangladesh (ADAB).[14]

However, despite claims of success among the NGOs in Bangladesh, one should be cognizant of the findings of some studies (NOVIB 1996, Rahman and Razzaque 2000, 3) that "the poorest of the poor were not reached through the existing programmes." This was largely because, according to Rahman and Razzaque (2000, 32), they have still been unable to "devise an appropriate strategy so that participation of the hardcore poor can be ensured in the social as well as credit programmes."

People Participation: The Saemaul Undong and Welfare Foundations in Korea

A classic illustration of people participation for poverty reduction is seen in the *Saemaul Undong*[15] in Korea. This has been considered as one of the major factors that led to the successful rural development and hence reduction of poverty in Korea (Chang-Soo 1993, Kee-Ok 1993, Yoon 2001). Mobilized by the spirit of self-help and voluntary labor among the poor, millions of Koreans have participated in the movement since the early 1970s resulting in the construction of thousands of hectares of rural roads, rural houses, roads and irrigation systems. The government provided resources (e.g., cement) to build the infrastructure such as local roads and houses, while local community residents provided their labor as counterpart. Since the project itself was under the office of the President, it was clothed with legitimacy, authority, and clout leading to relative ease of implementation. Initially a government-driven movement in the 1970s to contribute to nation-building and economic and rural development, the Saemaul Undong was eventually privatized in the 1980s and has since continued to enhance resident participation in regional and social development programs. Consequently, it has provided the context and basis for decentralization and local autonomy (Kee-Ok 1993) considering that the movement contributed toward the development of local capacities. A major reason for the successful implementation of the program was political will as exemplified by support from no less than the President. A second factor for the success of the program was ownership and commitment by the people who saw for themselves that it created jobs, contributed to the development of the rural areas, and helped alleviate poverty. Hence, when it was privatized, the citizens themselves sustained its implementation.

Another example of people's participation in poverty reduction is through the private sector. Yoon (2001) cites the participation of the private sector in various social welfare and relief programs, a number of which have been initiated by religious institutions, voluntary institutions, nonprofit foundations, and even big companies. Among them are the Buddhists, Christians, Korean Christian Church Federation, National Association of Disaster Protection, Korean Red Cross, Daewoo Foundation, and Adan Social Welfare Foundation of the Hyundai Group (Yoon 2001). One reason for the private sector's success was the fact that the government provided the appropriate policy context that nurtured their participation. Indeed in many cases, government simply has to provide the enabling environment for poverty reduction through policies and legislation that encourage, and not stifle, people participation.

Partnerships with Civil Society for Poverty Reduction in the Philippines

In the Philippines, the National Anti-Poverty Commission (NAPC) has taken the lead in the implementation of the National Anti-Poverty Agenda. The NAPC has representatives from the basic sectors as co-equal members of the Commission. The Commission itself is co-chaired by a representative from the basic sectors[16] seen as partners of the government in its poverty reduction efforts. The NAPC had its origins in the early to mid-1990s when the government embarked on the formulation of a social reform agenda aimed at reducing poverty in the country. A fundamental philosophy underlying the strategy was to get active civil society involvement by recruiting them as partners in the massive endeavor. In the mid-1990s, a Comprehensive and Integrated Delivery of Social Services (CIDSS) was implemented by the administration of President Ramos as a centerpiece of the Social Reform Agenda. A key feature of the CIDSS is the institutionalization of the partnership between the private and public sectors in the delivery of basic services at the community level. It was recognized that citizen participation was a key factor for this poverty reduction program to succeed and be sustained. Bautista (1999) concludes that this poverty reduction strategy made a difference in the areas where it was implemented. De Dios (1999) adds that the success could also be attributed to two additional factors: its relative depolitization and its low level of funding. More important, though, is De Dios' assertion that it was successful because of the mobilization of the community and its organizations. People participation was a key factor.

CONCLUSION

Existing literature concludes that good governance effected by public sector reforms can lead to the reduction of poverty. Public sector reform is typically characterized as administrative reform, citizen participation in governance, and decentralization (see Chapter 5). In all cases, implementation is critical and remains a major challenge confronting many ADCs.

Countries that have been relatively successful in their poverty reduction efforts have been among those that have carried out early public sector reforms. For the others, failure in implementation proved to be the pitfall. Many countries had poverty reduction frameworks, some more sophisticated than others. But their varied experiences have shown that partisanship, lack of political will, and graft and corruption have become serious obstacles to implementation. Related to this is the lack of continuity in the implementation of programs. Changes in leadership at the national and local levels usually stalled the continuity of programs.

Weak administrative capacities—both at the national and local levels—have also constrained the implementation of poverty reduction programs. More specifically, these included the lack of appropriate skills (especially at the local level) and the low salaries of government employees relative to those in the private sector. This has become a disincentive for qualified people to work in the bureaucracy, effectively depriving it of more qualified personnel. Increasing the salaries of government workers has therefore become a "standard" item in most government's administrative reform packages.

As frontline institutions, local governments play a key role in the implementation of poverty reduction efforts since they are logically positioned to deliver basic services to the people. As the cases would show, it is critical to develop the administrative capacities of institutions—including local governments—to enable them to meet their responsibilities as pivotal institutions in addressing poverty. Several areas have been identified as areas for capacity enhancement of local governments that would enable them to better confront the challenges of poverty reduction at the local level.

Capacity building for poverty reduction may also be directed at developing and strengthening citizen participation in governance. Among the areas for capacity building to strengthen partnerships are the following (UMP 2000): a sound understanding of the legal framework, laws, and regulations that govern local authorities; understanding and appreciation of fiscal administration matters such as sources of revenues and expenditures; and familiarity with the nature and processes of both government and nongovernment organizations to lay the foundation for smooth partnerships between government and civil society.

There is no "universal model" for poverty reduction, no one-size-fits-all solution that can be adopted globally. In fact, we have seen that the pace of implementation of administrative reforms varies across countries, as influenced by different political, social, cultural, and structural conditions. What can be done is to facilitate the sharing of experiences in public sector reform among the various countries and, where appropriate, approaches to public sector reform and poverty reduction adapted, and adopted, by others within the context of an enriched learning environment. The unique experiences of different countries must be placed and appreciated within their proper historical, social, cultural, political, and administrative context. Guided by its own needs, interests, and conditions, as well as insights from other countries' experiences, governments would thus be better able to mount public sector reforms and capacity-building modalities that would strengthen their poverty reduction efforts.

International agencies and institutions such as the Asian Development Bank, World Bank, United Nations agencies, and bilateral aid agencies can play a key role in enhancing poverty strategies by providing assistance in capacity building of public sector institutions, including national government agencies and local governments. This may cover such areas as local development planning, intergovernmental cooperation through integrated area development, skills training, and development and strengthening of technical information at the village level.

Notes

1. Parenthetically, it may be noted that the suggested relationships are more correlational rather than causal, as pointed out by Wescott (2001).
2. The notion of "reinventing" government gained worldwide prominence with the publication of the book of the same title (*Reinventing Government* by Osborne and Gaebler 1993). This book became the basis of many an attempt to reorient and reorganize many bureaucracies in the Third World, including the Philippines. "Reinventing the Government" is one of the chapters in Siddiqui (2001) that examines various aspects of governance in Pakistan. Siddiqui also has a chapter on "Retooling the Bureaucracy." Seoul Metropolitan Government has called its massive administrative reform procedure as "Reinventing Seoul City Government" (2000). The Seoul Reform Paradigm highlighted four major areas: small and efficient government; management that emphasized performance; an open administration that reaches out to citizens; and clear and transparent administration that includes an integrity pact and anticorruption index. In Thailand, Thamrongthanyavong (1998) refers to efforts to reform the Thai Bureaucracy as "reinventing the Thai Bureaucracy."
3. It must be recalled that the power of the bureaucrat is in the office occupied. An etymology of the term "bureaucracy" is helpful: *bureau* means "office" in French, and *cracy* is derived from the Greek word for "power." In other words, "the power is in the office" and any attempt to lessen the power (such as the implementation of civil service reforms) will be naturally resisted by the power wielder.
4. Comments made by a World Bank delegate during the Conference on Poverty, Growth, and the Role of Institutions held at the ADB, 10-12 October 2001.
5. Observation made by Clay Wescott in the session on "Public Sector Reform and Poverty Reduction" during the Conference on Poverty, Growth and the Role of Institutions, 10-12 October 2001.
6. Note that Viet Nam is quite bold in proclaiming that its ultimate objective is "poverty elimination" in contradistinction to those that target only "poverty reduction," or even more conservatively for others, "poverty alleviation."
7. Alan Whaites (2000) notes that, while the formulation of PRSPs is in the right direction, a potential weakness of the process of the preparation of the PRSPs lies in, among other things, the "interim" phase wherein participation seemingly becomes a formalism for the government. Indeed, the problem of formalistic participation continues to dog certain institutions and processes whose very foundations and raison d'etre are participation and empowerment. For instance, in a study of the Panchayat Raj in India, Gaiha et al. (2000) concluded that a number of policies, including the 73rd constitutional (amendment) Act essentially limited people participation in the formal structures of government, falling short of operationalizing meaningful participation and empowerment.

8. An issue that arises is the "ad hoc-ness" of such bodies. Depending on the capacities that are developed and technologies transferred, when do such bodies "self-destruct?" Or should they be converted into regular structures of the bureaucracy? The danger of course is that if they are converted into regular departments of the ministries themselves, they will evolve bureaucratic processes of their own and, paradoxically, be themselves targets of reform. A similar event occurred in Albania when they implemented their Rural Poverty Alleviation Pilot Project that essentially aimed to make available credit to the poor. The Project's relative success in reducing poverty was due to the fact that it was implemented through a transition agency outside government. See Nowak (1996).
9. Parenthetically, Koreans refer to this process as a "mental revolution" when they launched the Suhjongshoeshin Movement on the part of national (and local) bureaucrats that would be supportive of civil service reforms for poverty reduction amidst the professional and political dissonance (Rahman 1986).
10. As observed by Kim (1997, 5): "The Korean Civil Service System, once a leading force of industrialization and a guiding agent of social development in the country, has recently been criticized for becoming a barrier to development and a hindrance to competitiveness."
11. The *Participation Sourcebook* prepared by the World Bank (1996) identifies the following stages in the typical project cycle with the borrower and/or the World Bank as the key actors in each stage: identification, preparation, appraisal, negotiations, board approval, signing and loan effectiveness, implementation, project completion.
12. Although India is not included among the countries covered by the study, it is included considering that the Bangalore score card has been upheld as a model and is recognized internationally, and replicated by a number of other local governments as a model in promoting accountabilities and local government responsiveness.
13. It may be noted that the emergence and active involvement of NGOs in local development processes have also been considered as a mode of decentralization.
14. A similar coalition exists in the Philippines namely the Caucus of Development NGOs. Such a coalition has essentially served as a platform for legitimate NGOs in the country to participate in governance and influence policy-making processes, including, for instance, in the National Anti-Poverty Commission.
15. *Sae* means "new" and suggests innovativeness; *maul* means "villages."
16. These sectors are the artisans, fisherfolk, cooperatives, indigenous peoples, children, farmers and landless rural workers, nongovernment organizations, persons with disabilities, urban poor, women, workers in the informal sector, senior citizens, victims of disasters and calamities, workers in the formal sector and migrant workers, and youth and students.

APPENDIX TABLE 4.1: Administrative Reform in Selected ADCs

Bangladesh	Administrative Services Reform Committee and the National Pay Commission (1972-1975) Committee on Administrative Reform and the National Pay Commission II (1975-1981) Martial Law Committee for Examining Organizational Set-Up 1982 Committee for Administrative/Reorganization/Reform 1982 Public Administration Efficiency Study, November 1989 Public Administration Sector Study in Bangladesh, July 1993 Towards Better Government in Bangladesh, September 1993 Administrative Reorganizing (Nurun Nabi) Committee 1993-1996 Public Administration Reform Commission 1997
Korea	National Civil Service Act of 1947 Supreme Council for National Reconstruction 1961
Lao PDR	Committee for Organization and Personnel 1991 Department of Public Administration 1991 Committee for Government Organization Improvement 2000
Pakistan	Haffeez Pasha Report 1997 Commission on Administrative Restructuring 1999
Philippines	Government Survey and Reorganization Commission 1954-56 Integrated Reorganization Plan of 1972 Presidential Commission of Government Reorganization 1986 Reengineering the Bureaucracy 1992 Presidential Commission on Effective Governance 1999
Taipei,China	Committee for Studying Administrative Efficiency 1934 Committee for Improvement of Administrative Efficiency 1937 Three Connected States of Administration 1940 Regulation for the Structure of Position Classification Planning Committee 1956 Pushing Forth Administrative Reform and Establishing Clean and Efficient Government 2001
Thailand	Civil Service Act of 1928 Civil Service Act of 1975 Civil Service Act of 1992
Viet Nam	*Doi Moi* 1986 (that included governance reforms) Public Administration Review 2000

Sources: Shelley (2000); Ahmed and Khan (1990); Aminuzzaman (1992); Thamrongthanyavong (1998); Joong-Yand and Kyung-Bae (1994); Carino (1992); Sun and Gargan (1996); ADB (1999b); WB, ADB, and UNDP (2000); and UNDP/UNICEF (1996).

5 Decentralization and Poverty Reduction

RAGHAV GAIHA

INTRODUCTION

The term "decentralization" has been variously used to refer to the privatization, deconcentration, or devolution of political, administrative, and fiscal powers.[1] Decentralization as used here, however, refers only to devolution, whether or not powers are transferred simultaneously or in varying degrees. This chapter focuses on whether decentralization has helped the poor in Asia, and on the mechanisms through which the poor have benefited. Although several Asian countries have experimented with decentralization, experiences have varied considerably in their extent, forms and outcomes.[2] In several cases, the political dimension was dominant, with changing political circumstances and coalitions shaping the process of decentralization in important ways. By contrast, economic conditions were less crucial in decisions to decentralize. Nor was decentralization typically a response to mass pressure from the grassroots. Rather it was largely a top-down affair, guided mostly by the narrower interests of political leaders seeking legitimacy and mass support.[3] As a result, devolution has tended to be patchy or even temporary. Where inequality is extreme, it is common for local self-governing institutions to be "captured" by the elite. Nevertheless, a few successes may be cited where the poor indeed benefited. An objective of this chapter is to deepen understanding of the factors underlying these successes and the constraints that limit the benefits to the poor. From this perspective, both design and implementation aspects of decentralization will be reviewed.

The territorial domain of subnational governments varies greatly in Asia—a typical province in People's Republic of China (PRC) or India is larger than some countries. Consequently, federalism in the sense of devolution of power to provincial governments can still imply a fair amount of centralization of power. At the local level, units can be highly diverse, ranging from large cities to villages, with boundaries determined by accidents of history and geography and not necessarily by considerations of efficient decentralized administration. Although quantitative analyses of decentralization often stop short of the subprovincial level—mainly because of data limitations—it is often at this level that conflicts in, and failures of, decentralization in poverty alleviation are more glaring. Accordingly, this chapter focuses on some important actors at the local level, e.g., the local community. While recognizing their potentially important roles in designing and implementing programs for the poor, attention is also drawn to some of their limitations.[4]

The next section critically examines the rationale for decentralized redistribution, which rests on administrative and informational considerations. The third section reviews the nature and extent of decentralization and its impact on the poor in selected Asian countries. The fourth section distills from the rich diversity of country experiences strategic options in enhancing the political feasibility and effectiveness of decentralization in the context of poverty alleviation. Concluding observations from a broad policy perspective are made in the final section.

RATIONALE OF DECENTRALIZATION

Is There a Case for Decentralizing Redistribution?

A central rationale for state intervention is the redistribution of income and wealth to alleviate poverty. Redistribution policies may take either of two forms. A first set of policies seeks to provide basic primary or merit goods to individuals, including health care and education. Since the aim is to provide a minimum standard of access to primary goods[5] in the face of varying individual needs, policies of this type involve treating people unequally to ensure more equal outcomes. This may entail direct provision of goods rather than income support.[6] The second set involves income maintenance, aiming to redistribute income rather than ensuring access to specific commodities. The informational requirements of these two sets of policies are thus different, and it will be argued below that assigning these policies to two different levels of government is appropriate.

A case is often made for assigning redistribution policies to the central government based on two considerations (for a lucid exposition, see Helm and Smith 1989). First, if the extent of income redistribution is left to different levels of government, one level could "undo" the redistribution accomplished by another, a possibility that is minimized if such policies are assigned to a single level. Second, local redistributive policies induce a Tiebout process of migration, which could raise the costs of redistribution.[7] Migration could likewise restrict the use of redistributive taxes by local governments. In both cases, migration would limit the feasible range of redistributive policies and cause some loss of efficiency.

A difficulty with this argument, however, is that it rests on a sharp separation of efficiency and distribution. In practice, the two aspects are inextricably linked. The problem is illustrated by primary goods, many of which are mixed goods in the sense that they contain public good elements but are also provided in part on distributional considerations. Consider education, for example. Although distributional considerations are of considerable importance in its provision, it may contain both national and local public good elements (e.g., curricula may be set nationally while each province chooses its own medium of instruction). Where the local public good element is of substantial importance, it could be assigned to local government, despite the redistributional aspect. Transfers from central governments could ensure that the desired level of spending is achieved and the efficiency costs of migration are minimized.[8]

Another view holds that income redistribution is itself a local public good as it is essentially a preference by some over others, which displays the characteristics of nonexcludability and nonrivalrous consumption. Equity and efficiency objectives can thus be combined in a Pareto-efficient redistribution (for details, see Helm and Smith 1989). This, however, can be questioned on the ground that preferences are just one criterion for welfare judgment and that there are other more appealing nonefficiency criteria (Sen 1980, Dasgupta 1986).[9] In that case, equity is distinct from efficiency. If redistribution is not a local public good but a separate objective, it could be accomplished at any level of government.

Thus, assuming that redistributional goals are set by the central government, a case for their implementation by local governments rests largely on administrative and informational considerations.

An issue is whether the local government is superior to a provincial or regional branch of the central government in gathering and processing information. In principle, if central government agencies employed locally knowledgeable persons, they could perform this function with equal efficiency and avoid a possible clash of priorities. To the extent, however, that the local government is accountable to the local community, and the community is better placed to monitor and assess its performance, the local government is more likely to gather relevant information and to use it judiciously.[10] A related question is whether there are any advantages in assigning redistributional policies with national priorities to local governments with revenue-raising powers, as opposed to assigning them to, say, special locally elected boards (e.g., education boards) managing centrally-set budgets. Two reasons favor assignment to existing revenue-raising bodies: One is economies of scale in local administration, and another is the need for additional taxation to correct inappropriate national allocations, largely as a result of informational constraints (Helm and Smith 1989).

Fiscal Decentralization

An important consideration in devolving the power to tax to local authorities is that of encouraging greater fiscal responsibility among them and raising their stake in the cost-effectiveness of public expenditure. Devolution, however, may also cause inefficiencies and inequities. If there is a great deal of mobility across local jurisdictions, differences in taxes could misallocate the mobile factors. Inequities, on the other hand, may arise due to differences in fiscal capacities and preferences for redistribution. There is thus a need for central control to harmonize the tax system, to achieve a fairer redistribution, and to reduce the costs of tax collection. For these reasons, central governments in developing countries tend to retain control over direct taxes that apply to mobile factors (e.g., on capital) and that redistribute wealth (e.g., progressive taxation of income, wealth, and gifts). Some taxes are collected centrally but shared with lower levels of government, partly because of lower collection costs.[11,12] When there is an array of subnational taxes, e.g., different sales taxes at the state level in India, the efficiency gains of harmonizing these taxes may be substantial.[13]

By contrast, expenditure assignments are more decentralized than revenue collection, although there is often a vertical fiscal imbalance. As a result of economies of scale in tax collection by central governments and geographic concentration of economic activities, few local governments have access to elastic sources of tax revenue. They are thus perpetually dependent on central governments for transfers and grants, which restrict their financial autonomy. Transfers and grants are designed to correct fiscal imbalances, to reflect externalities—the interests that residents of other localities have in the spending decisions of a particular authority (e.g., in road building)—and to achieve equalization of living standards between different localities. Specific forms include conditional or matching grants, unconditional grants, and earmarking. Matching grants are appropriate when the provision of local services generates benefits for residents of other jurisdictions (i.e., spillovers). But they are seldom used because of their regressivity (since better-endowed regions/localities are more likely to use them fully). In contrast, unconditional grants are appropriate for fiscal equalization. Such grants channel funds from relatively wealthy jurisdictions to poorer ones. But under certain conditions these grants could be divisive. Finally, earmarking is a second-best solution by which the government makes a commitment that revenue from a particular source will be used exclusively for a particular purpose.

Resource Mobilization

Given limited fiscal devolution and a built-in tendency toward vertical fiscal imbalance, mobilization of local resources for poverty alleviation assumes considerable importance.[14] Yet this remains a major weakness of even moderately successful decentralization. This should not be taken to imply that there is limited potential for local resource mobilization. On the contrary, small, site-specific infrastructure projects often succeed in mobilizing local resources from their intended beneficiaries provided the latter are involved in it from the beginning. In a small community, problems of strategic revelation of preferences and free riding are unlikely to be serious. Some evidence from Bangladesh, for example, suggests that poorer groups were more willing to contribute to such projects than the better-off, provided of course that they were not required to bear a disproportionate share of the burden (for details, see Bardhan 1997). Besides, there is willingness to contribute if the services provided are good, there is no wastage or misappropriation of funds, and the central government does not renege on its contribution. However, local resource mobilization cannot be the mainstay of such projects/activities. The bulk of the funding must still come from the central government and donors.

Corruption, Capture, and Control

Corruption is commonly understood as the abuse of public power for personal benefit (World Bank 1997a). It is arguable that corruption in a decentralized system may be more costly in terms of efficiency than in a centralized system, as the latter internalizes the possible negative externality of one bribe transaction on other such transactions.[15] This is akin to Olson's (1993) idea that the distortionary effects of tax impositions of the state as a "stationary bandit" (with an "encompassing" interest in the domain over which the rent-extraction is carried out) will be smaller than those of the acts of a "roving bandit" will. It is, however, arguable that even centralized corruption is more distortionary than taxation, as the former uses up resources in concealing it and/or diverting resources to transactions/activities in which it is easier to avoid detection and punishment.[16]

The pervasiveness of corruption in local governments is attributable to the fact that arm's-length relationships among elected representatives, officials and the elite are relatively infrequent at the local level. Since collusion is easier to organize and enforce in small groups, the risks of detection and punishment are reduced. As elaborated in the case studies, the tight control over information relating to rural development and poverty alleviation programs is an effective rent-extraction mechanism. By contrast, at the national level, rent seeking is more competitive, and the capture of central government institutions is harder. Regional elites and interest groups neutralize one another; there are more stringent checks and balances; and general awareness levels are higher (Bardhan 1996, 1997).

In general, weak or nonexistent accountability mechanisms tend to perpetuate local corruption.[17] These weaknesses include the community's limited involvement in decision making and access to official records, over-elaborate procedures for removing corrupt officials/elected representatives, a weak opposition, and the absence of a vigilant press. In contrast, where democratic institutions are better developed and political processes more transparent, the theft of funds is likely to be smaller. A case in point is decentralization in Karnataka, as discussed below. Although the number of individuals involved in corrupt acts increased, the resources siphoned off were smaller (Crook and Manor 1998).

A major constraint on decentralization is the limited capacity of local governments in the area of redistribution. This is partly a consequence of the low quality of the bureaucracy. Central governments attract better talent partly because of better salaries, more attractive career prospects, a greater diversity of tasks, and partly also because of the self-reinforcing mechanisms of human capital emphasized in recent growth theory (Bardhan 1997). There is also a glaring mismatch in some cases (e.g., village *panchayats* or elected bodies in India) between the capabilities of local bodies and the tasks assigned to them.[18] Although line agencies are supposed to supplement their manpower resources, a dual authority structure prevails, which hampers their smooth functioning. This points to the need for incentive-compatible organizational structures that will minimize dissonance between elected representatives and line agencies.

Alternative Perspectives

Some recent contributions to the centralization versus decentralization debate have focused on the allocation of control rights in a framework of incomplete contracts. These yield rich insights, and what follows is a brief overview.

A few salient features of the basic model are the following: It assumes that electors cannot directly observe the actions of governments; it is further assumed that the welfare of electors is the result of both governments' exercise of power and of various random shocks, and that while welfare is observable by both governments and the electorate, it is not verifiable in the sense that it cannot be the subject of a clause in a contract; accordingly, governments cannot be directly or contractually punished or rewarded for the effects of their actions. What a constitution does is to grant electors the power to decide whether a government may be reelected to another term of office. The difference between centralized and decentralized government thus hinges on which groups of electors are collectively given the power to decide the government's reelection. Decentralization assigns control over policies to regional and local governments, with the right to reelect being vested in regional/local electors. Centralization assigns control over policies to a single government, with the right to reelect distributed across regions/localities.

Viewing decentralization as an allocation of control rights facilitates an understanding of its nature and extent. Constitutional provisions devolving power to local bodies are often either vague or implemented somewhat unevenly, depending on the bargaining power of various groups. These include not just the electors but special interest groups, local and central politicians, and bureaucrats. So the battles for control over policies are fought in several different arenas, such as parliament, state legislatures, and official agencies.[19] Some important dimensions include the intensity of electoral competition, awareness of voters, and the costs of organizing pressure groups at different levels. [20]

CASE STUDIES

These case studies aim to illustrate the nature and extent of decentralization, the political considerations that have shaped its course, coordination failures at different levels, the incentive incompatibility of organizational structures, the weak accountability mechanisms, corruption, and the potential of a few community-based initiatives in enhancing the well-being of the poor. From the diversity of experiences analyzed, strategic options in decentralization are then identified.

The Political Economy of Decentralization

Decentralization is essentially a political process, involving the distribution of power and resources both among different levels of the state and among different interests in their relationship to ruling elites, locally as well as nationally (Crook and Sverrison 1999). A central aspect is therefore the nature of the politics of central-local relations, in which two key elements are involved: (i) the configuration of the local power structure and (ii) the power bases of the national ruling elite, specifically the nature of alliances with local or regional elites. Connected with the first element is the issue of whether local governments are always bound to be captured by local elites, given an antagonistic relationship between them and the dominated groups (i.e., the poor and vulnerable). Evidence from the Indian state of West Bengal, however, points to a more complex relationship (for details, see Echeverri-Gent 1993). Within a competitive political system, the ruling Communist Party was able to consolidate its position by forming a broad-based alliance of the poor, middle peasants, and salaried employees. In the process it managed to supplant the old landlord class, as a power base.[21]

The role of interrelationships between national and local elites is no less complex. There are three distinct scenarios. First, the ruling elite or central authority may seek to build its power bases through an alliance with local elites that support its interests and enjoy some autonomy. This scenario entails bargaining and co-optation. Devolution of power and allocation of resources occurs, but pro-poor outcomes are unlikely. Many military regimes have sought to legitimize themselves in this way (e.g., Ghana in 1989-1992, Chile from 1975), as also established party regimes aiming to consolidate support (e.g., Colombia during the 1980s).

A second scenario is one where the central elite challenges or circumvents locally powerful groups. Here, elites at different levels of government may be divided by ideological rivalry, class, or ethnic conflict, and deep distrust. The challenge to entrenched local elites may follow a popular revolution (as in post-Marcos Philippines) or the coming to power of social democratic or communist parties (as in the Indian states of West Bengal or Kerala). A centrally funded antipoverty strategy is a typical mechanism, with the implementation assigned to decentralized bodies in a tightly controlled framework.

In a third scenario, the ruling elite may consolidate its position in a society where local elites exert no significant autonomous power (this draws upon Crook and Sverrisson 1999). Decentralization here primarily takes the form of deconcentration, indicating the power and effectiveness of the regime down to the local level. While pro-poor outcomes are possible, there is a danger of consolidating a system of corrupt patronage-based linkages (as in Bangladesh in the late 1980s and early 1990s).

The Nature of the Political Regime: A Comparative Analysis of Three Indian States

Along with the nature and extent of devolution, some characteristics of the political regime make a significant difference in poverty alleviation. This observation is illustrated by a comparative analysis based on fieldwork in three Indian states, viz., West Bengal, Uttar Pradesh (UP), and Karnataka during 1978-1979 and 1981 (Kohli 1987). During this period, these states were ruled by three different political parties, with varying degrees of commitment to, and capacity for, redistributive reform. Of these states, the performance of West Bengal's Communist government was most impressive. Its success was due to (i) a coherent and stable leadership, (ii) a clear pro-lower-class ideology, and (iii) a strong grassroots-level organization. However, while the Communist Party successfully carried out tenancy reforms, its record in redistributing surplus land was disappointing. This was partly due to the poor quality of land records. But, more fundamentally, it reflected the limited redistributive intent of the Communist Party in a democratic setting (for an elaboration of this argument, see Kohli 1987). In sharp contrast, the Janta regime in UP was characterized by a fragmented leadership, confused ideology, and weak organizational base. Not surprisingly, therefore, the poverty alleviation record of this regime was dismal (Kohli 1987). Karnataka represents an intermediate case. Under the Congress government, there was a modicum of redistributive success. In any case, a weak organization—dominated by propertied classes—could not support drastic redistribution.

While an analysis based on the above factors is persuasive, there is a need to probe into other factors influencing success or failure, including (i) the existence of bureaucratic impediments; (ii) the coverage of other programs, such as those involving health and education; and (iii) the nature and strength of coalitions that are activated by specific antipoverty interventions, with the potential for obstructing them.[22] Basically, these factors are in recognition of the generally accepted idea that poverty alleviation should not be confined to mitigating income deprivation.

Exclusion of the Poor in Bangladesh

The decentralization introduced by President H. M. Ershad in 1985 was designed to legitimize his military regime and to build support for a newly created party, the Jatiyo Party.[23] Rural landed elites and power brokers were co-opted to build a political power base, with limited power sharing. Two tiers of elected local councils were created: the directly elected union councils with populations of around 20,000, and the subdistrict (*upazila*) councils with an average population of 245,000. The new system combined elements of deconcentration and devolution. The councils largely depended on central funds, since they lacked powers to raise revenue.

There were no reservations or quotas for the poor or the disadvantaged. There was a provision for the appointment of three women at the subdistrict level, but who had no voting rights. Of a total of 4401 councillors, six women served as union chairwomen, with their husbands exercising real authority. Both the union and subdistrict councils were dominated by the affluent landed classes; the landless were excluded. Most of the affluent subdistrict chairmen spent much of their time in Dhaka, networking with influential politicians and civil servants. Soon after their election, 55 percent of the chairmen joined the Jatiyo Party.

Field evidence suggests that only a quarter of the respondents had contacted either their councillors, while about the same proportion had attended meetings (Crook and Manor 1998). An earlier survey, however, revealed that a majority of the respondents knew little about the upazila, and an insignificant proportion had attended any meetings (Ingham and Kalam 1992). Further, 64 percent of the respondents were "not at all satisfied" with either the union or the upazila councils, largely because of the corrupt and dictatorial behavior of their political leaders (Crook and Manor 1998). In the survey by Ingham and Kalam, as many as 75 percent of the elite respondents felt that NGOs and voluntary associations performed better than local governments, while 90 percent claimed to have had personal experience of corruption. Much of the funding was devoted to patronage-related activities that did not benefit the poor. But in some cases, especially those involving infrastructure, projects chosen by the councils were congruent with expressed needs (for details, see Crook and Manor (1998).

Whatever the gains to the Ershad regime of co-opting the local elites and power brokers through decentralization, however, these did not last long. In the 1990 elections, 90 percent of the upazila chairmen were rejected by the electorate, and a year later the regime itself collapsed.[24]

Reversal in the Philippines?

In the Philippines major decentralization was ushered in with the passage of the landmark Local Government Code in 1992 in accordance with the 1987 Constitution.[25] It curtailed the policy-making authority of both the President and the legislators in important ways (for details, see Brillantes 1998, Eaton 2001).

The Code also sought to foster the entrepreneurial spirit of local government units by enabling them to borrow in the market (by floating bonds), to enter into build-operate-transfer (BOT) arrangements with the private sector, and in general to adopt a competitive business outlook. An Oversight Committee was established to aid the implementation of the Code.

Central politicians faced particularistic incentives and their influence depended significantly on their role in negotiating fiscal transfers to their constituencies in a system of discretionary allocations.[26] Thus notwithstanding close relationships between central and local politicians—either as friends or relatives—decentralization posed a threat to the former.[27] Once the constellation of political forces brought about decentralization, the legislators attempted to reverse it and succeeded in bringing about "creeping centralization" through the following means.

First, the Code itself was designed to protect the interests of legislators. There was a provision for the Audit Commission to review and audit the fiscal accounts of each subnational government. Based on these annual reviews, legislators could then withdraw powers and revenues from a local executive in the event of abuse. Furthermore, local officials—including the auditors appointed by local executives—could be recalled. Finally, to protect the employment of bureaucrats who owed their jobs to national legislators, the subnational governments were required to pay the salaries of all government employees devolved from the central government.

Second, there were attempts at formal recentralization. Within a year of the introduction of the Code, 30 bills were introduced to amend various provisions. Attempts were made to recentralize a number of services such as health and agricultural research. In view of the President's opposition to such efforts, legislators turned their attention to "augmentation funds" meant to complement the local provision of certain services. These additional funds were distributed in a manner that allowed them to take personal credit for additional transfers. They also used their discretionary and enhanced pork-barrel funds in ways that competed with local government spending rather than complementing it.[28] When they ceased to be brokers of discretionary fiscal transfers, the legislators indulged in giving tax sops. Attempts were also made to divert tax revenues from automatic-revenue sharing systems to special infrastructure funds over which they had greater control.

As a result, despite a substantial expansion of the functions and responsibilities of local governments, their share of the national budget was a meager 14 percent in 1997. By contrast, the share of central government agencies rose, even though staff strengths and functional responsibilities had been reduced. Under provisions of the Code, 16,000 NGOs and POs were accredited to local bodies. Their participation has tended to stagnate in recent years. The receptiveness of local government officials to NGOs and POs has also been uneven.[29] Meetings of local bodies have become less frequent, and elections of representatives have not taken place yet. The capacities of local government units are not adequate for an expanded role, given the situation described above.

There are, however, a few illustrations of how greater local autonomy and NGO participation in poverty alleviation programs have resulted in significant improvements. The new initiatives in Naga City in Southern Luzon are a case in point (for a detailed exposition, see Robredo 2000).

Naga City evolved a partnership with civil society through two programs: (i) the Naga Socialized Program for Empowerment and Economic Development (Naga SPEED) and (ii) the Empowerment Ordinance. Briefly, Naga SPEED formalized the participation of local communities in identifying development priorities. The Empowerment Ordinance, on the other hand, authorized the Naga City People's Council (NCPC) to assign NGO representatives from its members to different boards, councils, committees, task forces, and other special bodies of the city government. These representatives play an important role in the design and implementation of city government programs.

Two examples of how this partnership has benefited the poor will suffice. One is the *Naga Kaantabay sa Kauswagan* (Partners in Development) Program, designed for the benefit of squatters and slum dwellers, who comprise 25 percent of the city population. Its achievements include: distributing 33 hectares of private and government land among 2017 poor families; upgrading 27 urban poor communities involving 2700 families; and securing, as part of its land banking strategy, a total of 25.4 hectares of land for future housing projects of the city government (Robredo 2000).

Another example is the formation of the Metro Naga Development Council (MNDC), a partnership between the city and 14 surrounding municipalities, designed to increase opportunities for employment and improve the delivery of basic services. Through a pooling of efforts and resources, MNDC contributed to the rehabilitation of some 50 kms of farm-to-market roads; the installation of 500 Level 1 water systems; the improvement of health service delivery; the extension of credit facilities; and the matching of local job-seekers and employment opportunities (Robredo 2000).

Assessments of the Local Government Code and the decentralization associated with it range from favorable to sceptical (for a favorable assessment, see Brillantes 2001). Without doubt, greater local autonomy and an expanded resource base are likely to be associated with some benefits to the poor, as exemplified by the new initiatives in Naga City. Doubts about the sustainability of such initiatives, however, cannot be set aside in view of "creeping centralization." More importantly, unless sufficient contrary evidence accumulates, available findings tend more to suggest that the poor did not benefit much, except in a few isolated cases. This conclusion is due both to the limited local autonomy in the design of the LGC and the distortions that crept in later.

Fiscal Decentralization

Although fiscal devolution is a key component of decentralization, it remains the weakest component in many developing countries. The two cases of fiscal devolution reviewed below point to a striking contrast. In the PRC, it resulted in rapid growth and poverty reduction while in Viet Nam the outcome appears to be greater inequity.

The PRC Experience

During the 1980s, the PRC fiscal system underwent significant changes. A unitary system, in which the central government had absolute control over revenue collection and budget appropriation, was decentralized so that revenues were shared between the central and provincial governments. Most of the provincial governments were required to remit a portion of their budget revenues to the central government. Provinces that were unable to cover the centrally determined expenditures received subsidies. Similar fiscal arrangements were made between successive tiers of governments at lower levels.

Under an initial revenue-sharing arrangement enacted in 1980, revenues were classified into central fixed revenues (e.g., customs duties, revenues remitted by centrally owned state enterprises); local fixed revenues (e.g., agricultural taxes, revenues remitted by locally owned state enterprises); and central-local shared revenues (e.g., profits of large scale enterprises under the dual leadership of central and local governments). Subsidies were provided for the poor and remote regions.

In 1985 although revenues still fell under the said three categories the criteria for division were changed. In this new scheme, central and local fixed revenues accounted for a relatively small part of the total government budget, and the shared revenue for a substantially larger part. This meant that the central government now relied on local governments to mobilize more revenues. The changes in the fiscal system were driven by three factors. One was the emergence of nonstate owned enterprises—township and village enterprises, joint ventures and private firms—with substantial revenue-generating potential.[30] Since state enterprises had become a drain on the fiscal system, the central government was forced to turn to alternative sources of revenue. Another was the greater local autonomy resulting from economic liberalization. It thus became natural for subnational governments to demand fiscal decentralization commensurate with their greater political autonomy. The third factor was essentially economic. Unless incentives are combined with local autonomy, local resource mobilization is likely to be sluggish.

Detailed econometric analysis (Lin and Liu 2000) bears out the significant effect of fiscal decentralization on per capita GDP growth.[31] Specifically, the growth rate rises by 3.62 percentage points in response to a fiscal reform that raises the marginal retention rate of budgetary revenue from 0 to 100 percent. This finding is confirmed in alternative specifications, involving different lags between growth rates and fiscal decentralization, reverse causality, and inclusion/exclusion of subsidies. Fiscal decentralization contributes to growth more by improving resource allocation efficiency than it does by inducing more investment. To the extent that growth of income is associated with poverty reduction,[32] the impact of fiscal decentralization on poverty cannot be insignificant. Evidence, however, points to a growing disparity between rich and poor regions in the provision of social and economic services at the local level.

The Viet Nam Experience

Economic liberalization or *doi moi*, initiated in Viet Nam in 1989, was instrumental in accelerating growth and poverty reduction (adopted from Rao 1999). However, the sustainability of rapid growth depends critically on infrastructure support and institutions for the provision of public services in accordance with diversified regional requirements. In this context, intergovernmental fiscal arrangements assume considerable importance, and for this reason the focus here is on the New Budget Law that became effective in 1997.

Prior to this law, the fiscal system was centralized and rigid, with hardly any provision for local initiative in providing public services. The delivery of public services to the poorer districts and communes was unsatisfactory, since the provinces made subprovincial allocations. Inevitably therefore these services were financed by contributions from the local community, resulting in a regressive system.

While the New Budget Law has efficiency-enhancing potential, some major concerns remain.[33]

Under the new system, local governments have an incentive to collect more tax revenues, since they are allowed to retain revenues in excess of targets. On the other hand, since tax officials get incentives for collecting taxes assigned to local governments, some distortions would occur if these officials concentrated only on these taxes.

At the commune level, there are three issues revolving around equity. Although community contributions impart greater flexibility in budget implementation, there is a risk of wide variation in the range and quality of services provided, depending on how rich the community is. The concurrence of expenditure at different levels could disadvantage poorer communes, especially during an economic downturn. When revenues fall, each level of government tends to shift some expenditure responsibilities to lower levels. Hence the poorer the commune, the harder it is to maintain an existing range and quality of services provided. Secondly, since transfers continue to be negotiated, in arriving at the expenditure requirements of local governments, bargaining skills play a greater role than equity considerations. Poorer provinces are thus likely to be at a disadvantage. One approach to the problem is, of course, to link transfers to fiscal disabilities, as determined through a transparent formula. Finally, there is evidence that the new system discriminates against poorer provinces receiving transfers in cash. While there is a provision to adjust the cash transfer to reflect increases in incomes and prices, the indexation is often incomplete. In 1999, for example, the cash transfers were adjusted by about 6 percent when the increase in real GDP alone was of that order, implying no adjustment for higher prices.[34]

Incentives, Accountability, and Capture

Incentives are central to the functioning of local governments and local bodies. While designing incentives for groups of officials and elected representatives is far from straightforward, some key elements may be identified. All too often the concern to make local governments and bodies accountable to higher authorities is exaggerated and unmatched by a corresponding concern for accountability to the local community. As a result, the capture of local governments by a few influential persons in a context of acute inequality of endowments is commonplace, with the poor often being the victims.

The New Panchayati Raj in India

The 73rd Constitutional Amendment Act of 1993, designed to revitalize the panchayats was a landmark. It provided for a uniform three-tier structure of panchayats at district, block, and village levels; mandatory elections every five years; proportional representation of SC/STs; a quota for women; periodic auditing of accounts; and a specification of areas of responsibility of the panchayats at the three levels. As these are broad guidelines, each state was required to modify its existing Acts accordingly. The village/*gram panchayat* has a major role in implementing two anti-poverty programs, namely, the Integrated Rural Development Programme (IRDP), a credit subsidy program, and the Jawahar Rozgar Yojana (JRY), a rural public works program. As the new structure was implemented, serious aberrations came to light. What follows is based on a review of state conformity Acts and their implementation in the states of Uttar Pradesh, Karnataka, and Maharashtra (for details see Gaiha et al. 2000).

Of the areas assigned to the panchayats under the UP Act, only rural sanitation was eventually assigned to them. All others remained under district/state agencies. To illustrate, the district agriculture officer was in charge of agriculture; an assistant engineer in the Minor Irrigation Department had the overall responsibility for minor irrigation schemes; the deputy director (extension) was responsible for land reform; the general manager of the District Industrial Corporation had overall responsibility for rural industries; and so on. Moreover, since the district magistrate chairs the District Rural Development Agency (DRDA) and District Planning Committee (DPC), the chief executive officer (CEO) of the district panchayat/*Zilla Parishad* is subordinate to him/her in the official hierarchy. Hence the district magistrate takes overall responsibility for some of the most important programs. The bureaucracy's ability to overextend its domain in violation of the state Act was largely due to an unstable party coalition (between the *Samajwadi Janta Party* and *Bhartiya Janta Party*) and to unsettled conditions in the hill areas. More generally, this points to the need to account for the distinct role of the bureaucracy in explaining and designing decentralization.[35]

The case of Karnataka points to another factor: the relative bargaining strengths and skills of the panchayats at different levels. As it turned out, most of the major schemes were monopolized either by the district or *zilla* panchayats, or the block/*taluk* panchayat, especially the latter, with a minimal role for the village panchayats. In agriculture, while the maintenance of agricultural seed farms was assigned under the state Act to both the zilla panchayat and taluk panchayat, it was in fact handled solely by the former. In livestock improvement, the promotion of dairy farming, poultry, and piggery was assigned to the gram panchayat but this was in fact dealt with by the zilla and taluk panchayats. The promotion of rural industries was assigned to all levels of panchayats but it was handled only by the zilla Panchayat. Finally, while the Act provided that the JRY be implemented by the gram panchayat, the responsibility for land reform still has to be transferred.

While incentive compatibility mechanisms can take a variety of forms, the issue is whether elected representatives have an incentive to respond to the needs of the community, especially the poor. More specifically, the question is whether the state Acts ensure that programs and schemes assigned to the panchayats are implemented in accordance with the needs or views of the community.

Both the 73rd (amendment) Act and the state Acts require the *gram sabha* (the village assembly) to meet at least twice a year to receive reports of development and other activities, and financial statements. Elections after five years are mandatory. The UP and Karnataka Acts also provide for dismissal of the chairperson following a no-confidence motion by the gram sabha. While these provisions cannot be dismissed as inconsequential, it would be naïve to overstate their importance.

There are a few other complications. First, since the gram panchayat is cast in a supporting role to the DRDA in implementing the JRY, it is unlikely that community needs would be accorded due importance; after all the DRDA is not accountable to the community in the same way gram panchayats are. Second, while the state Acts provide for dissolution of the panchayats for not fulfilling their roles, no such provisions apply to the official agencies (such as the DRDA). A similar incompatibility exists between the elected representatives of the panchayats and support staff drawn from state government departments. The incompatibility is more glaring at the level of the CEO (of the zilla panchayat). CEOs are usually members of the civil service and appointed by the state government. Although they are expected to work under the supervision of the chairperson, transfer and promotion decisions are vested in the parent state department.

Thus a dual authority structure prevails. As a result, there is often dissonance between the CEO and the chairperson, with the former playing a more independent role than required. To promote incentive compatibility, an obvious solution would be to require a common set of performance indicators clearly reflecting the community needs and applicable to both the panchayats and the official agencies on the one hand, and the elected panchayat members and support staff on the other. Achievements might then be judged with those of others in a group of peers (say, in a neighboring group of villages) (for an elaboration of this point, see Dasgupta 1993). This presupposes, however, that systems of monitoring and evaluation are already in place.

Although there is some inevitable overlap between incentives and accountability mechanisms, the latter are a subset of the former and may even be mandatory.

Accountability of the panchayats may be viewed either as: (i) accountability to funding authorities and to higher levels or (ii) accountability to the community. Here we focus largely on the former.

The state Acts emphasize financial accountability of the panchayats to the funding authority as reflected in the importance given to financial reporting, preparation of budgets, and auditing of accounts. The concern is not limited to the balancing of the revenue and expenditure but extends to compliance of expenditure with the guidelines/norms prescribed by higher authorities such as the DRDA for various schemes. For example, the distribution of expenditure on the JRY between wages and material costs must be in the proportion 60-40. It is debatable, to begin with, whether such rigid norms are economically justified. Furthermore, the limited autonomy allowed the panchayats has tended to delay implementation.

Serious doubts persist about the gram panchayat's accountability to the gram sabha (village assembly/ward). It is not obvious whether the gram sabha can perform the role assigned to it in villages without any tradition of corporate institutions or collective decision making. Unfamiliarity with the format and procedures of gram sabha meetings may become a serious impediment. Specific provisions for preserving the minutes of gram sabha meetings and for displaying their decisions in public places are missing. In the absence of a monitoring system, it is not obvious how the gram sabha can check whether expenditures are in accordance with decisions taken. Where there is deliberate default (e.g., embezzlement of funds), the gram sabha has no power to dissolve the gram Panchayat. Finally, whether five yearly elections will enforce greater accountability of gram panchayats in general seems unlikely. Specifically, when there is a multiplicity of goals and some are vaguely defined, it is difficult to assess the performance of an agency.[36] Also, to the extent that multiplicity of goals implies excessive responsibility, each activity has a relatively small weight in the decision of voters (on this, see Seabright 1996).

A survey in UP on the implementation of the JRY and IRDP (for details, see Gaiha et al. 1998, 2000) confirms large-scale resource diversion, producing only minimal benefits to the poor. With a local power structure dominated by the upper castes (especially *Brahmins* and *Thakurs*) and the poor lacking awareness and organization, rent-seeking behavior was unchecked. Regardless of whether the panchayat chairperson belonged to the upper or lower castes, there was little variation in the method and pattern of domination by locally powerful groups. Pessimism and a fear of violence discouraged any organized protest or resistance. Large segments of the rural population ironically continue to be at the mercy of a few powerful groups despite a drastic overhaul of the panchayats.

The survey brought to light some glaring shortcomings in the implementation of the JRY. The amounts received by the gram panchayats ranged from Rs16,000 to Rs18,000 in 1996-97, utilized mostly for making brick roads. The chairpersons claimed that 200-250 persons participated in this activity for seven to ten days each, with bricks supplied by the chairpersons.[37] Since the muster rolls were also maintained by the chairpersons, and none of the villagers interviewed were aware of how the JRY operated, the chairpersons and panchayat secretaries were asked to name a few participants. Some of the persons named denied receiving wages but admitted contributing free labor (*shramdan*) to prevent water logging in residential areas.

Other evidence indicates that the whole operation was masterminded by the chairpersons, panchayat secretaries, and village level workers for their personal benefit. The brick-laying activity was typically undertaken in busy months for agricultural laborers, resulting in their virtual exclusion. None of the panchayat members knew anything about the scheme and it is doubtful whether the poor benefited from the scheme at all. Indeed, in one case, the brick laying activity was completed well before the JRY grant was received.

The IRDP also failed dismally. Instead of the village assembly identifying the beneficiaries, the chairpersons selected them. In one instance, it was widely known that the chairperson extracted heavy fees; he subsequently absconded, following complaints. Even under the new chairperson, however, little seemed to change, and it was evident that a lack of awareness of the scheme and weak accountability mechanisms in the village community tended to perpetuate the status quo.

The role of the gram panchayat in other rural development schemes, such as village hygiene and sanitation, literacy, consolidation of holdings (*chakbandi*), and land transfers, reflected gross negligence or the unmistakable influence of a few dominant groups. Few of the panchayat members (including the chairperson) expressed concern about the lack of access to drinking water, primary health care facilities, poorly functioning schools, unhygienic conditions, and other development issues.[38] This fails to explain the many instances of chakbandi favoring a few influential and wealthy individuals that came to light during the survey. Large plots nearer the main road were assigned to a select few by the chairpersons in connivance with a few village officials, for a "fee." In another case, the cremation ground of a poor community was declared as farm land and allotted to an influential family.

Given the monopoly power of the panchayats in land allotment, employment, credit, health care, and education, there are ample opportunities for earning "rents," especially from affluent sections. The UP survey revealed a lack of transparency in panchayat decision-making even under the new system. Through the village-level workers, the chairpersons had access to information on various government schemes. Financial records were maintained by the panchayat secretary. To the extent that access to such information was limited to this group, monopoly rents accrued to it. It is therefore not surprising that important decisions were taken by this group, mostly without involvement of other panchayat members. Nor did the community play any significant role. Gram sabha meetings seldom took place and were reduced to mere rituals. The meetings were not publicized, their frequency was disputed, the agenda was manipulated, caste and other factors influenced important decisions, and intimidation and violence were frequently employed to force compliance. Under the new legislation, even accountability to higher authorities is ineffective because chairpersons can only be dismissed through a no-confidence motion. Meanwhile, a high degree of social stratification, with upper castes being dominant, limits the prospects of collective protest.

Agency Design and Incentives: A Comparison of Indian and Korean Irrigation Systems

The importance of agency design and incentives is illustrated in a striking way by comparing the Indian and the Korean irrigation systems.[39]

In the former, the canal patroller is a full-time employee and is not allowed to farm more than a small amount of land. He is usually not posted in his native village and is recruited by the Irrigation Department, which also pays his salary. He is not supposed to remain in one location more than six years. These features are meant to ensure that there is no collusion between irrigation staff and farmers.

The irrigation system is also subject to myriad checks and balances that are designed to check corruption but have the unintended effect of hampering its efficient functioning. Financial control and expenditure are rigidly separated. If, for example, a canal develops a breach, neither the foreman nor the assistant engineer may undertake repairs without the permission of the executive engineer. Under such an arrangement, it suits the assistant engineer to wait until the breach deteriorates and there is time to obtain a formal approval of funds for repairs.

Standing apart from the end-users and restricted in responding better to villagers' needs, canal patrollers are confined to routine tasks. Their bureaucratic superiors meanwhile are more concerned with political pressures, since the risk of unwelcome transfers is a real one. Requests from subordinates are typically ignored in favor of arbitrary or manipulative decisions imposed from above. These decisions could take the form of favoring farms belonging to large landowners and/or specific villages.

By contrast, the Korean system is managed by local associations with close links to the state as well as the communities. The president of an association is appointed by the Agriculture Ministry. Staff salaries and operational budgets of these associations are partly funded by the water charges collected by these associations. The professional staff are locally recruited, and the patrollers must themselves be end-users. Compared to one from India, a Korean patroller thus has stronger incentives to perform well—his own interest in obtaining water for irrigation, avoiding sanctions from his own community and preservation of his job. Not subject to transfers, he and his colleagues develop strong working relationships and exert peer pressure on one another.

Complementarity, Cooperation, and Coordination: Irrigation Associations in Taipei,China[40]

Irrigation systems in Taipei,China are among the best in the world. Their efficiency, however, is due less to the heavy investment by the government and more to the institutional arrangement that ensures a high degree of cooperation and coordination between the officials and farmers. In contrast to the preceding comparison, this case study demonstrates how appropriate incentives can be designed so that irrigation officials work closely with farmers' groups and respond to their concerns in a coordinated manner.

A feature of Taipei,China is abundant rainfall with uneven distribution in both space and time. Much of the rainfall is concentrated in the northeastern part while most of the cultivated land is on the west coast. Moreover, more than 80 percent of the rainfall occurs between June and October, with hardly any rainfall in the west coast during the winter season. Thus, effective irrigation management is vital for agricultural development. Another important feature is the small size of farms, i.e., an average of 1.1 hectares in 1992. As a consequence, collective action by a large number of small irrigators, and their coordination with irrigation officials are central to an effective irrigation management system.

The 17 Irrigation Associations (IAs) in Taipei,China manage and operate irrigation systems in one or more hydraulic regions. IAs are parastatal agencies legally owned and formed by farmers and supervised by government agencies at higher levels. IAs enjoy a measure of autonomy and are allowed to levy water fees. Within a region, a management station coordinates water allocation to different areas.

Within an irrigation district, the operation and maintenance are coordinated by a network of irrigation groups (IGs). An irrigation district is further divided into several irrigation blocks. Within each block, farmers are organized into irrigation teams (ITs) for operation and maintenance tasks. While both IGs and ITs are self-organized farmers' units, they appear in the organization chart as subsidiaries of the IAs. In fact, however, "the image that farmers are the boss of the IAs is very clear in the mind of IA officials" (Lam 1999, 1044).

Government agencies at various jurisdictional levels are also involved in the management of irrigation. At the local level, it is county governments; at the provincial level, it is the Provincial Water Conservancy Bureau; and at the national level, the Council of Agriculture is the lead agency.

Farmers can resolve conflicts at different levels of IAs. To reduce the potential for conflicts due to excessive participation, the scope of *farmers' participation* is carefully defined. For example, while farmers have much leverage in deciding water allocation within an irrigation block, the amounts of water allocated to particular blocks are determined by the IAs.

Various rules enhance the *complementarity* between the IAs and farmers. In a co-production process such as that involving irrigation, there is a strong complementarity between irrigation officials and farmers.[41] While officials might possess "scientific" knowledge about the physical aspects of irrigation, farmers possess time- and place-specific local knowledge of the system upon which their livelihood depends. Arrangements such as farmer representation, payment of water fees, and the status of IAs as juristic entities formed and owned by farmer members help sustain the mutual dependence between the IAs and the farmers.

A high degree of complementarity of interests also exists among the IA officials—specifically, the prevalence of lifetime careers aligns the careers of the officials with the fate of the organization. The stable membership of the organization allows the officials to adopt a longer time horizon in their relationships with one another.

The *asymmetries of interests and power* between those charged with authority and those supposed to obey may potentially encourage the former to abuse authority and dampen the incentives of the latter to perform better. An innovative feature dealing with such problems is that the alignment of authority and responsibility is backed not just by bureaucratic rules but also by norms and social sanctions. To illustrate, while a working station chief has *great* authority in handling water allocation within his jurisdiction, he is also responsible for what happens in the areas. If there is a persistent problem in these areas, he may face criticism from his colleagues. In addition, given the lengthy stay of the station chief, he may be subject to pressure from the local community to adopt corrective or remedial measures.[42]

Domains of *autonomy* at different levels allow problem-solving abilities to be applied. Within the IA, for example, the working stations determine water delivery and distribution in consultation with local farmers. At the field level, the irrigation groups (IGs) also retain a certain degree of autonomy in allocating water within irrigation blocks (Lam 1999). In addition, in areas with rotation irrigation, they decide how to finance the operation and maintenance activities at the local level.

Autonomy does not imply a hands-off mode of management. Instead, it is supported by various mechanisms. First, the scope of autonomy is clearly defined and understood, e.g., the autonomy of IGs from the IAs emphasizing the dominant position of farmers vis-à-vis the IAs. Second, autonomy at lower levels is nested within higher level institutions. If the IAs fail to manage irrigation satisfactorily, for example, the problems are transmitted to the next higher level. Thus, opportunities for problem solving are combined with backup by higher levels.

Irrigation Associations in Taipei,China offer significant lessons not just in efficient water delivery but also in the incentive structure that ensures cooperation and coordination between irrigation officials and farmers. The relevance of the latter in a broader context of decentralization is hard to dispute.

Decentralization, Corruption, and Poverty

As noted earlier, corruption refers to the abuse of public power for private benefit. Acts of corruption could be classified as: (i) bureaucratic or political, (ii) cost-reducing or benefit-enhancing to the briber, (iii) bribee- or briber-initiated, (iv) coercive or collusive (the latter is also sometimes referred to as corruption with theft),[43] (v) centralized or decentralized, (vi) predictable or arbitrary, and (vii) involving cash payment or not. Corruption is essentially a governance problem that results from a weak system of checks and balances, and the lack of accountability mechanisms in the government. It exists when individuals or organizations have monopoly power over a good or service, discretion over making decisions, limited or no accountability, and low levels of income (Klitgaard 1998).[44]

A number of studies have investigated the magnitude and mechanisms of corruption's effects on growth, inequality and poverty.[45] Mauro's (1995) pioneering work established a significant negative relationship between corruption and average annual economic growth rate, and between corruption and investment. If Bangladesh were to improve the integrity and efficiency of its bureaucracy to the level of that of Uruguay, its investment would be higher by 5 percentage points and its annual growth rate by about half a percentage point. In a subsequent study Mauro (1997) found that corruption also reduces expenditures on health and education. Tanzi and Davoodi (1997), on the other hand, report that corruption increases public investment at the expense of private investment, and skews the composition of public expenditure away from the maintenance of past investment towards new investment. Consequently, the productivity of public investment and infrastructure is reduced. Corruption also reduces the tax revenue because of the collusion between tax and customs officials, and their clients. Wei (1997a, b) confirms that corruption, acting like a tax, reduces foreign direct investment (FDI). Specifically, the less predictable the level of corruption (i.e., the higher is its variance), the greater is its impact on FDI as higher variance makes corruption act like an unpredictable and random tax that increases risk and uncertainty. Thus, increases in corruption and in its randomness are equivalent to a higher tax rate on enterprises. To illustrate, if India's corruption level were reduced to Singapore's level, it is equivalent to a reduction in the corporate tax rate of 22 percent.

While all of these point to the adverse effects of corruption on poverty through a dampening of growth, a detailed investigation of the effect of corruption on poverty was carried out recently by Gupta et al. (1998). They argue that corruption affects poverty in essentially two different ways, namely (i) by dampening economic growth, and (ii) by increasing inequality. Since the first has already been extensively discussed, we focus on the latter.

Higher corruption is associated with higher income inequality. A worsening of the corruption index of a country by one standard deviation (2.52 points on a scale of 0 to 10) is associated with an increase in the Gini coefficient of income distribution of about 4.4 points. This is equivalent to the effect on the Gini coefficient of a reduction in average secondary schooling of 2.3 years.[46] Although the effect varies with the specification used, corruption unambiguously increases poverty. A one standard deviation increase in the growth rate of corruption (a deterioration of 0.78 percentage points) is associated with a decline in income growth of the bottom 20 percent of the population of 1.6 percentage points per year.[47] Further, the negative effect of corruption on social spending (i.e., social security and welfare, education and health spending, and total social spending) is confirmed. In view of these effects, corruption is likely to aggravate poverty significantly.[48]

Recent literature is sharply divided on the relationship between decentralization and corruption. Wade (1997), for example, argues that India's over-centralized top-down structure is largely responsible for corruption in the irrigation bureaucracy. In contrast, Brueckner (1999) is emphatic that corruption is more likely to be a serious problem among local governments. In a comprehensive theoretical exposition, Bardhan and Mookerjee (2000a, b) argue that a centralized bureaucracy creates incentives to divert resources to the nonpoor, who can better afford to pay bribes. On the other hand, local governments are vulnerable to capture by the wealthy. The verdict on the relationship between decentralization and corruption must therefore rest largely on empirical evidence. Fisman and Gatti (2000) examine this relationship using cross-country data. The focus is on whether fiscal decentralization has any effect on corruption. The analysis confirms a strong negative effect of decentralization on corruption. Specifically, an increase of one standard deviation in decentralization is associated with a 40 percent improvement in the standard deviation of a country's corruption index. To correct for potential endogeneity bias, an instrumental-variable estimation technique is used, in which the legal tradition of a country—whether French (civil code) or British origin (common law)—serves as the instrument for decentralization.[49] Again, a higher degree of decentralization is associated with a lower measured corruption.

Although this is a useful analysis, the above has its limits. First is its aggregate nature; contextual specificity would have been crucial because the forms of corruption and processes involved differ greatly, as illustrated below. Second, it throws no light on *how* rents are extracted and therefore on *why* they remain unchecked. Case studies of Karnataka (an Indian state) and of Bangladesh offer useful insights (for details, see Crook and Manor 1998).

As a supplementary evidence, the case of Karnataka presents a paradox: While the number of people involved in corrupt acts increased significantly, the overall amount stolen decreased modestly. With decentralization, the number of people with influence increased. There were 3000 elected councillors in every district, as against more than a score of legislators, bureaucrats, and others previously. So the view that district and mandal panchayats/councils decentralized corruption is plausible. On the other hand, decentralization also meant greater transparency and accountability.

Before decentralization, a large fraction of the funds meant for development was siphoned off by ministers and legislators before reaching lower levels. At the lower taluk or subdistrict level, there was a Taluk Development Board consisting of directly elected members. But this was far weaker than the district and mandal councils, and its members had far less information about and influence over development programs. A few persons consisting of the chairman of the board, the taluk's state legislator, the block development officer, the chief engineer and the accounts officer, had access to information, and tight control over funds. These funds were surreptitiously misappropriated by this small circle among themselves and their friends and relatives.

Although new councillors continued to steal funds and accepted bribes under the new arrangement, the openness of the system made it harder to siphon off large amounts without risking discovery. Although notional estimates of corruption among the districts vary between 5 to 25 percent of council funds, there was greater concentration at the lower end.[50] By existing standards for developing countries, this is an impressive achievement (see Crook and Manor 1998 for details). Between the time this system lapsed in 1991 and the new one emerged after the 73rd Constitutional Amendment Act, there was a sudden increase in corruption, implying that decentralization played a role in reducing corruption.

In some ways, the Bangladesh case provides a striking contrast. The share of development funds stolen was much larger, ranging from 30 to 40 percent. The main beneficiaries were subdistrict chairmen and councillors, their clients and friends, contractors of public works projects, and bureaucrats at the district and subdistrict levels—in other words, it was mostly corruption with theft. The chairmen and councillors indulged in corruption as a means to recover the huge costs of their election; similarly, the bureaucrats had to bribe their recruiters; and the contractors colluded with the chairmen and councillors in inflating project expenses. High levels of corruption persisted in the absence of a vigilant press, and a competitive party system. However, many of the chairmen of subdistrict councils were rejected by the electorate after their first five-year term expired in 1990. Although it made sense for some new chairmen to steal as much as they could, fearing rejection after their five-year term, there were others who valued their reputation more. Despite all their shortcomings, elections ensured a degree of accountability and checked rampant corruption.

After subdistrict councils were abolished in 1991, some forms of corruption increased. For example, farmers seeking pump sets and other benefits from the government had to pay huge bribes, whereas before, councillors provided them free or for smaller payoffs. Thefts of wheat also increased sharply.

In sum, although decentralization increases the number of people involved in corruption, greater transparency and accountability of local governments helps curtail corruption after a time. In the event of a capture of the government by the elite, however, the poor may be no better off under decentralization than under centralization.

Role of the Community

The nature and extent of community involvement largely determines whether the provision of local public goods is efficient and whether the poor benefit from it. The value system, resources, institutions, and incentives shape these outcomes. Given the limited public awareness of the potential benefits of cooperation, lack of social cohesion, legal and other impediments, NGOs have an important role in mobilizing community support and in enhancing the well-being of the members. The case studies reviewed below examine the community's potential and the constraints that hamper it.

Values, Incentives, and Community Involvement in Primary Education: A Comparative Analysis of Two Villages in India and the PRC

There are well-known reasons why the provision of primary education cannot be left to the market forces (this case study draws upon Drèze and Saran 1995). These reasons include credit-market imperfections, positive externalities associated with education, and education being a merit good. For these reasons, markets would undersupply education. Illustrative evidence from the PRC and India points to marked variation in female literacy rates that are unrelated to differences in per capita income or the incidence of poverty. In rural India in 1991, the female literacy rate varied from 12 percent in Rajasthan to 85 percent in Kerala despite the absence of any significant difference in poverty. But the corresponding rate in Punjab was similar to that of West Bengal, although the incidence of poverty in the latter was three times that in the former. Similarly, in 18 out of 30 provinces in the PRC that had a rural per capita income between 400 and 600 *yuan* per year in 1989, rural female literacy rates varied from 11 to 75 percent. Moreover, it is striking that Kerala with a much lower level of per capita income than the PRC, is not only way ahead of the PRC in terms of rural literacy, it surpasses *every* province in that country.

Neither differences in private income nor differences in aggregate resources (i.e., the sum of public outlays on education and private income) are sufficient to explain the provision of primary education and its quality, a fact amply demonstrated by a comparison of Palanpur (a village in the Indian state of Uttar Pradesh) and She Tan (a village in the PRC province of Zhejiang). Palanpur has remained educationally backward despite a generous injection of resources, while She Tan has maintained an impressive record despite a resource crunch. This is not to suggest that resources do not matter. Instead what is emphasized here is that, given the resources, value system, incentives, and community's involvement matter more.

Education in Palanpur has been neglected over several generations. In 1981, the male literacy rate was 28 percent and the female rate barely 6 percent. These rates rose to 33 and 8 percent in 1991, respectively. By contrast, She Tan had already achieved impressive literacy rates in 1978, with little bias against females. Despite a resource crunch following the introduction of the household responsibility system, enrolment rates for adolescents in 1993, as in 1978, were maintained at close to 100 percent.[51]

Value systems differ markedly between Palanpur and She Tan. In the former, the discrimination in labor markets limits opportunities for low-caste households. Neglect of girls' education is linked to the kinship system and sexual division of labor. A girl shifts to her in-laws after marriage and only sons are supposed to provide filial support to the parents. Besides, women are expected to devote themselves exclusively to domestic chores, which require little education. By contrast, parents in She Tan attach high importance to the education of their children. The relative lack of gender bias in education is also partly associated with a higher degree of gender symmetry in employment, property rights, and marriage practices.

Incentives for educating children also differ between the two villages. In Palanpur, although the fees are not high, the opportunity costs are, given the value of child labor. Travel costs are also high for attending a better school in another village. On the supply side, disincentives such as the absence of a link between performance and remuneration of teachers have resulted in teacher absenteeism. In She Tan, by contrast, the disincentives are weaker but have the potential of dampening the demand for school education in the transition to the household responsibility system.

The role of the community presents yet another contrast. There is no effective village council or village government in Palanpur to supervise and mediate between the district administration and the village community. The caste-based fragmentary politics at the village level also prevents collective action or the development of responsive institutions. In She Tan, by contrast, there is a village government and a party organization that respond to the community's concerns and needs including improving the school's functioning and disciplining wayward teachers.

Legal Impediments: The Case of School Management Committees in Punjab, Pakistan

Legal impediments can thwart beneficiary participation in both the operation and management of elementary schools. This is strikingly illustrated in the following case (adapted from SPDC 2001).

School Management Committees (SMCs) were set up in Punjab, consisting of three nominated teachers, three locally influential persons or social workers, and three elected parents.[52] Fearing domination by outsiders, the SMCs were restricted to teachers and parents in a ratio of 1:3, with parents' representatives being elected. The mandate of the SMCs included improvements in the quality of school education, checking absenteeism of teachers, maintenance of school buildings and fund raising. Each SMC had its own bank account, operated by the president of the committee and one elected parent, thus ensuring transparency. The monitoring of teacher performance and attendance led to some improvement in the quality of teaching. Funds were mobilized to expand the facilities and to improve the physical infrastructure. However, following an attempt to empower SMCs to debit pay based on performance, the Punjab Teachers' Association filed a suit in the courts to have SMCs declared illegal entities. The courts upheld the petition, and the SMCs ceased to function.

Health and Education Programs in Bangladesh

Primary health care is largely a government responsibility in Bangladesh, although the quality of service leaves much to be desired. There is lack of hygiene and maintenance of equipment; irregular attendance by medical personnel; pervasive corruption in everything from a place in the consultation queue, to provision of medicine, access to hospital beds, and provision and quality of diet (Sobhan 1998). Many services are supposed to be provided free or at nominal costs, with the principal users of these facilities being the poorer classes. In practice, however, about 80 percent of a poor household's health expenditure is spent on private services providers that are frequently administered by faith healers, underqualified practitioners, and charlatans. Inefficiencies of the public system stem from weak administration, lack of accountability, and strong trade unionism among the medical staff.

In sharp contrast, the Bangladesh Rural Advancement Committee (BRAC), an NGO, provides a more effective although limited range of health services to the poor like maternal care, family planning, health and nutrition education primarily through community-based health workers. Considerable importance is given to the selection, training and performance of the staff. Selection and promotion are based strictly on merit. Community participation is encouraged to promote preventive health care. Some 73 percent of those registered in the BRAC program regularly use its facilities, as against the 15-25 percent who use public facilities.

Among the strengths of the BRAC programme are the accurate targeting of the poor, supervision and accountability of staff members, and active community involvement. A similar system is replicated by *Gono Shasto Kendro* (GSK) in an extensive health care and insurance facility for an upazila, Savar, and extended recently to North Bengal and the slums of Dhaka. Many smaller NGOs provide poor villagers and slum dwellers a range of medicare, including medical and family planning services immunization and small clinics.

A partnership has evolved between the government and BRAC, resulting in a remarkably successful expanded program of immunization (EPI) in Bangladesh. The latter complements the efforts of the former through awareness building and advocacy exercises, training, research, and monitoring.

The government is also the principal provider of primary education in Bangladesh. In 1994/1995, out of 62,617 primary schools, 60 percent were government-run schools, enrolling 72 percent of all students. The public system of primary education suffers from the lack of accountability of teachers, resulting in low standards of performance, contact hours, and quality of instruction. Overcentralized educational administration, rampant corruption, and lack of firmness in dealing with teachers' unions have had a crippling effect on the system. Consequently, even with larger educational outlays, the benefits to the poor are not likely to be substantial. By contrast, NGOs like BRAC have produced impressive results in nonformal education, with 11,000 schools dispersed across rural Bangladesh. The dropout rate in these schools is a mere 2 percent in a three-year program, as against 60 percent in government primary schools. Their schools are designed to suit the needs of the rural poor. Awareness building is combined with appropriate school hours and teaching methods, chosen in consultation with local communities. Supervision rests in a five-member local school committee, composed of teachers, community leaders, and BRAC officials. Responsiveness to community needs and its involvement in supervision distinguish BRAC schools from government schools, and account for the distinctly superior performance of the former. Partnerships between the government and NGOs in primary education are thus potentially of considerable importance for the poor.

Sustainable Development: The New Kerala Model

Kerala recently carried out a comprehensive decentralization program aimed at development, social improvement, and environmental sustainability,[53] making it a particularly interesting case for studying the community-based strategy for sustainable development.[54]

Following the 73rd Constitutional (Amendment) Act, Kerala allocated 35-40 percent of its 1996 annual budget for new development plans to the projects designed by local bodies. The latter were expected to match 25 percent of the grant with funds from beneficiaries and other sources and contributions of labor, material, or cash.

A striking feature of this new experiment was that *agency* was put before *structure*. Specifically, financial devolution preceded the division of functional responsibilities between the local bodies and the state government. The presumption was that the actual practice of participatory planning and implementation in the context of a mass campaign would evolve into an effective functional division. Another important feature was that the new participatory development programs emphasized joint productive interests to build up broad alliances among different interest groups. A third feature of decentralized planning was that it aimed to increase agricultural production, alleviate ecological problems, improve the quality of social infrastructure, and tackle gender injustice and deprivation in tribal groups.

In August 1996, the State Planning Board launched the "People's Planning Campaign" wherein 100,000 volunteers were trained to assist local bodies. In gram sabha meetings, more than two million people expressed their felt needs; voluntary experts and ward representatives identified the main problems and drafted development reports; based on these reports, sectoral task forces—comprising local officials, voluntary experts, and resource persons—drafted project proposals; village panchayats then prioritized these proposals within a broad set of guidelines for sectoral allocations; the local plans of 991 village panchayats were integrated in 152 block panchayat plans and 14 district panchayat plans; in consultation with district-level officers, block- and district-level panchayat representatives approved the plans in seminars; and, finally, district- and block-level expert committees gave the required technical sanctions.

The local plans in 1997/1998 produced nearly 68,000 projects, from repairing irrigation ponds, to developing cooperative vegetable gardens, establishing women's enterprises, building houses for squatter families, and reviving ritual traditions. Delays were solved through informal rules developed between different stakeholders. The adoption of productive and sustainability goals in the local plans shows a mixed record (Veron 2001). Compliance with prescribed sectoral allocations was weak since the majority of projects were consumption-oriented, individual beneficiary schemes were more common than group-based activities, and subsidy rates were high. The bulk of beneficiary contributions were mandatory contributions for receiving subsidized goods. Furthermore, the projects were partial interventions such as single-crop schemes that neglected ecology and marketing. In sum, most projects were qualitatively similar to those implemented by line agencies earlier (Veron 2001).

Among the few exceptions to this record, however, was the establishment of a "labor bank" through the initiative of an agricultural officer of a south Keralan village panchayat, designed to ensure assured supply of labor at short notice, a crucial requirement for paddy cultivation. A new body, the "Farmers' Helping Group", composed of representatives of panchayats, farmers and laborers, and government officers, was constituted. This group negotiated a fixed wage rate, provided training, and subsidized farm inputs. As a result, within a short period, there was agricultural intensification and employment generation, and reversal of environmentally unsound conversion of wetland. Both the participating laborers and farmers benefited.

Another exception relates to the integration of environmental concerns in some sectoral projects. For housing projects, for example, an NGO produced environment-friendly building materials. In a few cases committed government officers and scientists were instrumental in promoting the use of environment-friendly technology. In general, however, this was not the case (e.g., soil and water conservation projects failed as they were not part of an overall watershed management plan).

While decentralized planning thus expanded the scope for civil society, panchayats, NGOs, and officials to implement sustainable development projects, community participation alone did not lead to environmental projects. To some extent, the neglect of environmental impact assessment and monitoring of environmental standards by state institutions also contributed to the unimpressive record of decentralized planning in sustainable development.[55]

Although it was notable for its financial devolution and the involvement of communities in identifying, designing and implementing projects, the new Kerala model failed to produce the desired results for several reasons.

Despite the greater transparency in decision making, the network among locally influential persons led to an arbitrary selection of projects. One of the reasons was that, confronted with the often harsh trade-offs between immediate livelihood needs and long-term environmental protection, the former apparently became a stronger consideration. As a lesson borne out by decentralized planning in sustainable development, it bears repeating that sensitivity to environmental concerns cannot be taken for granted even in communities that depend heavily on natural resources. The immediate concerns expressed in village development plans need to be counterbalanced by the spatial and temporal externalities that would be articulated in higher-level planning. This is easier said than done, considering the difficulty of reconciling conflicting interests between popular participation and top-level planning.

A crucial requirement for community-based development is to clearly identify and strengthen areas of synergies between the state government, local bodies, and civil society. The Kerala model has tried to induct local civil servants into the process of decentralized planning. In addition, the transparency of financial allocations has also increased. Yet much depends on the commitment and dynamism of a few officials and development volunteers. Whether the development of line agencies under panchayats with some performance-linked incentives would make a difference deserves investigation.

In conclusion, while it would be premature to reject the Kerala model as inappropriate, the risk of "community failure" in environmental protection is indeed real and serious.[56]

Summing Up

The dominant thread running through all the cases discussed in this section has been the importance of community involvement. The comparison of primary education in a village in the PRC and India suggested that resources are less important than parental attitudes, community institutions, and accountability of teachers in explaining markedly lower literacy rates, especially among females. However, the community's response may be constrained by legal impediments, inertia, lack of cohesion, and ignorance regarding the potential benefits of cooperation.

Such constraints can be overcome through an imaginative nurturing of community involvement, as in the case of the Bangladesh's BRAC involved in health care and primary education. Of particular significance is the innovation of building social organizations around locally useful infrastructure projects.

Coalitions of the Poor

As a few case studies have illustrated, local governments or community-based organizations (CBOs) do not always adequately serve the interests of the poor, even when they are represented or when they are responsible for poverty alleviation programs. An important ingredient in transforming the nature of such organizations is a strong coalition of the poor. Some lessons from the literature are reviewed below (this draws upon Gaiha and Kulkarni 1999).

Paradoxically, cooperation today depends on whether cooperative action was successful in the past. The latter may be associated with shared norms of fairness, reciprocity and trust in a community.[57] Whether such norms will be observed in vertical social networks (as opposed to horizontal ones, involving people of similar status and power) is of course an open issue (for an important contribution, see Putnam 1993). In the Indian context, for example, caste hierarchies act as a barrier to cooperative or collective action among the poor. Some evidence, however, suggests that if the prospective gains are large, the disadvantages of a socially heterogeneous membership (e.g., the absence of a sense of collective identity) may be overcome. The problems of social heterogeneity are nevertheless sometimes compounded by economic inequalities. The capture of organizations such as village panchayats by the local elite, for example, remains unchallenged by the poor, since the latter are often trapped in interlocking transactions with the former (an agricultural laborer, for example, is usually in debt to his employer).

Ultimately, land reforms, or, more specifically, land redistribution through possibly a market-mediated mechanism could weaken the dominance of the elite and induce a more effective participation of the poor in panchayats. Bardhan (1997, 60) puts it succinctly:

> One beneficial by-product of land reform, underemphasized in the usual economic analysis is that such reform, by changing the local political structure in the village, gives more voice to the poor and induces them to become involved in local self-governing institutions and the management of local public goods.

A related issue is whether economic betterment should precede empowerment. Manor (1999) is somewhat sceptical of this view.[58] Participation of the poor in local self-governing institutions of course helps in evolving a sense of collective identity and inculcating a sense of public duty. But this process of empowerment is often slow and incremental, if not uncertain. A more rapid process of empowerment follows economic betterment.

Case studies in Carr et al. (1996) give a vivid portrayal of this process. Of particular interest are the roles of the Self-Employed Women's Association (SEWA) and the Cooperative Development Foundation (CDF) in India. Promotion of women's producer groups by SEWA and of women's credit and thrift societies by CDF—despite initial scepticism among the members—has led to more than moderate income gains among the members on a regular basis. Income gains, coupled with the experience of managing producer groups/cooperatives, have imparted to them greater self-confidence, security and independence both *within* and *outside* the household. There is a sense of solidarity among them, and caste divisions have weakened. Women now advise their husbands on cropping decisions. Their advice is also sought on community matters (e.g. sanitation). Greater political awareness has led to more active participation in local elections.[59, 60]

If the centrality of economic betterment in empowerment is accepted, the complementarity between Panchayats and other rural organizations (e.g., cooperatives, labor unions) acquires an added significance. As a result of economic betterment, through self-managed activities, the poorer/weaker sections become better equipped to play a more assertive role in the panchayats. On the other hand, to the extent that there are fixed costs in organizing the poor, through meetings, awareness campaigns, and dissemination of information, labor unions could reduce them significantly by enlarging their membership.[61]

STRATEGIC OPTIONS

Political Economy

As emphasized earlier, decentralization is often a political process, as it tends to disrupt the power and privileges of some influential groups. Depending on the strength of their coalitions, the process could be slow, uneven and uncertain. Broadly, therefore, a medium-term strategy of 10-15 years must be formulated, based on a careful identification of the allies and opponents of decentralization in a particular context, and an understanding of their motivations, and the mechanisms that could weaken the resistance to it. The pace of decentralization may have to be gradual if administrative and other capacities differ at subnational levels.[62] Political debates and mass campaigns to highlight the merits of decentralization, for example, have the potential to enlarge the constituency for it. Locally elected governments are not immune to pressures from above, especially if there are quotas for representatives of state assemblies and national parliaments. They often use their voting rights and political clout to sidetrack local priorities and build their own constituencies. Similarly, district- and state-level bureaucrats and civil servants represented in local government bodies have their own agenda that may not necessarily reflect local needs.[63] One option is to restrict their participation and withdraw their voting rights. Whether a competitive multi-party system can resolve some of these difficulties is not self-evident largely because there is a risk that local interests might get submerged in larger ideological battles. On the question of the inclusion of the poor, there are three priorities: (i) legislating inclusive democracy by requiring quotas for women and other disadvantaged groups; (ii) strengthening their local- and state-level organizations; and (iii) facilitating access to information.[64] The latter may also result in greater transparency of local governments and help curb corruption.[65]

Fiscal Devolution

Intergovernmental fiscal (IGF) relations are vital to the success of decentralization. IGF instruments are appropriately viewed as a source of a variety of incentives. They may help establish priorities, express government policies, ensure equity, and promote efficiency and accountability to both higher levels of government as well as local constituencies.[66] In designing these instruments, careful attention must be given to local requirements and fiscal capacities. Greater fiscal autonomy to local governments requires (i) a higher share of transfers as untied grants, (ii) converting these grants into a share of state revenues, (iii) defining through state legislation an equalization formula to allocate grants to local governments, and (iv) increasing the sources of own revenues through own and assigned taxes and strengthening their capacity to collect. Direct local government access to capital markets may also be facilitated, shifting from the current system where central government credit institutions subsidize interest rates and give loans projects that are often nonviable (Smoke 1999).[67] Equally important in the context of poverty alleviation is the need for greater flexibility in designing and implementing centrally sponsored schemes (such as rural public works) at the local level. Local governments must have an important role in choosing the mix and scale of services, delivery systems, financing, and remedial measures, if required. On the other hand, greater local autonomy must go hand in hand with greater accountability. Periodic audits must be combined with accountability of outcomes to the local community.

Coordination and Control

The choice of levels of government and functional responsibilities at different levels is a major priority for a decentralized system. An important issue is whether the potential benefits of decentralization can be delivered within the *existing* structure of government or whether some consolidation of levels/units or further subdivision of levels/units might be required. As far as assignment of functions is concerned, a priority is an unambiguous specification in the constitution or laws to avoid extension of control rights by higher levels of government.[68, 69]

Equally important, local governments are often burdened with responsibilities and functions that they are ill-equipped to perform. These may include activities that involve economies of scale and interjurisdictional externalities, and should not therefore be left entirely to local governments. An option in such cases may be simultaneous involvement of more than one level of government. Beyond that, however, two concerns arise, namely, who will coordinate their activities and how the coordination will be achieved. Central governments must avoid bypassing local governments in supporting user groups, since there is considerable potential for mutually beneficial relationships between local governments and user groups (e.g., revenue generation, enforcement of contracts, resource conservation). If there are nationally determined guidelines for poverty alleviation, any deviations can only be detected if there are appropriate performance indicators. Given the multiplicity of functions of local governments and their vague specification, reliance may have to be placed on some crude yardstick information. Other related issues are who will monitor and how frequently.[70]

Social Cohesion

In top-down initiatives, community involvement is often weak and tangential. As a consequence, targeting of local public goods and income redistribution activities may suffer, and potential cost reductions may not be realized. Where there is social apathy or mistrust and suspicion between different groups (belonging to, say, different castes and religions), careful attention must be given to overcoming these barriers. The spread of literacy is likely to help, along with social sensitization, and in both spheres NGOs may have a potentially important role.[71] The nature and duration of NGO involvement may, however, vary, depending, among others, on the degree of social stratification of a community. The participation of the poor or of backward groups in local governments through quotas may influence their functioning only over a period of time, as a sense of public duty is inculcated. Promoting mixed self-help groups in micro-credit schemes is another option, as successful ones have a strong demonstration effect. Whatever the options taken, however, the process of overcoming social barriers is likely to be slow and incremental.

Capacity Building

Learning horizontally is a promising option, as concrete solutions to specific problems in similar jurisdictions are often very instructive. From their peers, state and lower levels of government could learn how to identify demand, contract for delivery, and target the poor. In addition, training could be imparted to local governments in enhancing their governance capacity and fiscal responsibilities. An important concern is whether there are specific roles for NGOs and international donors. In addition, there is a need to synchronize the pace of decentralization with capacity building.[72]

CONCLUSION

The process of decentralization in Asia has been slow, and uneven. In most cases, it has been initiated from the top, and in a few motivated by an undisguised concern for political legitimacy. Such initiatives have ranged from sectoral experiments to comprehensive and ambitious blueprints for redefining and restructuring the roles of national and subnational governments. A few are of a very recent vintage and, for lack of documentation, cannot be reviewed in detail. In other cases, the quality of documentation is uneven. Subject to these caveats, however, an assessment of the role of decentralization in poverty alleviation is feasible.

The poverty alleviation outcome has been inconsistent. From the few successes as well as some failures, some insights may be gained into the factors that affect the well-being of the poor in the course of decentralization. These factors include the nature of the political regime and whether it challenges or tries to co-opt the local elite, the nature and extent of fiscal devolution, bureaucratic resistance, collusion among key functionaries of local governments, coordination at different levels of government, accountability of local governments to their constituents, and access to information about antipoverty programs. Given the focus on the role of the community as a key component of decentralization, its potential for providing health care and education despite resource constraints is of considerable significance. While resources matter, value systems, incentives, local institutions, and accountability mechanisms are no less significant. Equally instructive is the experience of extremely poor communities in building social organizations around locally useful infrastructure projects with some direction and assistance from outside. Escape from persistent poverty through community involvement is thus a real possibility. At the same time, it would be naïve to underestimate how the local power structure, the lack of trust and solidarity, and legal and other impediments can limit community involvement and the resulting benefits to the poor. From this perspective, coalitions of the poor have a critical role in ensuring more equitable outcomes.

A number of strategic options have been identified in the context of poverty alleviation. Broadly, these relate to political legitimacy of, and a constituency for, decentralization; formulating a medium-term strategy of decentralization; minimizing the influence of national and state-level politicians and civil servants; combining greater fiscal devolution with more stringent accountability of local governments to both higher authorities and constituents; administrative decentralization; putting in place an incentive structure to ensure greater cooperation among line agencies and local governments; strengthening capacities of local governments for governance; information dissemination to their constituents; revenue collection; building of trust and social cohesiveness; and coalitions of the poor.

While it is not yet evident that decentralization really benefits the poor, its potential for poverty alleviation cannot be disputed. How some strategic options are resolved and implemented may make a significant difference.

Notes

1. Deconcentration refers to the dispersal of agents of higher levels of government into lower levels of decision-making. Decentralization, on the other hand, involves devolution of political, administrative, and fiscal powers.
2. In the second half of the 20th century, nearly every country has experimented with some form of decentralization or local government reform with varying aims and outcomes (Cheema and Rondinelli 1983). The interest in decentralization continues to be pervasive, since "out of 75 developing and transitional countries with populations greater than 5 million, all but 12 claim to be embarked on some form of transfer of political power to local units of government" (Dilinger 1994, 8). What distinguishes, however, the present wave of decentralization from earlier attempts is the establishment of democratic institutions or extension of their role in many countries. In Latin America, in particular, military regimes have been replaced by elected civilian governments, and local government officials previously appointed are now elected (Parker 1995).
3. Manor (1999, 34) is emphatic that "no set of economic conditions has been a particularly important cause of decisions to decentralise." Instead, these have been more decisively influenced by the "hard-nosed calculations of self- interest" of political leaders (p. 37). Moreover, "Most decentralisers have conceived and implemented these reforms from above, on their own initiative, relatively free of pressure from below...." (p.43). Smoke (1999), however, has a broader and more persuasive view. In the Asian context, he notes, in some cases, international donor pressure without national commitment has been a key factor, while, in other cases, internal political and/or economic crises have played an important role, sometimes resulting in "quick-fix" decentralization programs that are neither carefully designed nor sustainable.

4. Parker (1995), for example, notes that many actors are involved in decentralization efforts. In particular, NGOs and community-level organizations have considerable potential in improving service delivery and in targeting disadvantaged groups.
5. In the capability approach pioneered by Sen (1980, 1987, 2000b), the emphasis shifts from primary goods to constituents of well-being—specifically, in this case, from health care to a healthy life.
6. Distinguishing between welfarism and positive freedom, Dasgupta (1986) elaborates that the former requires government allocation of positive rights goods (such as primary education and health care, as these are necessary for positive freedom) by means of transferable coupons, whereas doctrines appealing to positive freedom require their allocation in kind. This rests on a result due to Weitzman (1977). Specifically, rationing is the better mechanism if the dispersion in income is large in comparison with the dispersion in needs across the population, and the price mechanism is superior if the reverse is the case.
7. If, for example, local government in village A opted for a higher level of redistributive spending than did local government in a neighboring village B, the rich residents in A may move to B while the poor in B may move to A. Thus the cost of a given level of redistribution in A would rise.
8. If transfers from higher levels of government substitute for revenue collected through local taxation, the absolute level of redistribution that can be provided will be lower. In the Indian context, for example, the higher the share of central transfers in state government expenditure, the lower is the tax effort of state governments (Jha et al. 1998).
9. In an influential critique of utilitarianism, Sen (1980) draws attention to a fundamental anomaly. Suppose there is a cripple A who gets half the utility that another person B gets from any given level of income. Utilitarianism would then involve giving B more income than A such that marginal utilities are equated in the two cases. The cripple would thus be doubly worse off: both since he gets less utility from the same level of income and since he will also get less income. The superior efficiency of B in producing utility would divert income away from the less efficient but needier cripple.
10. Bardhan (1997, 47) puts it forcefully: "I practice, however, the local government still retains an informational advantage, and the main reason for this has to do with political accountability. In democratic countries, local politicians may have more incentive to use local information than national or provincial politicians, since the former are answerable to the local electorate while the latter have wider constituents where local issues may be diluted. Even in some authoritarian regimes, local politicians may be under more pressure than national politicians to be sensitive to local needs." It must, however, be noted that the comparative advantage of local voters in monitoring performance of local governments is

greater where important dimensions of performance involve unquantifiable aspects of service quality (Helm and Smith 1989). See Khemani (2001) for some corroborative evidence confirming that state governments' performance had a greater influence on their subsequent success in the polls than the central government—in other words, voters were better able to monitor and reward local governments for better performance.

11. On the general principles of tax assignments, see Bird (1999) and Oates (1999).
12. Until recently, the PRC differed from other developing countries in so far as local governments collected most of the revenues and "shared up" (Bardhan 1997).
13. For a detailed exposition of this and the preceding issues, see Bardhan (1997).
14. A recent study of decentralization in India draws pointed attention to limited fiscal devolution despite a landmark Constitutional (Amendment) Act to revive and restructure the Panchayats. Specifically, fiscal decentralization to village Panchayats (i.e., the share of village panchayat expenditure in total government expenditure in rural areas) in 1998/1999 ranged between 0.6 percent (Rajasthan) and 3.6 percent (Madhya Pradesh) in the states analyzed. Kerala was an exception with a share of 7.6 percent. This implies an expenditure by village panchayats of less than Rs100 per capita in most states (World Bank 2000). For a cross-country sample of estimates of subnational autonomy, see Shah (1994).
15. For an exposition, see Shleifer and Vishny (1993), and Bardhan (1997, especially Chapter 1). Bardhan (1997) provides an illustration, based on a comparison between post-communist Russia and the USSR. Formerly, the Communist Party centralized the collection of bribes, and checked any deviations from an agreed upon pattern. Today, various ministries, agencies, and officials charge their own bribes independently, with more disastrous consequences for the overall efficiency of the system.
16. Bureaucrats in poor countries, for example, often opt for imports of complex technology or goods in which over-invoicing is harder to detect than in a more standardized technology that might also be more appropriate. For similar reasons, there is also a strong preference for a few large defense contracts, as opposed to the setting up of a large number of small rural health clinics (Bardhan 1997).
17. *WDR 2001* points out that incomplete devolution of power to local levels may expand opportunities for corruption through a proliferation of regulations emanating from different levels of government.
18. As Bird (1995) puts it aptly, the central government may not know *what* to do, and the local government may not know *how* to do it.
19. For some illustrations in the Indian context see Gaiha et al. (2000).
20. For two important contributions focused on the capture of governments at different levels, see Bardhan and Mookherjee (2000a, b).

21. This is termed as the "political patronage hypothesis" by Echeverri-Gent (1993), according to which representative democratic participation generally results in the growth of organizations that capture the resources available to them, and are pushed by electoral logic to mediate the interests of the poor within a broader support base.

22. For example, the withdrawal of urban food subsidies and their replacement by income transfers to the poor or by producer subsidies is likely to be successfully resisted by urban groups, despite the support of all rural groups. For details, see de Janvry et al. (1992).

23. This case study relies largely upon Crook and Manor (1998) and Crook and Sverrisson (1999).

24. For a review of why more recent attempts at decentralization did not serve the poor better, see Westergaard and Alam (1995) and Khan (1999).

25. In the four decades following independence in 1946, there were attempts at deconcentration, which simply redistributed power within the central government bureaucracies over which the legislators and the presidents exerted much influence. As remarked by a politician, the Philippines remained a country where local governments had to appeal to national politicians to get windows fixed in the City Hall (Eaton 2001).

26. Since those seeking election to the lower House of Representatives can contest under any party label, national and subnational party leaders control neither access to the ballot nor the subsequent behavior of legislators in Congress. In this situation, electoral success depends on establishing personal reputations and delivering particularistic benefits to local constituents (Brilliantes 1998, Eaton 2001).

27. So much so that some authors regarded local governments as authoritarian enclaves (Brilliantes 1998).

28. The term "pork barrel" refers to local infrastructure projects in legislators' home districts for which they are able to secure funding from the central government.

29. In one case, the mayor was hostile, while the health department was sympathetic; in another, despite personal links to an NGO, the mayor was dismissive of their role in local governance; and, in a third case, officials had little time for NGO participation (Crook and Sverrisson 1999).

30. An analysis of the spectacular growth of township and village enterprises is carried out in a subsequent sub-section.

31. Using a production function approach, a two-way fixed-effects error-component model is estimated. The estimation is based on panel data from 28 of the 30 provinces in the PRC for the period 1970-1993. A distinctive feature of this analysis is the use of a marginal retention rate as a measure of decentralization, as opposed to the average share of government budgetary revenue retained by a province. For other details of the econometric analysis, see Lin and Liu (2000).

32. The poverty-growth elasticities range from 0.69 to 2.59, based on cross-country regressions, depending to some extent on whether economic inequalities are taken into account. For an exposition of why the range of the elasticities is so large, see Gaiha (2001a).
33. In a comment, Rondinelli (1999) objects to Rao's (1999) characterization of the new system as an "intergovernmental" system of finance, since local units are not local governments. He elaborates that since local units are branches of the central administration and do not have discretionary powers, the characterization is misleading. The New Law, however, does provide greater autonomy to all levels of government and therefore the characterization is not entirely inappropriate.
34. Rao (1999) seeks to establish the inequity of the new arrangement by regressing revenue and expenditure on GDP (all on a per capita basis) using province-level data for 1994 and 1996. Positive elasticities of revenue and expenditure to GDP are interpreted as confirming that richer provinces gained more than others. There are two difficulties with this analysis: one is that the periods precede the coming into force of the New Budget Law, and another is that there may be an omitted variable bias as interprovince income differences may be strongly correlated with efficiency in tax collection and utilization of revenues.
35. This is one failing of the Crook-Sverrisson framework (1999), for example.
36. As a result, a fuzzy equilibrium may prevail in which the agency in question does not get full credit for a good performance nor full stigma for a poor one (Tirole 1994).
37. In one case, it was reliably learnt that a relative of the chairperson owned the brick kiln.
38. Not surprisingly, some of the worst off in terms of unhygienic conditions were the poor settlements. In the villages covered by the Chiksson Gram Panchayat, for example, about 200 Muslim families shared a single drinking water tap.
39. For details, see Wade (1997) and for a review, see Das Gupta et al. (2000).
40. This draws upon Lam (1999).
41. The IA staff see themselves largely as government agents (although they do not have civil service status) and irrigation professionals (even though most of them do not have professional qualifications).
42. Recent research has drawn attention to the embeddedness of local IA officials in the local community as an important reason for the close relationship between them and farmers. IA officials are frequently residents of the local community. As a result, any irresponsible or negligent act that harms the community on their part attracts the ire of the community and could even result in social ostracism (Lam 1999).

43. As noted earlier, corruption with theft occurs when investors reap the benefits of a corrupt state machinery by forging patron-client relationships with that machinery and realize windfall gains, although the state loses revenue. An example is the collusion between customs officials and importers (Shleifer and Vishny 1993, and Bardhan 1997).

44. In private communication, D. Bromley disagrees with the view that corruption is essentially or largely a public sector phenomenon, since there is also a great deal of corruption in the private sector. He is also not persuaded that corruption causes poverty. Instead a reversal of causality i.e., poverty causes corruption is more plausible. As a detailed response cannot be given here, two brief observations are made. One is that corruption in the private sector could itself be the result of government interventions and weak enforcement of regulatory measures. On the direction of the causality, as noted in a review of the cross-country econometric evidence in this section, Bromley's conjecture is rejected.

45. Most of the econometric studies reviewed here are based on questionnaire-based surveys carried out by the Political and Economic Risk Consultancy, Transparency International and the Gallup Poll, among others. These surveys measure perceptions of corruption rather than actual corruption. The Transparency International index, for example, assesses the perception of corruption on a scale of 0 to 10. One attractive feature of different indices is that they are highly correlated among themselves (Tanzi 1998).

46. An IV estimation corroborates this result.

47. An IV estimation reinforces this result.

48. Another recent investigation of the effect of corruption on growth (Rahman et al. 2000) points out that, if Bangladesh were able to reduce corruption levels to those prevailing in advanced countries such as Canada, Denmark, and Norway, average annual growth rates could increase by 2.12-2.88 percentage points, implying per capita GNP levels of $592-$690 in 1997. An extra 2-3 percent increase in growth rate per annum could cut the incidence of extreme poverty from the current 36 percent to 11percent by the year 2020.

49. There are two possible reasons for the endogeneity bias. One is that corrupt officials of the central government may be reluctant to allow fiscal decentralization, as it would make it harder for them to extract rents. A more subtle reason is that different spending programs may have different potential for rent extraction. In that case, high-rent activities may remain with central governments while low-rent activities are assigned to local governments.

50. In general, the shares were 5 to 10 percent except in 2-3 remote districts where the shares approached 25 percent in bad years.

51. Under the household responsibility system, incomes derived from production are earned by households and not by the collective. Also, there are stringent limits to

the village government's power to tax. As a result, the financial basis of social services at the village level has weakened considerably (Dreze and Saran 1995).

52. Initially, there were 12 members. After a year, the number was reduced to nine (SPDC 2001).

53. For two recent reviews with different flavors, see Veron (2001) and Vijayanand (2001).

54. "Sustainable development is development that meets the needs of the present without compromising the ability of future generations to meet their own needs" (WCED 1987, 43). Or, as emphasized by Solow (2001, 278), "Sustainability as a moral obligation is a general obligation not a specific one. It is not an obligation to preserve this or preserve that. It is an obligation, if you want to make sense out of it, to preserve the capacity to be well-off, to be as well as we."

55. As Veron (2001) observes, the absence of private-public synergies at the macro level in regard to environmental protection counteracts the efforts of decentralized environmental planning, and may limit considerably Kerala's prospects in achieving sustainable development.

56. This is not inconsistent with Wade's (1987) influential analysis of collective action as a self-interested response in natural resource management in a sample of South Indian villages. Underlying this response were some agro-ecological conditions that favored collective action. In general, when spatial and temporal externalities are involved, cooperation may require some form of intervention.

57. For an elaboration with some illustrative evidence based on cooperatives in India, see Seabright (1997).

58. Commenting on de Janvry's (1981) view that the only reliable way to achieve an increase in participation and the collective action potential of poorer groups is to increase the resources available to them through redistributive policies, Manor (1999, 43) observes: Poor as well as prosperous people participate more and increase their collective action potential as a result of decentralization even where it works mainly to the advantage of the elites. Over time, the greater transparency offered by democratic systems at lower levels, the increased participation of poorer groups, and their developing skills at influencing those systems may well assist them in curbing the power of rural elites to appropriate benefits. The point of the evidence cited below, however, is that economic betterment induces a more rapid empowerment.

59. For similar evidence relating to self-help groups in the Maharashtra Rural Credit Project, see Gaiha (2000).

60. Some experimental studies suggest that social norms of trust and reciprocity, especially in a setting where there is communication between the parties, are just as effective in inducing cooperative behavior as externally imposed rules monitoring; besides, the norms are more effective in *sustaining* cooperative behavior (Ostrom 2000).

61. Attention may also be drawn to dynamic group network externalities among, say, rural organizations, i.e., the presence of a few successful ones induces the formation of others. Depending on the lags involved in this process, there could be sizeable reductions in the costs of organizing the poor (Gaiha 2001a, c).

62. The decentralized system in the Indian state of Kerala, for example, was developed and implemented incrementally. Nepal's Village Development Programme was also gradual. A challenge in each country is to develop an appropriate strategy that takes into account existing political imperatives, institutional structures, needs, and capacities (Smoke 1999).

63. In some cases, there are elections at all or most levels of decentralized government for leaders and/or councils, as in India. In other cases, such as Thailand, only certain levels elect officials to govern them. Even where there are local elections, some council members may be appointed by higher levels of government or serve *ex officio*, as with the Tambons in Thailand (Smoke 1999).

64. Apart from promoting self-help groups, other options that could strengthen the organizations of the poor include land reforms (Bardhan 1997) and rural public works along the lines of the Employment Guarantee Scheme in Maharashtra (Herring and Edwards 1983, Echeverri-Gent 1993, Gaiha 2001b).

65. Of particular significance in this context is the initiative of an NGO, Mazdoor Kisan Shakti Sangathan (MKSS), in improving the accountability of local governments/district administration through a sustained agitation for right-to-information in Rajasthan (an Indian state). MKSS demands, and sometimes succeeds, in gaining access to relevant records that are then subjected to a people's audit. Some of the records have revealed large-scale embezzlement of funds meant for the poor (Gaiha 2001a, IFAD 2001).

66. In fact, however, intergovernmental transfers are often unpredictable, the criteria of allocation are vague and there is rarely an effective link between local own-source revenues and resource transfers from higher levels of government. To illustrate, transfers to Tambons in Thailand and to communes in Cambodia (under an early donor-funded experiment) take the form of equal block grants regardless of differences in population or other measures of need (Smoke 1999).

67. In general, local governments in Asia have little or no direct access to capital markets or commercial lending, with the exception of a few cities in India and the Philippines. This reflects the underdevelopment of capital markets and the perception that few local governments are creditworthy.

68. In some cases, as in India, local governments are required to undertake limited functions but most other functions are "permissive" i.e., they can be undertaken subject to authorization from the state or center. There are also cases in which certain functions are assigned concurrently to more than one level of government, such as Indonesia and Viet Nam. In the most extreme scenario, local governments have few or no formally guaranteed independent rights or powers, as in Cambodia and the Lao PDR (Smoke 1999).

69. Smoke (1999) points to a dilemma: Should local governments aim for the provision of a few specific public services or for a broader range of functions involved in local area development? The issue is an important one, as decentralized programs aiming at both have not fared well. The Kecamatan Development Fund in Indonesia is a case in point. Two observations could be made. One is that local governments must not be overburdened with functions that they are ill-equipped to perform. Another, more specific, observation is that assignment of functions must be selective and based on sound economic criteria. So, the dilemma posed is an important one, as local area development may involve not only functions for which local governments are not well-equipped, but also activities with interjurisdictional externalities.

70. Some checks, however, can be built into the organizational structure. In West Bengal, for example, a multiplicity of committees such as the Public Health Standing Committee, the Village Education Committee, the Ration Committee, the Afforestation Committee, and the Night School Committee, with their rules and formal procedures, and their records and watchful members, have not only ensured an efficient division of responsibilities but also created an environment of transparency and self-policing (Mitra 2001).

71. As noted in the case studies of Bangladesh and Pakistan, NGOs and nonprofit organizations played an important role in promoting literacy and organizing the poor around local infrastructure projects. But it must be noted that they can be self-serving and elitist. They may even undermine the development of local governments, as they could pose a threat to their powerful position in the community.

72. As, for example, was illustrated by the freezing of district multiplication in the Lao PDR, as a direct consequence of manpower and other resource constraints.

PART II
Country Studies

6 Revisiting Growth and Poverty Reduction in Indonesia

ARSENIO M. BALISACAN, ERNESTO M. PERNIA, AND ABUZAR ASRA

INTRODUCTION

By international standards, Indonesia has done remarkably well in both economic growth and poverty reduction. For two decades prior to the Asian financial crisis in the late 1990s, economic growth averaged 7 percent per annum. This was the norm for East Asia and was substantially higher than the average growth rate of 3.7 percent for all developing countries. At the same time, Indonesia's poverty incidence fell from 28 percent in the mid-1980s to about 8 percent in the mid-1990s, compared with the drop from 29 percent to 27 percent in the poverty levels for all developing countries (excluding People's Republic of China [PRC]).[1] Indonesia's record also compares well with those of the PRC and Thailand whose economies grew even faster.

The Asian financial crisis, exacerbated by domestic political turbulence, hit hard the Indonesian economy, causing GDP per capita to contract in 1998 by 13 percent, effectively to what it was in 1994. Poverty rose sharply, as indicated by both official and independent estimates (e.g., ADB 2000c, Skoufias 2000, Suryahadi et al. 2000). Official figures show the proportion of people deemed poor increasing from 17.7 percent in 1996 to 24.2 percent in 1998. But just as the economic contraction caused a sharp increase in the poverty rate, the rebound in 1999 and 2000, albeit modest, led to a drop again in the poverty rate to nearly its pre-crisis level. Based on independent estimates (Suryahadi et al. 2000), poverty incidence in late 1999 was down to 10 percent, a level comparable to what it was in early 1996, after shooting up to 16 percent in mid-1998. These estimates suggest that poverty in Indonesia responds quite strongly and relatively quickly to large shocks.

While the Asian crisis adversely affected the welfare of the Indonesian people, the country's achievements in economic and human development during the past quarter-century remain impressive, especially seen against the performances of South Asia and other low and middle-income countries (Table 6.1). Indonesia's economic and social gains from the high–growth period could not be so easily wiped out by the crisis.

Indonesia's overall growth and poverty reduction experience appears to approximate the findings of studies based on cross–country regressions. Dollar and Kraay (2001), for example, show that the incomes of the poor move one–for–one with overall average incomes, suggesting that poverty reduction requires nothing much more than promoting rapid economic growth.

There is, however, more to the growth–poverty nexus than the national averages would imply. Growth and poverty reduction vary enormously across the island groups, provinces, and districts of Indonesia (Hill 1996 2002, Tadjoeddin et al. 2001, ADB 2000c, Booth 2000, Asra 2000).[2] In recent years, this variance appears to be widening, not converging, and is becoming a politically sensitive issue, given its ethnic dimensions (Hill 2002). Recent history is replete with examples showing that social or political tensions arising from economic disparities tend to dampen the return to high growth and, hence, winning the war against poverty.

An appropriate approach to socioeconomic disparities requires a clear understanding of policy and institutional factors that account for differences in the evolution of growth and poverty in the various

Table 6.1: Selected Social Indicators: Indonesia versus Other Developing Countries

INDICATOR	BEGINNING PERIOD	ENDING PERIOD
Average per Capita GDP (in 1999 PPP $)[a]	1970	2000
Indonesia	940	2,882
East Asia and Pacific	875	4,413
South Asia	1,051	2,216
Infant Mortality (per 1,000 live births)	1980	1999
Indonesia	90	42
East Asia and Pacific	55	35
South Asia	119	74
Low and middle income countries	86	59
Life Expectancy at Birth (years)		
Indonesia	55	66
East Asia and Pacific	65	69
South Asia	54	63
Low and middle income countries	60	64
Primary School Gross Enrolment Ratio (percent)[b]		
Indonesia	107	113
East Asia and Pacific	111	119
South Asia	77	100
Low and middle income countries	96	107
Secondary School Gross Enrolment Ratio (percent)[b]		
Indonesia	29	56
East Asia and Pacific	44	69
South Asia	27	49
Low and middle income countries	42	59
Adult Illiteracy (percent of people aged 15 and above)	M F	M F
Indonesia	13 27	9 19
East Asia and Pacific	13 29	8 22
South Asia	41 66	34 58
Low and middle income countries	22 39	18 32

Notes: M -Male, F -Female

a. Figures are three-year averages, centered on the year shown.

b. The most recent data pertain to 1997, instead of 1999.

Sources: World Bank (2001e) and IMF (2001).

districts of Indonesia. To what extent can differences in growth explain the observed differences in poverty reduction across provinces and districts? How important are government policies and programs, as well as geographic attributes and local institutions, in influencing poverty? What lessons can be learned from recent experience for promoting poverty reduction in the poorest areas?

Indonesia—as a case study for addressing the above questions—offers advantages that are not found in many developing countries. For one, as already noted, the country is diverse, both in geographic and institutional attributes and in economic performance. It is this diversity that permits an assessment of the influence of economywide policies and "initial" conditions on poverty. For another, comparable cross–sectional and time-series data on subnational units (provinces and districts) are available for the 1990s—a period characterized by marked changes in policy environment and economic performance. This facilitates a sufficiently disaggregative analysis and understanding of the determinants of growth and poverty reduction.

This chapter examines the key determinants of poverty reduction in Indonesia during the 1990s. The next section describes data and measurement issues. The third section uses consistently assembled district–level data to analyze the basic growth–poverty relationship. The fourth section probes the contribution of local attributes and time-varying economic factors to the variation in district–level economic performance vis-à-vis changes in poverty. A main interest here is to assess the extent to which certain policy measures can enhance or diminish the impact of growth on the living standards of the poor. The chapter concludes with implications for the design of pro-poor growth policies and institutions in Indonesia.

DATA AND MEASUREMENT ISSUES

The National Socioeconomic Survey (*Survei Sosial Ekonomi Nasional* or SUSENAS) is the main source of data for poverty and inequality analyses. The survey comes in two sets: the so-called *consumption module* and *core data* (hereafter referred to as SUSENAS module and SUSENAS core, respectively). The SUSENAS module provides detailed consumption data, is undertaken every three years, and allows disaggregation only up to the provincial level. For the 1990s, such data are available for 1993, 1996, and 1999. The SUSENAS core, on the other hand, covers not only consumption but also other socioeconomic indicators, though the specific indicators vary from year to year. Consumption data in the SUSENAS core are, however, not as detailed as those in the SUSENAS module. Indeed, consumption figures from the former are about 11 percent lower, on the average (for 1993-1999), than those from the latter. The advantage is that the data allow disaggregation up to the district level (urban district or *kotamadya,* rural district or *kabupaten*). Official government poverty figures calculated by the Central Bureau of Statistics (Biro Pusat Statistik [BPS]) are based on the SUSENAS module.[3]

We use the SUSENAS core as it yields a far greater number of observations for each survey year (285 districts versus 26 provinces).[4] However, to obtain the same aggregate poverty profile as that given by the SUSENAS module, we have adjusted the consumption data from the SUSENAS core such that the consumption expenditure means by quintile correspond to those obtained from the SUSENAS module.

On both conceptual and practical grounds, consumption is preferable to income as a measure of household welfare. Microeconomic theory suggests that since welfare level is determined by "life-cycle" or "permanent" income, and since current consumption is a good approximation of this income, current consumption is an appropriate measure of both current and long-term well-being. Indeed, measured consumption is typically less variable than measured income (Deaton 2001). For practical purposes, the difficulty of acquiring accurate information is less for consumption than for income, especially in developing countries where the governance infrastructure is weak and local markets are relatively undeveloped (Deaton 1997, Ravallion and Chen 1997, Srinavasan 2001).

The National Income Accounts (NIA) is also a distinct source of data on the country's average welfare. GDP per capita is widely used for this purpose. However, closer to the concept of average welfare, as measured by households' command over resources, is the level of personal consumption expenditure (PCE) per capita. In general, PCE, as measured in NIA, and household consumption expenditure (HCE), as measured in SUSENAS, do not necessarily correspond either as to their levels or their growth rates, largely because of differences in definitions, methods, and coverage.[5] PCE may, for example, exceed HCE simply because spending by the nonprofit sector (NGOs, religious groups, political parties) is often lumped with that by the household sector. At any rate, in the Indonesian case, average per capita levels of PCE and HCE move broadly in the same direction, at least for the 1990s (Figure 6.1).

The chosen indicator of household welfare, i.e., per capita consumption expenditure, has to be adjusted for spatial cost-of-living (SCOL) differences since prices in any given year vary substantially across provinces and districts of the country. The SCOL index is simply the ratio of the cost of attaining a level of utility in, say, province *k* to the cost of attaining the same in the reference province *r*. To the extent that spatial poverty lines are comparable in utility terms (i.e., they imply the same standard of living), then the ratio of the poverty line for province *k* to that for the reference province *r* is an appropriate SCOL index. For our purposes, we use the 1999 official poverty lines for urban areas to approximate SCOL differences for the 26 provinces as periodic surveys for consumer price index (CPI) construction cover only urban areas. Using urban poverty lines and Jakarta as the reference province (Jakarta=100), we find large interprovincial differences in cost of living, ranging from 74 percent in Southeast Sulawesi to 116 percent in Bengkulu (see Appendix Table 6.1).

Figure 6.1: Average Per Capita Expenditure: National Income Accounts versus SUSENAS (in '000 rupiah at current prices)

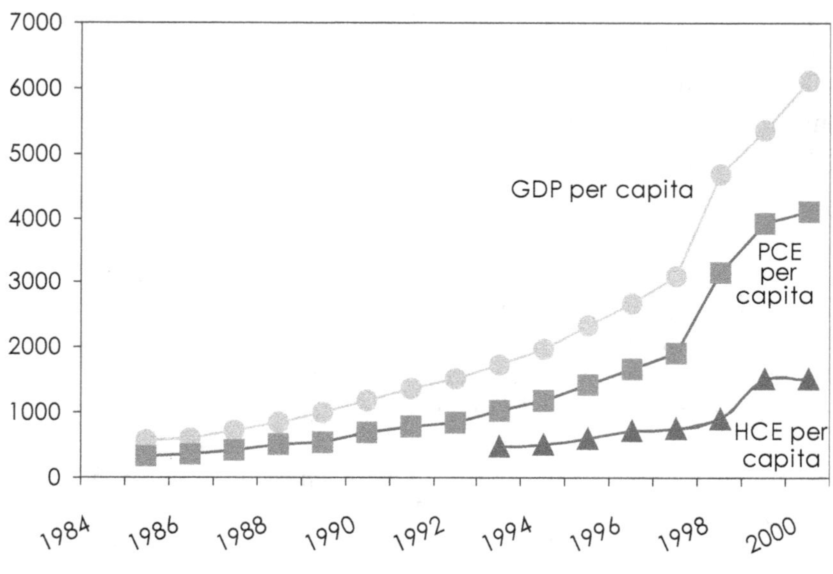

Comparison of household welfare over time also requires that the chosen welfare indicator, consumption expenditure, be adjusted for nominal price movements during the 1990s. A straightforward way to achieve this is to deflate the consumption expenditures using SCOL indices adjusted for province–specific CPI changes. For practical purposes, this would be sufficient if price movements were uniform across consumer goods during the period of interest. However, in reality the price movements vary across consumption items, especially during the economic crisis of the late 1990s.

We have constructed group–specific CPI to take account of the differential price regimes faced by the various population groups. The construction involves combining the information on province–specific price index with expenditure shares (weights), based on the 1996 SUSENAS core, for the following commodity groups: food, prepared food and beverage, housing, clothing, health, education and recreation, and transport and communication. Table 6.2 summarizes the average quintile–specific price indices for 1993-1999.

As a consequence of the sharp rupiah depreciation starting in July 1997, overall price inflation during 1996-1999 (121 percent) was much higher than in 1993-1996 (27 percent). In addition, while price changes between 1993 and 1996 (pre-crisis period) did not vary much across quintiles, they did so between 1996 and 1999 (crisis period). During the latter period, consumer price inflation was about 128 percent for the bottom quintile, while it was only 109 percent for the top quintile. The very high inflation rate for the poor during the crisis period was caused by the marked increases in the prices of food, par-

Table 6.2: CPI by Expenditure Quintile

				PERCENT CHANGE	
	1993	1996	1999	1993-96	1996-99
National Average	100.0	127.3	281.3	27.3	121.0
First (poorest)	100.0	128.2	292.2	28.2	128.0
Second	100.0	127.9	288.4	27.9	125.6
Third	100.0	127.6	284.6	27.6	123.1
Fourth	100.0	127.2	279.1	27.2	119.5
Fifth (richest)	100.0	126.1	264.0	26.1	109.4

ticularly rice, which accounts for a dominant share of the poor's consumption basket (Sigit and Surbakti 1999).[6]

The resulting national distributions of per capita consumption expenditures for the three SUSENAS years are shown in Figure 6.2. Note that the expenditures are in real terms (at 1999 prices) and have been adjusted for provincial cost-of-living differences. Thus, with the poverty line (in real terms) known, it is straightforward to obtain the poverty incidence from Figure 6.2 for the various years. For example, if the national-average (population-weighted) official poverty line of about Rp904,400 per person is used, the resulting poverty incidence would be 26 percent for 1993, 13 percent for 1996, and 16 percent for 1999.[7]

As shown by Foster and Shorrocks (1988), two nonintersecting cumulative distribution curves also suggest that the direction of poverty change is unambiguous even for all other plausible poverty indices that satisfy certain properties of a desirable poverty measure. This is the case for 1993 and 1996, as well as for 1996 and 1999. Thus, poverty is unambiguously higher in 1999 than in 1996, but still much lower than in 1993, for virtually all poverty norms and standard poverty measures that have been suggested in the literature.

Figure 6.2: Distribution of Living Standards

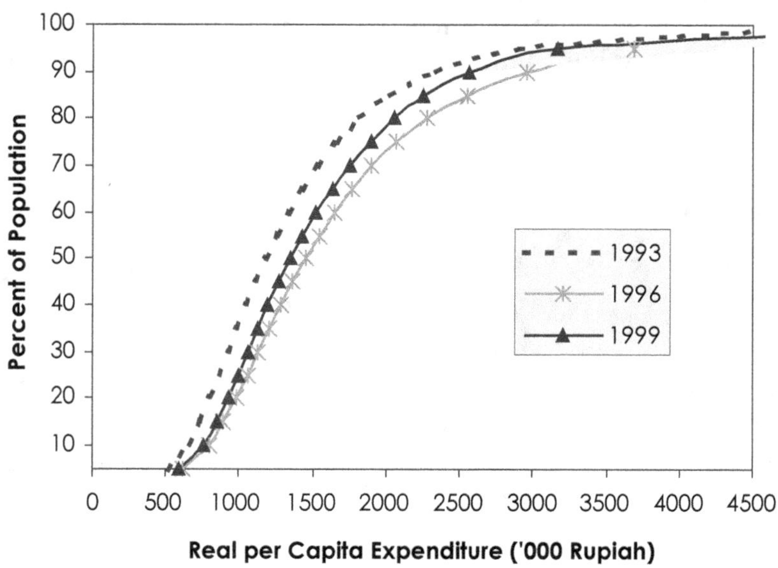

To some extent, the pattern of poverty change shown above is qualitatively consistent with the observations reported in previous studies. Using their "consistent" estimates, Suryahadi et al. (1999) showed that poverty increased by 6.5 percentage points between 1996 and 1999, while ADB's (2000c) estimate of the change, based on official poverty lines, was roughly 6 percentage points. Our estimate of the increase in poverty rate from 1996 to 1999 is approximately 3 percentage points. Note, however, that our estimate takes account of substantial interprovincial cost-of-living differences.

A caveat on the welfare distribution estimates for 1996 and 1999 is in order. The difference between the two years is strictly not an estimate of the extent of change *during* the crisis. The crisis did not begin in February 1996 and end in February 1999, which were the months covered by the SUSENAS data used in this chapter. Economic growth continued to be positive and surpass population growth (while inflation remained moderate) for nearly a year and a half after the early 1996 survey. This could have caused further decline in poverty, which was the norm in the 1980s and the first half of the 1990s. Thus, the increase in poverty during the crisis was likely higher than the 3 percentage points as reflected in Figure 6.2.

SUBNATIONAL DIFFERENCES IN WELFARE

Available data show large differences in natural endowment, agrarian structure, access to support services, institutions, and policies across the country's 285 districts. Figure 6.3 highlights these differences for a few indicators, namely, schooling, farm characteristics, and access to information, technology, and finance. The indicators (defined in the next section) pertain to district-level averages for the 1990s. In general, the values of these indicators are scattered widely around their overall (national) means. Moreover, even for districts with similar levels of real per capita expenditure, the dispersion is quite substantial.

District-level data covering the three survey years in the 1990s (a total of 855 observations) show a strong positive correlation between district-level average expenditure and average expenditure of the poorest 20 percent of the population (Figure 6.4).[8] The relationship is summarized by the fitted line, obtained by ordinary least squares (OLS) regression of the mean welfare of the poor on overall mean expenditure (income).[9] Note that both means are expressed in

Figure 6.3: District-level Differences for Selected Indicators

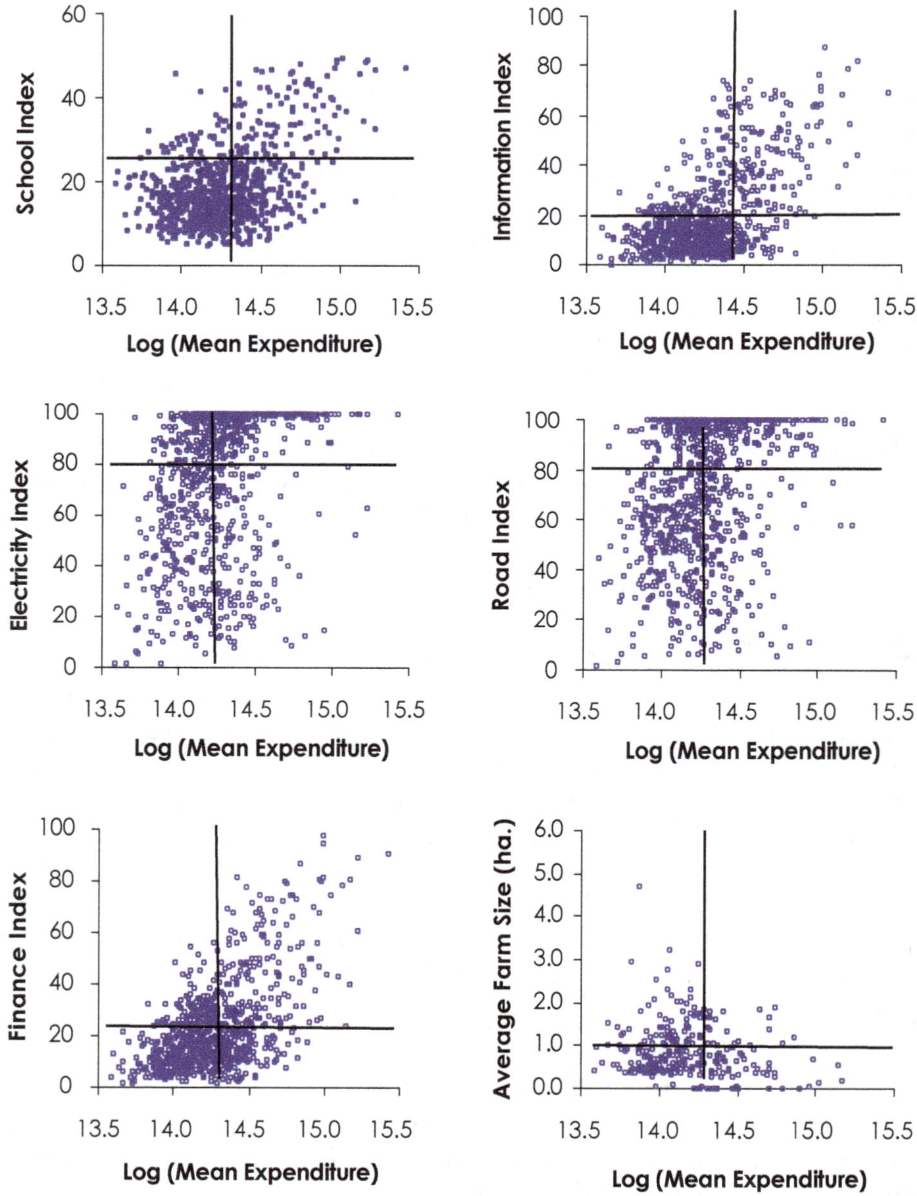

continued.

Figure 6.3. continued.

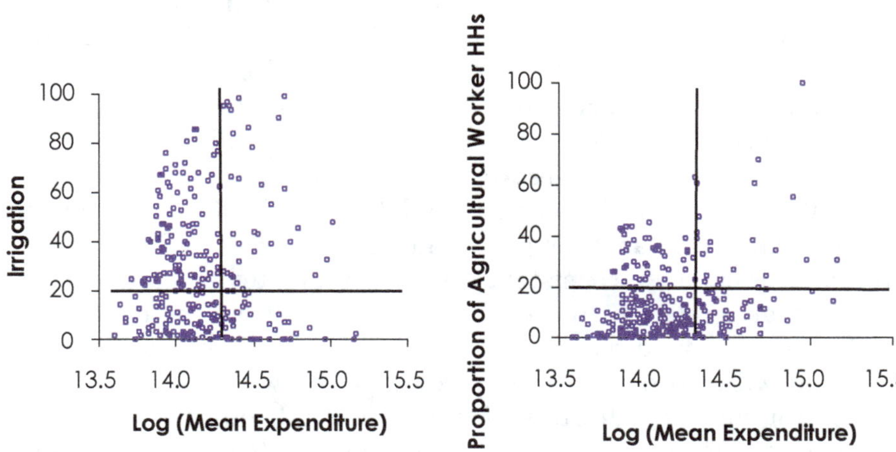

Notes:

School Index: District average for distance of villages to junior high school and distance to senior high school.

Information index: District average for proportion of villages with public phone, proportion of villages with TV, and proportion of villages with postal office.

Electricity index: Proportion of villages with access to state-run electricity.

Road Index: Proportion of villages with paved roads.

Finance index: District average for proportion of villages with banks and proportion of villages with cooperatives.

Irrigation: Ratio of total irrigated area to the total area comprising wetlands, garden drylands, shifting cultivation lands, and grasslands.

Proportion of agriculture worker households: Ratio of agricultural laborer households to total agricultural households.

Source: PODES 1993, 1996, and 1999, BPS Indonesia.

logarithms, hence, the slope of the fitted line can be interpreted as the elasticity of the average income of the poor with respect to the overall average income, henceforth referred to as the growth elasticity of poverty. This elasticity is about 0.8, indicating that a 10 percent increase in district-level income raises the living standards of the poor by 8 percent.[10] This result is strikingly similar to Bhalla's (2001) estimate based on cross-country analysis of poverty reduction from the late 1980s to the late 1990s.

However, simply regressing the per capita income of the poor on overall per capita income likely yields an inconsistent estimate of the growth elasticity of poverty. Measurement errors in per capita income (which is also used to construct our measure of the average income of the poor) bias the estimate of this elasticity. Moreover, it is possible that the incomes of the poor and overall incomes are jointly determined. Recent theory and evidence show a link between inequality (hence, incomes of the poor) and subsequent overall income growth. One school of thought suggests that income (or asset) inequality inhibits subsequent overall income growth (Alesina 1998, Deininger and Squire 1998), while another posits the reverse (Forbes 2000, Li and Zou 1998). Further, inconsistency of the parameter estimates of the growth-poverty relationship in Figure 6.4 arises from the omission of variables that have direct impact on the welfare of the poor and are correlated with overall average income, as shown in Figure 6.3. In addition, provincial indicators of human capital, infrastructure, and local institutions (e.g., social capital) also appear to correlate strongly with provincial mean incomes (Booth 2000, Kwon 2000, Garcia 1998).

We address these statistical problems by checking the robustness of the growth elasticity estimate and exploring other determinants of district-level poverty reduction. Figure 6.5 summarizes our empirical approach.

Figure 6.4: Welfare of the Poor versus District Mean Expenditure

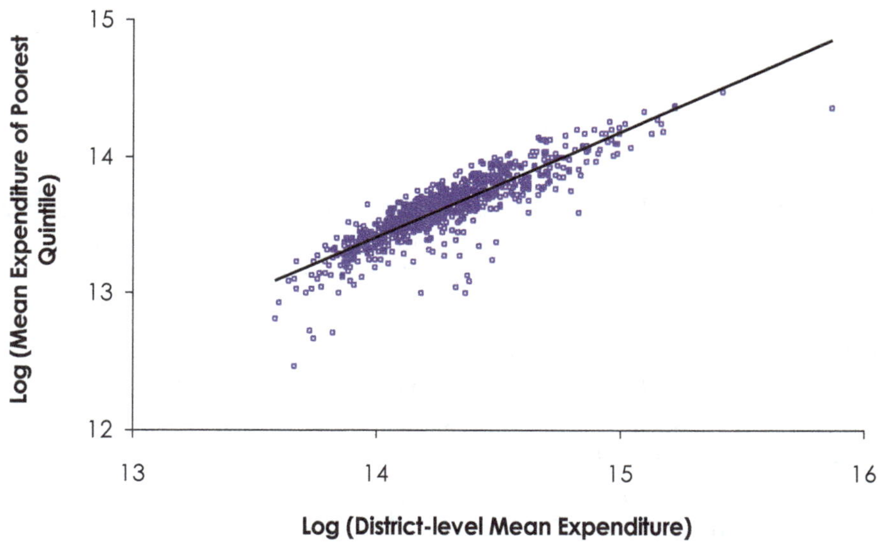

Figure 6.5: Empirical Framework

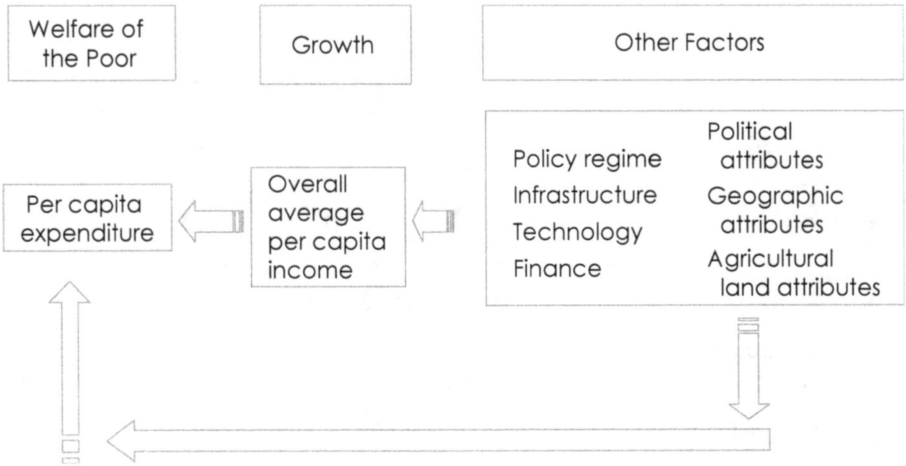

Note: Lagged endogenous variables (per capita expenditure and overall average per capita income) are not shown.

To deal with the measurement error, we could use average income to instrument for average expenditure. However, the income variable is not available at the district level. The alternative instrument is district-level expenditure growth, which also takes care of the endogeneity issue.[11] In the case of the omitted-variables bias problem, we exploit the longitudinal nature of the district-level data and employ panel estimation techniques to control for differences in time-invariant, unobservable province-specific characteristics. Specifically, we use two standard panel estimation models—the fixed-effects model and the random-effects model—suited for addressing unobserved fixed-effects problems, but doing so in such a way that the endogeneity of overall mean income is observed.[12] Table 6.3 summarizes the results of the estimation. For comparison, we also show the OLS regression estimates implied by the fitted line in Figure 6.4, as well as the instrumental variable (IV) regression estimates.

The panel estimation results indicate that, indeed, the unobserved district-specific effects are significant, leading to a reduction in the earlier OLS estimate of the growth elasticity of poverty at nearly 0.8 to about 0.7. This new elasticity estimate, including the values at 95

Table 6.3: Basic Specifications: Elasticity of the Income of the Poor to Overall Income

	OLS (1)	IV (2)	2SLS FIXED-EFFECTS (3)	2SLS RANDOM-EFFECTS (4)
Log of mean expenditure	0.774 (39.74)	0.764 (8.65)	0.712 (16.66)	0.714 (20.95)
Constant	2.583 (9.30)	2.729 (2.16)	3.474 (5.68)	3.442 (7.05)
95% confidence interval for growth elasticity	0.73-0.81	0.59-0.94	0.63-0.79	0.65-0.78
F-test that all district dummy coefficients are zero			5.58	

Note: Dependent variable is the logarithm of the mean expenditure for the bottom 20 percent of the population. Except for OLS, all estimations instrument for mean expenditure using lagged mean expenditure growth. Figures in parentheses are t-ratios. Data refer to the panel of 285 districts and three years covering the 1990s.

percent confidence interval, is roughly the same from both panel estimation techniques. Hence, we employ the panel estimation technique, in particular the fixed-effects model that also allows for the endogeneity of the overall income variable. The assumption of the random-effects model that the unobserved district-level effects and the explanatory variables are uncorrelated is not supported by the data. This correlation problem applies as well to the IV estimation technique.

To sum up, our growth elasticity of poverty estimate is not nearly the one-for-one correspondence between increase in the welfare of the poor and growth in overall income, as shown in studies employing cross-country regressions. However, the estimate for Indonesia is higher than that for the Philippines, for which a similar study finds this elasticity to be about 0.5 (Chapter 7). The comparison is instructive since the two countries are at roughly similar stages of economic development. Thus, while other factors appear to have direct (distributive) effects on the welfare of the poor, in the Indonesian case changes in the poor's welfare in response to overall economic growth seem fairly large. This could be explained by the relatively more labor-intensive and agriculture-based economic growth in Indonesia. Over the past two decades, growth of the agricultural sector was significantly faster in Indonesia than in the Philippines (3.7 percent in the 1980s and 2.2 percent in the 1990s for Indonesia versus 1.9 and 1.8 percent for the Philippines).

OTHER FACTORS INFLUENCING POVERTY REDUCTION

Certain economic and social factors influence poverty reduction at the local level. These include overall per capita income, relative price incentives, human capital, and access to infrastructure, technology, and finance. We use these variables to explain the wide differences in the per capita incomes of the poor across the country's 285 districts during the 1990s. Guiding our specifications are parsimony, development theory, and data availability.

The proxy for the human capital variable is the district-level average years of schooling of household heads, which is expected to directly influence the welfare of the poor (through income distribution), apart from its effect on district-level income growth. Numerous studies suggest that the higher the level of educational attainment, the higher is a person's expected earnings over a lifetime (e.g., Krueger and Lindhal 2001). For urban Java, the private rate of return on education is about 17 percent—higher than those found for most other countries (Byron and Takahashi 1989, as cited by Lanjouw et al. 2001). The social rate of return is also quite high, roughly 14 percent for junior secondary school and 11 percent for senior secondary school (McMahon and Boediono 1992).

Two alternative proxies for human capital are adult literacy and access to basic schooling. The first is defined as the proportion of the adult population who can read and write in Latin script. The second variable is defined as the average distance of villages to secondary (junior and senior high) schools. As is well known, since the late 1960s, Indonesia has witnessed an enormous expansion of educational opportunities at all levels. Duflo (2001) finds that each primary school constructed per 1,000 children led to an average increase of 0.12 to 0.19 years of education, as well as 1.5 to 2.7 percent increase in wages. Household data suggest, however, that while universal primary enrollment was reached as early as around 1986, secondary enrollment in the 1990s still varied quite enormously across provinces (Lanjouw et al. 2001; see also Figure 6.3). The large variation was true not only between islands, or between Java and the rest of the country, but also within major islands. For example, while West Kalimantan did badly in terms of education and poverty outcomes, the situation was far less worrisome in Central Kalimantan.

Roads represent access to markets, off-farm employment, and social services. This variable, defined as the proportion of villages with access to paved roads, may be seen as an indicator of spatial connectivity or, conversely, spatial isolation implying geographic "poverty traps." [13]

The presence of natural wealth (oil, gas, and minerals) is expected to influence growth and poverty reduction. This is defined in terms of the relative importance of oil, natural gas, and minerals in the local economy. The net effect of this variable on the welfare of the poor in resource-rich areas is, however, not *a priori* obvious.

The price incentives variable is given by the local terms of trade, defined as the ratio of prices of agricultural to nonagricultural products. Since poverty is concentrated in agriculture in developing countries (Pernia and Quibria 1999), including Indonesia (Asra 2000), this variable is expected to be positively related to the incomes of the poor.

Electricity is a proxy for access to technology, or simply the ability to use modern equipment. It is defined as the proportion of villages with state-run electricity. The communication-information variable also serves as indicator of access to technology. It is given here by a composite index representing the proportion of villages with access to all, or any combination, of the following: (i) public telephone, (ii) public television, (iii) post office, and (iv) news agent. We further combine the electricity and communication-information variables into a single composite index referred to simply as technology. This variable is also expected to positively influence the welfare of the poor, apart from its positive impact on overall growth.

Access to credit is critical to managing household consumption, particularly insofar as the poor are concerned, because it affords them the means to smooth their incomes in the event of unfavorable shocks. It is likewise key to securing working capital, maintaining assets, and expanding businesses. This variable is denoted by the proportion of villages in the district with either banks or credit cooperatives, or both.

Table 6.4 summarizes the results of the econometric estimation, including the results of the first-stage fixed-effects regression (FSFE), which indicate the response of overall growth to the exogenous variables. Appendix Table 6.2 provides the descriptive statistics on the variables.

After controlling for the influence of other factors (including unobserved district-specific fixed effects), the growth of overall income appears to exert a significant influence on the incomes of the poor. Indeed, the estimate of the growth elasticity is quite robust, consistently around 0.7 in the various specifications. Surprisingly, this estimate is close to that obtained in the basic specifications in which district-specific effects are controlled for (regressions 3 and 4 in Table 6.3).

Evidence on the direct effect of schooling is rather mixed. The mean years of schooling is insignificant (regression 1), although it is significant if the variable is defined for the poor only (regression 1a). It is possible that schooling years may not adequately reflect differences in human capital across the income spectrum. However, for the poor, schooling years may correspond well to achieved human capital since school quality may be less heterogeneous within the group.

Adult literacy also appears not to have a direct impact on the welfare of the poor (regression 2). However, it exerts a significant influence on overall growth, suggesting that improvement in human capital reduces poverty principally via the growth process. In other words, investment in human capital is good for growth and, indirectly, poverty reduction.

Price incentives matter to poverty reduction, as indicated by the positive and significant coefficient of the terms-of-trade variable. This means that changes in the price of agriculture relative to the price prevailing in other sectors of the local economy have an impact on the welfare of the poor, both directly by affecting income redistribution and indirectly through its positive effect on overall growth.[14] It is worth noting that the country's price and trade policy regimes in the 1980s and 1990s tended to penalize agriculture relative to manufacturing. Although significant trade reforms took effect in the 1990s, directly conferring some protection to the primary sector, the protec-

Table 6.4: Determinants of the Welfare of the Poor

EXPLANATORY VARIABLE	(1)	FSFE	(2)	FSFE	(3)	FSFE	(1a)	FSFE
Overall Mean Income (Y)	0.724 *** (13.12)		0.714 *** (13.42)		0.715 *** (13.42)		0.723 *** (13.76)	
Schooling								
Years of schooling	-0.039 (-0.40)	0.045 (0.60)					0.017 * (1.88)	-0.003 (-0.51)
Adult literacy			0.129 (0.74)	0.311 ** (2.32)				
Distance to schools					-0.017 (-1.19)	0.017 (1.50)		
Terms of Trade	0.001 * (1.77)	0.001 *** (4.83)	0.001 (1.35)	0.001 *** (4.57)	0.001 * (1.64)	0.001 *** (5.04)	0.001 * (1.63)	0.001 *** (4.94)
Technology	0.215 * (1.84)	0.029 (0.33)	0.206 * (1.77)	0.044 (0.50)	0.205 * (1.76)	0.040 (0.46)	0.227 ** (1.97)	0.032 (0.35)
Finance	0.035 (0.48)	-0.006 (-0.10)	0.043 (0.58)	-0.012 (-0.22)	0.034 (0.45)	-0.004 (-0.08)		
Roads	-0.014 (-0.52)	0.050 *** (2.34)	-0.165 (-0.56)	0.032 (1.41)	-0.012 (-0.42)	0.048 ** (2.26)	-0.018 (-0.79)	0.052 *** (2.53)
Oil and Gas	-0.193 (-0.90)	0.384 *** (2.35)	-0.295 (-1.36)	0.364 ** (2.21)	-0.228 (-1.09)	0.425 *** (2.64)	-0.269 (-1.28)	0.416 *** (2.56)
Lagged Growth of Y		0.457 *** (24.18)		0.468 *** (24.8)		0.461 *** (24.76)		0.458 *** (24.95)

continued.

Table 6.4 continued.

EXPLANATORY VARIABLE	(1)	FSFE	(2)	FSFE	(3)	FSFE	(1a)	FSFE
Intercept	3.278 ***	13.977 ***	3.266 ***	13.826 ***	3.296 ***	14.100 ***	3.163 ***	14.070 ***
	(4.23)	(101.54)	4.14	(131.32)	4.27	(277.83)	(4.15)	(280.79)
R-squared	0.741	0.785	0.739	0.789	0.732	0.787	0.733	0.785
F-ratio		145.11		145.23		146.37		169.81
Wald X2 (X1000)	24141		23759		24267		24507	
Prob > X2	0		0		0		0	
F-test that All Fixed Effects are Zero	4.49		4.69		4.67		3.46	
No. of Observations	570		558		570		570	

*** denotes significance at the 1 percent level.

** denotes significance at the 5 percent level.

* denotes significance at the 10 percent level.

Note: Estimation is by 2SLS fixed-effects regression in which the dependent variable is the logarithm of mean per capita expenditure of the poorest 20%. FSFE means first-stage fixed-effects regression in which the dependent variable is the logarithm of overall mean per capita expenditure. Figures in parentheses are z-ratios for the 2SLS fixed-effects regression and t-ratios for FSFE.

tion regime as a whole continued to tax agriculture, though to a lesser extent (Garcia 2000). This would have limited the income gains from trade reforms in provinces dependent on agriculture. Evidently, since agriculture is more tradable than either industry or services, and since agriculture is more labor-intensive than industry, reducing trade and price distortions promotes both poverty reduction and growth objectives.[15]

The access-to-technology variable is positive and significant, supporting the expectation that it matters to the incomes of the poor. Recall that this refers to the availability of electricity and publicly provided information channels at the village level. Villagers in areas where these services are absent may simply not have an important avenue for raising the productivity of their assets (in agriculture, mainly land and labor). The coefficient estimates, which average around 0.2, suggest that an improvement in access to these services by 10 percent raises the poor's incomes by roughly 2 percent, all other things being equal.

Surprisingly, the finance variable is insignificant, which runs counter to the common claim that access to formal financial intermediaries, particularly in agriculture, is critical for poor people. This variable, defined as the proportion of villages with banks or cooperatives, may be a poor proxy for access to credit.[16] The specific location and scale of these financial intermediaries vis-à-vis the village population may give a better indicator, but such variable is not available. Moreover, the proxy finance variable correlates strongly with the technology variable. Nevertheless, deleting the finance variable in the estimating model does not significantly change the parameter estimates of the remaining variables.

The roads variable does not appear to be significant, but it has a strong impact on overall growth. This is consistent with the observation (e.g., Hill 1996) that the public provision of roads has not been designed as a vehicle for achieving intradistrict (or province) redistribution but rather as a part of a development strategy for spurring economic growth, especially in the countryside.

The variable representing natural wealth is also not significant, although it does influence overall growth significantly. This supports the observation of Tadjoeddin et al. (2001) that there is no strong correlation between natural resource endowment and community welfare, defined in terms of HDI (human development indicators).[17] However, revenues generated from natural resources have been an important means for financing development projects, especially those aimed at keeping interregional inequality low. Indeed, the government's New Order equalization policy—which was achieved mainly through fiscal policy instruments, such as central government transfer, interregional transfer, and other initiatives within the *Inpres* scheme for provincial governments—was quite effective in spurring growth outside the Java-Bali enclave, especially in the Outer Island provinces.

DIFFERENTIAL EFFECTS ACROSS QUINTILES

Do the welfare effects of the economic and social factors discussed in the preceding section vary across income groups? The less-than-unity estimate of growth elasticity in Tables 6.3 and 6.4 indicate that those in the upper ranges of the income distribution tend to benefit more than proportionately from overall economic growth. What policies or institutional arrangements might enhance the benefits of growth for the poor?

We estimate the model for each of the other four income quintiles. In particular, we focus on the variant of the model in which the finance variable is dropped and the schooling variable pertains to the mean years of schooling for the relevant quintile.[18] Recall that in the earlier variant we used the mean schooling years of the first quintile, rather than the overall (all quintiles) mean schooling years, as a regressor. This education variable yielded a positive and significant impact on the welfare of the poor. The estimation results for each quintile are summarized in Table 6.5. For ready comparison, the results for the first quintile reported in Table 6.4 (column 1a) are reproduced as the first column in Table 6.5.

Results for the other quintiles generally do not diverge greatly from those for the first quintile. Apart from district mean income, average schooling in each income group directly and positively influences welfare of that group, as expected. Natural resource endowment (oil and gas), infrastructure (roads), and terms of trade exert their influence on welfare via their positive impact on overall income growth.

Growth elasticity of welfare tends to increase monotonically with income quintile, suggesting that indeed, those in the higher income

Table 6.5: Determinants of Average Welfare by Quintile

EXPLANATORY VARIABLE	Q1 (Poorest)	Q2	Q3	Q4	Q5 (Richest)
Overall Mean Income (Y)	0.723 ***	0.773 ***	0.832 ***	0.919 ***	1.190 ***
Years of Schooling	0.017 **	0.022 ***	0.021 ***	0.016 ***	0.016 ***
	(-0.003)	(0.003)	(0.011)	(0.006)	(-0.004)
Terms of Trade	0.001 *	0.000	0.000	0.000	0.000
	(0.001) ***	(0.001) ***	(0.001) ***	(0.001) ***	(0.001) ***
Technology	0.227 **	0.115	0.075	0.066	0.163 **
	(0.031)	(0.033)	(0.023)	(0.028)	(0.041)
Roads	-0.018 ***	0.022 **	0.004 **	0.015 **	-0.020 **
	(0.052)	(0.048)	(0.045)	(0.048)	(0.050)
Oil and Gas	-0.269 ***	-0.263 **	-0.176 **	0.028 **	0.028 ***
	(0.416)	(0.395)	(0.329)	(0.373)	(0.409)
Lagged Growth of Y	(0.458) ***	(0.459) ***	(0.454) ***	(0.455) ***	(0.465) ***
Intercept	3.163 ***	2.774 ***	2.125 ***	1.094 ***	-2.213 ***
	(14.071)	(14.043)	(14.003)	(14.021)	(14.091)
Wald X2 (X1000)	24504	54710	70432	94042	52379
Prob > X2	0	0	0		0

*** denotes significance at the 1 percent level.

** denotes significance at the 5 percent level.

* denotes significance at the 10 percent level.

Note: Estimation is by 2SLS fixed-effects regression. The dependent variable is the logarithm of the quintile mean per capita expenditure adjusted for provincial cost-of-living differences. Figures in brackets are results of first-stage fixed-effects regressions in which the dependent variable is the logarithm of the district mean per capita expenditure.

groups enjoy the benefits of growth more. Similar results have been found for the Philippines, except that the growth elasticities for the first two quintiles (bottom 40 percent of the population) are significantly higher for Indonesia. It is also worth noting that returns to schooling are quite similar across quintiles. An additional year of schooling raises per capita income by roughly 2 percent, other things being equal.[19] This result thus affirms the common claim in the development literature that education represents an important avenue for raising household welfare, even more so for the poor whose access to land and other assets is very limited. Finally, it appears that access to technology tends to directly influence the welfare of the poorest quintile and the richest quintile but not those in between.

CONCLUSION

Newly constructed panel data on Indonesia's 285 districts (kotamadyas and kabupatens) reveal huge differences in poverty changes, subnational economic growth, and local attributes. Econometric analysis of these data shows that the welfare of the poor responds quite strongly to overall income growth. The growth elasticity of poverty is about 0.7. This growth-poverty nexus seems significantly stronger than in the Philippines where the elasticity is estimated to be only about 0.5. This may be explained by the higher growth of agriculture in Indonesia, which is also likely to have been more employment-generating. Still, the growth-poverty relationship is far from the one-to-one correspondence revealed by studies based on cross-country regressions. Thus, growth is good for the poor in Indonesia as in the Philippines, but it is not good enough.

Besides economic growth, other factors exert direct distributive effects on the welfare of the poor, apart from their impact on growth itself. Among the critical ones are the terms of trade regime, schooling, infrastructure, and access to technology. Although often referred to in the literature as important to the poor, the access–to–credit variable as defined by available data did not come out significant. Future work has to go beyond physical indicators of financial services to include "meso" indicators pertaining to distribution of physical assets (particularly land) and social capital.

On the whole, this chapter has shown that there is more to poverty reduction than merely promoting economic growth. While fostering growth is evidently crucial and appears to be a relatively straightforward objective to pursue, a more complete poverty reduction strategy must take account of various institutional factors that matter, if the aim is rapid and sustained poverty reduction. Indeed, paying attention to these other factors will be good for both growth and poverty reduction.

Notes

The authors gratefully acknowledge the valuable assistance on the data provided by the P.T. Insan Hitawasana Sejahtera, in particular Swastika Andi Dwi Nugroho, and Lisa Kulp for advice. Gemma Esther Estrada provided very able research assistance.

1. This is according to World Bank's internationally comparable estimates based on a poverty line of approximately US$1 a day (in 1993 purchasing power parity). See Chen and Ravallion (2001).
2. These variations are also evident in other developing countries, both large and small (see, e.g., Fan et al. (2000) for the PRC, Ravallion and Datt (2002) for India, Chapter 7 for the Philippines, Chapter 8 for Thailand, and Chapter 9 for Viet Nam).
3. Although SUSENAS extends back to the 1960s, provincial-level data are strictly comparable only for the surveys beginning 1993 when the BPS implemented the heavily revised Core questionnaire and expanded the Core sample size from about 65,000 households prior to 1993 to around 200,000 households since then.
4. The classification of districts pertains to that prevailing in 1993. The data exclude East Timor.
5. Ravallion (2002) finds that, for developing and transition countries, the problem of comparability between survey and NIA data is more serious for income than for expenditure measures.
6. A notable feature of the economic crisis in the late 1990s was that food prices rose much more sharply than nonfood prices. Food CPI rose by about 160 percent between 1996 and 1999, while nonfood CPI increased by only 76 percent during the same period.
7. If no allowance was made for differences in provincial cost-of-living differences, i.e., if the only adjustment made on the SUSENAS expenditure data for the three survey years was on price changes over time, the estimate of poverty incidence would have been higher by 4.3 percentage points for 1993, 3.3 percentage points for 1996, and 3.4 percentage points for 1999.
8. Alternatively, as in common practice, poverty can be defined in terms of an explicit poverty line, below which a person is deemed poor. However, for our purposes, this practice is not particularly appealing, since it makes the estimate of poverty response sensitive to assumptions about the poverty line.
9. From hereon, for expositional purposes, we use the term "mean per capita income" or simply "per capita income" for "mean per capita expenditure" for consistency, unless otherwise specified. We also use the expression "mean welfare of the poor" or simply "welfare of the poor" or "living standards of the poor" for mean income or expenditure of the poor.

10. The estimated elasticity for each year—0.773 for 1993, 0.768 for 1996, and 0.775 for 1999—indicates that the overall estimate of 0.8 is robust.

11. The assumption is that the measurement error in overall mean expenditure is invariant to survey years.

12. The first model—the fixed-effects model—utilizes differences within each district across time. The technique is equivalent to regressing the average income of the poor on a set of intercept dummy variables representing the districts in the data, as well as on overall mean incomes. The second model—the random-effects model—is more efficient since it utilizes not only information across individual districts but also across periods. Its main drawback, however, is that it is consistent only if the district-specific effects are uncorrelated with the other explanatory variables.

13. In a somewhat related vein, Gallup et al. (1998) find that the geographic location of a country tends to influence the speed of its economic growth, noting in particular that landlocked countries tend to grow slower than those with direct access to sea transport.

14. As noted earlier, income poverty in Indonesia is largely a rural phenomenon. Of the rural poor, the large majority are dependent on agriculture for employment and income. As such, an improvement in the terms of trade in provinces where agriculture is a dominant component of the local economy tends to raise the welfare levels of the poor.

15. Since labor in Indonesia is quite mobile (Manning 1997), even farmers in resource-poor areas should benefit from trade and price reforms.

16. The proportion of villages with banks or cooperatives may not be a good indicator of access to finance since two districts with the same proportion of villages with banks or cooperatives could have different levels of accessibility (e.g., the number of banks or cooperatives may differ between them).

17. Indicators for the "19 enclave districts" such as consumption, health, and HDI are more or less similar to those of the national average, regardless of these districts' high level of per capita output. The 19 enclave districts include seven districts located in the four natural resource–rich provinces of Aceh, Riau, East Kalimantan, and Papua.

18. Using any of the other model variants reported in Table 6.4 will not substantially change the results in terms of the pattern of impact across quintiles.

19. Note that average schooling years vary by quintile.

APPENDIX TABLE 6.1:
Urban Poverty Line and Cost-of-Living Index by Province (1999)

	URBAN POVERTY LINE (RUPIAH)	COST OF LIVING INDEX (JAKARTA=100)
Aceh	78,286	0.869
North Sumatera	84,342	0.936
West Sumatera	100,131	1.111
Riau	90,609	1.006
Jambi	91,032	1.010
South Sumatera	88,533	0.983
Bengkulu	104,237	1.157
Lampung	96,635	1.072
DKI Jakarta	90,108	1.000
West Java	88,471	0.982
Central Java	80,369	0.892
DI Yogyakarta	92,037	1.021
East Java	83,223	0.924
Bali	94,190	1.045
West Nusa Tenggara	84,449	0.937
East Nusa Tenggara	79,473	0.882
West Kalimantan	95,767	1.063
Central Kalimantan	95,220	1.057
South Kalimantan	87,134	0.967
East Kalimantan	79,350	0.881
North Sulawesi	85,886	0.953
Central Sulawesi	83,579	0.928
South Sulawesi	77,513	0.860
Southeast Sulawesi	66,290	0.736
Maluku	95,556	1.060
Irian Jaya	76,250	0.846

APPENDIX TABLE 6.2: Descriptive Statistics

VARIABLE	MEAN	STD. DEV.	MIN	MAX
Income of the poor: log(average per capita Expenditure of bottom 20 percent) [a]	13.623	0.249	12.458	14.482
Overall mean income: log(average per capita expenditure) [a]	14.270	0.282	13.585	15.864
Lagged growth of Y: growth of per capita expenditure in *t*-3 period, where *t* is current year [a]	0.053	0.191	-0.441	0.502
Years of schooling: [a]				
Average schooling years of adult heads	6.545	1.188	4.200	10.390
Average schooling years of female adult heads	5.369	1.261	2.670	9.140
Average schooling years of adult heads in poorest 20 percent	4.182	1.373	2.500	16.000
Adult literacy: proportion of adults in district who can read and write [b]	0.823	0.119	0.215	0.999
Distance to schools: distance of secondary schools from village [c]	0.094	0.107	0.001	0.704
Terms of trade: agricultural output deflator/nonagricultural output deflator [d]	108.992	13.712	86.410	156.770
Technology: composite index representing the presence of public phone, television, postal office, news agent, and electricity in village [e]	0.190	0.167	0.002	0.875
Finance: proportion of villages with banks and cooperatives [f]	0.227	0.171	0.016	0.977
Roads: proportion of villages with paved roads [g]	0.708	0.269	0.018	1.000
Mineral: proportion of oil and gas in total provincial output [h]	0.102	0.161	0.002	0.659

Notes/data sources:

[a]Computed from SUSENAS Core (1993, 1996, and 1999).

[b]Estimates of ADB for 1993, 1996, and 1999.

[c]District average for distance of villages to junior high school and distance of villages to senior high school; computed from the PODES district data for 1993, 1996, and 1999.

[d]Computed from *Gross Regional Domestic Product of Provinces in Indonesia by Industrial Origin* (BPS 1993, 1996, 1999).

[e]District average of the following: proportion of villages with public phone (approximated by the presence of at least one of the following in the village: coin public phone, card public phone, telephone kiosk, post and telephone kiosk); proportion of villages with television; proportion of villages with postal office; proportion of villages with news agent; and proportion of villages with electricity; computed from PODES 1993, 1996, and 1999 district data.

[f]District average of the (a) proportion of villages with banks and (b) proportion of villages with cooperatives; computed from PODES 1993, 1996, and 1999 district data.

[g]Source is PODES district data for 1993, 1996, and 1999.

[h]Computed from *Gross Regional Domestic Product of Provinces in Indonesia by Industrial Origin* (BPS 1993, 1996, and 1999).

7 Poverty, Inequality, and Growth in the Philippines

Arsenio M. Balisacan and Ernesto M. Pernia

INTRODUCTION

Recent research suggests that economic growth is key to poverty reduction in developing countries. Some results indicate that the growth-poverty relationship is invariant to economic cycles, i.e., whether the economy is expanding or contracting (Dollar and Kraay 2001). From a policy perspective, this suggests that poverty reduction involves nothing more than creating an environment conducive to rapid economic growth. Indeed, Bhalla (2001) asserts that "growth is sufficient."

Is this all there is to poverty reduction? Probably not. To begin with, much of the earlier empirical work on the growth-poverty nexus has been based on cross-national averages. As Ravallion (2001) argues, however, there is much more to this nexus than the cross-country averages imply. Indeed, looking beneath such averages, one sees highly diverse experiences, even in countries at similar stages of economic development. Moreover, within a country, there are often large variations in the growth-poverty performance across subnational units (regions, states, provinces). These variations are evident in large countries, such as People's Republic of China (Fan et al. 2000); India (Datt and Ravallion 1998, Ravallion and Datt 2002, Chand 2001); and Indonesia (Hill 1996; Chapter 6), as well as in moderately sized countries such as the Philippines (Balisacan 2000); Thailand (Chapter 8); and Viet Nam (Glewwe et al. 2000; Chapter 9).

In revisiting the lessons from the so-called East Asian miracle countries, Quibria (2001) concludes that: (i) the main lever for poverty reduction in the miracle economies was not any radical improvement in income distribution but rapid economic growth; (ii) growth, in turn, was invariably spurred by openness to trade and technology in conjunction with prudent macroeconomic principles, labor market flexibility, and a set of efficiency-enhancing institutions; (iii) neither land reform nor an initially high level of human capital was a precondition to sustained growth and poverty reduction; and (iv) growth in agriculture per se was not critical to the reduction of poverty. These conclusions are debatable, however. The finding, for example, that neither the endowment of human capital nor the growth of agriculture mattered clashes with the received wisdom about the centrality of human capital and agricultural development in poverty reduction.

To the extent that the foregoing observations are based on studies using cross-country averages, they are not surprising. As noted above, one must proceed beyond cross-national averages to determine the robustness of conclusions about the poverty-growth relationship. Is it the case, for example, that the initial distribution of land and other assets does not affect growth and poverty reduction in the regions or provinces within a country? Not only do simple cross-country averages tend to mask the true story of growth and poverty; the problem is compounded because the data used are based on concepts and definitions of income, poverty, and inequality that vary greatly across countries.

Clearly, a deeper understanding of the economic and institutional determinants of poverty reduction requires probing beneath cross-national averages, i.e., hence, an investigation of subnational units. Key questions of interest include:

(i) Why are some subnational units/provinces more successful than others in achieving growth, or in translating growth into poverty reduction, or in achieving both growth and poverty reduction?

(ii) What specific institutional arrangements or features of the local economy and polity facilitate or inhibit growth and poverty reduction? How do these interact with macroeconomic and/or external shocks? And how do they influence poverty reduction directly or through access to basic social services?

(iii) Can the experience of relatively successful subnational units be replicated in other areas?

A subnational approach has advantages over cross-country regression analysis in understanding the poverty-growth nexus. First, cross-country regression is prone to omitted-variable bias and measurement errors (Forbes 2000, Ravallion 2001). Numerous variables tend to correlate systematically with growth and poverty reduction, but these are usually difficult to measure and to include in cross-country regressions. Some variables pertain to politics and institutions, culture and social norms, macroeconomic and trade regimes, and perhaps even geographic and population attributes. The variety of these variables makes it difficult to predict a priori how they might affect estimates of the relationship between growth and poverty. In subnational work, however, it is reasonable to assume that these variables are largely common across subnational units; thus their omission will not bias estimates of the poverty-growth nexus. It is also reasonable to assume that systematic measurement errors are far more problematic in cross-country than in subnational data. These errors could result in either a negative or positive bias in the estimate of the response of poverty to growth, depending on the correlation between the measurement error and the growth variable (as well as the other variables in the regression). If countries with high inequality grow slower than low-inequality countries but also tend to underreport their inequality statistics, the probable outcome would be a negative bias in cross-country estimates of the poverty-growth relationship.

Second, comparable cross-section and time-series data on subnational units of developing countries have increasingly become available. In the Philippines, the periodic conduct of comparable household surveys in the last 15 years has allowed the construction of a panel of subnational units, especially at the regional level. This development facilitates systematic analysis of the determinants of growth and poverty reduction.

Third, cross-country work does not directly address the important issue of how growth is related to poverty reduction within a single country. Indeed, as Rodrik (2000, 8) notes, all that is demonstrated by the high correlation between growth and incomes of the poor "is that the income distribution tends to be stable and rather unresponsive to policy changes." The practical question is not whether growth is good for poverty reduction, or vice versa. Rather, it is whether the welfare of the poor should enter as a separate determinant of policy choices, in addition to growth-promoting policies, such as macroeconomic stability and good governance. Subnational work using panel estimation offers a direct approach to establishing the link between poverty and policy choices.

This chapter attempts to shed light on the above issues using subnational data on the Philippines. The focus is on the 1980s and 1990s, a period characterized by spells of economic growth and decline, as well as by fundamental changes in the policies and institutions. The next section describes economic growth and poverty changes at the national level. The third section then uses consistent provincial data to examine the robustness of the poverty-growth relationship. The fourth section extends the analysis by examining the contribution of certain physical attributes, political economy, and time-varying economic factors to the observed variation in provincial poverty performance. The chapter concludes with implications for policy.

AGGREGATE GROWTH AND POVERTY CHANGES

For most of the 1980s and early 1990s, the Philippine economy performed poorly, especially against the backdrop of the other East Asian economies. During this period, growth spurts were often followed by bust and stagnation. Not surprisingly, the country's per capita GNP at the beginning of the 21st century was just about the same as that in the early 1980s (Figure 7.1).

Figure 7.1: Per Capita GNP (at 1985 prices)

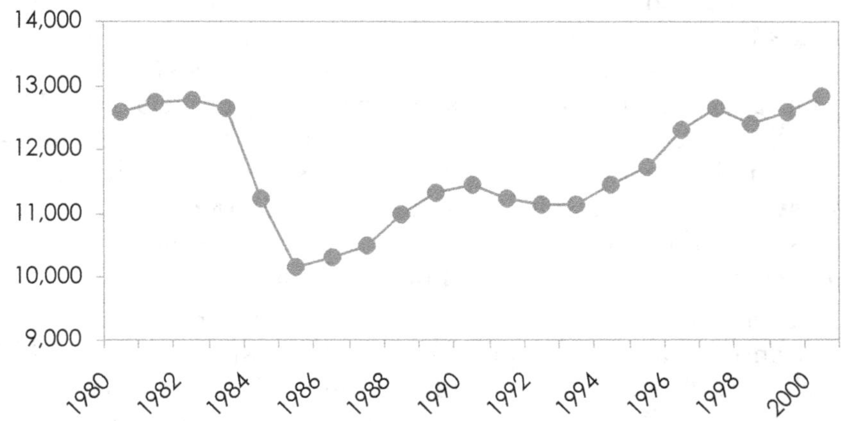

However, the growth episodes in the 1990s appear to have been fundamentally different from previous ones. Growth took place in an environment of political stability, economic deregulation, and institutional reforms. While policy coordination problems persisted (e.g., in public investments), it could be said that the country at the end of the 20th century was closer to a market economy than it ever was in the past (see Bautista and Tecson 2003). We focus on four distinct phases of the growth process from the mid-1980s to the late 1990s. Fortuitously, the available household surveys needed for examining the poverty performance across provinces roughly correspond to the end-points of these phases.

The first phase was a brief period of economic growth (1986-1989) after a sharp contraction in 1984 and 1985, when per capita GDP shrank by an average of 10 percent a year. The next four years (1990-1993) were a period of bust and stagnation, punctuated by political instability, natural disasters, and macroeconomic mismanagement. The three succeeding years (1995-1997) witnessed a recovery, coinciding with the restoration of political stability and deepening of policy and institutional reforms. However, per capita GDP fell again at the end of the decade owing to the combined impact of the Asian economic crisis and the El Niño that ravaged agriculture in 1998.

The data for poverty and inequality comparisons come mainly from the various *Family Income and Expenditures Survey* (FIES) rounds from the mid-1980s to the late 1990s. Conducted every three years since 1985, these surveys are undertaken by the government's primary statistical agency, the National Statistics Office (NSO). While earlier surveys covering the 1960s and early 1970s are also available, they have been excluded since they are either beset by technical problems or available only in published form.[1] By contrast unit record data are available for the 1985-1997 surveys. The FIES provides data for the two popular broad indicators of household welfare, namely, current income and current consumption expenditure.

In the Philippines, as in Indonesia, average per capita personal consumption expenditure, as measured in the National Income Accounts (NIA), and household consumption expenditure, as measured in FIES, move in the same direction, at least for the 1980s and 1990s (Figure 7.2). The chosen indicator of household welfare must be adjusted for spatial cost-of-living differences, since prices vary significantly across provinces and regions. Previous poverty and income inequality studies on the Philippines have been largely unsuccessful

Figure 7.2: Personal Consumption Expenditure (PCE) vs Household Consumption Expenditure (HCE)

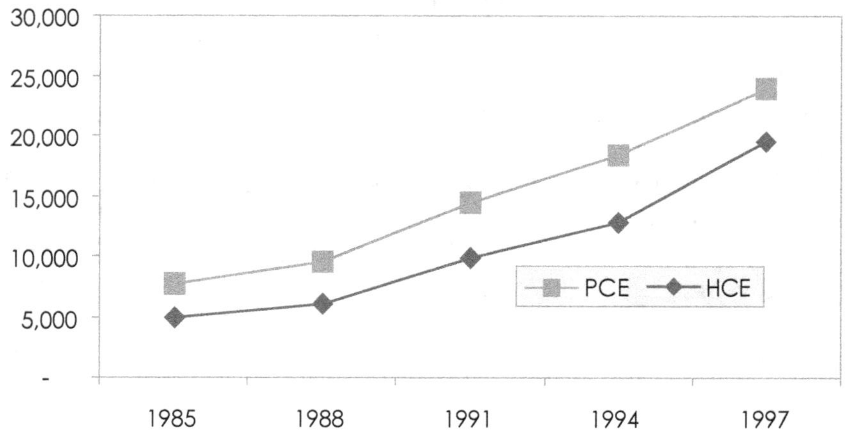

Sources: PCE: National Income Accounts
HCE: Family Income and Expenditures Survey

in making adjustments to either household incomes or expenditures, owing mainly to the absence of appropriately constructed spatial cost-of-living indices. For this chapter, we employ the 1997 provincial cost-of-living indices reported in Balisacan (2001). The reference province is Metro Manila (i.e., the cost-of-living index for this province is 100), although any other province may serve the same purpose. Since we are also concerned with welfare comparisons over time, we have updated these indices to reflect nominal price movements during the 1980s and 1990s. This was done by applying the regional consumer price index (CPI) to the provincial cost-of-living indices.[2]

The resulting national distributions of per capita consumption expenditures for the various FIES years are shown in Figure 7.3. The expenditures are in real terms (at 1997 prices) and have been adjusted for provincial cost-of-living differences. Thus, with a given poverty line

Figure 7.3: Distribution of Living Standards

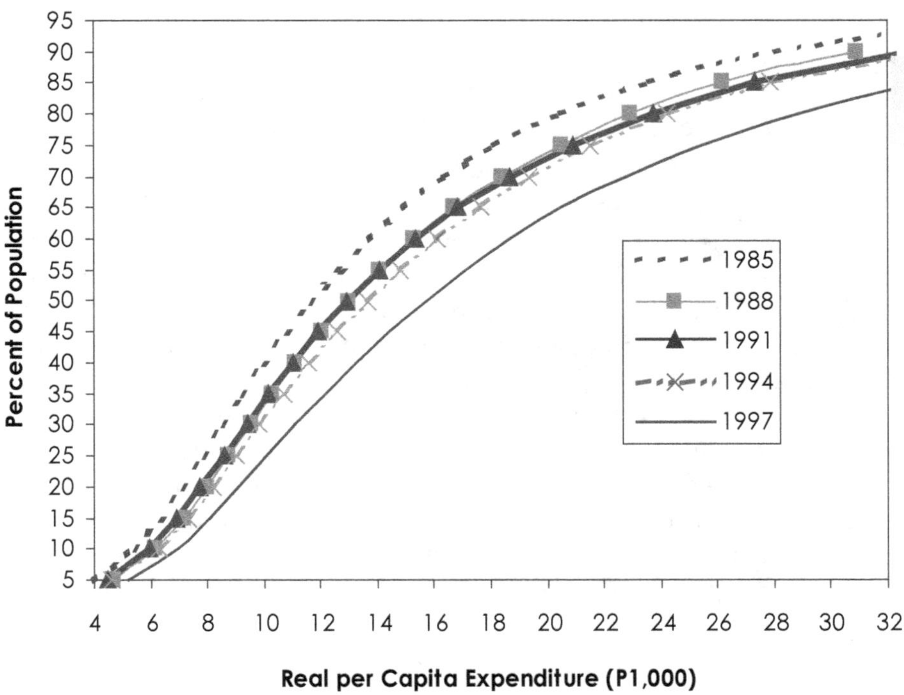

(in real terms), it is straightforward to obtain the poverty incidence from Figure 7.3 for the various years. The national average official poverty line of P11,319 per person implies a poverty incidence of 49 percent for 1985, 45 percent for 1988, 45 percent for 1991, 41 percent for 1994, and 37 percent for 1997.[3] Aggregate poverty is unambiguously lower in 1997 than in any of the other years, regardless of the assumed poverty norm.

Unlike in the Indonesian case, an ambiguity in poverty change is evident, however, for the comparison between 1988 and 1991, as well as between 1991 and 1994, a period of virtually zero growth (see Figure 7.3). In these cases, poverty in the initial year is either higher or lower than that in the last year, depending on whether the poverty line is drawn to the left or to the right of the intersection of the pair of cumulative distribution curves. Note that this ambiguity is peculiar to periods when overall mean income growth was low, as in 1988-1991 (1.6 percent a year), or when it was nil or negative, as in 1991-1994.

It is evident from Figure 7.3 that significant poverty reduction occurred between 1985 and 1997. Applying the spatially consistent poverty lines suggested by Balisacan (2001) to the distribution of per capita expenditures, we obtain a poverty incidence of 41.5 percent for 1985 and 25.0 percent for 1997, or an average decline of about 1.4 percentage points a year. The decline occurred in tandem with rising mean per capita income, averaging 4.2 percent a year.[4] How important was this growth to the observed change in poverty?

The change in poverty during a given period can be decomposed into two components. One is the pure growth effect in mean living standards, defined as the change in poverty if all consumption groups share equally in growth. The other component is the redistribution effect, defined as the change in poverty if the mean consumption of the population remains constant, given the redistribution that occurs. Table 7.1 gives the estimates of these components for the observed poverty reduction between 1985 and 1997.[5] Growth clearly accounted for the bulk of the poverty reduction observed during the period. Without the increase in the Gini ratio from 0.41 to 0.45, the decline in poverty incidence would have been even more rapid (i.e., 20.5 percentage points instead of 16.5 percentage points). A similar result is suggested by the depth-of-poverty measure.

Table 7.1: Growth and Redistribution Components of Poverty Change

YEAR/CHANGE	INCIDENCE	DEPTH
1985	41.5	12.4
1997	25.0	6.4
Change	-16.5	-6.0
Due to growth	-20.5	-8.0
Due to redistribution	4.0	2.0

Source: Authors' estimates.

The ambiguity in poverty change for some periods makes it necessary to examine the various segments of the income distribution for conclusions regarding the relationship between growth and poverty. Thus, below, we explore the link between overall growth and poverty not only with respect to changes in poverty indices (which depend on specific poverty lines) but also in terms of the changes in average per capita expenditures of the various population subgroups.

The above decomposition appears to confirm what has typically been found at the national level regarding the close link between growth and poverty reduction. We now turn to subnational evidence.

PROVINCIAL DIFFERENCES IN LIVING STANDARDS

Changes in living standards among the poor during the 1980s and 1990s vary greatly across provinces. Figure 7.4 shows the extreme ranges (top 10 and bottom 10 provinces) of the distribution of changes in mean per capita expenditure for the 72 provinces.

At the provincial level, the living standards of the poor appear to be closely associated with overall mean income. In Figure 7.5, provincial data covering the five survey years (a total of 360 observations) show a strong positive correlation between overall incomes and living standards of the poor. The growth elasticity of poverty is about 0.7, indicating that a 10 percent increase in overall incomes raises living standards of the poor by 7 percent. This elasticity is lower than Indonesia's 0.8 (Chapter 6).

We examine the robustness of the growth elasticity estimate and explore other determinants of provincial performance in poverty reduction. The results indicate that unobserved province-specific effects

Figure 7.4: Change in Mean Expenditure of Poorest Quintile between 1991 and 1997

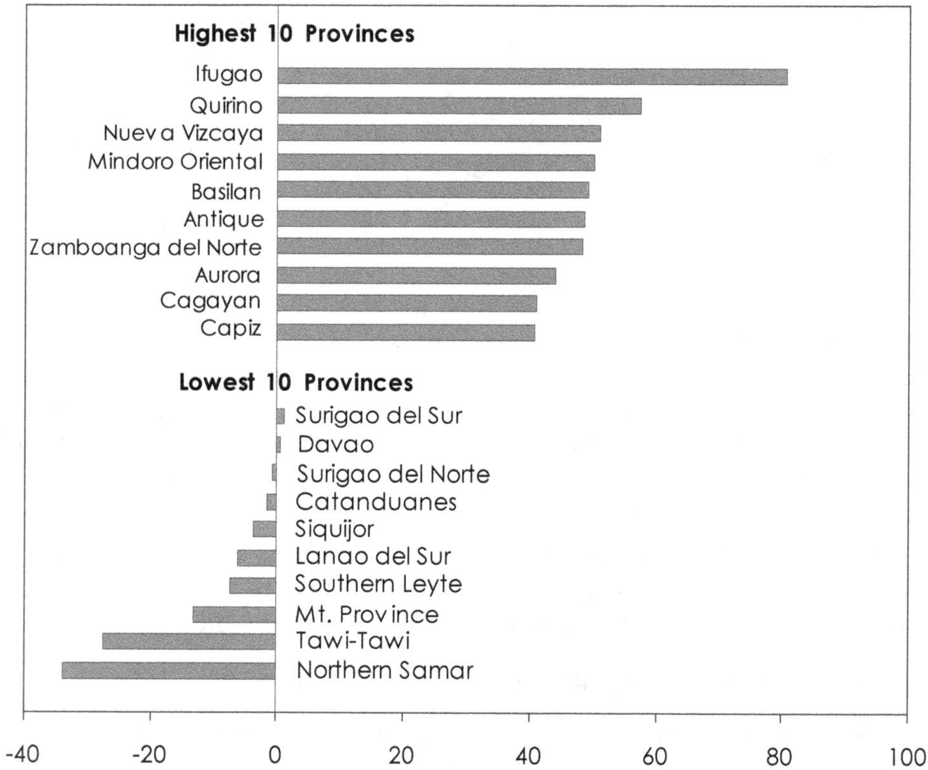

are significant. The estimates, given in Table 7.2, suggest a somewhat weaker response than that reflected in Figure 7.5: the elasticity estimate falls from 0.7 to as low as 0.55.

As is well known, panel estimation assumes certain structures for the unobserved fixed effects. This assumption is rejected by the data. For example, the assumption that the error terms are not correlated with the explanatory variable is rejected by the provincial panel data.

An alternative procedure is to directly estimate the elasticity from differences in variable values over time. Such estimation yields an elasticity estimate of 0.54 (not shown in the table), which is of a magnitude generally comparable to those obtained from panel estimations.

Figure 7.5: Average Expenditure of Bottom Quintile versus Overall Provincial Mean Income

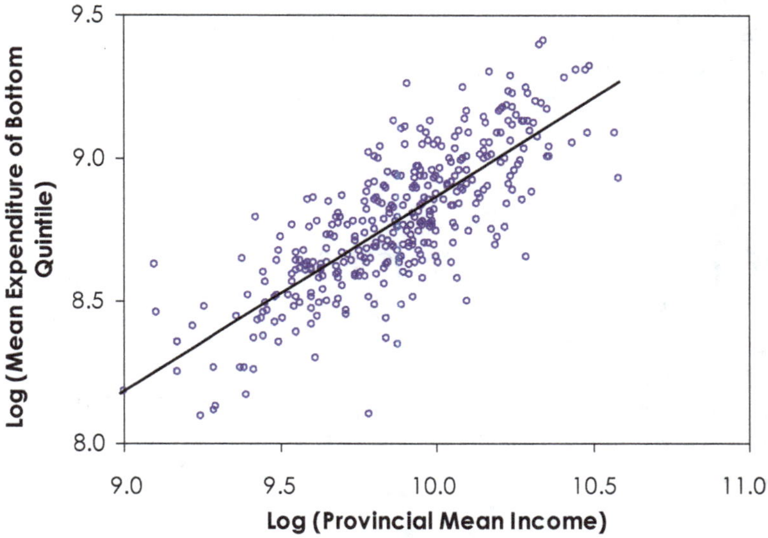

Table 7.2: Average Expenditures of Bottom Quintile versus Provincial Mean Income: Basic Specifications

ITEM	OLS	FIXED EFFECTS	RANDOM EFFECTS
Log of mean income	0.704 (.029)	0.553 (.033)	0.610 (.030)
Constant	1.833 (.286)	3.328 (.331)	2.758 (.293)
F-test		F=5.86	
Hausman specification test			x^2=13.49

Note: Dependent variable is the logarithm of the mean expenditure for the bottom 20 percent of the population ranked by per capita expenditure. The F-test statistic pertains to a test of the null hypothesis that all provincial dummy coefficients are zero. The Hausman specification test statistic pertains to a test of the null hypothesis that the difference in coefficients between the random and the panel effects estimations is not systematic. Both hypotheses are rejected at the 1 percent significance level. Figures in parentheses are robust standard errors. Data refer to the panel of 72 provinces and five years covering the 1980s and 1990s.

We noted earlier that there may be reverse causation in the poverty-growth relationship, i.e., overall mean income may systematically respond to changes in the average living standards of the poor. Here it appears that overall average income is not exactly exogenous, as has so far been assumed in the above regressions. The above elasticity estimates may thus be biased and inconsistent.

Table 7.3: Basic Specifications: Endogenous Mean Income

ITEM	IV ESTIMATION		SYSTEM
	LEVEL	DIFFERENCE	
Slope	0.502	0.622	0.700
	(.088)	(.100)	(.033)
Constant	3.832		1.861
	(.870)		(.331)

Note: IV means instrumental variable. Figures in parentheses are robust standard errors. Data refer to the panel of 72 provinces and five years covering the 1980s and 1990s.

We thus reestimate the poverty-growth relationship by using instruments for mean income, namely, lagged mean income growth. For the difference form of the poverty-growth relationship, we instrument for the difference of mean income over three years using the initial mean income in the current three-year period and the growth of mean income for the past three years prior to the current period. The resulting parameter estimates are summarized in the second and third columns of Table 7.3. These yield a growth elasticity of 0.50 for the levels form and 0.62 for the differences form.

By construction, the slope for the levels form and that for the differences form should be equal. Conventional tests indicate that the two slopes are indeed not statistically different from each other (using a 95 percent confidence level).

Dollar and Kraay (2001) suggest that combining the information on both data levels and differences helps resolve the dilemma of choosing and estimating either a levels or a differences form of model. We follow this mode of analysis and estimate a system involving both levels and differences, but imposing the restriction that the coefficients in the levels and differences equations are equal. The parameter estimates for the basic specification are shown in the last column of Table 7.3. The estimate of the growth elasticity is 0.7; the 95 percent confidence interval for this coefficient is [0.63, 0.76].

To sum up, the estimates of the growth elasticity of poverty are far from suggesting a one-to-one correspondence between growth in the average living standards of the poor and overall average income growth. Other factors appear to have direct distributive effects on the living standards of the poor, apart from the impact of these factors on overall income growth. This result is consistent with those based on state-level and province-level analyses in India (Datt and Ravallion 1998, Ravallion and Datt 2002), Indonesia (Chapter 6), and Thailand (Chapter 8).

OTHER DETERMINANTS OF POVERTY REDUCTION

We assess the impact of certain economic and institutional factors on poverty in the various provinces. As in the previous section, the variable to be explained is the average per capita expenditures of the poor—defined initially to be those in the bottom quintile of the expenditure distribution—which varied widely across provinces during the 1980s and 1990s.

Because provincial data on explanatory factors are less complete for the 1980s than for the 1990s, we first proceed to estimate a system involving only a limited set of variables but utilizing the complete panel (72 provinces and five years covering the 1980s and 1990s). We then reestimate the system utilizing the full set of variables but focus on a partial panel (63 provinces and three years covering only the 1990s). We refer to the former as the full panel and the latter as the partial panel.

The explanatory variables for both full and partial panels are categorized into two groups, namely, initial-condition variables and time-varying policy variables. Included in the first group are province-specific human capital endowment, farm and land characteristics, social capital, geographic attributes, and political economy characteristics.

The time-varying variables, on the other hand, include relative price incentives, road access and electricity, agrarian reform, and overall per capita income.

The proxy used for initial human capital endowment is the (three-year lagged) average years of schooling of household heads. Expected to be positively correlated with the living standards of the poor, this variable is available for the full panel (1980s and 1990s). An alternative proxy is the access of the villagers (*barangay* residents) to school establishments. This variable is available for the early 1990s and is used in the partial panel.

Farm characteristics are represented by average farm size and irrigation. The latter, expressed as the ratio of irrigated land to total farm area, is a proxy for the quality of agricultural land. It is expected that both variables are positively correlated with per capita expenditure of the poor. Data on these variables are available only for the early 1990s and are thus used for the partial panel.

Geographic attributes available for the full panel are spatial isolation or high transport costs (represented by a dummy variable indicating whether a province is landlocked or not) and the average frequency of typhoons hitting the province. These variables are intended to capture geographic "poverty traps." It has been observed, for example, that areas most frequented by typhoons are among the poorest areas in the country (see, e.g., Balisacan 2001). Using cross-country regressions, Gallup and Sachs (1998) also find that the geographic location of a country tends to influence the speed of its economic growth, noting in particular that landlocked countries tend to grow slower than those with direct access to sea transport.

The initial political economy variables reflect the quality of local governance and access to fiscal resources. One variable for the full panel is local political dynasty, defined as the local officials related to each other by blood or affinity as a proportion of the total number of elective positions. This variable reflects the extent of collusion or competition in local politics. We expect that political dynasty inhibits poverty reduction through its negative effect on the efficient operation of markets (i.e., restricting competition in local markets and creating rents for the political clan) and on the access of the poor to public goods.[6] The other variable pertains to the political party affiliation of the provincial chief executive. This is represented by a dummy variable indicating whether the provincial governor belongs to the national president's political party. The expectation is that more resources for infrastructure, employment generation, and poverty reduction tend to flow to local governments that have direct ties to the ruling political party.

The time-varying price incentives variable is given by the agricultural terms of trade, defined as the ratio of the price of agricultural to nonagricultural products. Since poverty in developing countries is concentrated in agriculture (Pernia and Quibria 1999)—an observation that also holds for the Philippines (Balisacan and Pernia 2002)—the price-incentives variable is expected to be positively related to the living standards of the poor. The variable is available for the full panel analysis.

The time-varying infrastructure variables pertain to road access and electricity.[7] Roads represent access to markets, off-farm employment, and social services. The variable is defined as quality-adjusted road length per square kilometer of land area. Electricity, on the other hand, is a proxy for access to technology, or simply the ability to use modern equipment. It is defined simply as the proportion of households with access to electricity. Both variables are available for the full panel analysis.

A time-varying policy variable related to the government's redistribution (and empowerment) program is the Comprehensive Agrarian Reform Program (CARP). The agrarian reform variable, defined as the proportion of cumulative agrarian reform accomplishments out of total potential land reform area, serves as a proxy for households' ability to smooth consumption during shocks, given imperfections in credit markets. The variable is expected to be positively related to the living standards of the poor and is available for the full panel regression.

Certain variables may have strong complementarities, i.e., the impact of one variable on the welfare of the poor may be influenced by other variables. Endogenous growth theory, for example, asserts that the rates of return to investment in technology are conditioned by the level of human capital stock. To allow for this possibility, we have introduced interaction terms on certain variables, as appropriate.

Detailed descriptions of the above variables are given in Appendix Table 7.1 and the estimating model is spelled out in Appendix 7.2. All the regression models are estimated as a system, i.e., both the levels equations (initial-condition and time-varying variables) and differences equations (time-varying variables) are estimated jointly, taking into account the endogeneity of overall mean income and its difference. Some variants of the model take account of the possibility that agrarian reform is endogenous, as suggested by Otsuka's (1991) earlier assessment of Philippine land reform implementation. The results for the full panel are summarized in Table 7.4, while those for the partial panel are given in Table 7.5.

In either the full panel or partial panel regressions, the response of the living standards of the poor (bottom quintile) to overall income growth is far lower than that suggested by cross-country studies (e.g., Dollar and Kraay 2001, Timmer 1997). The growth elasticity is only slightly higher than 0.5, suggesting that a 10 percent increase in overall per capita income raises the per capita expenditure (or welfare) of the poor by just about 5 percent. This result suggests that the quality or type—not just the pace—of growth also matters for poverty reduction. It further implies that the same growth brings about disproportionately higher welfare gains for the upper quintiles of the population. We return later to the differential responses of the various quintiles to growth and other factors.

The agrarian reform variable is significant in three of four variants of the model. Interestingly, the estimated coefficient is positive and highly significant when the specification allows for the possibility that agrarian reform is endogenous and uses initial land inequality and tenancy as additional instruments (variant 4). Note that in the full panel, these instruments, as well as irrigation and farm size, are not used since values for these variables are available only for the 1990s. It is thus plausible that the agrarian reform variable in the full panel regression either captures the effects of the omitted variables (variant 1) or is inadequately instrumented (variant 2). For this reason, the specification given in variant 4 is suggestive of the positive impact of agrarian reform on the welfare of the poor.

Apart from its direct impact on overall income, overall schooling per se does not seem to have a direct impact on the well-being of the poor. The schooling coefficient is not significantly different from zero in all variants of the regression model. However, when schooling is taken in conjunction with the roads variable (a proxy for access to markets and social services), the coefficient is positive and significant in all re-

Table 7.4: Determinants of Average Living Standards of the Poor (Bottom Quintile), Full Panel (1980s and 1990s)

EXPLANATORY VARIABLE	VARIANT 1			VARIANT 2 (Agrarian Reform is Endogenous)		
	Coefficient	t-ratio		Coefficient	t-ratio	
Initial Conditions						
Schooling	0.061	0.66		0.080	0.86	
Local dynasty	-0.124	-3.76	***	-0.124	-3.76	***
Political party	0.027	1.69	*	0.033	2.06	**
Landlocked	-0.067	-3.53	***	-0.067	-3.53	***
Typhoon	-0.038	-2.11	**	-0.054	-2.70	***
Time-varying Variables						
Per capita income (Y)	0.535	12.16	***	0.499	11.09	***
Terms of trade (Pa/Pna)	0.092	2.04	**	0.108	2.40	**
Roads	-0.320	-3.37	***	-0.295	-3.07	***
Electricity	0.110	1.29		0.121	1.41	
Agrarian reform	2.800	2.80	***	6.300	3.94	***
Interactions						
Schooling*Roads	0.157	3.14	***	0.144	2.82	***
Schooling*Electricity	0.058	1.53		0.035	0.90	
Y*year91	0.001	0.50		0.003	1.50	
Y*year94	-0.001	-0.50		-0.000	0.00	
Intercept	3.241	8.27	***	3.542	8.72	***
R-squared	0.719	0.40		0.707	0.377	

*** denotes significance at the 1 percent level.

** denotes significance at the 5 percent level.

* denotes significance at the 10 percent level.

Note: Estimation is by three-stage least squares. Instruments are actual values of schooling, roads, electricity, political economy and geographic variables, agrarian reform (except in variant 2), terms of trade, and lagged values of the other variables, including twice-lagged value of average income growth. Data are for full provincial panel covering five years of three-year intervals in the 1980s and 1990s. The *R*-squared values apply to the level and the difference form of the estimated log (per capita expenditure) function.

Table 7.5: Determinants of Average Living Standards of the Poor (Bottom Quintile), Partial Panel (1990s)

EXPLANATORY VARIABLE	VARIANT 3		VARIANT 4 (Agrarian Reform is Endogenous)	
	Coefficient	t-ratio	Coefficient	t-ratio
Initial Conditions				
Schooling	-0.072	-0.79	-0.010	-0.11
Local dynasty	-0.101	-3.48 ***	-0.104	-3.47 ***
Political party	0.026	1.73 *	0.029	1.93 *
Landlocked	-0.062	-3.26 ***	-0.067	-3.53 ***
Typhoon	-0.042	-2.47 **	-0.064	-3.37 ***
Irrigation	0.309	7.92 ***	0.233	5.07 ***
Farm size	0.008	0.44	0.010	0.53
Time-varying Variables				
Per capita income (Y)	0.602	13.68 ***	0.544	11.57 ***
Terms of trade (Pa/Pna)	0.118	2.81 ***	0.140	3.26 ***
Roads	-0.208	-2.19 **	-0.212	-2.21 **
Electricity	0.051	0.59	0.049	0.57
Agrarian reform	-0.500	-0.50	4.100	2.41 **
Interactions				
Schooling*Roads	0.109	2.14 **	0.110	2.16 **
Schooling*Electricity	0.016	0.43	0.007	0.18
Intercept	2.865	7.44 ***	3.324	8.19 ***
R-squared	0.771	0.394	0.758	0.385

*** denotes significance at the 1 percent level.

** denotes significance at the 5 percent level.

* denotes significance at the 10 percent level.

Note: Estimation is by three-stage least squares. Instruments are actual values of schooling, roads, electricity, political economy and geographic variables, agrarian reform (except for variant 4), terms of trade, and lagged values of the other variables, including twice-lagged value of average income growth. For variant 4, two additional instruments are lagged land inequality and tenancy. Data are for provincial panel covering three years of three-year intervals in the 1990s. The *R*-squared values apply to the level and the difference form of the estimated log (per capita expenditure) function.

gressions. This suggests that returns to schooling depend on the availability of complementary factors.

The coefficient for roads is significant but surprisingly has a negative sign, implying that access to markets and information per se may not necessarily have a favorable effect on the plight of the poor. This could suggest that roads do not reach the areas where most of the poor are found or if they do, they could exert an adverse impact on the poor through such channels as factor-market and political-economy processes. As pointed out, however, road access can improve the well-being of the poor provided they have sufficient human capital to take advantage of it.

Electricity, as well as its interaction with education, is insignificant in all regressions. This result is somewhat puzzling, considering the importance often attributed to access to technology as a factor in poverty reduction. It is possible that this variable is a poor proxy for access to technology.

As expected, the terms of trade variable is positive and significant, indicating that changes in agricultural prices relative to those in other sectors of the local economy benefit the poor.[8] This result reflects the favorable effects on the poor of the trade and exchange rate reforms in the 1990s. These reforms effectively reduced the degree of overvaluation of the local currency, thereby improving the price incentives for tradables relative to nontradables. That is, since the output of agriculture is largely either exportable or import-substituting compared to that of services and, to a lesser extent, industry, the policy shift would have improved the relative profitability of agriculture. Further, since agriculture is more labor-intensive than industry, the reforms would have benefited the poor.[9]

Initial farm size is not significant but irrigation is. This suggests that land quality, not farm size per se, positively influences the living standards of the poor. This result conforms to the commonly held view that investment in land improvements, such as irrigation and drainage, is an important measure for poverty reduction in land-scarce, labor-abundant developing areas.

Interestingly, local political dynasty is highly significant and has the negative sign, indicating that the welfare of the poor tends to be lower in provinces governed by political dynasties than in provinces characterized by competitive politics, other things being equal. This is consistent with the view that dynasty in local politics inhibits economic performance—through its effects on economic efficiency—and restricts the access of the poor to basic services. The other political economy variable—political party affiliation of local chief executives—is likewise significant, suggesting that resources for employment generation and poverty reduction tend to flow more favorably to local governments run by administrators with direct ties to the country's ruling party.

The frequency of typhoons tends to depress the average living standards of the poor: the coefficient of the typhoon variable in all variants of the regression model is consistently negative and highly significant. Another geographic "poverty trap" is high transport costs, as evidenced by the estimated negative relationship between the living standards of the poor and the variable "landlocked."

DIFFERENTIAL EFFECTS ACROSS QUINTILES

As in the Indonesian case, we ask whether the welfare effects of the variables vary across income groups? If the upper ranges of the income distribution tend to benefit more than proportionately from overall economic growth, what policies or institutional arrangements might enhance the benefits of growth for the poor?

We address these issues by estimating variant 4 of the model for each of the other four income quintiles. Recall that in variant 4, agrarian reform is endogenous and the model is estimated using the partial panel data (i.e., the full set of variables but covering the 1990s only). The estimation results for each quintile are summarized in Table 7.6. For ready comparison, the last column in Table 7.5 is reproduced for the first quintile in Table 7.6.

In general, the results for the second quintile closely resemble those for the first quintile. This is significant considering the wide variation in estimates of Philippine poverty—from 20 to 40 percent—depending on, among other things, the poverty norm employed. The official estimate roughly corresponds to the bottom 40 percent of the population.

Other observations are also worth noting. First, the growth elasticity of poverty increases monotonically with income quintile. This confirms what has already been noted above: the benefits of growth are unevenly spread throughout the various income groups. Second, an

Table 7.6: Determinants of Average Living Standards by Income Quintile, Partial Panel (1990s)

EXPLANATORY VARIABLE	1ST QUINTILE (poorest)	2ND QUINTILE	3RD QUINTILE	4TH QUINTILE	5TH QUINTILE (richest)
Initial Conditions					
Schooling	-0.010	0.080	0.107	0.075	-0.139
Local dynasty	-0.104 ***	-0.069 ***	-0.055 **	-0.029	0.041
Political party	0.029 **	0.013	0.022 *	0.022 *	0.030 **
Landlocked	-0.067 ***	-0.077 ***	-0.070 ***	-0.061 ***	0.041 **
Typhoon	-0.064 ***	-0.055 ***	-0.046 ***	-0.048 **	0.059 ***
Irrigation	0.233 ***	0.157 ***	0.093 ***	0.008	-0.115 **
Farm size	0.010	-0.012	-0.011	0.010	0.072 ***
Time-varying Variables					
Per capita income (Y)	0.544 ***	0.621 ***	0.676 ***	0.798 ***	1.045 ***
Terms of trade (Pa/Pna)	0.140 ***	0.149 ***	0.135 ***	0.119 ***	-0.051
Roads	-0.212 **	-0.264 ***	-0.215 **	-0.051	0.478 ***
Electricity	0.049	0.098	0.162 **	0.143 **	-0.006
Agrarian reform	4.100 **	3.300 **	2.900 **	2.600 *	-0.900
Interactions					
Schooling*Roads	0.110 **	0.133 ***	0.102 ***	0.015	-0.251 ***
Schooling*Electricity	0.007	0.019	0.009	0.002	0.002
Intercept	3.324 ***	2.760 ***	2.418 ***	1.625 ***	0.491
R-squared	0.758; 0.385	0.833; 0.498	0.864; 0.576	0.879; 0.610	0.854; 0.686

*** denotes significance at the 1 percent level.

** denotes significance at the 5 percent level.

* denotes significance at the 10 percent level.

Note: Estimation is by three-stage least squares. Instruments are actual values of schooling; roads; electricity; political economy and geographic variables; terms of trade; and lagged values of other variables including land Gini, tenancy, and twice-lagged value of average income growth. Data are for provincial panel covering three years of three-year intervals in the 1990s. The *R*-squared values apply to the level and the difference form of the estimated log (per capita expenditure) function.

improvement in the terms of trade for agriculture tends to raise the living standards in all quintiles, except the top. The welfare of those in the richest quintile does not respond directly to changes in the relative price of agriculture, since they depend mainly on the nonagriculture sectors of the local economy for employment and income.

Third, the roads variable is significant but has a negative sign for the first three quintiles, suggesting that roads by themselves directly reduce the welfare of the poor unless complementary factors like schooling are present. By contrast, this variable is significant and positive for the top quintile, indicating that roads raise directly the welfare of the richest group in society.

Figure 7.6: Schooling and Road Impact

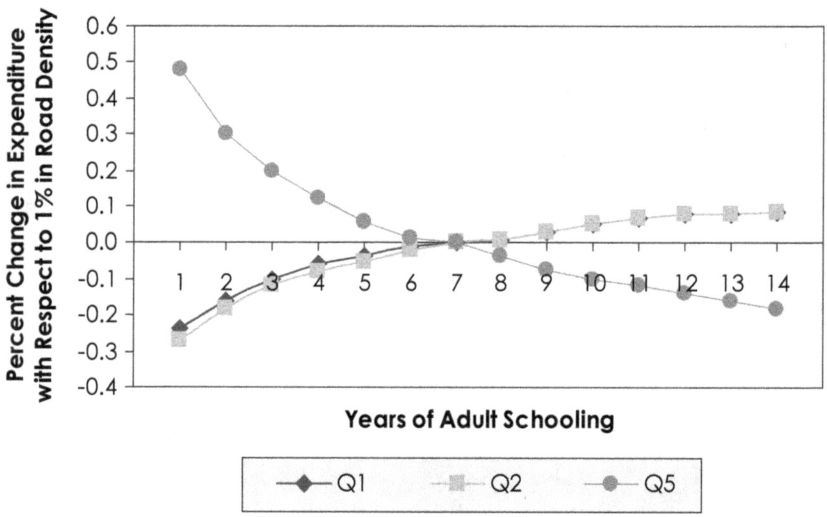

Fourth, overall schooling has no direct, significant effect on the well-being of any quintile. As noted above, however, in conjunction with roads, schooling tends to raise the well-being of the first three quintiles. This suggests again that complementarity does matter. In Figure 7.6, the impact of raising average province-level schooling on returns (in terms of changes in quintile mean expenditures) to roads is shown for the bottom two and the top quintiles. The contrast suggests that higher schooling confers direct benefits to the poor only if complementary factors, such as overall road development, are likewise accessible to them.

Fifth, other things being equal, agrarian reform raises the welfare of all quintiles, except the top one. Again, as mentioned earlier, those in the top quintile typically do not depend on agriculture for employment and income.

Sixth, irrigation tends to have a pro-poor bias. Farm size has no significant effect on the welfare of any but the richest group, implying that it is land quality, not farm size per se, that favorably affects the welfare of the lower-income groups.

Finally, the local political economy appears to influence differently the welfare of the various quintiles. Lack of political competition (the presence of political dynasties) hurts the lower income groups, particularly the poorest.

CONCLUSION

Newly constructed panel data for the Philippines spanning the 1980s and 1990s reveal substantial differences in the evolution of poverty across provinces. Our econometric results based on these data indicate that the response of poverty to overall income growth is far more subdued than reported by cross-country analyses. The growth elasticity of poverty is just above 0.5, indicating that income growth does not proportionately benefit the poor. Rather, changes in poverty over time depend not only on the *rate* of economic growth but also on the *type* of growth. Put differently, the poor would benefit more from growth if institutions and policies are reformed to favor them, or are at least made neutral. This result is consistent with those of similar subnational analyses for India, Indonesia, and Thailand.

Apart from economic growth, other factors influence the welfare of the poor via income distribution. This chapter has highlighted the importance of education, infrastructure, terms of trade, agrarian reform, governance, and certain geographic attributes. Schooling, if accompanied by complementary public investments, raises the welfare of the poor, apart from its indirect effect through economic growth. So do the implementation of agrarian reform, investments to improve land quality, and the removal of price distortions that diminish the profitability of agriculture relative to nonagriculture. Political dynasties appear to prejudice the poor, since they not only constrain local economic growth but also restrict access of the poor to basic services. High transport costs act as geographic "poverty traps" that prevent the poor from taking advantage of economic opportunities elsewhere.

On the whole, economic growth explains a great deal but not everything about poverty. The balance is accounted for by institutions and other factors. Thus, while growth may indeed be good for the poor, it is not good enough.

Notes

The authors thank Anil Deolalikar, Nobu Fuwa, Gunter Hecker, and Mario Lamberte for valuable comments, as well as Gemma Esther Estrada and Pilipinas F. Quising for excellent research and technical assistance.

1. See Balisacan (1994a, 2001) for an extensive discussion on the comparability of the FIES data. Of special note here is the problem posed by the periodic regional regroupings of provinces and the occasional splitting of provinces, as well as the decadal reclassification of initially "rural" areas into "urban" areas. This problem makes the published tables unsuitable for spatial comparison of poverty reduction performance. In this paper, the unit record data of the FIES were used to reconstruct *spatially comparable* poverty profiles, i.e., geographical boundaries of the provinces were kept constant throughout the period of interest.
2. Provincial CPIs are not available.
3. Note that these estimates do not correspond to the officially published poverty estimates. The official approach to poverty estimation uses current income rather than consumption expenditure as the welfare indicator, as well as poverty lines that vary in real terms across regions and between urban and rural areas. As shown in Balisacan (2001), this approach fails the consistency test for poverty lines. Hence, it is not suitable for national poverty monitoring or assessing comparative performance across regions, provinces, or areas of the country—if the main policy objective is to reduce absolute poverty.
4. In comparison, mean per capita expenditure rose by 41 percent between 1985 and 1997, or an average of 3.4 percent a year. The increase of real per capita GDP during the same period was much lower at 1.2 percent a year.
5. In deriving these estimates, we have applied the procedure suggested by Kakwani (1997) and Kakwani and Pernia (2000) to identify the components of poverty change.
6. Put differently, local governance under a political dynasty may facilitate the concentration of economic power and control, thereby causing or perpetuating high income inequality. High income inequality, in turn, may inhibit subsequent

growth in the local economy, as suggested by recent development literature. Moreover, such governance structures may make public services less accessible to the poor.

7. Government expenditures on infrastructure would have been preferred to levels of physical infrastructure. The former variables would have related a policy handle—spending on infrastructure—directly to the average living standards of the poor.
8. As shown elsewhere (see Balisacan 2001), income poverty in the Philippines is a largely rural phenomenon, regardless of the poverty norm employed. Nearly two thirds of the rural poor depend on agriculture for employment and income. Improvements in the terms of trade in provinces where agriculture is a dominant component of the local economy therefore tend to raise the welfare levels of the poor.
9. The severe overvaluation of the peso in the 1970s and 1980s disproportionately penalized agriculture and the export-oriented manufacturing sector (see Bautista and Tecson 2003).

APPENDIX TABLE 7.1: Variable Definitions and Data Sources

VARIABLE NAME	DEFINITION	SOURCE OF BASIC DATA
Mean expenditure	Log (average per capita expenditure of bottom 20 percent, adjusted for provincial cost-of-living differences)	FIES-NSO(1985-1997)
Mean income	Log (average per capita income, adjusted for provincial cost-of-living differences)	FIES-NSO (1985-1997)
Roads	Log (concrete-equivalent roads per square kilometer)	DPWH and NSO (1989, 1997)
Electricity	Proportion of households with access to electricity	FIES (1985-1997)
Agrarian reform	Proportion of cumulative CARP accomplishments to 1990 potential land reform area	DENR and DAR CARP Accomplishment Reports (1988-1997)
Farm size	Log (average farm size, in hectares)	NSO, 1991 Census of Agriculture
Irrigation	Proportion of irrigated farm area to total farm area	NSO, 1991 Census of Agriculture
Tenancy	Proportion of tenanted farm area to total farm area	NSO, 1991 Census of Agriculture
Land Gini	Log (Gini ratio of agricultural landholding)	NSO, 1991 Census of Agriculture
Education	Log (mean years of schooling of household heads)	FIES-NSO (1985-1997)
Terms of trade	Log (ratio of implicit price deflator for agriculture to implicit price deflator for nonagriculture)	NSCB regional accounts (1988-1997)
Local dynasty	Proportion of provincial officials and district representatives related by blood or affinity	COMELEC records and Congressional interviews
Political party	Dummy variable (equal to 1 if the governor's party is the same as that of the president, 0 otherwise)	COMELEC Election Reports
Landlocked	Dummy variable (equal to 1 if province is landlocked, 0 otherwise)	Philippine map
Typhoon	Average annual number of typhoons for 1948-1998	PAGASA

APPENDIX 7.2: The Estimating Model

The estimating model of the determinants of average household welfare at the provincial level has the general form

$$y_{pt}^{Qi} = \alpha_0 + \alpha_1 y_{pt} + \alpha_2' x_{pt} + \alpha_3' z_p + v_p + \varepsilon_{pt}, \qquad i = 1,2,...,5 \qquad (1)$$

where the subscripts *p* and *t* are indices for provinces and years, respectively; y^{Qi} is the logarithm of mean per-capita expenditure for quintile *i*; *y* is the logarithm of overall mean per-capita income; *x* is a vector of time-varying factors other than income; *z* is a set of observed province-specific factors; and $v+\varepsilon$ is a composite error term, including unobserved province effects. This paper's main interest is the determinants of the mean per capita expenditure for *Q1*, the poorest quintile of the provincial population.

As discussed in the text, the appropriate household welfare indicator is consumption expenditures normalized by household size. For consistency, the overall welfare indicator on the right-hand side of equation (1) should also be formulated in terms of expenditures, not incomes. However, doing so would introduce correlations in any measurement errors between the right-hand side variable and the error terms ε_{pt} since this variable and the left-hand side variable come from the same distribution. The effect would be biased estimates of the parameters of interest. By using incomes as an instrument for expenditures, this source of potential biases is eliminated.

The difference-form of equation (1) shows growth in the mean per capita expenditure of the poor in province *p* over the time period from *t*-3 to *t* as a function of growth in overall income, as well as of changes in *x* variables, i.e.,

$$\left(y_{pt}^{Qi} - y_{pt-3}^{Qi}\right) = \alpha_1\left(y_{pt} - y_{pt-3}\right) + \alpha_2'\left(x_{pt} - x_{pt-3}\right) + \tau_{pt}, \qquad (2)$$

where $\tau_{pt} = (\varepsilon_{pt} - \varepsilon_{pt-3})$. Direct OLS estimation of this equation gives unbiased estimates of the growth elasticity of poverty as well as responses of average welfare to other time-varying factors, but at the expense of losing information on the influence of certain fixed effects which are also of interest.

In equations (1) and (2), the level of average income and its rate of growth influence the poor's average welfare level and its growth. But the reverse causation is also possible. One strand of the recent growth-empirics literature, for example, suggests that increasing the current welfare of the poor through, say, redistribution policies enhances subsequent overall growth. To see this, suppose, as in standard formulation of Barro-type growth regressions, that the overall per-capita income at time *t* is a function of initial income and initial income inequality, among other variables. Let the measure of income inequality be represented by the income share of the poor (here, the bottom quintile Q1) Then the overall per capita income can be expressed as

$$y_{pt} = \beta_0 + \beta_1 \ln\left(\frac{Q1_{pt-k}}{0.2}\right) + \beta_2 y_{pt-k} + \beta_3' w_{pt} + \eta_p + \mu_{pt} \quad (3)$$

where *w* is a vector of other determinants of overall per capita income.

Clearly, from equations (1) and (3), the welfare level of the poor (y^{Q1}) also influences overall per capita income (y), provided β_1 is not equal to zero. For example, a high realization of *v* in equation (1) causes the incomes of the poor to rise relative to those of the nonpoor, which, in equation (3), then raises the overall per capita income if $\beta_1 > 0$, or lowers it if $\beta_1 < 0$.

When obtaining estimates of a_1 (as well as other parameters), the usual practice is to estimate either equation (1) or equation (2) by OLS. Given fixed effects, the disadvantage of estimating equation (1) is well known. On the other hand, estimating equation (2) directly to obtain the parameters of the time-varying variables (y and x) results in loss of information. Following Dollar and Kraay (2001), this paper combines information from both levels of, and changes in, the data by estimating equations (1) and (2) simultaneously. Specifically, the system is estimated using three-stage least squares; the estimation imposes the restriction that coefficients in the levels and differences equations are equal.

One of the time-varying *x* variables is agrarian reform, which is treated in the paper as an endogenous variable. Instruments for this variable are land inequality—given by the landholding Gini ratio—and tenancy incidence, as well as lagged values of per capita expenditure of the poor and of overall per capita income.

8 Poverty, Growth, and Inequality in Thailand

ANIL B. DEOLALIKAR

INTRODUCTION

While the thesis that economic growth reduces poverty has existed for some time, it has only been in the last few years that a large empirical literature has arisen on the nature of the relationship between poverty and growth. These studies have attempted to measure the sensitivity of poverty to growth, i.e., the "growth elasticity of poverty", to ask the question—do the poor in particular, as opposed to all segments of society, share the benefits of economic growth proportionally? Virtually all such studies are based on cross-country data.

There are two main problems with the use of cross-country data to analyze this relationship, however. First, there are enormous problems of comparability when data are pooled from a large number of countries that differ from one another in the quality, frequency, and type of poverty data collected (e.g., whether data are obtained from national income accounts or household surveys), not to mention differences in concepts, measurement, and definitions of key variables. These differences are likely to introduce systematic measurement errors in the estimation of poverty-growth elasticities.

Second, cross-country studies neglect the fact that the growth-poverty relationship is likely to be highly country-specific; the "average" elasticity estimated by various studies is thus unlikely to capture the wide range of country experiences. In some countries, economic growth has been associated with rapid poverty reduction, while in others it has not. Even in a given country, growth can be sharply poverty-reducing at one time yet have a much smaller effect on poverty at a different time.

These problems can be mitigated to some extent by using intracountry data—data on regions, provinces, or districts within a country. Since data on different regions of a country are typically derived from the same statistical survey or administrative data collection system, data are more comparable across units of observation. In addition, subnational entities such as provinces often share the same political and policy framework and are socially and culturally more similar to each other than are individual countries. The estimation of an average poverty-growth elasticity for a country, though not perfect, makes more sense than an average elasticity for the entire developing world.

In addition to the use of highly aggregate cross-country data, another shortcoming of the poverty-growth literature is the omission of changes in the distribution of income as a factor in poverty. As well as economic growth, changes in income inequality affect the rate of poverty reduction. The impact of growth on poverty will be smaller if growth is associated with a worsening income distribution.[1] The vast majority of studies on the poverty-growth relationship ignore the contemporaneous effect on poverty of changes in income inequality.

This chapter uses provincial data from Thailand to explore the impact of economic growth and changes in income distribution on poverty reduction between 1992 and 1999. Thailand is an ideal country for which to estimate an intracountry relationship between growth and poverty for three reasons. First, the number (76) of administrative provinces in the country offers a relatively large sample for estimation purposes. Second, the country conducts at regular intervals a nationally representative household consumption and income survey (the Socioeconomic Survey), the sample size for which is large enough to calculate reliable provincial means. The survey has employed the same concepts and definitions of income since 1988, making data for different time periods comparable. Third, Thailand experienced large changes in mean income and income inequality over the period 1992-1999. While the period 1992-1996 saw rapid economic growth and a modest reduction in income inequality, the period during the Asian economic crisis (1997-1999) was associated with a sharp decline in mean income and a sharp increase in income inequality. These changes offer a unique opportunity to study the effects of both growth and distributional changes on poverty reduction.

POVERTY IN THAILAND

Poverty Line

A number of different poverty lines have been used in Thailand over the last 20 years. In 1996, however, the National Economic and Social Development Board (NESDB) developed a new poverty line that was officially accepted by the Thai cabinet[2] and is now used as the standard poverty line in most poverty analyses in the country. This official line is used throughout this chapter, unless otherwise noted. Not only does this poverty line vary across rural and urban areas and across the five regions to reflect geographical variations in the cost of living, it also varies across households of different sizes and demographic composition, as subsistence needs are assumed to differ by age and sex of individuals. The national average of the official poverty line was B878 per person per month in 1998 and B886 per person per month in 1999.

In 1999, the poverty line (which had an average value for the entire country of B10,632 per capita per annum) was only about one seventh (14.4 percent) of gross domestic product (GDP) per capita. Converted to a daily figure, the poverty line is significantly lower than the minimum wage, constituting less than one fourth of the minimum wage in 1999 (which averaged about B135 nationally). In United States (US) dollars, the official Thai poverty line in 1999 was approximately $0.75 per day.[3]

Extent of Poverty and Changes in Poverty

Headcount Ratio

Data from the Socioeconomic Survey (SES) show a sharp decline in the incidence of poverty (or headcount ratio) from 1988 to 1996 (Figure 8.1).[4] The headcount ratio fell from 32.6 percent to 11.4 percent, with the number of the poor declining from about 18 million to 7 million. On average, 1.4 million persons were annually being lifted out of income-poverty between 1988 and 1996. The onset of the economic crisis halted these impressive rates of poverty decline. The headcount ratio of income-poverty instead increased from 11.4 percent in 1996 to 13 percent in 1998 and 15.9 percent in 1999.[5] This means that one million more persons became poor in 1998, with another two million persons joining them in 1999.

Figure 8.1: Measures of Income-Poverty, 1988-1999

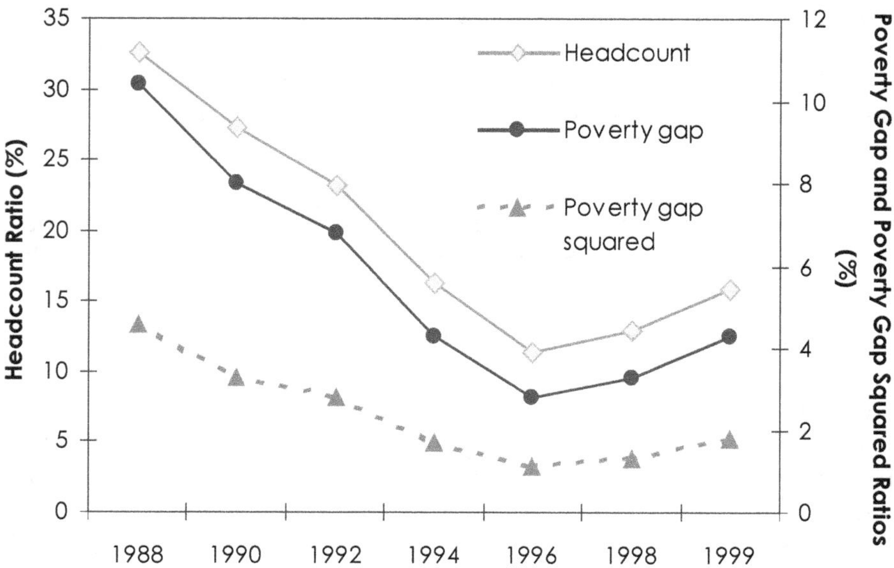

Poverty Gap

One shortcoming of the headcount ratio is that it says nothing about the depth of poverty, viz., the extent to which the incomes of the poor fall below the poverty line. The poverty gap index addresses this shortcoming by measuring the shortfall between the incomes or consumption expenditures of poor households and the poverty line. The sum of all individual poverty gaps in a sample can be interpreted as the minimum amount of income transfers needed to bring all of the poor just up to the poverty line in the presence of perfect targeting.[6] A poverty gap of 4.3 percent for Thailand in 1999, as shown in Figure 8.1, suggests that, if perfect targeting were possible, an income transfer of B38 (= 0.043 × national poverty line of B886) per person per month would be required to eliminate poverty. The total volume of income transfers required to bring all of the poor to an income level just above the poverty line would then be B28 billion (= B38 × 12 months × 61.66 million persons).[7]

The poverty gap measure for Thailand roughly displays the same trend through time as the headcount ratio. There was a small increase in the poverty gap between 1996 and 1998 but a much sharper increase from 1998 to 1999.

Severity of Poverty

The poverty gap index has its own disadvantage in being insensitive to the distribution of income among the poor and hence to the severity of poverty. Redistributing income from a destitute individual to someone much better off though still below the poverty line would leave the poverty gap index (as well as the headcount index) unchanged, although it is clear that this redistribution increases the severity of poverty among the population. The poverty gap-squared index, which belongs to the broader family of Foster-Greer-Thorbecke (FGT) indices, is sensitive to the distribution of income among the poor, since it weights the shortfall between an individual's income and the poverty line more heavily the further below the poverty line that individual's income falls. A shortcoming of this index, however, is that unlike the headcount and the poverty gap indices, it does not lend itself to an easy interpretation. Its use, therefore, lies mainly in comparing the severity of poverty over time or across different subgroups in the population.[8]

Like the headcount ratio and the poverty gap index, the poverty gap-squared index in Thailand showed a falling trend from 1988 to 1996, which reversed itself in 1998 and 1999. The deterioration in all three measures of poverty in 1998 and 1999 due to the economic crisis was sufficient to erase a considerable amount of progress achieved in poverty reduction and push the country back to where it was in 1994 in terms of poverty outcomes.

Regional Variations in Poverty

In Thailand, as in most other countries, large regional differences exist in both the level of poverty and the rate at which poverty has been reduced over time. Historically the Northeast has been the country's poorest region, followed in order by the South, North, Central region, and Bangkok. In 1988, for instance, nearly one half (48.4 percent) of all Northeasterners were poor, as compared to only 6 percent of Bangkok residents (Figure 8.2). By 1996—the year before the economic crisis—poverty incidence had declined in all regions although the Northeast continued to be the poorest region in the country. In the period since the crisis, the ranking of regions by poverty incidence has remained roughly similar, reflecting the fact that relatively poorer regions did not experience more rapid poverty reduction.

In fact, the evidence suggests exactly the opposite, that is, poverty has declined more rapidly in the better-off regions than in the poorer ones. This is clear from Figure 8.3, which shows headcount ratios of poverty from 1988 to 1999 across the five regions, starting from a common base of 100 in 1988. Figure 8.3 shows the Northeast experiencing the smallest relative decline in poverty between 1988 and 1996, with poverty incidence in 1996 being 40 percent of its 1988 level. The South and the North were also relative laggards, with poverty rates in 1996 that were about a third of the corresponding 1988 levels. Bangkok performed best, reducing its 1996 poverty headcount to only 10 percent of the level in 1988.

Regional disparities in poverty reduction trends actually widened with the onset of the crisis. Between 1996 and 1999 poverty incidence increased sharply in the Northeast, rose somewhat in the South and Central regions, and declined in Bangkok and in the North.

Thus by 1999 the poverty headcount in the Northeast was up to two thirds its 1988 level, while the corresponding ratio for Bangkok was a mere 3 percent. The North lay between these, with a poverty headcount in 1999 that was one third of its 1988 level.

The sharp adverse impact of the crisis on poverty reduction in the Northeast, South, and North may seem puzzling since the economic crisis of 1997 originated in the financial center, Bangkok. However, labor migration played an important role in transmitting the impact of the financial crisis to regions outside Bangkok. As the financial shock spread to the real economy shortly after July 1997, aggregate demand fell, and firms responded by cutting back on employment and reducing wages. This resulted in a decrease in the remittances that migrant workers in Bangkok sent to their families in the Northeast. In addition, although there was no large return migration of workers out of Bangkok, there nonetheless was a sharp slowdown

Figure 8.2: Headcount Ratio of Income-Poverty by Region, 1988, 1996, and 1999 (percent)

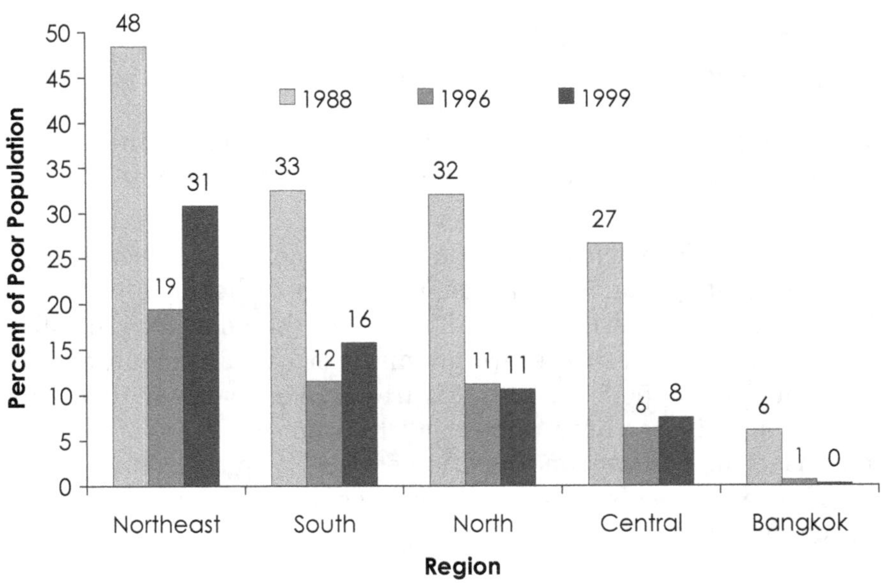

Figure 8.3: Headcount Ratio of Income-Poverty by Region, 1988-1999 (1988 poverty headcount=100)

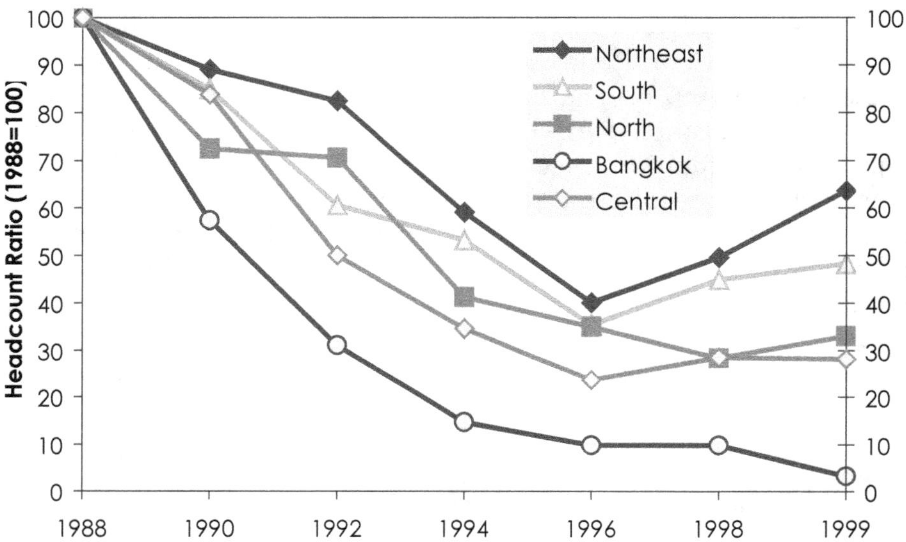

in the migration out of the Northeast, which had been a mainstay of Thai labor markets in the last two decades. The decline in remittances and the reduced outflow of migrants from the poorer to richer regions probably accounted for the decline in household income and the increase in poverty in the Northeast, North, and South during 1998 and 1999.

Interprovincial variations in poverty incidence are even greater than those among regions. The average poverty headcount ratio of 30.8 percent in the Northeast in 1999 masks the enormous disparity in poverty rates between the two provinces of Ubon Ratchathani (8.7 percent) and Surin (50.5 percent). Figure 8.4 is a poverty map of Thailand that highlights these provincial differences. The Northeast is seen to have the highest concentration of poverty in the country. High levels of poverty are also observed in a few of the Northern and Southern provinces.

ECONOMIC GROWTH, INEQUALITY, AND POVERTY ACROSS PROVINCES

What are the reasons for the large provincial and regional differences in poverty levels and poverty reduction in Thailand? To what extent are these differences in poverty performance attributable to provincial differences in economic growth rates?

Figure 8.4: Poverty Map of Thailand

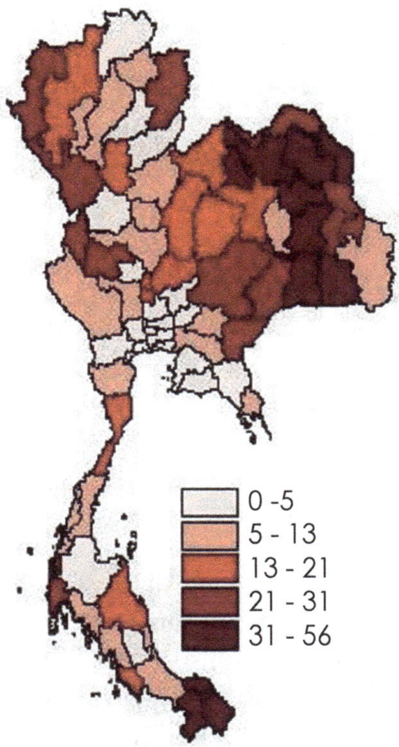

As already noted in the previous section, a large literature is emerging on the relationship between growth and poverty, which argues that economic growth is one of the important determinants of poverty reduction across countries. This point has been empirically established for a cross-section of developing countries as well as for some individual countries over time. But little is known about the effect of economic growth on poverty reduction in Thailand.

Clearly, aggregate poverty has fallen rapidly in Thailand during periods of strong economic growth and has increased during periods of weak or negative growth (Figure 8.5). However, one problem with analyzing the relationship between growth in per capita GDP and changes in poverty at an economywide level is that there are relatively few data points to permit a precise estimate of the relation-

Figure 8.5: Growth Rate per Capita GDP and Changes in Incidence of Consumption-Poverty, 1988-1999

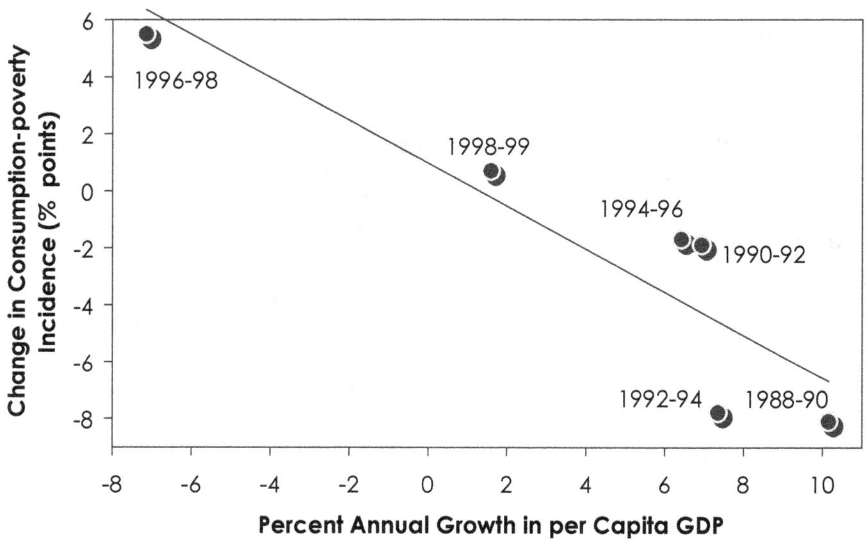

ship. Another problem is that the scatter plot in Figure 8.5 does not control for contemporaneous changes in income inequality that may also be important in influencing changes in poverty.

Here an attempt is made to use household survey data from five different rounds of the Thai Socioeconomic Survey (SES)—1992, 1994, 1996, 1998 and 1999—in estimating the relationship between economic growth, poverty headcount ratio, and income inequality at the provincial level.[9] The household survey data are used to construct the (sample-weighted) incidence of income-poverty (i.e., headcount ratio), mean household income per capita, and the Gini coefficient of per capita income inequality for each of the 76 Thai provinces. The cross-province data are then used to estimate the econometric relationship between changes in poverty incidence, on the one hand, and economic growth (proxied for by changes in mean per capita income) and distributional changes (proxied by changes in the Gini coefficient), on the other.[10] In addition to the three variables—mean income per capita, Gini coefficient of income inequality, and poverty incidence—

we also calculate and use provincial means of selected demographic variables (such as household size, proportion of children aged 0-15 years in the population, and proportion of the elderly aged 60 years and over) and socioeconomic variables (e.g., average schooling of adults, proportion of population residing in female-headed households, and proportion of population that is urban) on which data are readily available in the SES.

Relationship between Levels of Poverty, Inequality, and Mean Income

A scatter plot of poverty incidence against mean per capita income (Figure 8.6) shows a strong log-linear relationship between the two variables. The "levels" regression produces a growth elasticity of poverty of -2.2, indicating that a 1 percent increase in mean per capita income is associated with more than a 2 percent decrease in the per-

Figure 8.6: Cross-provincial Relationship between Poverty Incidence and Mean per Capita Income Growth, 1992-1999

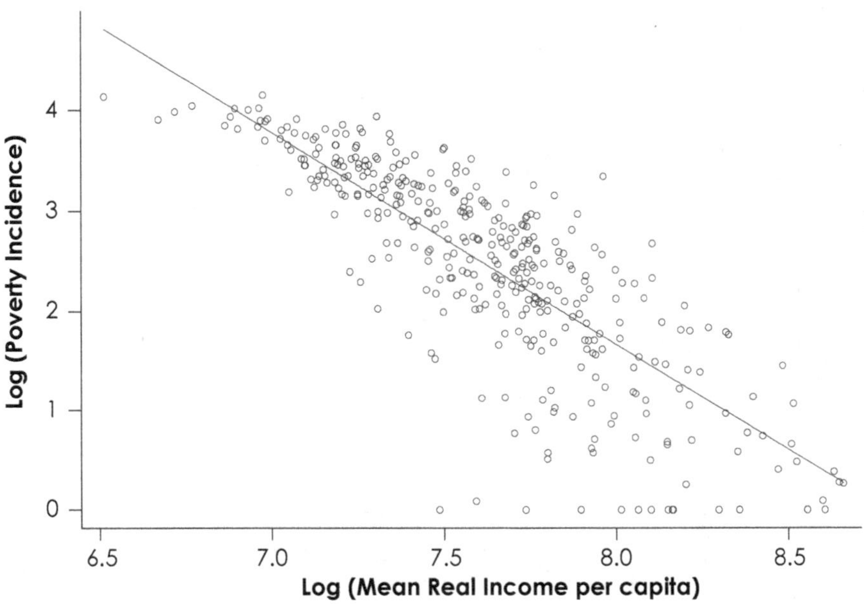

centage of population that is poor (Table 8.1).[11] This suggests that the poverty level in a province is strongly influenced by mean per capita income. As may be seen in Figure 8.7, however, poverty is also strongly associated with income inequality (measured by the Gini index of income). The association is positive, implying that, controlling for mean income, a more unequal distribution of per capita income is associated with a sharply higher level of poverty. The estimated distributional elasticity of poverty is 3.2, indicating a three-for-one increase in poverty incidence with an increase in the Gini coefficient of income inequality.

When other socioeconomic and demographic variables are included as additional determinants of poverty (see Equation 2 in Table 8.1), there is little change in the estimated growth and distributional elasticities. The coefficients of mean income and the Gini index retain their signs as well as their significance. The only other signifi-

Figure 8.7: Cross-provincial Relationship between Poverty Incidence and Income Inequality, 1992-1999

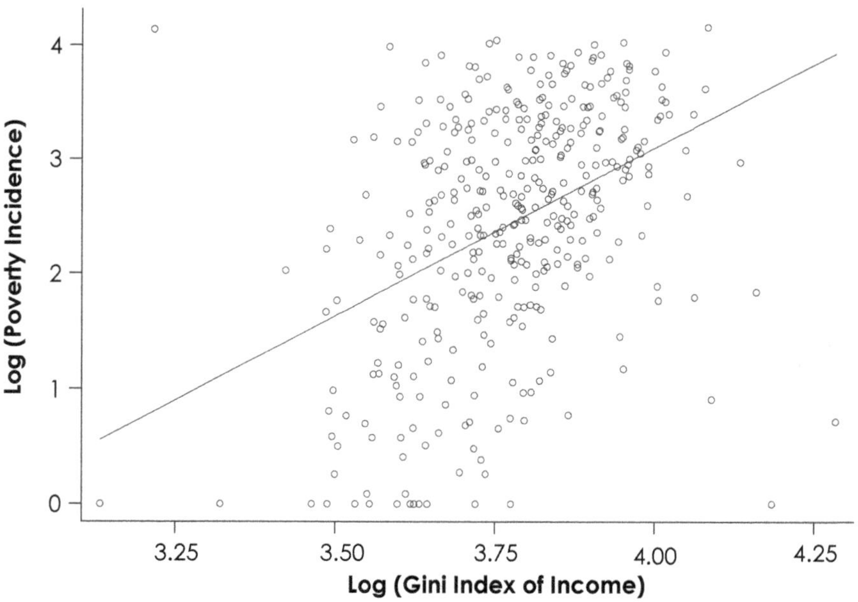

Table 8.1: Determinants of Poverty across Provinces, Pooled 1992-1999 Data (levels estimates)

INDEPENDENT VARIABLE	LOG OF POVERTY HEADCOUNT RATIO							
	OLS LEVELS ESTIMATES						2SLS LEVELS ESTIMATES	
	EQUATION 1		EQUATION 2		EQUATION 3			
	Coeff.	t-ratio	Coeff.	t-ratio	Coeff.	t-ratio	Coeff.	t-ratio
Log mean income per capita	-2.174	-37.14 ***	-2.456	-20.39 ***			-2.094	-17.04 ***
Log Gini coefficient	3.220	18.05 ***	3.391	18.21 ***			2.868	1.91 *
Mean age of household head (years)			-0.002	-0.17	0.077	2.71 ***		
Percent of population residing in female-headed households			0.003	0.74	-0.022	-2.48 **		
Mean schooling years of adults (18 years and older)			0.089	2.23 **	-0.387	-6.49 ***		
Percent of urban population			-0.001	-0.69	-0.004	-1.04		
Mean household size			-0.131	-1.84 *	0.002	0.01		
Percent of population aged 0-15 years			-0.011	-1.40	0.073	5.47		
Percent of population aged 60 years and over			-0.014	-1.24	-0.073	-2.54 **		
Time (1=1992, ..., 8=1999)	-0.029	-0.78	-0.006	-0.16	-0.192	-2.73 ***	-0.031	-0.39
Time squared	0.004	0.89	0.000	0.09	0.026	3.38 ***	0.004	0.42
Intercept	6.910	8.20 ***	9.115	7.33 ***	-0.105	-0.10	7.643	1.22
Number of observations	377		377		377		377	
F-ratio	499.78		234.03		72.00		161.44	
Significance level of F-ratio	0		0		0		0	
R-squared	0.875		0.882		0.560		0.557	

continued.

Table 8.1 continued.

INDEPENDENT VARIABLE	FIRST-STAGE OLS LEVELS ESTIMATES			
	LOG OF MEAN INCOME PER CAPITA		LOG OF GINI COEFFICIENT	
	Coeff.	t-ratio	Coeff.	t-ratio
Log mean income per capita				
Log Gini coefficient				
Mean age of household head (years)	-0.031	-3.36 ***	0.001	0.22
Percent of population residing in female-headed households	0.005	1.99 **	-0.004	-3.02 ***
Mean schooling years of adults (18 years and older)	0.187	10.44 ***	-0.005	-0.34
Percent of urban population	0.002	1.93 *	0.001	1.56
Mean household size	-0.046	-1.12	0.006	0.22
Percent of population aged 0-15 years	-0.028	-7.00 ***	0.005	1.75 *
Percent of population aged 60 years and over	0.026	2.82 ***	0.001	0.31
Time (1=1992, ..., 8=1999)	0.117	5.66 ***	0.030	2.05 **
Time squared	-0.014	-6.16 ***	-0.003	-1.59
Intercept	8.693	25.80 ***	3.578	16.23 ***
Number of observations	377		377	
F-ratio	94.17		2.92	
Significance level of F-ratio	0		0	
R-squared	0.731		0.067	

*** denotes significance at the 1 percent level.

** denotes significance at the 5 percent level.

* denotes significance at the 10 percent level.

cant variables in the relationship are household size and adult education. Household size is inversely associated with poverty while education is positively associated. The latter result may seem counterintuitive but simply indicates that an improvement in the mean level of schooling in a province is associated with greater poverty *after controlling for improvements in mean per capita income.*

In both of the above equations, a large proportion (about 88 percent) of the interprovincial variation in poverty is "explained" by variations in mean per capita income and in income inequality. Of this, approximately three quarters (i.e., 67 percent) is explained by variations in mean income alone, with the remainder being explained by variations in income inequality.

Equation (3) in Table 8.1 estimates a "reduced-form" relationship between poverty on the one hand and socioeconomic and demographic variables on the other (with mean income and income inequality omitted as regressors). Four main findings emerge. First, mean education has a strong negative effect on poverty in the reduced-form poverty equation, indicating that education affects poverty through mean income, income inequality, or both. Therefore, if mean schooling reduces poverty, it does so mainly by raising mean income.[12]

Second, poverty is inversely associated with residence in female-headed households, with a one percentage point increase in female-headedness in a province being associated with a 2.2 percent decrease in that province's incidence of poverty. Third, although mean household size is no longer a significant determinant of poverty, the age composition of the population is. A larger proportion of children aged 15 years and below in the population is associated with significantly higher levels of poverty, but a larger population share of the elderly (i.e., those aged 60 years or more) is actually associated with lower levels of poverty. This could reflect the fact that the elderly are active income contributors within households, or that the elderly take care of children and perform household chores, thus freeing middle-aged adults, especially women, to seek employment outside the home.

Finally, the results indicate that provincial poverty incidence has been falling over time, but at a diminishing rate. In the early 1990s, poverty was declining at an annual rate of 16.6 percent, but the rate had already slowed down to 6 percent by 1996, the year before the onset of the economic crisis. During the crisis years, poverty reversed its decline and started rising.

It is quite likely that mean provincial income and provincial income inequality may not be exogenous with respect to poverty incidence. Certain unobserved provincial variables, such as "social capital" or initial endowments, may affect mean income, income inequality, and poverty simultaneously. Additionally, high levels of poverty may be the cause of low mean income (rather than the other way around), as a high incidence of poverty may mean that a large proportion of the population is effectively outside the market and production economy of the province. One way around this problem would be to employ instrumental-variable (IV) methods to estimate the poverty-growth relationship, treating both mean income and the Gini index as endogenous variables. The demographic and socioeconomic variables already discussed above could be used as instruments for mean income and income inequality.

The absolute magnitudes of the 2SLS estimates are only slightly smaller than the OLS estimates—a growth elasticity of poverty of 2.1 and a Gini coefficient elasticity of poverty of 2.9 (Table 8.1). The robustness of the estimated poverty elasticities across alternative specifications is reassuring and suggests a strong cross-provincial relationship between poverty, on one hand, and mean income and income inequality, on the other.

Relationship between Changes in Poverty, Inequality, and Mean Income

Level-regressions have a disadvantage of not being able to control for unobserved provincial heterogeneity.[13] To the extent that factors unique to a province (such as location, quality of land, proximity to power centers, historical circumstances, institutions, administration, and culture) jointly affect its poverty incidence, its mean level of per capita income, and its level of income inequality, a "levels" regression of the type reported in Table 8.1 would be biased, and might simply reflect a spurious correlation between poverty and mean income and between poverty and income inequality. A solution to this problem would be to use fixed-effects estimation techniques that effectively control for unobserved and time-invariant heterogeneity across provinces. Obviously, fixed-effects estimation, which involves allowing each province to have its own intercept in the regression, is only possible with the availability of longitudinal (or panel) data on provinces.

The fixed-effects estimate of the growth elasticity of poverty is virtually identical to the levels estimate (viz., 2.2), but the fixed-effects estimate of the Gini elasticity of poverty is somewhat smaller (3.0 versus 3.2) (Table 8.2). These estimates are again virtually un-

Table 8.2: Determinants of Poverty across Provinces, Pooled 1992-1999 Data (provincial fixed-effects estimates)

INDEPENDENT VARIABLE	LOG OF POVERTY HEADCOUNT RATIO											
	PROVINCIAL FIXED-EFFECTS ESTIMATES									2SLS FIXED-EFFECTS ESTIMATES		
	EQUATION 1			EQUATION 2			EQUATION 3					
	Coeff.	t-ratio		Coeff.	t-ratio		Coeff.	t-ratio		Coeff.	t-ratio	
Log mean income per capita	-2.171	-17.30	***	-2.159	-14.85	***				-2.087	-5.63	***
Log Gini coefficient	2.956	16.75	***	2.997	16.41	***				2.011	1.84	*
Mean age of household head (years)				-0.026	-1.69	*	-0.038	-1.72	*			
Percent of population residing in female-headed households				0.004	1.03		0.002	0.25				
Mean schooling years of adults (18 years and older)				0.002	0.04		-0.264	-3.35	***			
Percent of urban population				-0.013	-2.59	***	-0.010	-1.38				
Mean household size				-0.072	-0.77		0.117	0.88				
Percent of population aged 0-15 years				-0.002	-0.20		0.033	2.34	***			
Percent of population aged 60 years and over				0.010	0.72		0.024	1.25				
Time (1=1992, ..., 8=1999)	-0.028	-0.78		-0.058	-1.49		-0.253	-5.01	***	-0.018	-0.28	
Time squared	0.003	0.94		0.006	1.54		0.025	4.57	***	0.002	0.35	
Intercept	7.884	9.62	***	9.274	7.41	***	4.382	3.41	***	10.803	3.09	***
Number of observations	377			377			377			377		
F-ratio	137.29			51.71			12.96			28.06		
Significance level of F-ratio	0			0			0			0		
R-squared	0.917			0.920			0.830			0.828		

continued.

Table 8.2. continued.

INDEPENDENT VARIABLE	LOG OF POVERTY HEADCOUNT RATIO — PROVINCIAL FIXED-EFFECTS ESTIMATES — EQUATION 1 Coeff.	t-ratio	EQUATION 2 Coeff.	t-ratio	EQUATION 3 Coeff.	t-ratio	2SLS FIXED-EFFECTS ESTIMATES Coeff.	t-ratio
F-test for significance of provincial fixed effects	1.97		1.81		6.22		7.47	
Significance level of provincial fixed-effects F-test	0		0		0		0	

INDEPENDENT VARIABLE	FIRST-STAGE FIXED-EFFECTS ESTIMATES — LOG OF MEAN INCOME PER CAPITA Coeff.	t-ratio	LOG OF GINI COEFFICIENT Coeff.	t-ratio
Log mean income per capita				
Log Gini coefficient				
Mean age of household head (years)	0.008	1.12	0.002	0.31
Percent of population residing in female-headed households	-0.004	-2.24 **	-0.004	-2.64 ***
Mean schooling years of adults (18 years and older)	0.173	6.75 ***	0.036	1.75 *
Percent of urban population	0.003	1.31	0.003	1.73 *
Mean household size	-0.149	-3.45 ***	-0.044	-1.29
Percent of population aged 0-15 years	-0.006	-1.20	0.008	2.11 **
Percent of population aged 60 years and over	-0.005	-0.79	0.001	0.25
Time (1=1992, ..., 8=1999)	0.136	8.27 ***	0.033	2.51 **
Time squared	-0.014	-7.55 ***	-0.004	-2.44 **
Intercept	7.083	16.97 ***	3.470	10.44 ***
Number of observations	377		377	
F-ratio	31.92		2.32	
Significance level of F-ratio	0		0.01	
R-squared	0.880		0.433	
F-test for significance of provincial fixed-effects	4.83		2.52	
Significance level of provincial fixed-effects F-test	0		0	

*** denotes significance at the 1 percent level.

** denotes significance at the 5 percent level.

* denotes significance at the 10 percent level.

changed when changes in demographic and socioeconomic variables are added to the regression. The addition of provincial fixed effects obviously increases the explanatory power of the regressions, although the provincial effects add a total of only four more percentage points to the explanatory power of the model. This does not, however, mean that sociocultural and institutional factors (which are reflected in the provincial fixed effects) are relatively unimportant in explaining differences in poverty, since they are important in determining mean income growth and distributional changes. [14]

Figures 8.8 and 8.9 show the relationship between *changes* in poverty, income inequality, and mean income. (These graphs effec-

Figure 8.8: Cross-provincial Relationship between Annual Changes in Poverty and Annual Changes in Mean Real Income per Capita, 1992-1999

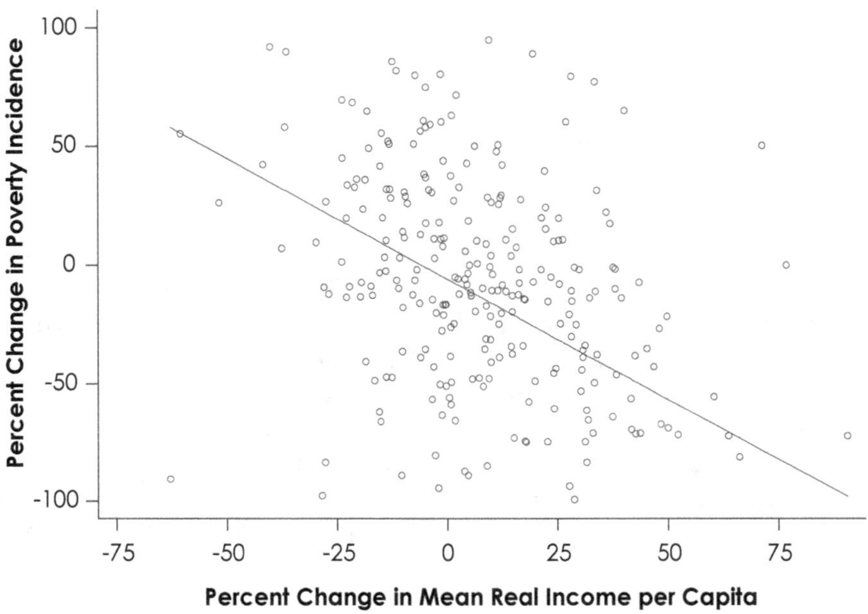

Figure 8.9: Cross-provincial Relationship between Annual Changes in Poverty and Annual Changes in Income Inequality, 1992-1999

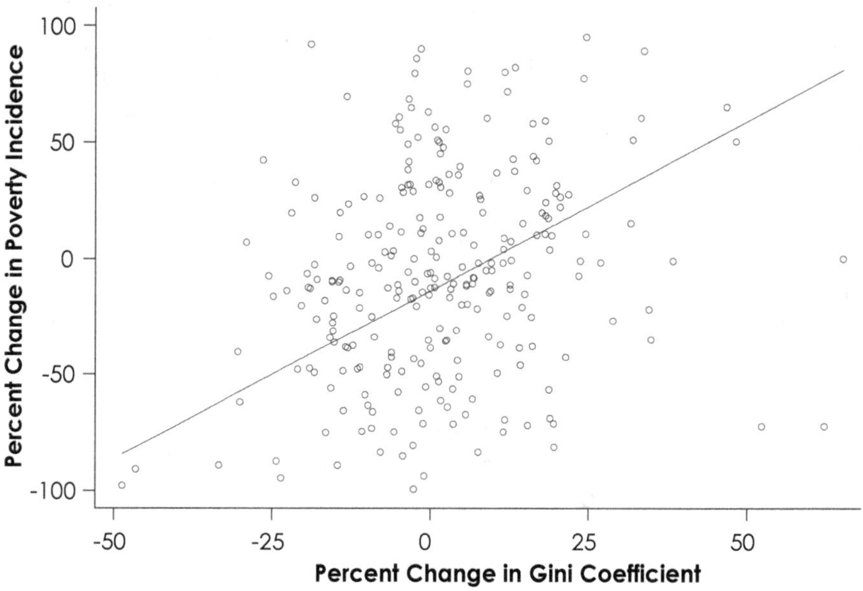

tively show the fixed-effects relationship between the relevant variables.) The relationship between poverty, and mean income and inequality, remains surprisingly strong.

These results powerfully demonstrate that while a strong relationship exists between poverty reduction and income growth, it is a *ceteris paribus* relationship. In other words, mean income growth reduces poverty substantially *only if the distribution of income does not change substantially during the process of growth.* Otherwise the effect of growth is significantly reduced since increases in inequality have an even stronger effect on poverty. Consider a hypothetical province with a mean provincial monthly income per capita of B2,500, a Gini coefficient of 45 percent, and a poverty incidence of 20 percent.

The results suggest that a 5 percent increase in mean income per capita would reduce poverty incidence to 17.8 percent as long as there were no changes in income inequality. But if the Gini coefficient of income inequality were to simultaneously increase by 5 percent along with mean income per capita, poverty incidence in the province would actually increase from 20 to 20.8 percent. Thus, worsening income inequality can substantially offset—even reverse—the beneficial effect of economic growth on poverty reduction.

Effect of Initial Inequality on Economic Growth

In both the "levels" and fixed-effects analysis discussed in the two earlier sections, one maintained assumption is that economic growth and income inequality are independent of each other. In a recent paper, however, Barro (2001) has raised the possibility that initial levels of inequality have a negative effect on subsequent growth rates in developing countries, although he does not find a similar effect for more developed economies. Human capital investments are one mechanism through which improvements in the distribution of income may foster growth. In developing countries, credit constraints may prevent the poor from making human-capital investments (e.g., schooling) that offer high rates of return. In such a situation, a redistribution of assets and incomes from the rich to the poor would result in more human-capital investment, which in turn would raise the average productivity of investments and thereby the growth rate of the economy.

Provincial data for Thailand strongly support Barro's findings (Table 8.3). Lagged levels of inequality, as measured by the Gini coefficient, are observed to have a strong negative effect on the growth of mean real income per capita, with or without controls for other socioeconomic and demographic variables. The regression estimates indicate that a 1 percent increase in the initial level of the Gini coefficient is associated with a 0.5 percent decline in the subsequent growth of real income per capita. This effect is large and implies that income inequality affects poverty reduction in two ways, namely: first, higher inequality is associated with increased poverty, controlling for economic growth; and second, high levels of initial inequality reduce future growth rates in the economy, thereby impeding the poverty reduction that would have taken place in the presence of rapid growth.

Table 8.3: Effect of Lagged Inequality on Growth of Mean Income per Capita across Provinces, Pooled 1992-1999 Data

INDEPENDENT VARIABLE	EQUATION 1		EQUATION 2	
	Coeff.	t-ratio	Coeff.	t-ratio
Log Gini coefficient	-0.529	-5.71 ***	-0.514	-5.64 ***
Mean age of household head (years)	-0.016	-1.79 *		
Percent of population residing in female-headed households	0.004	1.44		
Mean schooling years of adults (18 years and older)	-0.089	-3.96 ***		
Percent of urban population	0.001	0.83		
Mean household size	0.097	2.08 **		
Percent of population aged 0-15 years	-0.009	-1.90 *		
Percent of population aged 60 years and over	-0.004	-0.52		
Time (1=1992, ..., 8=1999)	0.027	0.62	0.030	0.67
Time squared	-0.005	-1.13	-0.007	-1.46
Intercept	3.063	5.97 ***	2.057	5.96 ***
Number of observations	301		301	
F-ratio	8.68		20.83	
Significance level of F-ratio	0		0	
R-squared	0.230		0.174	

*** denotes significance at the 1 percent level.

** denotes significance at the 5 percent level.

* denotes significance at the 10 percent level.

Note: All independent variables are expressed as once-lagged values of the corresponding variable. Dependent variable is percent growth of real mean income per capita across each survey period (i.e., 1992-94, 1994-96, 1996-98, and 1998-99).

CONCLUSION

Throughout much of its recent history, rapid economic growth in Thailand worked to extricate large numbers of people from poverty. This occurred despite increasing income inequality because growth was very strong. However, just as growth stalled and eventually turned negative with the onset of the economic crisis of 1997, the distribution of income began to worsen. The combination of negative growth and worsening income inequality has resulted in a sharp increase in poverty incidence in the country since 1997. It is unclear whether the increase in inequality is transitory or the beginning of a new trend (since income inequality, after a large increase from the 1970s to the early 1990s, had been declining from 1992 to 1998).

Analysis of provincial data from 1992 to 1999 suggests that while income growth has had a positive effect on poverty reduction, income inequality had a sharply negative effect. For any given rate of economic growth, increased inequality will be associated with increased poverty. But high levels of initial inequality will also reduce future growth rates, thus impeding the poverty reduction that would have taken place.

All of this suggests that income inequality can play a critical role in poverty reduction, especially in a low-growth environment. Given that the near-term prospects for growth in Thailand (and in most countries of the region) do not look very promising, it may be more strategic to refocus poverty reduction efforts toward improving income inequality, or at least prevent it from worsening. This could be accomplished among others by expanding educational opportunities for students from low-income families, investing in infrastructure in historically poor and disadvantaged areas, and providing fiscal and other incentives to encourage private-sector investment in backward areas.

Notes

1. What matters for poverty reduction, of course, is not the degree of overall income inequality but the inequality of incomes in the vicinity of the poverty line.
2. The poverty line is based on a technique developed by Kakwani and Krongkaew

3. Note that this figure differs from the commonly used "dollar-a-day" poverty line, since that line refers to a dollar in 1993 purchasing power parity-adjusted terms. Thailand's official poverty line in 1999 was equivalent to $1.60 in terms of 1993 PPP.

4. The analysis in this chapter is based on primary data from the Socioeconomic Surveys (SES). See Appendix 8.1 for a description of the SES.

5. Since the SES of 1999 was a special survey that was conducted only during four months (June-September 1999), results from earlier SESs are not strictly comparable unless data from the earlier SESs are analyzed only for the second and third quarters (covering the period June-September). It was observed, however, that whether data for two or four quarters are used for earlier SES samples, the results differ little from those presented in this chapter. Therefore, unless otherwise noted, statistics presented here for years other than 1999 are based on data covering all four quarters, while those for 1999 are based on two quarters of data.

6. Perfect targeting implies that each individual below the poverty line would receive a transfer that would permit his or her income or consumption to reach the level of the poverty line and that no one above the poverty line would receive any transfers.

7. It should be noted that these are hypothetical numbers. Besides the fact that perfect targeting is rarely practicable, few developing-country governments would choose to continue making income transfers to the poor in perpetuity, in part because of the significant disincentive effects of making transfers to each poor individual based on his or her income shortfall (relative to the poverty line).

8. All three measures discussed here—headcount ratio, poverty gap index, and poverty gap squared index—are fully decomposable across different subgroups in the population.

9. Unfortunately, the relatively small size of the SES sample at the provincial level means that it is not possible to calculate, with any degree of precision, mean values of any variable for population subgroups in a province (such as income quintiles), although mean values for the entire province can be measured fairly precisely. Consequently, no attempt is made here to analyze the impact of mean income growth on the growth of income of the poorest income quintile.

10. Since the poverty headcount ratio, mean real income per capita, and the Gini coefficient all summarize different facets of the cumulative distribution of real income per capita in the population, they are bound to show strong co-movements with each other. However, they are not related to each other in the form of an identity, so a regression of the poverty headcount ratio on mean income per capita and the Gini coefficient is still valid.

11. Interestingly, this estimate is close to the growth elasticity of poverty incidence estimated by a number of cross-country studies (Ravallion 2000, Ravallion and Chen 1997, and Bruno et al. 1998).
12. Indeed, this is confirmed by looking at the estimates of the log mean income equation shown in the fourth column from the right in Table 8.2.
13. To some extent, the 2SLS estimates presented earlier do control for heterogeneity, but, as is well known, 2SLS estimates treat the unobserved provincial effect as a random—not fixed—effect. This means that the provincial effect is assumed to be uncorrelated with the other right-side variables, such as mean income and income inequality. This is an assumption that is likely to be invalid, as one would expect unobserved provincial heterogeneity to be correlated with provincial mean income and provincial inequality.
14. Indeed, a comparison of the levels and fixed-effects estimates of mean income and the Gini index (in Tables 8.2 and 8.3) shows that the provincial fixed effects account for 15 percent of the interprovincial variation in log mean per capita and for 37 percent of the cross-provincial variation in the Gini coefficient.

APPENDIX 8.1: The Thai Socioeconomic Surveys

The first Socioeconomic Survey (SES) was conducted by the National Statistical Office (NSO) in 1957. It was only in 1988 that the survey began to be undertaken every two years (the interval used to be five years between 1957 and 1987). The SES is undertaken throughout the year, and has a typical sample size of about 25,000 households. For instance, the 1998 SES surveyed a total of 23,549 households comprising 86,058 individuals. In 1999, the NSO conducted a special (periodic) SES to gauge the effects of the economic crisis on household income and consumption. This survey had a much smaller sample size than the usual SESs (7,789 households), as it was conducted only during four months of the year (viz., June-September 1999).

The SES typically obtains information on household income and household expenditure, household consumption patterns, changes in assets and liabilities, ownership of durable goods, and housing characteristics. In its stratified two-stage sampling design, the primary sampling units are the blocks for municipal areas, and villages for nonmunicipal areas, while the secondary sampling units are the households within each of these blocks/villages.

9 Economic Growth and Poverty Reduction in Viet Nam

Arsenio M. Balisacan, Ernesto M. Pernia, and Gemma Esther B. Estrada

INTRODUCTION

Viet Nam's emergence as one of the fastest growing economies in Asia over the last two decades has been widely hailed. This has been attributed to a series of reforms, known as the *doi moi*, which started in the latter part of the 1980s. Reforms began primarily in the agricultural sector which, at the time, accounted for close to 40 percent of gross domestic product (GDP) and 70 percent of total employment. The country's reform effort focused initially on the dismantling of collective farms, redistribution of land to peasant households through long-term leases, and abolition of price controls on goods and services. It then eliminated production and consumption subsidies and streamlined the public sector (Dollar and Litvack 1998, Weinns 1998). Further, the reform effort included the stabilization of inflation and liberalization of foreign trade and investment (Dollar 2002).

The series of reforms paved the way for the country's spectacular growth in the 1990s. During that decade, GDP growth averaged 7.9 percent a year, remarkably higher than the 5.5 percent growth average for East Asia and Pacific region (excluding People's Republic of China [PRC]) or the 5.6 percent growth for South Asia. The growth of agriculture, averaging 4.8 percent a year, was likewise impressive, exceeding the 3.1 percent average for the East Asia and Pacific region.

Viet Nam's reforms appear to have been broad-based, thus benefiting the poor. During most of the 1990s, the incidence of absolute poverty fell by an average of 4.1 percentage points a year. In contrast, the average reduction for the East Asia and Pacific region was only 2 percentage points a year (Table 9.1). Likewise, marked improvement in quality of life was manifested by the relatively high literacy (92.9 percent) and life expectancy (69 years), as well as low mortality (37 per 1,000 live births) in the latter 1990s.

It appears that economic growth has been the key determinant of poverty reduction in Viet Nam, a finding that seems consistent with the results of cross-country regressions (e.g., Dollar and Kraay 2001). Nevertheless, it is important to go beyond cross-country averages to determine the robustness of the conclusions about the growth-pov-

Table 9.1: Poverty Reduction: Viet Nam vs. Other Asian Developing Countries

	PERIOD	PERCENTAGE-POINT REDUCTION PER YEAR	AVERAGE GROWTH OF PER CAPITA GDP (%)
Viet Nam	1993-98	-4.1	6.8
East Asia and Pacific	1993-98	-2.0	5.6
Bangladesh	1992-96	-1.7	2.8
Cambodia	1994-97	-1.0	2.6
PRC	1993-98	-2.5	10.4
India	1992-97	-1.4	3.8
Philippines	1994-97	-1.3	1.9
Indonesia	1990-96	-2.1	6.4
Thailand	1992-96	-1.0	7.2

Source: Viet Nam Living Standards Survey (1992-1993 and 1997-1998) and World Bank (2001e).

erty relationship. In this chapter, we explore the determinants of poverty reduction at the subnational level in Viet Nam during the 1990s, using household panel data. In particular, we examine the impact of local economic growth and other factors, including initial endowments and policy conditions, on the welfare of the poor.

DATA AND MEASUREMENT ISSUES

The main source of data is the Viet Nam Living Standards Survey (VLSS) conducted in 1992-1993 and 1997-1998 by the Viet Nam General Statistics Office (GSO), with funding from the United Nations Development Program and the Swedish Development International Development Authority. Technical assistance was provided by the World Bank in line with the Living Standards Measurement Study household surveys conducted in a number of developing countries.

The 1992-1993 VLSS covered 4,800 households, while the 1997-1998 VLSS was administered to 6,000 households. The latter survey was designed to update the information on households surveyed in the first VLSS; thus, the two surveys constitute a household panel data set. Out of the total number of households surveyed in the 1992-1993 VLSS, about 495 households were not re-interviewed due to a change in sampling weights, transfer of residence or temporary absence from the commune, or some other reasons. About 4,302 households or 90 percent of the original respondents constitute the large panel data set.[1]

The surveys were conducted at the household and commune levels. Topics covered at the household level included education, employment, health and fertility, migration, agricultural activities, income and expenditures, and credit and savings. On the other hand, the commune level surveys were administered mainly to rural areas[2] and comprised questions on demographics, physical and economic infrastructure, education, health, and agriculture. Extensive price data were likewise gathered from both urban and rural areas at the commune level.

In characterizing household welfare, we use household consumption expenditure data. The VLSS contains a rich account of food and nonfood expenditures of households, including amounts spent on holidays, primarily Tet (New Year) which is often characterized by unusually high expenditures on some food items (World Bank 2000d).

Apart from consumption, income is widely used to measure household welfare. While the VLSS captured household income, the survey in 1997-1998 covered a more extensive account of household income compared to 1992-1993.

As in the Indonesian and Philippine cases, the chosen indicator of household welfare, consumption expenditure, has to be adjusted for spatial cost-of-living differences and nominal price movements over time. For adjustment in spatial price variation, we employed the cost-of-living indices constructed by the GSO for urban and rural areas in each of the country's seven regions (see Appendix Table 9.1). For adjustment in price changes during the VLSS survey period, we used the monthly food and nonfood price indices calculated by the GSO (see Appendix Table 9.2).

The resulting cumulative distribution (CD) curves of per capita expenditures (at January 1998 prices) for the two survey years are shown in Figure 9.1. Given the national poverty line of 1,789,781 Vietnamese dong (at 1998 prices), the poverty incidence would be roughly 61 percent in 1993 and 37 percent in 1998[3]. Note that the two CD curves do not intersect, suggesting that the direction of poverty change is unambiguous, regardless of the assumed (but plausible) poverty

Figure 9.1: Distribution of Living Standards: Viet Nam

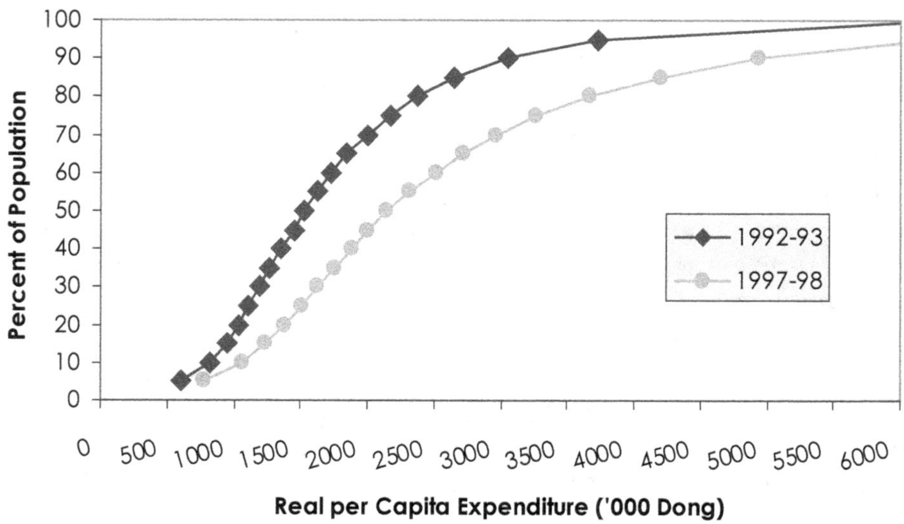

norm and even for all other poverty indices that satisfy certain properties of a desirable poverty measure (see, for example, Foster and Shorrocks 1988). Thus, in Figure 9.1, poverty is unambiguously lower in 1998 than in 1993. The decline in poverty was accompanied by a significant increase in mean per capita expenditure, averaging 8.5 percent a year.[4]

The change in poverty during a given period can be decomposed additively into growth and redistribution components (as done in the Philippine case). The growth component pertains to the change in poverty if all consumption groups had shared equally in the growth that occurred. The redistribution component, on the other hand, is defined as the change in poverty if the mean consumption were to remain the same but income distribution had changed as observed during the period. Table 9.2 summarizes the estimated components of poverty change between 1993 and 1998.[5] Estimates of changes in both poverty incidence and depth show that growth accounts for the bulk of poverty reduction. If not for the increase, albeit slight in the Gini ratio from 0.31 to 0.35 during the period, the reduction in poverty incidence would have even been faster, i.e., 27.1 percentage points instead of the observed 23.2 percentage points. Similarly, the reduction in the poverty depth index would have been 13 percentage points instead of the observed 9.5 percentage points. It is worth noting that while the growth process in Viet Nam was accompanied by a mild deterioration in income distribution, its level of inequality during the latter 1990s was still lower than in most developing East Asian countries (Table 9.3).

Table 9.2: Growth and Redistribution Components of Poverty Change

	INCIDENCE	DEPTH
1993	60.6	19.0
1998	37.4	9.5
Overall Change	-23.2	-9.5
Due to growth	-27.1	-13.0
Due to redistribution	3.9	3.5

Source: Authors' estimates.

As shown in Table 9.2, the period between 1993 and 1998 witnessed a substantial reduction in poverty. An examination of the changes in mean expenditures by decile, using the complete data set for 1992-1993 and 1997-1998 VLSS, however, reveals that the increase in mean expenditure has been the least for the lowest income group (Figure 9.2). While the increase in the living standards of the poorest decile was close to 30 percent, that for the top decile was about 60 percent (see Bhushan, Bloom, and Thang 2002).

Table 9.3: Gini Ratio for Viet Nam and Other East Asian Developing Countries

	SURVEY YEAR	GINI RATIO	SURVEY INDICATOR
Viet Nam	1998	0.35	Consumption
Cambodia	1997	0.40	Consumption
PRC	1998	0.40	Income
Indonesia	1999	0.32	Consumption
Malaysia	1997	0.49	Income
Philippines	1997	0.46	Consumption
Thailand	1998	0.41	Consumption

Sources: 1997-1998 VLSS and World Bank (2002).

Figure 9.2 should, however, be interpreted with caution since households belonging to the poorest decile in 1992-1993 may not be the same households in that decile in 1997-1998. Some households may have moved into higher deciles while those in the upper deciles could have moved into lower income groups.[6] Indeed, the panel data suggest that the poorest group in the 1992-1993 survey had the highest mean expenditure growth, while the richest group had the lowest (Figure 9.3).

As expected, given geographic differences in initial conditions (including resource endowments and local institutions), changes in the living standards of the poor vary markedly across regions (Figure 9.4). The highest increase occurred in the Southeast region (140 percent), which also had the lowest initial poverty incidence and ac-

Figure 9.2: Percent Change in Mean Expenditures by Decile, Complete Data

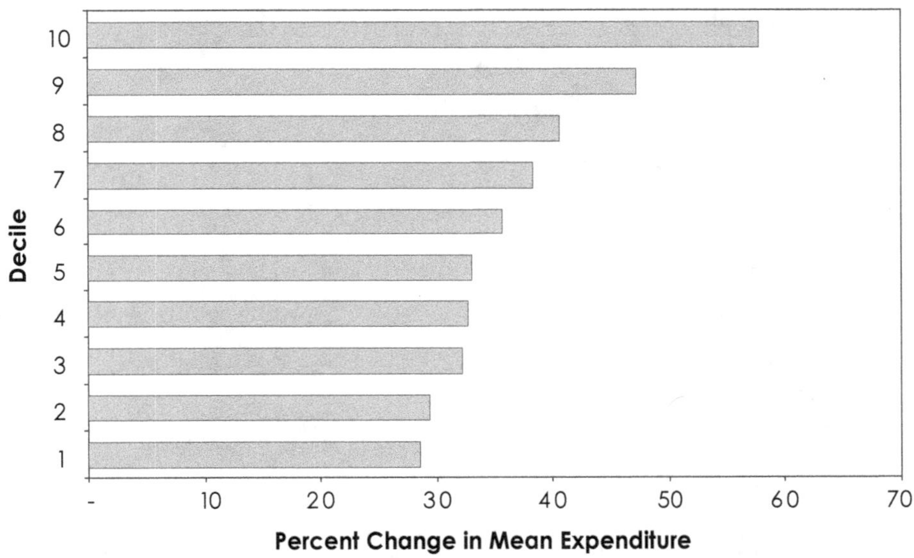

Figure 9.3: Percent Change in Mean Expenditures by Decile, Panel Data

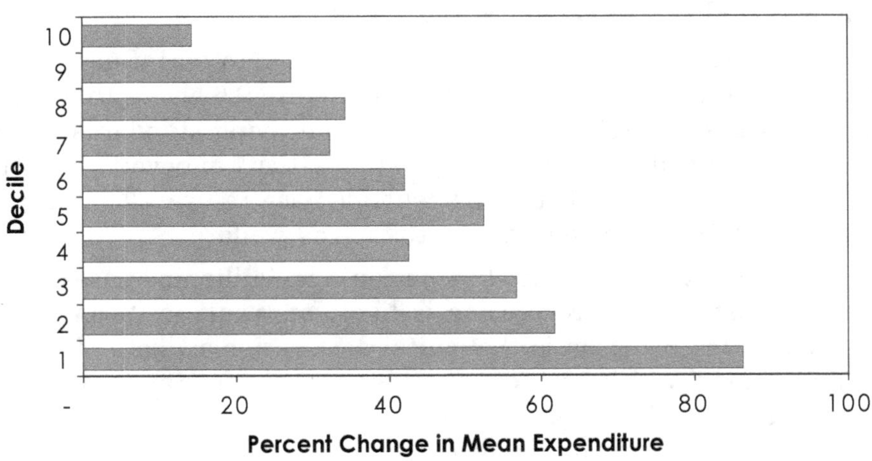

Figure 9.4: Percent Change in Mean Expenditures of the Poorest Quintile, Panel Data

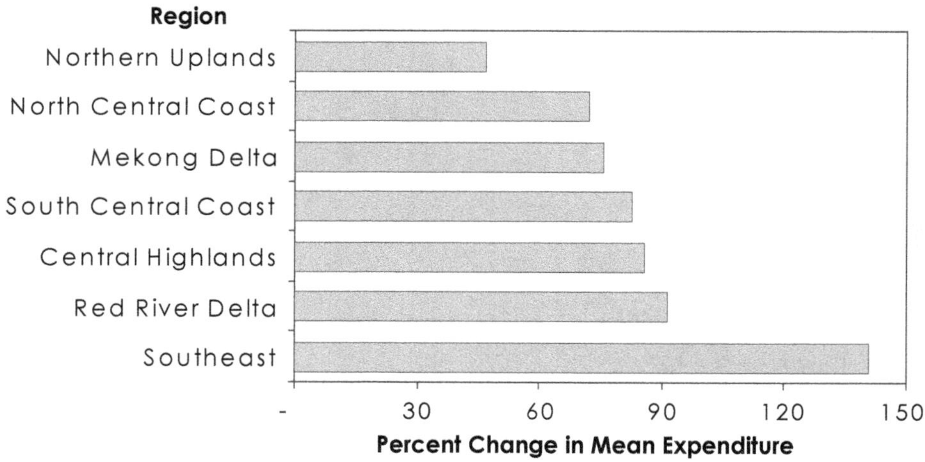

counted for only about 3.5 percent of the poor (Figure 9.5). This region had comparatively good transport facilities and power infrastructure (Dollar and Glewwe 1998). On the other hand, the lowest increase (about 45 percent) took place in the poorest region, Northern Uplands. This region accounted for 20.6 percent of the poor in 1992-1993 and 28.1 percent in 1997-1998.

DETERMINANTS OF POVERTY REDUCTION

We expect the living standards of the poor to be influenced directly by local economic growth.[7] Indeed, Figure 9.6 shows that there is a strong positive relationship between the living standards of the poor and provincial incomes.[8] The growth elasticity of poverty is about 0.7, which indicates that a 10 percent increase in overall income is associated with a 7 percent rise in the poor's welfare.

However, as noted in the Indonesian and Philippine cases, such ordinary least squares regression is likely to result in inconsistent estimates. A main reason is the omission of variables, both observed and unobserved, which have direct impacts on living standards of the poor and are correlated with overall average incomes. Below, we exploit the longitudinal nature of the two surveys and employ panel

Figure 9.5: Poverty Incidence by Region, 1992-1993 and 1997-1998

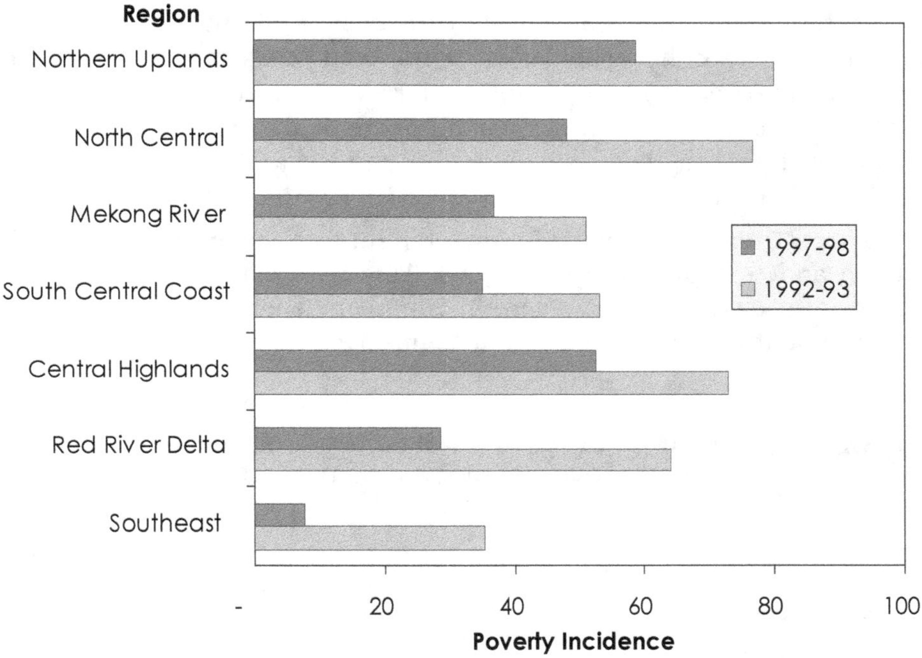

estimation techniques to obtain consistent estimates of the growth elasticity of poverty and other parameters of interest.

Specifically, we use the fixed-effects model to control for differences in time-invariant, unobservable household-specific characteristics. This technique removes any bias resulting from the correlation between these characteristics and overall average income or any other explanatory variable. Other explanatory variables included in the model are household demographics, geographic location, schooling, infrastructure, and farm characteristics.

The estimation model has two variants. The first is a regression involving a subsample of 3,494 rural households wherein information on commune characteristic (quality of roads) is available. The second is a regression making use of all households in the panel data set (4,302 households) but excluding the commune-related regressor. In both cases, the observations are unit record data of the poorest 20 percent of the population based on the expenditure distribution in the 1992-1993 survey.

Differences in household welfare may be systematically related with differences in household composition and characteristics (Deaton 1997). The estimation model controls for these effects by including as regressors household size; number of dependents; number of female members of working age; as well as age, gender, and marital status of the household head.

The estimation likewise allows for interaction between overall growth and certain initial conditions. This is to explore whether the impact of growth on the welfare of the poor depends in part on the "environment" which the poor find themselves in. In India, Ravallion

Figure 9.6: Average Expenditure of Bottom Quintile versus Overall Provincial Mean Income

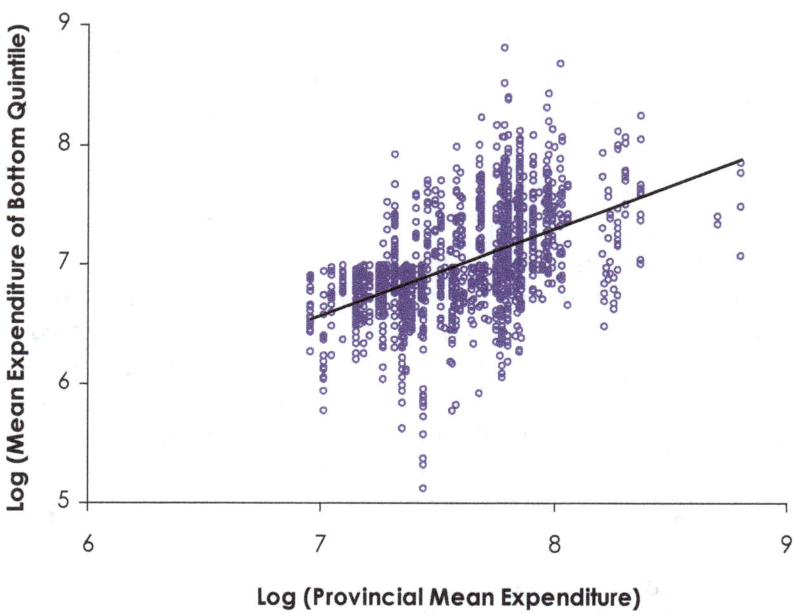

and Datt (2002) find that the growth process was more pro-poor in states with initially higher literacy rates, higher farm productivity, lower landlessness, and lower infant mortality. In this paper, we examine whether the growth elasticity of poverty is higher with more schooling years, presence of electricity, lower incidence of impassable roads, bigger land size, and better irrigation development.

Correspondingly, interaction terms on growth and regional classification are included in the model to account for regional variation in the growth elasticity of poverty. It is expected, for example, that the elasticity is higher for the Red River Delta than for Central Highlands, with the former having remarkably higher initial consumption expenditure, literacy, access to electricity and water, sanitation, and health (see Dollar and Glewwe 1998).

The economic opportunities created by the *doi moi* could have strengthened the role of education in raising overall living standards. Moock, Patrinos, and Venkataraman (1998) find that private rates of return to primary and university education in Viet Nam are 13 and 11 percent, respectively. Using cross-sectional data, Glewwe, Gragnolati, and Zaman (2000) have shown that an additional year of schooling of household heads raises household consumption per capita by about 3 percent. Their use of panel data indicates that an additional year of general schooling is associated with a 0.6 percentage point increase in consumption expenditures. We attempt to estimate the impact of schooling on living standards of the poor, using years of schooling of household heads as a regressor.

The presence of roads represents access to markets and mobility to explore nonfarm income opportunities. In Viet Nam, about 68.9 percent have access to roads. In terms of road quality, however, only 53.9 percent have access to passable roads more than half of the year. We represent roads in the regression as the number of months in a year that roads are impassable in the commune.

In Viet Nam, a high proportion of the poor (82 percent) live in communities with some electricity. Electricity facilitates commercialization, as well as growth of off-farm employment opportunities. It also allows access to improved technology and enables the use of modern equipment.

In Viet Nam, about two-thirds of population are in the agriculture sector. Land is an important asset that households may use to help smooth consumption during shocks, given imperfections in the credit market.[9] Limited landholding or landlessness has been strongly associated with poverty in Viet Nam (Weins 1998, World Bank 1999). We represent land size in the regression by type of farmland, namely, annual crop land, perennial land, and water surface land.[10] We also include irrigation, represented here by the proportion of irrigated annual crop land, to account for differences in land quality.

The results of the regression are presented in Table 9.4 (Appendix Table 9.4 shows the descriptive statistics on the variables). As expected, local economic growth exerts a strong impact on the welfare of the poor. The estimated coefficient in both models suggest a more than one-to-one correspondence between growth and welfare of the poor, markedly higher than those obtained for Indonesia (Chapter 6) and the Philippines (Chapter 7), and even higher than that reported by Dollar and Kraay (2001) using cross-country averages. This result indicates that in Viet Nam growth has been a particularly potent determinant of poverty reduction.

Household composition and characteristics also influence welfare levels. In particular, male-headed household and age of household head are positively associated with the welfare of the poor in both variants of the regression. As expected, household size and number of dependents are negatively associated with household welfare.

Interaction effects between growth and regional classification appear to be insignificant for most regions except for two regions in the South. Controlling for provincial income growth, household demographics and initial conditions, the South Central Coast and Mekong Delta regions are characterized by higher growth elasticity of poverty relative to the reference region.

While schooling does not come out statistically significant in the two variants of the regression for the poorest quintile, it becomes highly significant in the regression for the other quintiles, as discussed in the next section. The interaction effects between growth and other initial conditions (i.e., electricity, roads, and land) also appear to be insignificant. This does not, however, discount the importance of these factors to the welfare of the poor in Viet Nam. As in the

Table 9.4: Determinants of the Welfare of the Poor (bottom quintile)

EXPLANATORY VARIABLE	MODEL 1 (RURAL PANEL HOUSEHOLDS)			MODEL 2 (ALL PANEL HOUSEHOLDS)		
	Coeff.	t-ratio		Coeff.	t-ratio	
Overall Mean Income (Y)	1.3679	7.70	***	1.3052	8.63	***
Age of household head	0.0236	2.98	***	0.0246	3.23	***
Age Squared	-0.0002	-3.25	***	-0.0003	-3.46	***
Household Size	-0.4070	-5.84	***	-0.4612	-7.04	***
Number of Dependents	-0.0339	-2.33	**	-0.0241	-1.80	*
Number of Female Members at Working Age	-0.0104	-0.48		0.0128	0.66	
Male-headed household	0.2092	2.81	***	0.1884	2.89	***
Marital status of head	0.0392	0.62		0.0802	1.36	
Interaction of Y with Region:						
Y*Northern Uplands	0.0993	0.65		0.1675	1.21	
Y*Red River Delta	0.0989	0.64		0.1654	1.19	
Y*North Central Coast	0.1398	0.89		0.1990	1.36	
Y*South Central Coast	0.5163	2.64	***	0.6038	3.47	***
Y*Central Highlands	0.1702	0.83		0.2494	1.29	
Y*Mekong Delta	0.8380	4.19	***	0.8231	4.57	***

continued.

Table 9.4 continued.

EXPLANATORY VARIABLE	MODEL 1 (RURAL PANEL HOUSEHOLDS)			MODEL 2 (ALL PANEL HOUSEHOLDS)		
	Coeff.	t-ratio		Coeff.	t-ratio	
Interaction of Y with "Initial Conditions":						
Y*Schooling	0.0139	0.31		0.0465	1.10	
Y*Electricity	0.0903	0.90		0.0965	1.09	
Y*Impassable Road	-0.0024	-0.19				
Y*Annual Crop Land	-0.1081	-0.67		-0.1364	-1.00	
Y*Perennial Land	-0.2647	-3.21	***	-0.2462	-3.22	***
Y*Water Surface Land	-0.0859	-0.77		-0.0998	-0.95	
Y*Irrigation	-0.1065	-0.91		-0.1547	-1.42	
Intercept	-1.6172	-1.35		-1.4934	-1.53	
R-squared (within)	0.718			0.712		

*** denotes significance at the 1 percent level.
** denotes significance at the 5 percent level.
* denotes significance at the 10 percent level.

Note: Estimation is by fixed effects regression in which the dependent variable is the logarithm of mean per capita expenditure of the poorest 20 percent. Model 1 refers to the poorest 20 percent of all rural households, while Model 2 (without road variable) pertains to the poorest 20 percent of the complete panel data set.

cases of Indonesia (Chapter 7) and the Philippines (Chapter 8), their effects on the poor tend to work via the growth process.

DIFFERENTIAL EFFECTS ACROSS QUINTILES

Using the same set of variables as that for the bottom quintile based on the panel of rural households (Model 1), we fitted similar regressions for the other four income quintiles. The estimation results for each quintile are summarized in Table 9.5. For ease of comparison, the result for the first quintile given in Table 9.4 is reproduced in Table 9.5.

The regression results show that the growth elasticity is lower for the upper four quintiles than for the first quintile. The growth elasticity drops substantially as one moves from the first to the second quintile. As seen in Appendix Table 9.3, a similar pattern emerges if we construct quartiles instead of quintiles. The results imply that the impact of growth is highest for the poor, which is the reverse of that found for Indonesia and the Philippines where growth elasticity tends to increase with income level.

Among the household demographic characteristics, those found to be statistically significant in most quintiles are household size and number of household dependents. As expected, both were found to be negatively related to per capita income.

Estimation results also reveal that for the second and fourth quintiles, households in Northern Uplands, Red River Delta, and North Central Coast have lower growth in incomes compared with those in the Southeast. The effect of regional location, however, no longer appears to be important for the third and fifth quintiles, except for the growth–Mekong Delta interaction variable.

While the higher quintiles have lower growth elasticity compared with the first quintile, they respond strongly to interaction effects between growth and initial conditions. In particular, growth is more welfare-enhancing when combined with access to schooling for the second, third, and fourth quintiles, indicating that middle-income households benefit significantly from schooling. This finding is particularly relevant in view of the declining school enrollments in rural areas (Glewwe and Jacoby 1998) where measures to encourage investment in education could be critical.

For the third, fourth, and fifth quintiles, growth has a stronger impact on welfare when combined with access to electricity. By its ability to increase productivity levels, electricity (denoting access to technology) can be an effective tool in raising incomes.

The interaction between growth and the number of months that roads are impassable has a negative and significant coefficient for the second, third, and fourth quintiles. This suggests that middle-class households benefit directly from the complementarity between growth and access to good roads. For the poor, other modes of transport may be more important. For example, in the South and in the

North where a large proportion of the poor are found, canals and waterways are widely used for transportation (van de Walle 1998).

As with the first quintile, initial land size does not appear to exert a positive direct effect on the welfare of the other four quintiles. Interaction between growth and perennial land size has a significant, albeit negative, coefficient for the first to the third quintiles; at the same time, initial annual crop land size is found to be insignificant. Viet Nam has achieved an equitable distribution of land use rights (Ravallion and van De Walle 2001), but it is land quality that matters

Table 9.5: Determinants of Average Welfare by Quintile

EXPLANATORY VARIABLE	Q1 (POOREST)	Q2	Q3	Q4	Q5 (RICHEST)
Overall mean income (Y)	1.3679 ***	0.8081 ***	0.7609 ***	0.8702 ***	0.5548 ***
Age of household head	0.0236 ***	-0.0060	0.0057	0.0015	0.0169 **
Age squared	-0.0002 ***	0.0001	0.0000	0.0000	-0.0001 *
Household size	-0.4070 ***	-0.3563 ***	-0.3308 ***	-0.2124 ***	-0.2190 ***
Number of dependents	-0.0339 **	-0.0267 *	-0.0102	-0.0821 ***	-0.0631 ***
Number of female members at working age	-0.0104	0.0121	0.0501 **	-0.0124	-0.0652 ***
Male-headed household	0.2092 ***	0.0151	0.0284	0.0544	0.1148 *
Marital status of head	0.0392	0.0202	0.1157 *	-0.0768	-0.0531
Growth Interaction with Region					
Y*Northern Uplands	0.0993	-0.2432 **	-0.1761	-0.3194 ***	-0.0848
Y*Red River Delta	0.0989	-0.2404 **	-0.1713	-0.3113 ***	-0.0540
Y*North Central Coast	0.1398	-0.2041 *	-0.1735	-0.2018 *	-0.1659
Y*South Central Coast	0.5163 ***	0.0952	-0.0264	-0.1200	-0.1093
Y*Central Highlands	0.1702	0.1020	0.2971	-0.4036	0.1841
Y*Mekong Delta	0.8380 ***	0.4314 ***	0.3718 **	-0.0244	-0.5081 ***

continued.

Table 9.5 continued.

EXPLANATORY VARIABLE	Q1 (POOREST)	Q2	Q3	Q4	Q5 (RICHEST)
Growth Interaction with "Initial Conditions"					
Y*Schooling	0.0139	0.1639 ***	0.0991 ***	0.1196 ***	-0.0094
Y*Electricity	0.0903	0.1109	0.1535 *	0.1849 ***	0.2417 ***
Y*Impassable Roads	-0.0024	-0.0251 **	-0.0290 ***	-0.0269 ***	0.0035
Y*Annual Crop Land	-0.1081	0.0697	0.0161	-0.1621	-0.0551
Y*Perennial Land	-0.2647 ***	-0.1564 **	-0.1295 *	-0.0905	0.0013
Y*Water Surface Land	-0.0859	-0.1031	0.1098	0.0515	-0.0058
Y*Irrigation	-0.1065	0.1875 *	0.0005	-0.0742	-0.1748
Intercept	-1.6172	0.4704	1.5290	4.5605 ***	5.9777
R-squared (within)	0.718	0.646	0.533	0.517	0.276

*** denotes significance at the 1 percent level.

** denotes significance at the 5 percent level.

* denotes significance at the 10 percent level.

Note: Estimation is by fixed effects regression in which the dependent variable is the logarithm of mean per capita expenditure of the poorest 20 percent. Data refer to a panel of 3,494 rural households covering the 1992-1993 and 1997-1998 VLSS.

rather than land size per se. As observed for the second quintile, irrigation is found to be significant but not annual crop land size.

CONCLUSION

By international standards, Viet Nam has achieved remarkable poverty reduction and broad-based economic growth appears to be the key. As the provincial panel data suggest, the growth process that occurred had a strong pro-poor bias, i.e., the proportionate increases in the incomes of the poorest 20 percent of the population were appreciably larger than those of the top 20 or 40 percent. The institutional and policy reforms that began in the late 1980s appear to have paved the way for greater participation of the poor in the growth process in Viet Nam than in other Asian developing countries in recent decades. An alternative or additional explanation is that the socialist social infrastructure that remained enabled the poor to benefit from the rapid economic growth.

A caveat is in order. The provincial panel data used in this chapter pertain largely to rural areas. As such, the regression results may not fully reflect the broader nationwide picture. Nevertheless, the concentration of poverty in Viet Nam, as in other developing countries, is in rural areas. Further, policy and institutional reforms were under way prior to the period covered by the provincial panel survey, but these reforms had to be well in place before they could exert a significant impact on both economic growth and poverty reduction.

Finally, the findings for Viet Nam relative to those for the other countries suggest that the higher the growth rate, the lesser becomes the role of distributive factors that directly influence the poor's well-being. Still, these factors could contribute to reinforcing both growth and poverty reduction in the long run.

Notes

The authors gratefully acknowledge the valuable advice on the data provided by Sarah Bales and comments by Erik Bloom.

1. Three panel households with insufficient expenditure information are not counted here. For a detailed description of the two surveys, see World Bank (2000d, 2001d).
2. The 1992-1993 VLSS surveyed 120 rural communes, while the 1997-1998 VLSS covered 156 communes in rural and minor urban areas.
3. The official poverty estimate for 1993 is slightly lower, at 58.2 percent, based on a poverty line of 1,160,363 Vietnamese dong (at 1993 prices).
4. In comparison, real per capita GDP during the same period increased by 7.4 percent a year.
5. The components of poverty change have been estimated using the procedure suggested by Kakwani (1997) and Kakwani and Pernia (2000).
6. Breaking the panel households into quintiles, Glewwe and Nguyen (2002) find that only 10 percent of those in the poorest quintile in 1992-1993 remained in the same quintile in 1997-1998. They contend though that the observed economic mobility may well overestimate the true mobility because of measurement errors.
7. For the rest of this section, the poor refer to the bottom 20 percent of the population based on the ranking in the 1992-1993 VLSS.

8. A total of 51 provinces were covered in the 1992-1993 VLSS. Newly created provinces in the 1997-1998 VLSS were reclassified back to their 1992-1993 original definitions.
9. While land is primarily owned by the state, the issuance of the 1993 Land Law gives households the right to sell or rent out the right to use the land allocated to them by the state for long-term use.
10. *Annual crop land* refers to the area used by households to cultivate annual cash crops such as rice, corn, and cassava. *Perrenial land* is that used for growing long-gestating crops such as coconut, coffee, and tea. *Water surface land* refers to such areas as ponds, lakes or marshes used to raise aquatic products.

APPENDIX TABLE 9.1: Regional Price Indices for VLSS 1992-1993 and 1997-1998

REGIONS	1992-1993		1997-1998	
	URBAN	RURAL	URBAN	RURAL
Northern Uplands	1.113	0.968	0.993	1.018
Red River Delta	1.072	0.934	1.056	0.816
North Central	1.019	0.912	1.025	0.938
Central Coast	1.066	0.953	1.053	0.974
Central Highlands	-	1.086	-	1.060
Southeast	1.223	1.049	1.134	0.965
Mekong Delta	1.107	0.100	1.013	1.027

Note: No price index was used for urban areas in the Central Highlands since there were no respondents coming from the urban areas of this region in both survey years.

Source: General Statistics Office.

APPENDIX TABLE 9.2: Monthly Price Indices for VLSS 1992-1993 and 1997-1998

	1992-1993			1997-1998	
	FOOD AND FOODSTUFF	NONFOOD		FOOD AND FOODSTUFF	NONFOOD
October 92	0.577	0.773	December 97	0.979	0.992
November 92	0.573	0.789	January 98	1.000	1.000
December 92	0.584	0.807	February 98	1.030	1.009
January 93	0.595	0.817	March 98	1.022	0.998
February 93	0.624	0.812	April 98	1.046	1.001
March 93	0.621	0.805	May 98	1.068	1.004
April 93	0.631	0.799	June 98	1.067	1.005
May 93	0.627	0.807	July 98	1.059	1.006
June 93	0.627	0.802	August 98	1.074	1.011
July 93	0.630	0.798	September 98	1.085	1.017
August 93	0.627	0.799	October 98	1.089	1.019
September 93	0.577	0.799	November 98	1.086	1.027

Source: General Statistics Office.

APPENDIX TABLE 9.3:
Determinants of Average Welfare by Quartile

EXPLANATORY VARIABLE	Q1 (poorest)	Q2	Q3	Q4 (richest)
Overall Mean Income (Y)	1.2660 ***	0.7476 ***	1.0032 ***	0.5207 ***
Age of household head	0.0251 ***	-0.0054	0.0002	0.0176 **
Age Squared	-0.0003 ***	0.0001	0.0000	-0.0002 **
Household Size	-0.4006 ***	-0.2964 ***	-0.3218 ***	-0.1903 ***
Number of Dependents	-0.0320	-0.0160	-0.0476 ***	-0.0717 ***
Number of Female Members at Working Age	-0.0098	0.0432 **	0.0158	-0.0671 ***
Male-headed household	0.1918 ***	-0.0298	0.0760	0.0920 *
Marital status of head	0.0103	0.0810	-0.0159	-0.0281
Interaction with Regions				
Y*Northern Uplands	0.0420	-0.2722 ***	-0.2820 ***	-0.0570
Y*Red River Delta	0.0402	-0.2675 ***	-0.2700 ***	-0.0308
Y*North Central Coast	0.0762	-0.1777	-0.2297 **	-0.1125
Y*South Central Coast	0.5209 ***	-0.1017	-0.0960	-0.0715
Y*Central Highlands	0.1722	0.1303	-0.0660	-0.2067
Y*Mekong Delta	0.6885 ***	0.5174 ***	0.1709	-0.4446 ***

continued.

Appendix Table 9.3 continued.

EXPLANATORY VARIABLE	Q1 (poorest)	Q2	Q3	Q4 (richest)
Interaction with "Initial Conditions"				
Y*Schooling	0.0156	0.1294 ***	0.0984 ***	0.0005
Y*Electricity	0.0879	0.1944 ***	0.0524	0.2893 ***
Y*Impassable Roads	-0.0054	-0.0313 ***	-0.0347 ***	0.0020
Y*Annual Crop Land	-0.0555	0.1636	-0.1690	-0.0826
Y*Perennial Land	-0.2494 ***	-0.1605 ***	-0.1670 ***	0.0372
Y*Water Surface Land	-0.1194	0.0141	0.1202	0.0255
Y*Irrigation	-0.0279	0.0816	-0.0241	-0.1770 *
Intercept	-1.4067	-0.1956	4.1068 ***	5.7180 ***
R-squared (within)	0.710	0.597	0.521	0.302

*** denotes significance at the 1 percent level.

** denotes significance at the 5 percent level.

* denotes significance at the 10 percent level.

Note: Estimation is by fixed effects regression in which the dependent variable is the logarithm of mean per capita expenditure of the poorest 20 percent. Data refer to a panel of 3,494 rural households covering the 1992-1993 and 1997-1998 VLSS.

APPENDIX TABLE 9.4: Summary of Variables

VARIABLE	MEAN	STD. DEV.	MIN	MAX
Income of the Poor: *log(Average per capita expenditure of bottom 20%)*	7.4877	0.5064	5.1232	10.1018
Overall Mean Income: *log (Average per capita expenditure of the province)*	7.6195	0.3171	6.8269	8.7164
Age: *Age of household head*	46.4837	14.3599	16.0000	95.0000
Age Squared	2366.9120	1444.3720	256.0000	9025.0000
Household Size	1.4986	0.4718	0.0000	3.2189
Number of Dependents: *household members aged less than 15 years old and above 65*	2.0947	1.4904	0.0000	13.0000
Number of Female Members of Working Age: *with ages 15 to 65*	1.4870	0.8867	0.0000	7.0000
Male	0.7728	0.4191	0.0000	1.0000
Married	0.8173	0.3865	0.0000	1.0000
Overall Income *Northern Uplands	1.2833	2.8019	0.0000	7.8633
Overall Income *Red River Delta	1.8435	3.2673	0.0000	8.5892
Overall Income *North Central Coast	1.1786	2.7285	0.0000	7.8406
Overall Income *South Central Coast	0.8238	2.3805	0.0000	8.0489
Overall Income *Central Highlands	0.2454	1.3317	0.0000	7.7494
Overall Income *Mekong Delta	1.5641	3.1067	0.0000	8.0159
Overall Income* Years of Schooling of Household Head	10.4022	9.1788	0.0000	103.0706
Overall Income* Access to Electricity	2.9359	3.7306	0.0000	8.7164
Overall Income* Number of Months Roads are Impassable	16.3603	32.6064	0.0000	99.9686
Overall Income* Annual Crop Land	13.7613	5.2197	0.0000	19.3473
Overall Income* Perennial Land	7.3101	6.9042	0.0000	19.1096
Overall Income* Water Surface Land	2.8998	5.3203	0.0000	18.5727
Overall Income* Proportion of Irrigated Land	4.7668	3.3895	0.0000	8.7164

Note: Household size and land variables are also expressed in logarithms.

References

Ahmed, S. G., and M. M. Khan., 1990. "Bangladesh." In V. Subramanian, ed., *Public Administration in the Third World: An International Handbook.* Connecticut: Greenwood Press.

Alesina, A., 1998. "The Political Economy of High and Low Growth." In B. Pleskovic and J. Stiglitz, eds., *Annual World Bank Conference on Development Economics.* World Bank, Washington, D.C.

Aminuzzaman, S., 1992. "Administrative Reforms and Their Impact on Training the Public Bureaucracy in Bangladesh." *Governance. An International Journal of Policy and Administration* 5(4, October):438-58.

Anand, K., 2000. *Governance.* United Nations University Annual Report.

Asian Development Bank (ADB), 1994. *Escaping the Poverty Trap: Lessons from Asia.* Manila, Philippines.

______, 1999a. *Fighting Poverty in Asia and the Pacific: The Poverty Reduction Strategy of the Asian Development Bank.* Manila, Philippines.

______, 1999b. *Governance in Thailand: Challenges, Issues and Prospects.* Manila, Philippines.

______, 1999c. *Reducing Poverty: Major Findings and Implications.* Manila, Philippines.

______, 1999d. "A Study of NGOs: Regional Overview Report." Manuscript.

______, 2000a. Addressing Poverty in Bangladesh. Bangladesh Economic Policy Paper 1, Bangladesh Resident Mission, Dhaka, Bangladesh.

______, 2000b. *Anti-Corruption Policy. Description and Answers to Frequently Asked Questions.* Manila, Philippines.

______, 2000c. "Assessment of Poverty in Indonesia." Processed.

______, 2000d. "Country Economic Review: Socialist Republic of Vietnam." Manila, Philippines.

______, 2000e. *Lao Education Sector Development Plan.* Manila, Philippines.

______, 2000f. *Social Exclusion or Inclusion: Development Challenges for Asia and Europe.* Manila, Philippines.

______, 2001a. "Basic Parameters of Governance in Pakistan." Manuscript.

______, 2001b. Rural Development Policy Paper. Agriculture and Social Sectors Department (East), Asian Development Bank, Manila, Philippines.

Asian Productivity Organization (APO), 1998. *Productivity and Quality Improvement in the Civil Service.* Tokyo, Japan.

Asra, A., 2000. "Poverty and Inequality in Indonesia: Estimates, Decomposition and Key Issues." *Journal of the Asia Pacific Economy* 5(1):91-111.

Atinc, T. M., 1998. "Responding to the Global Financial Crisis: Social Consequences of the East Asian Financial Crisis." Manuscript.

______, 2000. "Coping with Crises: Social Policy and the Poor." Available: http://www.worldbank.org/eapsocial/asemsocial/ keypapers.htm.

Balisacan, A. M., 1994a. *Poverty, Urbanization and Development Policy: A Philippine Perspective.* Quezon City: University of the Philippines Press.

______, 1994b. "Urban Poverty in the Philippines: Nature, Causes and Policy Measures." *Asian Development Review* 12(1):117-52.

______, 1999. "What We Really Know—Or Don't Know—About Poverty and Economic Inequality in the Philippines." In A.M. Balisacan and S. Fujisaki, eds., *Causes of Poverty Myths, Facts and Policies.* Quezon City: University of the Philippines Press.

______, 2000. "Growth, Redistribution, and Poverty: Is the Philippines an Exception to the Standard Asian Story?" *Journal of the Asia Pacific Economy* 5(1,2):125-40.

______, 2001. "Poverty in the Philippines: An Update and Reexamination." *Philippine Review of Economics* 38(1):16-51.

Balisacan, A.M., R. Edillon, A. Brillantes, and D. Canlas, 2000. "Approaches to Targeting the Poor." National Economic and Development Authority and the United Nations Development Program. Manuscript.

Balisacan, A.M., and N. Fuwa, 2001. Growth, Inequality, Poverty, and Politics: Philippines, 1988-1997. Discussion Paper No. 0109, School of Economics, University of the Philippines.

Balisacan, A.M., and E.M. Pernia, 2002. "The Rural Road to Poverty Reduction: Some Lessons from the Philippine Experience." *Journal of Asian and African Studies* 37(2, July):147-67.

Bandopadhyaya, D., 1985. "A Study on Poverty Alleviation in Rural India through Employment Creation Programmes." ARTEP, New Delhi. Mimeo.

Banerjee, A., 2000. "Land Reforms: Prospects and Strategies." Background paper for *World Development Report 2000.*

Bardhan, P., 1984. *The Political Economy of Development in India.* Oxford: Blackwell.

______, 1996. "Decentralised Development." *Indian Economic Review* 31:139-56.

______, 1997. *The Role of Governance in Economic Development: A Political Economy Approach.* Development Centre, OECD, Paris.

Bardhan, P., and D. Mookherjee, 2000a. "Capture and Governance at Local and National Levels." *American Economic Review (Papers and Proceedings)* 90 (May):135-9.

______, 2000b. "Decentralising Anti-Poverty Programme Delivery in Developing Countries." Department of Economics, University of California, Berkeley. Mimeo.

Barenstein, J., 1994. *Overcoming Fuzzy Governance in Bangladesh. Policy Implementation in Least Developed Countries.* Dhaka: University Press Ltd.

Barro, R. J., 2001. "Human Capital and Growth." *American Economic Review (Papers and Proceedings)* 91(May):12-7.

Bautista, R. M., and G. Tecson, 2003. "International Dimensions." In A.M. Balisacan and H. Hill, eds., *The Philippine Economy.* Quezon City: Ateneo de Manila University Press.

Bautista, V. A., 1999. *Combating Poverty Through the Comprehensive and Integrated Delivery of Social Services (CIDSS).* Quezon City: National College of Public Administration and Governance, University of the Philippines.

Besley, T., and S. Coate, 1992. "Workfare vs. Welfare: Incentive Arguments for Work Requirements in Poverty-Alleviation Programs." *American Economic Review* 82(1):249-61.

Bhalla, S., 2001. *Imagine There Is No Country: Globalization and Its Consequences for Poverty.* Institute of International Economics, Washington, D.C.

Bhushan, I., E. Bloom, and N. Minh Thang, 2002. Unequal Benefits of Growth in Viet Nam. ERD Policy Brief Series No. 3, Economics and Research Department, Asian Development Bank.

Binswanger, H., K. Deininger, and G. Feder, 1995. "Power, Distortions, Revolts and Reforms in Agricultural Land Relations." In J. Behrman and T. Srinivasan, eds., *Handbook of Development Economics,* Vol. IIIB. Amsterdam: North Holland.

Bird, R.M., 1995. "Decentralizing Infrastructure: For Good or for Ill?" In A. Estache, ed., *Decentralizing Infrastructure: Advantages and Limitations.* World Bank, Washington D.C.

______, 1999. Rethinking Sub-National Taxes: A New Look at Tax Assignment. IMF Discussion Paper, Fiscal Affairs Division, Washington, D.C.

Biro Pusat Statistik (BPS), various years. *Gross Regional Domestic Product of Provinces in Indonesia by Industrial Origin.* Jakarta.

______, various years. *National Socioeconomic Survey.* Jakarta.

______, various years. *Village Potential Statistics (PODES).* Jakarta.

Booth, A., 1999. "Initial Conditions and Miraculous Growth: Why Is South East Asia Different from Taiwan and South Korea?" *World Development* 27(2):301-21.

______, 2000. "Poverty and Inequality in the Soeharto Era: An Assessment." *Bulletin of Indonesian Economic Studies* 36(1):73-104.

Breman, J., and S. Mundle, eds., 1991. *Rural Transformation in Asia.* Delhi: Oxford University Press.

Brillantes, A.B., 1998. "Local Governance and Decentralization: The Philippine Experience." *Philippine Journal of Public Administration* 42.

______, 2001. "Public Sector Reform and Poverty Reduction." Asian Development Bank, Manila. Mimeo.

Brueckner, J., 1999. "Fiscal Decentralization in LDCs: The Effects of Local Corruption and Tax Evasion." Department of Economics, University of Illinois at Urbana-Champaign. Mimeo.

Bruno, M., M. Ravallion, and L. Squire, 1998. "Equity and Growth in Developing Countries: Old and New Perspectives on the Policy Issues." In V. Tanzi and K.Y. Chu, eds., *Income Distribution and High Quality Growth.* Cambridge, MA: MIT Press.

Caiden, G., 1991. "Administrative Reform." In A. Farazmand, ed., *Handbook of Comparative and Development Public Administration.* New York: Marcell Dekker Inc.

Canadian International Development Agency (CIDA), 2000. *Enquiry into Poverty Reduction in Asia: Who Cares for Asia's Poor?* Quebec.

Carino, L. V., 1992. *Bureaucracy for Democracy.* Manila: College of Public Administration, University of the Philippines.

Carr, M., M. Chen, and R. Jhabvala, eds., 1996. *Speaking Out: Women's Economic Empowerment in South Asia.* New Delhi: Vistaar Publications.

Carroll, J. J., S.J., 1997. "Foreword." In C. C. Goño, Peasant Movement-State Relations in New Democracies: The Case of the Congress for a People's Agrarian Reform (CPAR) in Post-Marcos Philippines. Pulso Monograph No. 18, Institute on Church and Social Issues, Quezon City.

Chand, R., 2001. "Regional and Sectoral Disparities in Economic Growth and Income in India." In S.S. Acharya and D.P. Chaudhri, eds., *Indian Agricultural Policy at the Crossroads: Policies and Agenda.* Jaipur and New Delhi: Rawat Publications.

Chang, C., 2000. "Premier Chang Announces Determination on Administration Reform." Government Information Office. Available: http://www.gio.gov.tw/taiwan-website/4-oa/chang/press 1229.htm.

Chang-Soo, L., 1993. "Local Administration and the Saemaul Undong in Korea." In R. de Guzman and M. Reforma, eds., *Decentralization Towards Democratization and Development.* Manila: EROPA Secretariat, pp. 34-39.

Chaudri, 2000. Interim Poverty Reduction Strategy Paper. Pakistan, April.

Cheema, G.S., and D.A. Rondinelli, eds. 1983. *Decentralization and Development: Policy Implementation in Developing Countries.* Beverly Hills: Sage.

Chen, S., and M. Ravallion, 2001. "How Did the World's Poorest Fare in the 1990s?" *The Review of Income and Wealth* 47(3):283-300.

Chenery, H., M.S. Ahluwalia, C.L.G. Bell, J.H. Duloy, and R. Jolly, 1974. *Redistribution with Growth: Policies to Improve Income Distribution in Developing Countries in the Context of Economic Growth.* World Bank and the Institute of Development Studies, University of Sussex. London: Oxford University Press.

Cho, M. H., 1989. *Korea and the Major Powers: An Analysis of Power Structures in East Asia.* Research Center for Peace and Unification of Korea, Seoul.

Cook, S., N. Kabeer, and G. Suwannarat, 2001. "Social Protection in Asia: Addressing Exclusion, Challenging Orthodoxy." Paper prepared for The Ford Foundation.

Crook, R.C., and J. Manor, 1998. *Democracy and Decentralisation in South Asia and West Africa: Participation, Accountability and Performance.* Cambridge: Cambridge University Press.

Crook, R.C., and A.S. Sverrisson, 1999. "To What Extent Can Decentralised Forms of Government Enhance the Development of Pro-Poor Policies and Improve Poverty Alleviation Outcomes?" Mimeo.

Dancel, R.C., 2001. "Filipinos Poorer Due to Crisis–NSCB." *Philippine Daily Inquirer.* 4 August. Page B1.

Dasgupta, P., 1986. "Positive Freedom, Markets, and the Welfare State." *Oxford Review of Economic Policy* 2(2):25-36.

______, 1993. *An Inquiry into Well-being and Destitution.* Oxford: Clarendon Press.

Datt, G., and M. Ravallion, 1998. "Why Have Some Indian States Done Better than Others at Reducing Rural Poverty?" *Economica* 65(257):17-38.

David, I.P., A. Asra, and M. de Castro, 1999. Poverty Incidence in the Asian and Pacific Region: Data Situation and Measurement Issues. EDRC Briefing Note No. 17, Asian Development Bank, Manila, Philippines.

De Dios, E. S., 1997. Economic Outcomes and Philippine Democratization. In F. Miranda, ed., *Democratization: Philippine Perspectives.* Quezon City: University of the Philippines Press.

______, 1999. "Combating Poverty through CIDSS." *Philippine Journal of Public Administration* XLIII, 3 & 4 (July-October).

De Dios, E.S., and P. Hutchcroft, 2003. "Political Economy." In A. M. Balisacan and H. Hill, eds., *The Philippine Economy: Development, Policies and Challenges.* New York: Oxford University Press.

de Haan, A., 1994. "Bibliographical Review of Social Exclusion in South Asia." International Institute for Labour Studies of the International Labour Organization. Available: http://www.ilo.org/public/english/bureau/inst/papers/1994/dp77/ch1.htm.

de Janvry, A., 1981. *The Agrarian Question and Reformism in Latin America.* Baltimore: Johns Hopkins University Press.

de Janvry, A., and E. Sadoulet. 2000. "Growth, Poverty and Inequality in Latin America: A Causal Analysis, 1970-94." *Review of Income and Wealth Series* 46(3): 267-87.

de Janvry, A., A. Fargeix, and E. Sadoulet, 1992. "The Political Feasibility of Rural Poverty Reduction." *Journal of Development Economics* 37:351-67.

Deaton, A., 1997. *The Analysis of Household Surveys: A Microeconometric Approach to Development Policy.* Baltimore: Johns Hopkins University Press for the World Bank.

______, 2001. "Counting the World's Poor: Problems and Possible Solutions." *World Bank Research Observer* 16(2):125-47.

Deininger, K., and L. Squire, 1998. "New Ways of Looking at Old Issues: Inequality and Growth." *Journal of Development Economics* 57:259-87.

Dennis, J. V., 2000. *A Review of National Social Policies in Lao PDR.* Regional Environment Technical Assistance 5771, Poverty Reduction and Environmental Management in Remote Greater Mekong Subregion (GMS) Watersheds project (Phase 1). Asian Development Bank, Manila, Philippines.

Deolalikar, A. B., 1988. "Do Health and Nutrition Influence Labor Productivity in Agriculture? Econometric Estimates for Rural South India." *Review of Economics and Statistics* 70:406-13.

Department of International Development (DFID), 2001. "Eliminating World Poverty: Making Globalisation Work for the Poor." A white paper on international development, London.

Dilinger, W., 1994. Decentralization and its Implications for Urban Service Delivery. Urban Management Program Discussion Paper No. 16, World Bank, Washington D.C.

Dollar, D., 2002. Reform, Growth, and Poverty Reduction in Vietnam. Policy Research Working Paper No. 2837, World Bank, Washington, D.C.

Dollar, D., and P. Glewwe, 1998. "Poverty and Inequality in the Early Reform Period." In , D. Dollar, P. Glewwe, and J. Litvack, eds., *Household Welfare and Vietnam's Transition.* Regional and Sectoral Studies, World Bank, Washington, D.C.

Dollar, D., and A. Kraay, 2001. Growth is Good for the Poor. World Bank Policy Research Paper No. 2587, Washington D.C.

Dollar, D., and J. Litvack, 1998. "Macroeconomic Reform and Poverty Reduction in Vietnam." In D. Dollar, P. Glewwe, and J. Litvack, eds. , *Household Welfare and Vietnam's Transition.* Regional and Sectoral Studies, World Bank, Washington, D.C.

Drèze, J., and A.K. Sen, 1989. *Hunger and Public Action.* New York: Oxford University Press.

Dreze, J., and M. Saran, 1995. "Primary Education and Economic Development in China and India: Overview and Two Case Studies." In K. Basu, P. Pattanaik, and K. Suzumura, eds., *Choice, Welfare and Development*. Oxford: Clarendon Press.

Duflo, E., 2001. "Schooling and Labor Market Consequences of School Construction in Indonesia: Evidence from an Unusual Policy Experiment." *American Economic Review* 91:795-813.

Eaton, K., 2001. "Political Obstacles to Decentralisation: Evidence from Argentina and the Philippines." *Development and Change* 32:101-27.

Echeverri-Gent, J., 1993. *The State and the Poor*. Berkeley: University of California Press.

Eid, U., 2000. "Good Governance for Poverty Reduction." Paper prepared during the ADB Seminar on The New Social Policy and Poverty Agenda for Asia and the Pacific, Chiang Mai, Thailand, 5 May.

Ellison, K., 1998. "Emerging Styles of Governance: A Global Context." *Philippine Journal of Public Administration* 42,1 & 2 (January-April):1-16.

Fan, S., L. Zhang, and X. Zhang, 2000. "How Does Public Spending Affect Growth and Poverty? The Experience of China." Paper presented at the Second Annual Global Development Network Conference, Tokyo, 11-13 December.

Farazmand, A., 1998. "Comparative and Development Public Administration 2000: Introduction to the Symposium." *International Journal of Public Administration* 21(12):1647-65.

Farrington, J., and D. J. Lewis, eds., with S. Satish, and A. Miclat-Teves, 1993. *Non-Governmental Organizations and the State in Asia; Rethinking Roles in Sustainable Agricultural Development*. London and New York: Routledge.

Finance Minister of Pakistan, 2001. Speech delivered before the Pakistan Development Forum, Islamabad, 12 March.

Fisman, R., and R. Gatti, 2000. "Decentralization and Corruption: Evidence across Countries." Development Research Group, World Bank, Washington, D.C. Mimeo.

Forbes, K. J., 2000. "A Reassessment of the Relationship between Inequality and Growth." *American Economic Review* 90(September):869-87.

Foster, J. E., and A. F. Shorrocks, 1988. "Poverty Orderings." *Econometrica* 56:173-77.

Gaiha, R., 2000. *The Exclusion of the Poorest: Emerging Lessons from the Maharashtra Rural Credit Project, India*. International Fund for Agricultural Development (IFAD), Rome.

______, 2001a. "Are DAC Targets of Poverty Reduction Useful?" *Oxford Development Studies*. Forthcoming.

______, 2001b. "Rural Public Works and the Poor—A Review of the Employment Guarantee Scheme in Maharashtra." International Food Policy Research Institute (IFPRI). Mimeo.

______, 2001c. "Deprivation amidst Opportunity: Lessons from Mewat Area Development Project." International Fund for Agricultural Development. Forthcoming.

Gaiha, R., and V. Kulkarni, 1999. "Policy Reforms, Institutions and the Poor in Rural India." *Contemporary South Asia* 8(1):7-28.

Gaiha, R., P.D. Kaushik, and V.Kulkarni, 1998. "Jawahar Rozgar Yojana, Panchayats, and the Rural Poor in India." *Asian Survey* 38(10):928-49.

______, 2000. "Participation or Empowerment of the Rural Poor: The Case of the Panchayats in India." In V.Damodaran and M. Unnithan-Kumar, eds., *Post Colonial India*. Delhi: Manohar.

Gallup, J.L., S. Radelet, and A. Warner, 1999. Economic Growth and the Income of the Poor. Consulting Assistance on Economic Reform II Discussion Paper No. 36, Harvard Institute for International Development, Cambridge, MA.

Gallup, J.L., J. D. Sachs, with A. D. Mellinger, 1998. "Geography and Economic Development." In B. Pleskovic and J.E. Stiglitz, eds., *Annual World Bank Conference on Development Economics.* World Bank, Washington, D.C.

Garcia, J. G., 1998. "Why Do Differences in Provincial Incomes Persist in Indonesia?" *Bulletin of Indonesian Economic Studies* 34(1):95-120.

______, 2000. "Indonesia's Trade and Price Interventions: Pro-Java and Pro-Urban." *Bulletin of Indonesian Economic Studies* 36(December):93-112.

Glewwe, P., and H. Jacoby, 1998. School Enrollment and Completion in Vietnam: An Investigation of Recent Trends. In D. Dollar, P. Glewwe, and J. Litvack, eds., *Household Welfare and Vietnam's Transition.* Regional and Sectoral Studies, The World Bank, Washington, D.C.

Glewwe, P., and P. Nguyen, 2002. Economic Mobility in Vietnam in the 1990s. Policy Research Working Paper No. 2838, World Bank, Washington, D.C.

Glewwe, P., M. Gragnolati, and H. Zaman, 2000. Who Gained from Viet Nam's Boom in the 1990s? An Analysis of Poverty and Inequality Trends. Policy Research Working Paper 2275, World Bank, Washington, D.C.

Gelbach, J. B., and L. H. Pritchett, 1995. Does More for the Poor Mean Less for the Poor? The Politics of Tagging. World Bank Working Paper 1523, Washington, D.C.

Goño, C., 1996. Peasant Movement-State Relations in New Democracies: The Case of the Congress for a People's Agrarian Reform, CPAR, in Post-Marcos Philippines. Pulso Monograph No. 12, Institute of Church and Social Issues, Quezon City.

______, 1998. Peasant Movement - State Relations in New Democracies: The Case of the Congress for a People's Agrarian Reform (CPAR) in Post-Marcos Philippines. Pulso Monograph No. 18, Institute on Church and Social Issues, Quezon City.

Grindle, M., ed., 1980. *Politics and Policy Implementation in the Third World.* New Jersey: Princeton University Press.

______, ed., 1997. *Getting Good Government. Capacity Building in the Public Sectors of Developing Countries.* Boston: Harvard Institute for International Development; Harvard University Press.

Gupta, S., H. Davoodi, and R. Alonso-Terme, 1998. "Does Corruption Affect Income Inequality and Poverty?" International Monetary Fund, Washington, D.C. Mimeo.

Habermas, J., 1975. *Legitimation* Crisis. Boston: Beacon Press.

Haggard, S., 1990. *Pathways from the Periphery—The Politics of Growth in the NICs.* Ithaca, NY: Cornell University Press.

Helm, D., and S. Smith, 1989. "The Decentralised State: The Economic Borders of Local Government." In D. Helm, ed., *The Economic Borders of the State.* Oxford: Oxford University Press.

Herring, R., 2000. "Political Conditions for Agrarian Reform and Poverty Alleviation." Background paper for *WDR 2000.*

Herring, R., and R.M. Edwards, 1983. "Guaranteeing Employment to the Rural Poor: Social Functions and Class Interests in the Employment Guarantee Scheme in Western India." *World Development* 11(7):575-92.

Hill, H., 1996. *The Indonesian Economy since 1966: Southeast Asia's Emerging Giant.* Cambridge: Cambridge University Press.

______, 2002. "Spatial Disparities in Developing East Asia: A Survey." *Asian-Pacific Economic Literature* 16(1):10-35; Oxford: Blackwell Publishers Ltd.

Ho, S. P.S., 1978. *Economic Development of Taiwan, 1860-1970.* New Haven: Yale University Press.

Housing and Urban Development Coordinating Council (HUDCC), 2001. *Magnitude of Informal Settlers in Metro Manila: Summary by LGU (Local Government Unit) as of 11 April.* Tables.

Hwa, L., 1991. "The Public Administration of the Republic of China on Taiwan." In A. Farazmand, ed., *Handbook of Comparative Development Administration.* New York: Marcell Dekker Inc.

Iglesias, G. U., ed., 1976. *Implementation: The Problem of Achieving Results.* Manila: Eastern Regional Organization for Public Administration.

Illo, J., 1997. "Women in the Philippines." Country Briefing Paper. Asian Development Bank, Manila, Philippines.

Ingham, B., and A.K.M. Kalam, 1992. "Decentralisation and Development: Theory and Evidence from Bangladesh." *Public Administration and Development* 12:373-85.

Institute for Popular Democracy (IPD), 1991. *Political Clans and Electoral Politics in the Philippines: A Study on Elites and Power Relations.* Manila.

Institute on Church and Social Issues, 2000. "An Analysis of Contemporary Developments in Philippine Society as of 22 December 1999." *Intersect* 15(2, February).

International Fund for Agricultural Development (IFAD), 2001. *Rural Poverty Report 2001: The Challenge of Ending Rural Poverty.* New York: Oxford University Press.

International Labor Organization (ILO), 1977. *Poverty and Landlessness in Rural Asia.* Geneva.

International Monetary Fund (IMF), 2001. *The World Economic Outlook Database.* Available: http://www.imf.org/external/ pubs/ft/weo/2001/02/data/ index.htm#5a.

Irfan, M., and R. Amjad, 1984. "Poverty in Rural Pakistan." In A.R. Khan and E. Lee, eds., *Poverty in Rural Asia.* International Labour Organisation, Bangkok.

Isham, J., D. Kaufmann, and L. H. Pritchett, 1997. "Civil Liberties, Democracy, and the Performance of Government Projects." *The World Bank Economic Review* 11(2):219-42.

Islam, N., 1990. "Pakistan." In V. Subramanian, ed., *Public Administration in the Third World.* New York: Greenwood Press.

Jansen, K., 2000. "Vietnam, Macroeconomic Policies and Poverty." 30 October. Manuscript.

Jensen, R., 1998. Public Transfers, Private Transfers, and the 'Crowding Out' Hypothesis: Evidence from South Africa. Kennedy School of Government Faculty Research Working Paper #R98-08.

Jha, R., M. Mohanty, S. Chatterjee, and P. Chitkara, 1998. "Tax Efficiency in Selected Indian States." *Empirical Economics* 24(4):641-54.

Jomo, K.S., and L.H. Aun, 2000. "Some Social Consequences of the 1997-98 Economic Crisis in Malaysia. Social Impacts of the Asian Economic Crisis." Thailand Development Research Institute.

Joong-Yand, K., and P. Kyung-Bae, 1994. "Future Development of the Korean Public Administration System." *Asian Review of Public Administration* 6 (1-2, January-December):123-63.

Kakwani, N., 1997. On Measuring Growth and Inequality: Components of Changes in Poverty with Application to Thailand. Discussion Paper, The University of New South Wales, Sydney.

Kakwani, N., and M. Krongkaew, 1996. "Final Report: Establishment of Key Indicators System for the 8th Plan Monitoring and Evaluation – Paper II: Specific Issues." DED, NESDB, Bangkok. Mimeo.

Kakwani, N., and E. M. Pernia, 2000. "What is Pro-Poor Growth?" *Asian Development Review* 18(1):1-16.

Karaos, A. M. A., 1997. Future of Asian Cities. *Intersect* 12(1, January).

Kee-Ok, K., 1993. "Privatization of the Saemaul Movement." In R. de Guzman and M. Reforma, eds., *Decentralization Towards Democratization and Development.* EROPA Secretariat, Manila.

Kelles-Viitanen, A., 2001. "Comment to Sociocultural Factors Affecting Poverty Reduction." Paper presented at the Conference on Poverty, Growth and the Role of Institutions. Manila, Asian Development Bank.

Kemal, A.R., 2001. "Structural Adjustment, Macroeconomic Policies, and Poverty Trends in Pakistan." Paper presented at the Asia and Pacific Forum on Poverty: Reforming Policies and Institutions for Poverty Reduction. Manila, Asian Development Bank.

Kerkvliet, B. J. T., 1990. *Everyday Politics in the Philippines: Class and Status Relations in a Central Luzon Village.* Berkeley, CA: University of California Press.

Khan, A.R., and E. Lee, eds., 1984. *Poverty in Rural Asia.* Bangkok: ILO.

Khan, Z. R., 1999. "Decentralized Planning and Financing of Rural Development in Bangladesh." *Regional Development Dialogue* 20:43-57.

Khandker, S.R., 1998. *Fighting Poverty with Micro Credit—Experience in Bangladesh.* New York: Oxford University Press.

Khemani, S., 2001. Decentralization and Accountability: Are Voters More Vigilant in Local than in National Elections. Policy Research Department Working Paper No. 2557, World Bank, Washington, D.C.

Khundker, N., W. Mahmud, B. Sen, and M. U. Ahmed, 1994. "Urban Poverty in Bangladesh: Trends, Determinants, and Policy Issues." *Asian Development Review: Studies of Asian and Pacific Economic Issues* 12(1):1-31.

Kim, J. G., 1994. "Urban Poverty in the Republic of Korea: Critical Issues and Policy Measures." *Asian Development Review: Studies of Asian and Pacific Economic Issues* 12(1): 90-116.

Kim, P. S., 1999. "Public Sector Reform in Korea: Some Policy Implications." *NIRA Review,* Spring. Available: http://www. nira.go.jp/publ/review/ 99spring/kim.html.

Kim, Y. P., 1997. "The Korean Civil Service System." A country report presented at the Research Consortium of Civil Service Systems in Comparative Perspective, Indiana University, Bloomington, Indiana, 5-8 April. Available: http://www.indiana.edu/ ~csrc/kim1html.

Klauss, R., 1997. "Laos: The Case of the Transitioning Civil Service System in a Transitional Economy." A country report presented at the Research Consortium of Civil Service Systems in Comparative Perspective, Indiana University, 5-8 April.

Klitgaard, R., 1998. "International Cooperation against Corruption." *Finance and Development* 35:3-6.

Knowles, J. C., E. M. Pernia, and M. Racelis, 1999. "Social Consequences of the Financial Crisis in Asia." Economics and Development Resource Center, Asian Development Bank, Manila, Philippines. Processed.

Kohli, A., 1987. *The State and Poverty in India.* Cambridge: Cambridge University Press.

Kpundeh, S., 1997. "Political Will in Fighting Corruption." In UNDP and OECD Development Center, *Corruption and Integrity Improvement Initiatives in Developing Countries.* Report of the conference held at the OECD headquarters in Paris, 24-25 October.

Kpundeh, S., and I. Hors, 1997. "Overview." In UNDP and OECD Development Center, *Corruption and Integrity Improvement Initiatives in Developing Countries.* Report of the conference held at the OECD headquarters in Paris, 24-25 October.

Krueger, A., and M. Lindhal, 2001. "Education for Growth: Why and For Whom?" *Journal of Economic Literature* 39(4):1101-36.

Kwon, E., 2000. "Infrastructure, Growth, and Poverty Reduction in Indonesia: A Cross-Sectional Analysis." Asian Development Bank, Manila, Philippines. Processed.

Lam, W. F., 1999. "Institutional Design of Public Agencies and Co-production: A Study of Irrigation Associates in Taiwan." *World Development* 24(6):1039-54.

Lanjouw, P., M. Pradhan, F. Saadah, H. Sayed, and R. Sparrow, 2001. "Poverty, Education and Health in Indonesia: Who Benefits from Public Spending?" World Bank, Washington, D.C. Processed.

Lanjouw, P., and M. Ravallion, 1998. Benefit Incidence and the Timing of Program Capture. World Bank Working Paper 1956, Washington, D.C.

Lao PDR, 1998. *Lao People's Democratic Republic Country Report.* September.

______, 2000a. "Fighting Poverty through Human Resource Development, Rural Development and People's Participation." Government Report to the Seventh Roundtable Meeting, Vientiane, 21-23 November.

______, State Planning Committee, 2000b. *Poverty in the Lao PDR. Participatory Poverty Assessment (PPA).* October.

______, 2001. "Interim Poverty Reduction Strategy Paper." A government paper prepared for the Executive Boards of the IMF and the WB, 20 March.

Li, H., and H. Zou, 1998. "Income Inequality Is Not Harmful for Growth: Theory and Evidence." *Review of Development Economics* 2(3):318-34.

Lin, J.Y., and Z. Liu, 2000. "Fiscal Decentralisation and Economic Growth in China." *Economic Development and Cultural Change* 49(1):1-22.

Little, I. M. D., T. Scitovsky, and M. Scott, 1970. *Industry and Trade in Some Developing Countries: A Comparative Study.* London: Oxford University Press.

Lustig, N., and N. Stern, 2000. "Broadening the Agenda for Poverty Reduction: Opportunity, Empowerment, Security." *Finance and Development* 37(4, December):3-7.

Mahbub-ul-Haq Human Development Centre, 1999. *Human Development in South Asia Report: The Crisis in Governance.* Oxford: Oxford University Press.

______, 2000. *Human Development in South Asia 2000.* Oxford: Oxford University Press.

Mangahas, M., 1999. "Monitoring Philippine Poverty by Operational Social Indicators." Paper presented to the World Bank's Poverty Reduction and Economic Management (PREM) Network, PREM Week 99, July 13-14, 1999, University of Maryland University College, College Park, Maryland.

______, 2001. "Voicing Poverty As Well As Votes." *Social Climate*, 6 April. Available: http://www.sws.org.ph/apr01.htm.

Manning, C., 1997. Regional Labor Markets during Deregulation in Indonesia. Policy Research Working Paper 1728, World Bank, Washington D.C.

Manor, J., 1999. *The Political Economy of Democratic Decentralization.* World Bank, Washington D.C.

Mauro, P., 1995. "Corruption and Growth." *Quarterly Journal of Economics* 110(3):681-712.

______, 1997. "The Effects of Corruption on Growth, Investment and Government Expenditure: A Cross Country Analysis." In A.E. Kimberly,ed., *Corruption and the Global Economy.* Institute for International Economics, Washington D.C.

McMahon, W. W., and Boediono, 1992. "Universal Basic Education: An Overall Strategy of Investment Priorities for Economic Growth." *Economics of Education Review* 11(2):137-51.

Migdal, J. S., 1988. *Strong Societies And Weak States: State-Society Relations and State Capabilities In The Third World.* Princeton, NJ: Princeton University Press.

Ministry of Labour, Invalides and Social Affairs (MOLISA), 2000. "Hunger Eradication and Poverty Reduction Strategy in the 2001-2010 Period." 22 November.

Mitra, S.K., 2001. "Making Local Government Work: Local Elites, Panchayati Raj, and Governance in India." In A. Kohli, ed., *The Success of India's Democracy.* Cambridge: Cambridge University Press.

Moock, P., H. A. Patrinos, and M. Venkatamaran, 1998. Education and Earnings in a Transition Economy: The Case of Vietnam. Policy Research Working Paper 1920, The World Bank, Washington, D.C.

Moon, H., H. Lee, and G. Yoo, 1999. The Social Impact of the Financial Crisis in Korea. Economics and Development Resource Center, Asian Development Bank, Manila, Philippines. Processed.

Morley, S., 2000. "La Distribution del Ingreso en America Latina y el Caribe.' *Fondo de Cultura Economica.*

Narayan, D., 1999. *Bonds and Bridges: Social Capital and Poverty.* The World Bank, Washington D.C.

Narayan, D., R. Chambers, M. Shah, and P. Petesch, 2000. *Voices of the Poor: Crying Out for Change.* New York: Oxford University Press.

Narayan, D., A. Rademacher, K. Schafft, R. Patel, and S. Koch-Schulte, 2000. *Voices of the Poor: Can Anyone Hear Us?* New York: Oxford University Press.

Naseem, S.M., 1977. "Rural Poverty and Landless in Pakistan." In ILO Report on Poverty and Landlessness in Asia. International Labour Office, Geneva.

National Anti-Poverty Commission (NAPC), 1999. *Breaking Free from Poverty.* Office of the President, Manila, Philippines.

______, 2001a. "Anti-Poverty Targeted Interventions (Social Safety Nets)." 17 April.

______, 2001b. *Strategizing the Anti-Poverty Program of the GMA Administration.* Office of the President, Manila, Philippines.

______, 2001c. "Updates on the Government's Poverty Reduction Strategy and the National Anti-Poverty Commission." 14 July.

National Statistical Coordination Board (NSCB), 1997. *Final Philippine Poverty Statistics.*

National Economic and Social Development Board (NESDB), 1999. *Indicators of Well-being and Policy Analysis* 3:1.

National Statistics Office, 1999. *Annual Poverty Indicators Survey 1999.* Available: http:www.census.gov.ph/data/sectordata/ 2000/ap991004.htm.

Ngolaban, G., 1999. "Urban Poor Issues and Concerns." Paper presented at the Public Forum on the Philippines entitled The Estrada Government Amidst the Crisis: Can It Deliver Its Promise to the Poor?, Utrecht, the Netherlands, 23 April.

North, D. C., 1990. *Institutions, Institutional Change, and Economic Performance.* Cambridge: Cambridge University Press.

NOVIB, 1996. *Bangladesh Country Policy Document: Summary Proceedings of the Mid-term Review Workshop.* As cited by A. Rahman and A. Razzaque, "On Reaching the Hardcore Poor: Some Evidence on Social Exclusion in NGO Programmes." *Bangladesh Development Studies* 26(1, March):1-35.

Nowak, M., 1996. "Albania: Rural Poverty Alleviation Pilot Project." In *The*

World Bank Participation Sourcebook. The International Bank for Reconstruction and Development, Washington D.C.

Oates, W.E., 1999. "An Essay on Fiscal Federalism." *Journal of Economic Literature* 37(3):1120-49.

OECD, 2000. "The Governance Factor." *OECD Observer,* December.

Ofosu-Amaah, R. Soopramanien, and K. Uprety, 1999. *Combating Corruption. A Comparative Review of Selected Legal Aspects of State Practice and Major International Initiatives.* International Bank for Reconstruction and Development, World Bank, Washington, D.C.

Okidebe, N., 2001. "Rural Poverty: Trends and Measurement." Background study prepared for the 2001 update of the World Bank's Rural Development Strategy.

Olson, M., 1993. "Dictatorship, Democracy and Development." *American Political Science Review* 87(3):567-75.

Osborne, D., and T. Gaebler, 1993. *Reinventing Government. How the Entrepreneurial Spirit is Transforming the Public Sector.* New York: Penguin Books.

Ostrom, E., 2000. "Collective Action and the Evolution of Social Norms." *Journal of Economic Perspectives* 14(3):137-58.

Otsuka, K., 1991. "Determinants and Consequences of Land Reform Implementation in the Philippines." *Journal of Development Economics* 35: 339-55.

______, 1993. "Land Tenure and Rural Poverty." In M.G. Quibria, ed., *Rural Poverty in Asia: Priority Issues and Policy Options.* Hong Kong: Oxford University Press for the Asian Development Bank.

______, 2000. "Land Tenure, Land Reform and Rural Poverty in Asia." Paper presented at the IAAE conference in Berlin, August. Mimeo.

Paitoonpong, S., 1999. "Consultations with the Poor: National Synthesis Report: Thailand." Preliminary Draft.

Pakistan Government, Planning Commission, 2001a. *Three Year Poverty Reduction Programme 2001-04.* Islamabad, Pakistan.

______, 2001b. Pakistan Interim Poverty Reduction Strategy Paper (I-PRSP). Prepared jointly with the Poverty Reduction Cell, Planning Commission, Policy Wing, Finance Division, March.

Park, C., and M. Kim, 1998. *Current Poverty Issues and Counter Policies in Korea.* Seoul, Korea: Korea Institute for Health and Social Affairs and the United Nations Development Programme.

Parker, A.N., 1995. "Decentralization: The Way Forward for Rural Development?" World Bank, Washington, D.C. Mimeo.

Paul, S., 1996. *Making Voice Work: The Report Card on Bangalore's Public Services.* World Bank, Washington, D.C.

Pernia, E.M., ed., 1994. *Urban Poverty in Asia: A Survey of Critical Issues.* Hong Kong: Oxford University Press for the Asian Development Bank.

______, 2001. Is Growth Good Enough for the Poor? ERD Policy Brief Series No. 1, Economics and Research Department, Asian Development Bank, Manila.

Pernia, E.M., and M.G. Quibria, 1999. Poverty in Developing Countries. In P. Cheshire and E. Mills, eds., *Handbook of Regional and Urban Economics.* Amsterdam: North-Holland.

Phongpaichit, P., 1998. "Corruption and Its Effect on Thailand's Economy and Political Institutions: Focus on Thailand." *Asian Perspectives Series.* The Asia Foundation.

Population Reference Bureau, 2000. "2000 World Population Data Sheet." Available: http://www.worldpop.org.

Pradhan, M., and N. Prescott, 1998. A Poverty Profile of Cambodia. World Bank Discussion Paper 373, Washington, D.C.

Prud'homme, R., 1995. "The Dangers of Decentralization." *World Bank Research Observer* 10(2):201-20.

Psacharopoulos, G., and M. Woodhall, 1985. *Education for Development: An Analysis of Investment Choice.* Oxford: Oxford University Press.

Putnam, R., 1993. *Making Democracy Work.* Princeton: Princeton University Press.

Putzel, J., 1992. *A Captive Land: The Politics of Agrarian Reform in the Philippines.* Manila: Ateneo de Manila University Press and London: The Catholic Institute for International Relations.

Quibria, M.G., ed., 1993. *Rural Poverty in Asia: Priority Issues and Policy Options.* Hong Kong: Oxford University Press for the Asian Development Bank.

______, 2001. Growth and Poverty: Lessons from the East Asian Miracle Revisited. Asian Development Bank Institute (ADBI) Research Paper No. 33, ADBI, Tokyo.

Racelis, M., 1999. "Cities for Twenty-First Century People: A Regional Perspective on Urban Poverty in Asia." *Regional Development Dialogue* 20(1, Spring):1-15.

______, 2000a. "Fighting Urban Poverty in Asia through Effective Partnerships." Paper presented at the ADB Asian Mayors Forum in Shanghai, 26-29 June.

______, 2000b. "New Visions and Strong Actions: Civil Society in the Philippine." In M. Ottaway and T. Carothers, eds., *Funding Virtue: Civil Society Aid and Democratic Promotion.* Carnegie Endowment for International Peace, Washington, D.C.

Racelis, M., W. F. Arce, A. M. Karaos, L. L. Lim, and A. Dizon, 1999. *Urban Poverty from the Perspectives of the Urban Poor.* Quezon City: Institute of Philippine Culture.

Racelis-Hollnsteiner, M., 1963. Reciprocity in the Lowland Philippines. IPC Paper No. 2, Ateneo de Manila Institute of Philippine Culture, Manila.

______, 1979. "Mobilizing the Rural Poor through Community Organization." *Philippine Studies* 27:387-416.

Rahman, A., G. Kisunko, and K. Kapoor, 2000. "Estimating the Effects of Corruption: Implications for Bangladesh." South Asia Region, World Bank, Washington, D.C. Mimeo.

Rahman, A.T. R., 1986. "Legal and Administrative Measures Against Bureaucratic Corruption in Asia." In L. Cariño, ed., *Bureaucratic Corruption in Asia: Causes, Consequences and Controls.* Manila: College of Public Administration.

Rahman, A., and A. Razzaque, 2000. "On Reaching the Hardcore Poor: Some Evidence on Social Exclusion in NGO Programmes." *Bangladesh Development Studies* 26(1, March):1-35.

Raksasataya, A., 1989. "Anti-Corrupt Measures in Thailand." In R. de Guzman, M. Reforma, and D. Reyes, eds., *Public Administration in a Changing National and International Environment.* Manila: EROPA Secretariat General.

Rao, M.G., 1999. "Intergovernmental Fiscal Arrangements in a Transitional Economy: The Case of Vietnam." *Regional Development Dialogue* 20 (2):119-31.

Rashid, S., and M.G. Quibria, 1995. "Is Land Reform Passe? With Special Reference to Asian Agriculture." In M.G. Quibria, ed., *Critical Issues in Asian Development: Theories, Experiences and Policies.* Hong Kong: Oxford University Press for the Asian Development Bank.

Ratanakomut, S., C. Ashakul, and T. Kirananda, 1994. "Urban Poverty in Thailand: Critical Issues and Policy Measures." *Asian Development Review: Studies of Asian and Pacific Economic Issues* 12(1):204-24.

Ravallion, M., 2000. "Growth and Poverty: Making Sense of the Current Debate." World Bank, Washington D.C. Mimeo.

______, 2001. "Growth, Inequality and Poverty: Looking Beyond Averages." *World Development* 29:1803-15.

______, 2002. "Measuring Aggregate Welfare in Developing Countries: How Well Do National Accounts and Surveys Agree?" *Review of Economics and Statistics.* Forthcoming.

Ravallion, M., and S. Chen, 1997. "What Can New Survey Data Tell Us About Recent Changes in Distribution and Poverty?" *World Bank Economic Review* 11(2):357-82.

Ravallion, M., and G. Datt, 1995. "Is Targeting through a Work Requirement Efficient? Some Evidence from Rural India." In D. van de Walle and K. Nead, eds., *Public Spending and the Poor: Theory and Evidence.* Baltimore: The Johns Hopkins University Press.

_______, 2002. "Why Has Economic Growth Been More Pro-Poor in Some States of India than Others?" *Journal of Development Economics* 68(2):381-400.

Ravallion, M., and B. Sen, 1994. "Impacts on Rural Poverty of Land-Based Targeting: Further Results for Bangladesh." *World Development* 22(6): 823-38.

Ravallion, M., and D. van de Walle, 2001. Breaking up the Collective Farm: Welfare Outcomes of Vietnam's Land Privatization. Policy Research Working Paper 2710, World Bank, Washington, D.C.

Reyes, C. M., 2002. "The Poverty Fight: Have We Made an Impact?" Paper presented at the Symposium Series, Philippine Institute for Development Studies, September.

Reyes, C. M., R. G. Manasan, A. C. Orbeta, and G. G. de Guzman, 1999. "The Social Impact of the Financial Crisis in the Philippines." Economics and Development Resource Center, Asian Development Bank, Manila, Philippines. Processed.

Robredo, J., 2000. "Local Governments and National Poverty Alleviation." In *The New Social Policy Agenda in Asia (Proceedings of the Manila Social Forum*). Asian Development Bank and the World Bank, Manila Philippines.

Rodrik, D., 2001. "Growth versus Poverty Reduction: A Hollow Debate." *Finance and Development* 37(December):8-9.

Roemer, M., and M. Gugerty, 1997. Does Economic Growth Reduce Poverty? Consulting Assistance on Economic Reform II Discussion Paper No. 4, Harvard Institute for International Development, Harvard.

Rondinelli, D.A., 1999. "Comment on Intergovernmental Fiscal Arrangements in a Transitional Economy: The Case of Viet Nam." *Regional Development Dialogue* 20(2):132-33.

Rosegrant, M. W., and P. B. R. Hazell, 2000. *Transforming the Rural Asian Economy: The Unfinished Revolution.* New York: Oxford University Press.

Sahn, D. E., and H. Alderman, 1988. "The Effect of Human Capital on Wages, and the Determinants of Labor Supply in a Developing Country." *Journal of Development Economics* 29:157-83.

San Juan, K., 1996. "Strategic Roles of Philippine NGOs." In A. G. Alegre, ed., *Trends and Traditions, Challenges and Choices: A Strategic Study of Philippine NGOs.* Quezon City: Ateneo Center for Social Policy and Public Affairs.

Schultz, T. P., 1988. "Education Investments and Returns." In H. Chenery and T.N. Srinivasan, eds., *Handbook of Development Economics,* Vol. 1. Amsterdam: North Holland.

Scott, J. C., 1985. *Weapons of the Weak: Everyday Forms of Peasant Resistance.* New Haven: Yale University Press.

Seabright, P., 1996. "Accountability and Decentralisation in Government: An Incomplete Contracts Model." *European Economic Review* 40:61-89.

______, 1997. "Is Cooperation Habit Forming?" In P. Dasgupta and K.G. Maler, eds., *The Environment and Emerging Development Issues.* Oxford: Clarendon Press.

Sen, A. K., 1980. "Equality of What?" In *Tanner Lectures on Human Values,* 1, S. McMurrin, ed. Cambridge: Cambridge University Press.

______, 1981. *Poverty and Famines: An Essay on Entitlement and Deprivation.* Oxford: Clarendon Press.

______, 1987. "The Standard of Living." In G. Hawthorn, ed., *The Standard of Living.* Cambridge: Cambridge University Press.

______, 2000a. *Beyond the Crisis—Development Strategies in South Asia.* Institute of South East Asian Studies, Singapore.

______, 2000b. *Development as Freedom.* New Delhi: Oxford University Press.

______, 2000c. Social Exclusion: Concept, Application, and Scrutiny. Social Development Paper No. 1, Asian Development Bank, Manila.

Sen, B., 2000. "Bangladesh Poverty Analysis: Trends, Policies and Institutions." Mimeo.

______, n.d. "Poverty in Bangladesh: A Review." Available: http://www.bids-bd.org/poverty.htm.

Seoul Metropolitan Government, Bureau of Administrative Reform, 2000. *Reinventing Seoul City Government.*

Shaban, R. A., 1987. "Testing between Competing Models of Sharecropping." *Journal of Political Economy* 95:893-920.

Shah, A., 1994. *The Reform of Intergovernmental Fiscal Relations in Developing and Emerging Market Economies.* World Bank, Washington D.C.

Shelley, M. R., 2000. "Governance and Administration: Challenge of New Millennium." In H. Abdul Hye, ed., *Governance. South Asian Perspectives.* Karachi: Oxford University Press.

Shin, G-W., 1998. "Agrarian Conflict and the Origins of Korean Capitalism." *The American Journal of Sociology* 103(5):1309-51.

Shleifer, A., and R. Vishny, 1993. "Corruption." *Quarterly Journal of Economics* 108:599-617.

Siddiqi, K., ed., 1994. *Local Government in Bangladesh,* Revised 2nd ed. Dhaka: The University Press Ltd.

______, ed., 1995. *Local Government in South Asia: A Comparative Study.* Dhaka: University Press Ltd.

Siddiqui, T. A., 2001. *Towards Good Governance.* Oxford: Oxford University Press.

Sigit, H., and S. Surbakti, 1999. "The Social Impact of the Financial Crisis in

Indonesia." Economics and Development Resource Center, Asian Development Bank, Manila, Philippines. Mimeo.

Silver, H., 1995. "Reconceptualizing Social Disadvantage: Three Paradigms of Social Exclusion." In G. Rodgers, C. Gore, and J. Figueiredo, eds., *Social Exclusion: Rhetoric, Reality, Responses.* International Institute for Labour Studies, Geneva.

Skoufias, E., 2000. "Changes in Household Welfare, Poverty and Inequality during the Crisis." *Bulletin of Indonesian Economic Studies* 36(August):97-114.

Smillie, I., 1997. *Words and Deeds. BRAC at 25.* Dhaka: Bangladesh Rural Action Committee.

Smoke, P., 1999. "Understanding Decentralization in Asia: An Overview of Key Issues and Challenges." *Regional Development Dialogue* 20(2):1-17.

Smolensky, E., R. Plotnick, E. Evenhouse, and S. Reilly, 1994. "Growth, Inequality and Poverty: A Cautionary Note." *Review of Income and Wealth* Series 40(2): 217-22.

Sobhan, R., 1998. How Bad Governance Impedes Poverty Alleviation in Bangladesh. OECD Development Center Technical Paper No. 143, November.

Social Policy and Development Centre (SPDC), various years. *Social Development in Pakistan, Annual Review.* Oxford: Oxford University Press.

Socialist Republic of Vietnam, 2000. *Country Economic Review.* November.

Soco, A. M., 2000. "Manila's Poor." *Intersect* 15(6, June).

Solow, R., 2001. "Sustainability: An Economist's Perspective." In U. Sankar, ed., *Environmental Economics.* New Delhi: Oxford University Press.

Srinivasan, T.N., 2001. "Comment on 'Counting the World's Poor' by Angus Deaton." *World Bank Research Observer* 16:157-68.

Stern, N., 2001. "Investing for Growth and Poverty Reduction: Institutions and People." Paper delivered in Islamabad, 29 March.

Strauss, J., 1986. "Does Better Nutrition Raise Farm Productivity?" *Journal of Political Economy* 94:297-320.

Streeten, P., 1995. The Political Economy of Fighting Poverty. Issues in Development Discussion Paper 1, International Labour Organisation, Geneva.

Sun, T-W., and J. Gargan, 1996. "A Strategic Perspective on Public Administration Problems in Taiwan." *Asian Journal of Public Administration* 18(1, June):96-117.

Suphachalasai, S., and D. Patmasiriwat, 1991. Poverty and Government Policy in Thailand. Working Paper No. 91/12, National Center for Developing Studies.

Suryahadi, A., S. Sumarto, Y. Suharso, and L. Pritchett, 2000. "The Evolution of Poverty during the Crisis in Indonesia, 1996 to 1999." Social Monitoring and Early Response Unit, Jakarta. Processed.

Tadjoeddin, M. Z., W. I. Suharyo, and S. Mishra, 2001. "Regional Disparity and Vertical Conflict in Indonesia." *Journal of the Asia Pacific Economy* 6(3):283-304.

Tai, H-C., 1974. *Land Reform and Politics: A Comparative Analysis.* University of California Press.

Taipei, China, Government Information Office (GIO), 2001. *The Republic of China's New Comprehensive Approach. Fruits of Twenty ROC Governmental Policies.*

Tanzi, V., 1998. "Corruption around the World: Causes, Consequences, Scope, and Cures." Fiscal Affairs Department, International Monetary Fund, World Bank. Mimeo.

Tanzi, V., and H. Davoodi, 1997. *Corruption, Public Investment and Growth.* International Monetary Fund, Washington, D.C.

Thailand Development Research Institute, 2000. The Process Of Formulating Poverty Reduction Strategies in Thailand. Working Paper.

Thamrongthanyavong, S., 1998. "Reinventing the Thai Bureaucracy in the Next Decade." In M. Ahmad, ed., *Public Service Management: Achieving Quality Performance in the 21st Century.* Kuala Lumpur: National Institute of Public Administration (INTAN).

Tiep, N. T., 1998. "Government Reform for Socio-Economic Development in Vietnam." *Asian Review of Public Administration* 10(1-2, Jan-Dec.): 172-86.

Timmer, C. P., 1997. How Well Do the Poor Connect to the Growth Process, Consulting Assistance on Economic Reform II Discussion Paper No. 17, Harvard Institute for International Development, Cambridge, MA.

Tirole, J., 1994. "The Internal Organisation of Government." *Oxford Economic Papers* 46:1-29.

Tsai, P-L., 2001. "Poverty Reduction in Taiwan: The Postwar Experience." Paper prepared for the ADB study on Pro-Poor Growth. June.

un Nabi, R., D. Datta, S. Chakrabarty, M. Begum, N. J. Chaudhury, 1999. "Consultations with the Poor: Participatory Poverty Assessment in Bangladesh." Report of the Bangladesh NGO Working Group to the World Bank, Voices of the Poor Project headed by Deepa Narayan.

UN-ESCAP, 1998. "Asia and Pacific into the 21st Century: Prospects for Social Development." Theme of the 54th session of ESCAP, 20-28 April. Available: http://www.unescap.org/sps/poverty. htm.

UNICEF, 1996. *The State of the World's Children 1996.* Available: http://www.unicef.org/sowc96.

United Nations (UN), 1970. Towards Accelerated Development—Proposals for the Second United Nations Development Decade. United Nations Publication No. E.70.II.A.2, New York.

United Nations Commission on Human Settlements (UNCHS), 2001. Statistical Annexes to the *Global Report on Human Settlements 2001*. Available: http://www.unchs.org/habrdd/statannexes. htm.

United Nations Development Programme (UNDP), 1997. Reconceptualizing Governance. Discussion Paper 2 (January). Management Development and Governance Division, Bureau for Policy and Programme Support, UNDP, New York.

______, 1998a. *Human Development Report 1998.* New York: Oxford University Press.

______, 1998b. *Integrity in Governance in Asia.* Report of Workshop in Bangkok, Thailand, 29 June-1 July.

______, 1998c. *Public Sector Management Reform in Asia and the Pacific. Selected Experiences from Seven Countries.* Regional Bureau for Asia and the Pacific in cooperation with Management Development and Governance Division. UNDP, New York.

______, 1999. *Human Development Report 1999.* New York: Oxford University Press.

______, 2000. *Poverty Report 2000. Overcoming Human Poverty.* New York.

UNDP Vietnam, 1996. "Vietnam Fact Sheet on Poverty." Available: http://www.undp.org.vn/undp/docs/fact/english/pov_fact. htm.

UNDP/UNICEF, 1996. *Catching Up. Capacity Development for Poverty Elimination in Vietnam.* UNDP/UNICEF, Hanoi.

United Nations in Viet Nam, 1999. *Looking Ahead: A United Nations Common Country Assessment of Viet Nam.* Office of the United Nations Resident Co-ordinator, Ha Noi, Viet Nam.

Urban Management Programme (UMP), 2000. *Asia News* 3(2, Fall).

Urban Resource Centre, 2001. "Evictions in Karachi." Available: http://www.urckarachi. org/evic.htm.

van de Walle, D., 1995. Public Spending and the Poor: What We Know, What We Need to Know. World Bank Working Paper 1476, Washington, D.C.

______, 1998. "Infrastructure and Poverty in Vietnam." In D. Dollar, P. Glewwe, and J. Litvack, eds., *Household Welfare and Vietnam's Transition.* Regional and Sectoral Studies, World Bank, Washington, D.C.

Veron, R., 2001. "The 'New' Kerala Model: Lessons for Sustainable Development." *World Development* 29(4):601-17.

Vietnam Socialist Republic, 2000. *Interim Poverty Reduction Strategy Paper.* Hanoi.

Vietnam-Sweden Mountain Rural Development Programme, ActionAid, Save the Children Fund (UK) and Oxfam (GB), 1999. *A Synthesis of Participa-*

tory Poverty Assessments from Four Sites in Vietnam: Lao Cai, Ha Tinh, Tra Vinh & Ho Chi Minh City.

Vijayanand, S.M., 2001. "Poverty Reduction through Decentralization: Lessons from the Experience of Kerala State in India." Paper presented at the Asia and the Pacific Forum on Poverty, Asian Development Bank, Manila, Philippines. Mimeo.

Wade, R., 1987. *Village Republics.* Cambridge: Cambridge University Press.

______, 1997. "How Infrastructure Agencies Motivate Staff: Canal Irrigation in India and the Republic of Korea." In A. Mody, ed., *Infrastructure Strategies in East Asia: The Untold Story.* World Bank, Washington D.C.

Wei, S., 1997a. *How Taxing is Corruption on International Investors?* National Bureau of Economic Research, Cambridge, MA.

______, 1997b. *Why is Corruption So Much More Taxing than Tax? Arbitrariness Kills.* National Bureau of Economic Research, Cambridge. MA.

Weinns, T. B., 1998. "Agriculture and Rural Poverty in Vietnam." In D. Dollar, P. Glewwe, and J. Litvack, eds., *Household Welfare and Vietnam's Transition.* Regional and Sectoral Studies, World Bank, Washington, D.C.

Weitzman, M.L., 1977. "Is the Price System or Rationing More Effective in Getting a Commodity to Those Who Need it Most?" *Bell Journal of Economics* 8(2):517-24.

Wescott, C. G., ed., 2001. *Key Governance Issues in Cambodia, Lao PDR, Thailand and Vietnam.* Programs Department (West), Asian Development Bank, Manila, Philippines.

Westergaard, K., and M.M. Alam, 1995. "Local Government in Bangladesh: Past Experiences and Yet Another Try." *World Development* 23(4):679-90.

Whaites, A., 2000. *PRSPs: Good News for the Poor? Social Conditionality, Participation and Poverty Reduction,* World Vision International, UK.

World Bank, 1990. *World Development Report 1990.* New York: Oxford University Press.

______, 1996a. Thailand: Growth, Poverty and Income Distribution: An Economic Report. Report No. 15689-TH, World Bank, Washington DC.

______, 1996b. *The World Bank Participation Sourcebook.* International Bank for Reconstruction and Development, World Bank, Washington D.C.

______, 1997a. Helping Countries Combat Corruption: The Role of the World Bank. PREM. Mimeo.

______. 1997b. "Poverty and Inequality—The Other Face of the Asian Miracle." News Release No. 98/1450, 26 August. Washington, D.C.

______, 1998. "Bangladesh: From Counting the Poor to Making the Poor Count." Poverty Reduction and Economic Management Network, South Asia Region.

______, 1999. *Vietnam Development Report 2000. Attacking Poverty.* Joint Report with Government of Vietnam-Donor-NGO Working Group. Consultative Group Meeting for Vietnam, 14-15 December.

______, 2000a. *World Bank Quarterly.* September 18.

______, 2000b. *World Development Report 2000/2001: Attacking Poverty.* New York: Oxford University Press.

______, 2000c. *Social Monitor III: Thai Workers and the Crisis.* World Bank, Bangkok.

______, 2000d. *Vietnam Living Standards Survey.1992-93 Basic Information.* Available: http://www.worldbank.org/html/prdph/lsms/ country/ vn93/vn93bid.pdf.

______,2001a. *Administrative and Civil Service Reform. Bangladesh: Governance Score Cards.* Available: http://www.worldbank .org/ publicsector/civilservice/in-bangladesh.htm.

______, 2001b. Philippines: Filipino Report Card on Pro-Poor Services. Sector Report No. 22181, Environment and Social Development Sector Unit, East Asia and Pacific Region, World Bank, Washington, D.C.

______, 2001c. *Vietnam Development Report. Vietnam 2010: Entering the 21st Century: Overview.* Joint report with the Asian Development Bank and UNDP.

______, 2001d. *Vietnam Living Standards Survey. 1997-98 Basic Information.* Available: http://www.worldbank.org/ mhtml/prdph/lsms/ country/ vn98/vn98bif.pdf.

______, n.d. *Global Poverty Monitoring.* Available: http://www. worldbank.org/research/povmonitor.

______, n.d. *Global Development Network Growth Database.* Available: http://www.worldbank.org/research/growth/GDNdata.

______, various years. *World Development Indicators.* World Bank, Washington, D.C.

Yoon, S. B., 2001. *Pro-Poor Growth and Institutional Constraints on Poverty Reduction in DMCs: The Case of Korea.*

Yu, S. O., 1994. Supporting the Informal Sector: Cases of NGO Assistance Programs. Pulso Monograph No. 13(February). Institute of Church and Social Issues, Quezon City.

Author Index

Subject Index

www.ingramcontent.com/pod-product-compliance
Lightning Source LLC
LaVergne TN
LVHW011517200926
848484LV00001B/56
* 9 7 8 1 4 0 3 9 1 8 0 6 2 *